Sophia Studies in Cross-cultural Philosophy of Traditions and Cultures

Volume 24

The Sophia Studies in Cross-cultural Philosophy of Traditions and Cultures focuses on the broader aspects of philosophy and traditional intellectual patterns of religion and cultures. The series encompasses global traditions, and critical treatments that draw from cognate disciplines, inclusive of feminist, postmodern, and postcolonial approaches. By global traditions we mean religions and cultures that go from Asia to the Middle East to Africa and the Americas, including indigenous traditions in places such as Oceania. Of course this does not leave out good and suitable work in Western traditions where the analytical or conceptual treatment engages Continental (European) or Cross-cultural traditions in addition to the Judeo-Christian tradition. The book series invites innovative scholarship that takes up newer challenges and makes original contributions to the field of knowledge in areas that have hitherto not received such dedicated treatment. For example, rather than rehearsing the same old Ontological Argument in the conventional way, the series would be interested in innovative ways of conceiving the erstwhile concerns while also bringing new sets of questions and responses, methodologically also from more imaginative and critical sources of thinking. Work going on in the forefront of the frontiers of science and religion beaconing a well-nuanced philosophical response that may even extend its boundaries beyond the confines of this debate in the West – e.g. from the perspective of the 'Third World' and the impact of this interface (or clash) on other cultures, their economy, sociality, and ecological challenges facing them – will be highly valued by readers of this series. All books to be published in this Series will be fully peer-reviewed before final acceptance.

More information about this series at http://www.springer.com/series/8880

Gordon F. Davis

Editor

Ethics without Self, Dharma without Atman

Western and Buddhist Philosophical
Traditions in Dialogue

 Springer

Editor
Gordon F. Davis
Department of Philosophy
Carleton University
Ottawa, ON, Canada

ISSN 2211-1107   ISSN 2211-1115   (electronic)
Sophia Studies in Cross-cultural Philosophy of Traditions and Cultures
ISBN 978-3-319-67406-3   ISBN 978-3-319-67407-0   (eBook)
https://doi.org/10.1007/978-3-319-67407-0

Library of Congress Control Number: 2018940871

Printed on acid-free paper

This Springer imprint is published by the registered company Springer International Publishing AG part
of Springer Nature.
The registered company address is: Gewerbestrasse 11, 6330 Cham, Switzerland

Preface

There is a familiar conundrum in philosophy that arises out of our complex relationship to the history of philosophical concepts and their diverse cultural origins. Philosophers use several terms deriving from ancient languages that encompass both metaphysical and ethical significations, resulting in not only conceptual richness but also ambiguity. (A prime example is the family of terms deriving from the Greek term *telos*, e.g. 'teleological'.) This polysemy can be revealing, if not fertile; but in some contexts, the metaphysical and the ethical stand in a problematic relation to each other. We find a similar tension in certain contexts in which *dharma* is invoked as a guiding ideal in ancient Indian philosophy. The cosmic order of *dharma* was sometimes assumed to underpin the moral *dharma*, but various Indian philosophical traditions questioned such assumptions, including the Buddhist tradition. Admittedly, the phrase *dharma without ātman*, in our title, may sound incongruous to those who think of the Hindu tradition as the primary source of the ethical notion of *dharma*. But Buddhists also retained a version of this notion, calling Buddha's teachings the *buddha-dharma*. However, unlike that of the Hindu tradition, this *dharma* was not only divorced from assumptions about selfhood or cosmic self (*ātman*), but *based on* a vision of reality without self or selves (*an-ātman*). Albeit with an imperfect repertoire of concepts, contemporary philosophers continue to debate both the question of personal identity and the question of the bearing (if any) of metaphysics on ethics.

This volume has three main aims. The first aim is to explore interconnections between metaphysical questions about the nature of selfhood and ethical questions concerning the practical implications of revising or subverting various traditional conceptions of selfhood and personhood. Another aim, much more general but equally important, is to raise problems and new prospects for both comparative philosophy and cross-cultural philosophy. The focus on Buddhist philosophy, in particular, highlights a third aim of our project: to throw light on the ways in which Buddhist philosophy in particular has either anticipated, echoed or contributed to seminal episodes in the history of Western philosophy. Many of the chapters here focus on philosophical ideas without belabouring historical details (though the first offers an overview of the historical connections that link the history of Buddhist philosophy – at certain points – with the history of Western philosophy). Several of our chapters engage in *doing* Buddhist philosophy; but at the same time, these chapters directly or indirectly highlight the potential for treating the Buddhist tradition as an element in a comparative case study. We raise, albeit tentatively in some cases, the questions of whether, and why, two independent traditions of philosophy would end up tackling similar philosophical problems, not to mention tackling what might be the same *meta-problem* – namely, of how the metaphysical problems and the ethical problems do or should relate to each other.

Following the overview in the first chapter, a first trio of essays (Chaps. 2, 3, and 4) examines various parallels between ancient Indian Buddhist philosophy and ancient Greek philosophy. The next three chapters shift to modern philosophy, and cover what might be called the 'pre-contact' phase of Western philosophy, given that Spinoza, Hume and Kant were probably unaware of specific texts and ideas from the Buddhist philosophical tradition. (Nonetheless, parallels with Śāntideva's selfless altruism, in particular, are explored especially with respect to the role of benevolence in the ethics of Spinoza and Hume.) Channels of communication had been opened up by Jesuits in East Asia, decades before Spinoza's time, establishing a sort of contact between European and Buddhist philosophical traditions; but specifically Buddhist themes took some time to be disentangled from elements of other Asian traditions. Translations of Buddhist texts did not become available until the nineteenth century, so they were indeed quite novel when Schopenhauer encountered them. The next three essays can thus be construed as looking at 'post-contact' reactions and inspirations; these essays discuss five Western philosophers: Schopenhauer, Nietzsche, Heidegger, William James and Bertrand Russell. Finally, the last three essays address themes from Buddhist metaphysics and ethics in contemporary philosophy.

In his essay on contemporary forms of altruism, for example, Stephen Harris scrutinizes various ways of reading Śāntideva as drawing a *moral* conclusion based on a kind of reductionism about selfhood, and proceeds to consider whether a different reading might resonate better with a broader understanding of *ethics*. In the following, penultimate chapter, Ashwani Peetush likewise discusses ethical values that – in a socio-political context – go beyond considerations of narrow forms of justice. And in the last chapter, Davis and Sahni return to a certain kind of putative moral obligation, based on environmental concerns, that has nonetheless been grounded in wide-ranging ethical reflections, often in ways directly inspired by Buddhist sources. In some ways, these contemporary themes are foreshadowed in the opening trio of essays, which begin with the Socratic origins of Western philosophy. Considering themes that run through Socrates, Plato and Aristotle, Michael Griffin explores various resonances with Buddhist ethics, including ethics in the narrow 'moral' sense that concerns interpersonal obligations (as well as broader senses). Pivoting to ethics in the broader sense, Emily McRae considers the 'therapeutic' orientation of ancient Stoicism and a related set of problems that kindred strands of Buddhist ethics address, in some cases more effectively, she argues. And in the third of those essays, after examining the relationship between religious practice and ethics (again in the broader sense), Ethan Mills traces parallels between a Nagarjunian scepticism and a Pyrrhonist scepticism, each of these being more reconcilable to ethical praxis than many have assumed. Ancient Stoics were often at loggerheads with ancient sceptics in the West; but ethical tendencies that more or less reconciled them are also traceable, as these early chapters make out, *mutatis mutandis*, in certain Buddhist traditions.

In the ancient Greek context, those ethical reflections fell under the heading of theories of *eudaimonia*. Proceeding to the modern context, meanwhile, a somewhat different set of problems comes to the fore, of a more explicitly *moral* nature. Although these moral themes are more associated with Kant and the 'British Moralists' than figures like Spinoza, in the fifth chapter Davis and Renaud consider some neglected moral reflections in Spinoza's works, and compare these to themes in Mahāyāna philosophy. Like several other chapters that discuss Śāntideva's ethics, chapters five and six focus on themes in Mahāyāna Buddhism, with Jay Garfield addressing Madhyamaka specifically, in his chapter on Hume's ethics. Meanwhile, in exploring 'contemplative strategies' of self-analysis in both Buddhist and Kantian ethics, Emer O'Hagan draws mainly on texts from the Pali Canon, thus addressing pre-Mahāyāna as well as Mahāyāna themes. The next three chapters then bring us back to the scene of contemporary ethical theory, both 'continental' and 'analytic' – in chapter nine, via Heidegger; and in chapter ten, via Bertrand Russell. Leading up to this crossroads, Douglas Berger discusses Schopenhauer and Nietzsche, but instead of recounting the usual narrative of how these figures were inspired by Buddhist sources, Berger underlines some deep ethical differences. Sonia Sikka also highlights contrasts, in her case between Buddhist metaphysics and Heidegger's early writings (with allowance made for different emphases in his later writings). With Nalini Ramlakhan's survey of William James and Bertrand Russell, we come full circle, in the sense that, in the twentieth century, Western thinkers could finally claim to have some substantial first-hand knowledge of Buddhist texts; and as the chapters proceed from there, many of the key figures we discuss in the final stretch, so to speak, can themselves be described as scholars of Buddhist philosophy, and in some cases as full-fledged practitioners of Buddhist ethics.

Many of us had the opportunity to present early versions of our chapters at various venues in North America, Europe and Asia. I would like to thank my fellow contributors for their participation in panels on these themes, and for their patience as other contributors proceeded to present at other venues in later stages of this process. On behalf of all the contributors I would like to thank, for their feedback and encouragement, audiences at the Canadian Philosophical Association and the International Association of Buddhist Studies, as well as groups of fellow travellers at Carleton University, the University of Ottawa, SUNY Binghamton, the University of Hawaii, the University of Delhi, the University of Vienna and Leiden University, among others. I would also like to thank the anonymous referees for their valuable advice and comments, the editorial team at Springer for much patience and assistance, and personally, my own family – Leo, Catherine, Margaret and Gordon. Finally, to close with *śrāddha*, for some fellow travellers, in memoriam: John Leroux, David Chappell, Daya Krishna, Derek Parfit, Jiyuan Yu and Sarah Marquardt.

Ottawa, ON, Canada   Gordon F. Davis

Contents

Contributors

Douglas L. Berger is Professor of Comparative Philosophy at Leiden University in the Netherlands. His primary areas of research and teaching are classical Brāhmiṇical and Indian Buddhist thought, Classical Chinese philosophy, and cross-cultural philosophical hermeneutics. He is the author of *Encounters of Mind: Luminosity and Personhood in Indian and Chinese Thought* (SUNY Press, 2015), *"The Veil of Māyā:" Schopenhauer's System and Early Indian Thought* (Global Academic Publications, 2004), and coeditor, with JeeLoo Liu, of *Nothingness in Asian Philosophy* (Routledge, 2014). He has authored dozens of essays and book chapters on the areas of his research and is chief editor of the University of Hawai'i Press book series "Dimensions of Asian Spirituality." He has also served as the president of the Society for Asian and Comparative Philosophy (2014–2016).

Gordon F. Davis is Associate Professor of Philosophy at Carleton University in Ottawa, Canada. His research focuses on ethical theory, meta-ethics, history of ethics, and comparative philosophy, including comparative treatments of rival philosophical schools within the Buddhist tradition. Recent publications include "Moral Realism and Anti-realism Outside the West" (in the journal *Comparative Philosophy*), "Traces of Consequentialism and Non-consequentialism in Bodhisattva Ethics" (*Philosophy East and West*), and "The Atipada Problem in Buddhist Meta-Ethics" (*Journal of Buddhist Ethics*).

Jay L. Garfield is Doris Silbert Professor in the Humanities and Professor of Philosophy, Logic and Buddhist Studies and Director of the Buddhist Studies and Logic programs at Smith College. He is also Visiting Professor of Buddhist Philosophy at Harvard Divinity School, Professor of Philosophy at Melbourne University, and Adjunct Professor of Philosophy at the Central University of Tibetan Studies. Professor Garfield's research addresses topics in the philosophy of mind, ethics, epistemology, the philosophy of logic, methodology in cross-cultural interpretation, and Buddhist philosophy, particularly Indo-Tibetan Madhyamaka and Yogācāra. He is currently working on a book with Y. Deguchi, G. Priest, and R. Sharf, *What Can't Be Said: Paradox and Contradiction in East Asian Philosophy*;

a book on Hume's *Treatise of Human Nature, The Concealed Operations of Custom: Hume's Treatise from the Inside Out*; and a large collaborative project on Geluk-Sakya epistemological debates in fifteenth to eighteenth century Tibet. His most recent books are *The Essential Jewel of Holy Practice* (a translation of Patrul Rinpoche's text of that name, with Emily McRae); *Minds Without Fear: Philosophy in the Indian Renaissance* (with Nalini Bhushan); *Engaging Buddhism: Why It Matters to Philosophy* (OUP); *Dignāga's Investigation of the Percept: A Philosophical Legacy in India and Tibet* (with Duckworth et al.); and two volumes coauthored with the Cowherds (OUP).

Michael Griffin is Associate Professor of Classics and Philosophy at the University of British Columbia. His research focuses on Ancient Greek philosophy in late antiquity, particularly philosophical education. He is coeditor, with Richard Sorabji, of the *Ancient Commentators on Aristotle* project. He is author of *Aristotle's Categories in the Early Roman Empire* (OUP, 2015) and a two-volume translation of the Neoplatonist Olympiodorus' introduction to Platonic philosophy, *Olympiodorus: On Plato's Alcibiades* (Bloomsbury, 2014 and 2016).

Stephen Harris is Assistant Professor (Universitair Docent 2) at Leiden University's Institute for Philosophy. He specializes in cross-cultural and Indian philosophy, with a particular interest in Buddhist ethical texts. He has published articles in a number of academic journals, including *Journal of Buddhist Ethics*, *Journal of Indian Philosophy*, *Philosophy East and West*, and *Sophia*.

Emily McRae is an Assistant Professor of Philosophy at the University of New Mexico. She specializes in Tibetan Buddhist philosophy, ethics, moral psychology, and feminism. She has published articles on issues in comparative moral psychology in both Western and Asian philosophical journals and volumes, including *American Philosophy Quarterly*, *History of Philosophy Quarterly*, *Journal of Religious Ethics*, *Philosophy East and West*, and *The Oxford Handbook of Buddhist Ethics*. She is currently coediting, with Dr. George Yancy, a volume on Buddhism and whiteness. Her translation, with Jay Garfield, of the nineteenth-century Tibetan master Patrul Rinpoche's *Essential Jewel of Holy Practice* will be published by Wisdom Books.

Ethan Mills has been Assistant Professor of Philosophy at the University of Tennessee at Chattanooga since 2014. He specializes in Indian philosophy, Buddhist philosophy, and ancient and modern skepticism. He has published in journals including *Philosophy East and West*, *Asian Philosophy*, *Comparative Philosophy*, and *The International Journal for the Study of Skepticism*. He is currently working on a book on skepticism in classical India focusing on Nāgārjuna, Jayarāśi, and Śrī Harṣa.

Emer O'Hagan is Associate Professor at the University of Saskatchewan. Her primary interests include the role of self-knowledge in moral agency and moral development, constitutivism in metaethics, and Kantian ethics. Some of her recent publications include "Self-Knowledge and the Development of Virtue," in N. Birondo and S. Braun (eds.), *Virtue's Reasons: New Essays on Virtue, Character, and Reasons* (Routledge, 2017); "Shmagents, Realism and Constitutivism About Rational Norms," in *The Journal of Value Inquiry* 2014; "Self-Knowledge and Moral Stupidity," in *Ratio* 2012; and "Animals, Agency, and Obligation in Kantian Ethics," in *Social Theory and Practice* 2009.

Ashwani Peetush is Associate Professor of Philosophy at Wilfrid Laurier University in Waterloo, Ontario. His research areas encompass ethics, political philosophy, and Indian philosophy; particular themes of interest include human rights, pluralism, and the metaphysics of the self and consciousness in Advaita Vedānta and Buddhism. His recent publications include *Human Rights: India and the West* (edited with Jay Drydyk, OUP, 2015); "Justice, Diversity, and Dialogue: Rawlsian Multiculturalism" in *Multiculturalism and Religious Identity*, ed. S. Sikka and L. Beaman (McGill-Queens Press, 2014); and "The Ethics of Radical Equality" in *The Bloomsbury Research Handbook of Indian Ethics*, ed. S. Ranganathan (Bloomsbury, 2017).

Nalini Ramlakhan recently finished her Ph.D., researching moral psychology in the Cognitive Science Department at Carleton University (dissertation entitled "Emotion and Morality: Understanding the Role of Empathy and Other Emotions in Moral Judgment and Moral Behaviour"). She works on a variety of empirical and conceptual issues concerning the moral dimensions of addressing psychopathology, as well as ethics and moral psychology in general. Her publications include "An Argument in Favour of a Universal Moral Grammar and Its Weaknesses," *International Journal of Arts and Sciences* (2011), and "On the Nature of Moral Judgment," *Cognitive Science Proceedings* (2014).

Mary D. Renaud is a Ph.D. Candidate in Philosophy at Brown University. Her primary research focuses on the intersection of metaethics and the philosophy of action, with a particular focus on moral responsibility and the semantics of normative statements. She has additional interests in ethical and metaphysical themes in Buddhist philosophy and in the metaphysics of personal identity. Her current research topics include the treatment of righteous anger in Theravāda and Mahāyāna Buddhism as evidence for a character consequentialist interpretation of the Buddhist normative framework, the information-sensitivity of deontic modals, and a critique of top-down causation arguments for free will libertarianism.

Pragati Sahni is Associate Professor of Philosophy at the University of Delhi. Her research interests include environmental philosophy, ethics, and early Buddhist philosophy. She is the author of *Environmental Ethics in Buddhism: A Virtues Approach* (Routledge, 2011) and is coeditor (with Vibha Chaturvedi) of *Understanding Ethics* (Motilal Banarsidass, 2015).

Sonia Sikka is Professor of Philosophy at the University of Ottawa. Her primary areas of research are German philosophy, multiculturalism, secularism, religion, and race. Dr. Sikka's recent publications include *Heidegger, Morality and Politics* (in press, Cambridge University Press); "Heidegger's Argument for the Existence of God?" (*Sophia*, 2016); "On Translating Religious Reasons: Rawls, Habermas and the Quest for a Neutral Public Sphere" (*Review of Politics*, 2016); *Living with Religious Diversity*, ed. with Bindu Puri and Lori Beaman (Routledge, 2015); and *Multiculturalism & Religious Identity: Canada and India*, ed. with Lori Beaman (McGill-Queen's Press, 2014).

Chapter 1
Self-Sceptical Ethics and Selfless Morality: A Historical and Cross-Cultural Overview

Gordon F. Davis

It is natural to think that, if the ego is an illusion, then egoism cannot stand. This is more than just natural, perhaps, if the 'ego' is simply the self referred to in first-person terms, and if 'egoism' is a generalized claim, for example a claim intended in an ethical (or some normative) sense.[1] If egoism 'cannot stand', in some such sense, this would not amount to denying that 'self-serving' patterns of behaviour might predominate regardless; and even where they seem restrained or muted, nothing in such an unmasking of illusion would rule out that roughly 'selfish' motives may underlie generosity, cooperation and the like. The fact that many such motives are unconscious may mean that, for better or worse, a better theoretical understanding of identity and personhood might not dislodge them. But the natural thought, the idea that egoism 'cannot stand', is rather that egoism could not be *valid* if the ego is an illusion.[2] That is to say, egoism – *qua* fundamental normative standard – would seem to be left without any prospect of justification if 'ego' and 'self' turn out to be illusory and thus disqualified from providing any ontological or referential basis for such posits as 'egoism' and 'self-interest'.

Moreover, normative egoism may not be the only view that would turn out to lack justification; the same disqualification might apply also to conceptions of duties that are alleged to depend fundamentally on who one happens to be: someone's legal

---

[1] It would seem that 'psychological egoism' would be even more of a non-starter, as it probably is in any case; but the qualification in my next sentence complicates the task of explaining how and why that would be so.

[2] The (different) question of whether egoism is *morally* justifiable might not even arise, if in this sense egoism is not *theoretically* valid – that is, lacking the metaphysical credentials that would be required for a place in any ontology.

G. F. Davis (✉)
Department of Philosophy, Carleton University, Ottawa, ON, Canada
e-mail: Gordon.Davis@carleton.ca

© Springer International Publishing AG, part of Springer Nature 2018   1
G. F. Davis (ed.), *Ethics without Self, Dharma without Atman*, Sophia Studies
in Cross-cultural Philosophy of Traditions and Cultures 24,
https://doi.org/10.1007/978-3-319-67407-0_1

guardian, heir, senior officer, etc.[3] Some would even say that the disqualification should go global, in the sense that, once selfhood has been debunked, the subversion must – supposedly – be seen as undermining all of ethics. In the absence of a 'self' for any kind of genuine self-orientation, they say, nothing at all could be justified, at least in the sort of ultimate sense discussed by moral theorists and their detractors – detractors such as existentialists who flirt with a moral anti-realism of this kind.[4] Yet most would feel that this reaction goes too far. A global rejection of all ethics, besides being so alien a notion as to be almost irrelevant to theorist and layperson alike,[5] hardly seems to follow from scepticism about only one particular kind of entity, such as 'the self'. Nonetheless, a transformation in our understanding of self-hood might well have profound ethical implications – implications *within* ethics.

Some of these ideas for adjusting our ethical orientation(s) may be 'natural' ways of responding to the claim that the ego is an illusion, but there are two sets of problems to consider: (a) Could any argument be robust enough and convincing enough to justify reconceptualizing what we mean by a sense of *self* or *identity*, let alone debunking such basic elements of common sense as these (e.g. relegating the common reference of 'I' and 'me' to the status of a mere illusion)? And (b) Even if there are grounds for debunking the notion of personal identity, be they philosophical or scientific, and even if they seem to be decisive with respect to ontology, must there be any ethical implications, let alone any outright disqualification of moral outlooks that already structure many people's lives?[6] Here I mainly consider the second question; but, reflecting the structure of this volume as a whole, I shall begin and end with some historical context for these questions.

---

[3] These so-called 'agent-relative' duties (conceived as *justified* by their alleged agent-relativity) would also be disqualified by moral consequentialists – who hasten to add, though, that such duties can be important (even crucial) in serving a larger purpose, such as overall well-being. Illusionists about selfhood, not to mention those who critique notions of identity in more nuanced ways, could make the same accommodation, if they share that purpose. There are other views, situated some-where between egoism and agent-relative deontology, which often go by the name of 'individual-ism', and which underlie certain liberal views in political philosophy; many of those views would also seem to be threatened – in their foundations – by any unmasking of the self as an illusion.

[4] We are here concerned primarily with ethics and only secondarily with meta-ethics, so concerns with moral anti-realism will remain mostly in the background; I do include at the end of this chapter, however, a few comments on the intersection of meta-ethics and the metaphysics of person-hood (see also notes 34, 37 and 38 below).

[5] The term 'ethics' will be used here in such a way as to cover more than 'morality'. Global rejec-tions of *moral* truth warrant consideration, at least for theorists. Some other chapters in this volume also take seriously Pyrrhonist rejections – even those that go beyond their more usual *suspen-sions* – of moral belief; and yet, insofar as the Pyrrhonist goal is *ataraxia*, which is meant to be a *desirable* state of mind, this goal can itself be considered ethical in a broad axiological sense.

[6] Perhaps most ambitiously, Charles Goodman (2009) argues that a morally demanding form of impartial consequentialism follows from reductionism about personal identity (in conjunction with other elements of Buddhist axiology); cf. earlier work in this vein by Siderits (2000). For the most part, in this volume, we consider more modest ethical claims – sometimes prudential claims having to do with value(s) agents can find in their own lives, sometimes a moral altruism that leaves open the full shape of whatever moral theory should prevail. Claims like Goodman's, however – focused on impartiality and/or cosmopolitan concern – surface in Chaps. 2, 5, 10, 11 and 13, respectively by Griffin, Davis & Renaud, Ramlakhan, Harris and Davis & Sahni.

Western philosophers became more closely familiar with these issues when word spread – rather slowly – about David Hume's scepticism about personal identity in the mid-eighteenth century (primarily concerning (a)). Prior to Hume, there may have been a fainter degree of familiarity (again mostly focused on (a)), via isolated references in Plutarch, medieval Averroists and Michel de Montaigne. However, these have appeared as outliers, and even in the wake of both Hume's and Kant's attacks on rational psychology, careful consideration of these issues was slow in coming. Partly thanks to seminal books in the 1980s by Derek Parfit, Thomas Nagel and Charles Taylor,[7] discussion has sharpened over recent decades. Meanwhile, in the Buddhist philosophical tradition, there has been intensive discussion of these issues for millennia. As a result, Buddhists and other Asian philosophers can draw on a long-standing terminology for distinguishing different views about selfhood, whereas our terms in the West remain embryonic and are not widely recognized outside of specialized subdisciplines. In analytic philosophy, the most widely discussed kind of illusionism about selfhood in the West often goes by the unwieldy term 'anti-realism about diachronic personal identity' (which, moreover, extends only rather awkwardly to the influential approach called 'reductionism'). But for present purposes, when not using Pali or Sanskrit terms, we shall use a simpler and more generic term, which can apply equally to Buddhists, Montaigne, Hume, Parfit and others, calling their views '*self-sceptical*'.[8]

Anti-egoism in the ethical sense, meanwhile, can be cast in terms of a commitment to social justice, or in terms of a widening circle of moral concern, or more expansively, as a call for compassion for all beings, a construal recognizable to anyone familiar with Buddhist beliefs. Perhaps not as often highlighted among those beliefs – but equally important within the Buddhist worldview – is the idea that the most enlightened way to grasp the need for *karuṇā* (compassion) is via an understanding of *anattā / anātman* ('no-self' or 'not-self'). This way of connecting insight and praxis[9] is often described as a spiritual transformation, but has also been expressed as a rational argument, with *anātman* as a premise and altruism as a conclusion. Once the premise is granted, in a form that preserves value(s), the conclusion seems to fol-

---

[7] Parfit (1984/1987), Nagel (1986) and Taylor (1989).

[8] This term is far from perfect, not only because it might seem to use 'self' indexically rather than as a general noun (so that any such view would sound unduly sceptical about *itself*), but also because many of the views with revisionist potential, and especially many Buddhist ones, are anti-realist rather than sceptical in the sense of suspending judgment while keeping an open mind about the reality of the self. For better or worse, the term at least resonates with its counterpart, 'free will scepticism', which is generally intended to cover anti-realist views and not just classical scepticism. (Note also that reductionism, such as the kind explored by Parfit, can also be called 'self-sceptical' even though it differs in certain ways from both scepticism and anti-realism; and the same applies to most forms of fictionalism and illusionism about personal identity.)

[9] Or as we might put it, connecting *metaphysics and ethics*; however, many Buddhists are uneasy about entanglements with metaphysics, for various reasons. Comparative philosophers who construe the connection in terms of metaphysics may run the risk of imposing alien categories in Buddhist contexts; nonetheless, at least some Buddhist philosophers embrace a role for metaphysics (and meanwhile, problems and prospects of engaging in comparative metaphysics are at stake in many of the following chapters).

low: provisionally accepting a conventional distinction between 'self' and 'others', 'I' must see the welfare of 'others' as making demands on 'my' attention that are as important and as justified as those of 'my' welfare, once this distinction is exposed as having no deep or ultimately real basis. In that formulation, this rational connection between insight and praxis may sound distinctly modern, echoing thinkers ranging from Schopenhauer to Parfit. But this reason-based approach is already clearly evident in the works of the eighth-century Buddhist monk Śāntideva, as well as in numerous Indian and Tibetan commentaries on Śāntideva.[10] Indeed, this connection is familiar not only to students of Asian religions and of course to Buddhists, but also familiar to most contemporary philosophers, at least as an important possibility, thanks to the writers just mentioned. However, the extent to which these issues are new to the Western context, or perhaps not as new as is generally supposed, has not been closely investigated. As we show here, self-sceptical approaches to ethics have existed in earlier phases of Western philosophy, though they have largely been overshadowed or suppressed. Some of those approaches did not even address the reality of persons in general; some, for example, addressed tensions between individuality and immortality in accounts of immaterial intellection, while others were sceptical just by virtue of suspending judgment on the nature of selfhood.

Some reductionists are quick to remind us that their view preserves the simple truths we seem to express when we use personal pronouns, and even the truth of statements about a 'same' person across long stretches of time; their reservations only concern, they say, the facts and entities that can make such statements true (when indeed true). In apparent contrast to this, many would be inclined to boil down the Buddhist approach to the straightforward assertion that 'the self' (ātman) simply does not exist; the idea would be to deny that such statements are ever really true.[11] This simple denial does capture one aspect of the Abhidhamma / Abhidharma scriptures, which contain some of the oldest written philosophical reflections in the Buddhist tradition. Whether ātman is conceived cosmically or individually, the Abhidharma view of early Buddhism is that no such essence exists, in either form. Personal identity over time – the persistence of the things we seem to refer to with our personal pronouns (e.g. me, myself) – is a notion that Abhidharma Buddhists take to be illusory. In Pali, it is said that anattā is true of everything; in Sanskrit, that anātman is true of everything – or simply true. We are without self, they say, but we are not without path(s) in life. Like many other moral systems, what the orthodox traditions in India call 'dharma' seems to call for revision, if we humans – whether on a path of dharma or not – are not the sort of agents, let alone souls or spirits, that

---

[10]Śāntideva's most famous formulation of the argument is in verses 90–103 of Chapter 8 of his *Bodhicaryāvatāra* (quoted in full in Jay Garfield's chapter here, i.e. Chap. 6 below); the fact that he does not focus on *karuṇā* in this passage calls for resorting to a more general concept, such as 'altruism'.

[11]These two approaches can be reconciled within Buddhist metaphysics by appealing to the distinction between conventional and ultimate truths. Regarding persons, there are no ultimate truths – so say almost all Buddhists – but Abhidharmists also allow conventional truths where (e.g.) 'first-personal facts' are reducible to impersonal facts that may correspond to ultimate truths (cf. the early chapters of Siderits 2015).

most of us had been unreflectively or dogmatically taking ourselves to be. Other revisions might be expected as well; and indeed, many Buddhists regard the 'no-self' or 'not-self' insight as life-changing, and even the kernel of supreme spiritual liberation. If we assume that this liberation does not involve the kind of global res-ignation I referred to in my second paragraph above (and thus does not and should not involve a 'transcendence of all values'[12]), then there may be warrant for a *dharma without ātman*, as our book's title suggests.

Those who associate the concept of 'dharma' with Hinduism may find a phrase like '*dharma without ātman*' to be counterintuitive, if not incoherent. But the mes-sage of the Buddha – his 'system', however that might be conceived in different contexts – is typically called *buddhadharma*. Indeed, the philosophical elaboration just referred to is called Abhi-*dharma*; and most Mahāyāna schools featured a simi-lar philosophical discourse about the Buddha's *dharma*. Buddhadharma is meant to supersede not only orthodox 'dharma' but also the entire value-system of which, in ancient India, that was merely one element.[13] For Buddhists, then, 'dharma without ātman' is not only possible, but required; they generally believe, and their philoso-phers generally argue, that an ethical reorientation is necessary, purged of assump-tions about an ultimate referent for diachronic personal identity. To reiterate this in the simpler terms of my opening sentence, and in terms that reach beyond the Buddhist context: if it is an illusion that persons have egos (selves, as opposed to self-images), then any ethics that reflects reality must set aside the notion of ego-ism – at least at a foundational level – and the premises of moral philosophy must then deploy concepts of a quite different provenance.

1.1 Self-Sceptical Reflections in the Western Tradition

David Hume is often considered one of the only philosophers in the early modern Western tradition to have mounted a critique of the notion of personal identity. Rather than wade into the ongoing debate about the nature of his critique,[14] I pro-

---

[12] As Keown (2001) points out, some Buddhists have favoured a kindred notion of 'transcendence'; Goodman (2009) has deepened the debate about this, highlighting insights on both sides, but Keown's critique of this 'transcendence' – as an interpretation of Buddhism – remains persuasive, at least enough to shift the burden of argument, or so I would argue. Nietzschean 'transvaluation' is very different, but Douglas Berger's critique of Nietzsche (in Chap. 8 in this volume) could be construed along similar lines.

[13] Bilimoria (1997) points out, however – echoing others who have expored the implications of Advaita Vedanta – that elements of the Hindu tradition converge with some readings of Buddhist *anātman* (see also n. 30 below). In his chapter here (Chap. 12), Ashwani Peetush considers this possibility as well.

[14] For a recent sympathetic account of his critique, see G. Strawson (2011); and for historical back-ground, see Udo Thiel's *Early Modern Subject: Self-Consciousness and Personal Identity from Descartes to Hume* (2011). A recent comparative study of Hume (on selfhood) and Buddhism is Long (2012); cf. Garfield's Chap. 6 in this volume.

pose here to take a historical step back, noting that scepticism about selfhood, or even about the ultimate reality of *persons*, was not entirely absent from Western philosophy prior to Hume. The philosophical scene of the late Middle Ages in Europe had its Averroists, who contended that the highest form of the intellect could not ultimately be individuated, and that the mind, if not 'the soul', must really be one shared, impersonal intellect, rather than a phenomenon embodied in plural instantiations.[15] (Technically, this was 'dogmatic' rather than 'sceptical', as were Stoic versions of this view; but as we shall see presently, even some Stoics put their thoughts in a sceptical form.) Was it inevitable that this ultimate reality, as construed in the sub-traditions deriving from Averroes, would be seen as something mental or intellectual? Medieval apophatic traditions, *inter alia*, would cast some doubt on this, perhaps injecting a form of scepticism into the debate. Spinoza would also eventually question this, in a different way; for him, the mental is only one attribute, and not necessarily a fundamental one, of a single, infinite – and impersonal – substance.[16] Nonetheless, these forms of monism cast doubt on the notion of individuated selfhood, and even though they occupy the opposite end of the spectrum, in a sense, from Hume's reductionist tendency, they seem equally subversive with respect to the kind of ego that would have to underpin egoism (or at least, egoism as a putative ultimate truth).

It could be argued, meanwhile, that the ancient Greek schools of philosophy problematized the notion of selfhood as much or more than Hume did. As Richard Sorabji argues in his book *Self* (2006), Plato was not as affirmative as Aristotle about the reality of individual selfhood; and even Aristotle raised doubts of a different kind, by casting doubt on the notion of an individual afterlife. Sorabji also points out that some Stoic philosophers wondered whether the person who will wake up in 'my' bed tomorrow morning will be the same person that 'I' take 'myself' to be (2006, 41); and the Stoics' famed equanimity (*apatheia*) was thought to be available to those who get some critical distance from the notion of a persisting self or subject that would always be burdened with apparently inescapable expectations and regrets. A more systematic suspension of judgment might be expected from Pyrrhonist sceptics such as Sextus Empiricus; but on several related questions, Sextus seems to shift between suspension of judgment and outright denial (cf. Bett 2000). He comments that some thinkers had already denied the existence of the soul, including Dicaearchus of Messene (Sextus 2000, 75). He then argues that for philosophers who find the matter undecidable, they must "grant the inapprehensibility of the soul; [whereas] if they say that it is decidable… [t]hey cannot decide it with perception… [and to decide via intellect is to try] to decide and confirm what is less a matter of investigation by what is more a matter of investigation – which is absurd", i.e. because matters of intellect are "the most unclear" (2000, 75–76). Thus, Sextus says, "the dispute about the soul will not be decided with the intellect. Therefore with nothing. But if this is so, souls are actually inapprehensible" (76).

---

[15] As Herbert Davidson shows (1992, 338–40), this view had a plausible basis in Averroes's writings.

[16] For more detail on Spinoza, see Chap. 5 here (Davis & Renaud, in this volume).

Later in his *Outlines*, he questions any relation between 'the good' and 'the soul', commenting: "The soul is perhaps unreal; and even if it is real, [Dogmatists must admit that] it is not apprehended… [hence] how can they say that the good comes about in the soul?" (193; Bk. III: 186–87).

Epicureanism may be one natural recourse for those reeling from this critique. Indeed, the next remark by Sextus himself, following the question above, turns to consider an Epicurean approach: "Epicurus," he says, "locates the aim in pleasure and says that the soul is composed of atoms…" (ibid., 193). Sextus is, of course, just as critical of Epicureanism as any other ethical perspective.[17] But by the sixteenth century, some philosophers were willing to entertain unique syntheses of scepticism, hedonism and altruism. As for altruism, it is worth considering its role in the works of the sixteenth century's most important Pyrrhonist – or perhaps crypto-Pyrrhonist – Michel de Montaigne. In his late essay 'On Vanity' (1588), he juxtaposes doubts about personal identity with a variety of moral intuitions. Elsewhere in his essays, we find self-sceptical reflections on personal values, often overshadowing moral values. But in 'On Vanity', Montaigne expresses a cosmopolitan moral concern for all fellow humans, saying "I reckon all men my fellow-citizens, embracing a Pole as I do a Frenchman, placing a national bond after the common universal one" (2003, 1100). Typical self-sceptical remarks are interspersed throughout, and then the essay ends, as does the more famous 'Apology for Raymond Sebond', with thoughts that echo Plutarch's, questioning the notion of an underlying individual essence that would guarantee a person's identity from one day to the next. These essays represent a unique episode in the history of Western philosophy. But part of their uniqueness consists in their not having been followed up in the century that followed Montaigne's (at least not in the form of a universalist moral philosophy[18]); and anyway, Montaigne does not connect the metaphysical and the moral segments of his reflections in the form of an argument. Even if we give up on the search for an argument structure (as perhaps a reader of Montaigne should in any case), we cannot be entirely sure that his moral idea of 'universal bonds' is at all connected to his scepticism about selfhood. It is very tempting to think that these were connected, in his mind; but it is worth noticing that we would then find ourselves (for better or worse) in a counterpart of the situation that many Western philosophers claim to find frustrating while grappling with Buddhists philosophical texts.[19] One thing that

---

[17] Even in its most radically sceptical phases, Sextan practice can resemble some Buddhist forms of spirituality, as Ethan Mills shows in his chapter here (Chap. 4 in this volume).

[18] Of those who were marked by Montaigne's writings, Blaise Pascal was arguably not theoretical enough (particularly in ethics), while 'les philosophes libertins' were arguably not concerned enough with Montaigne's altruism, to count as successors in this respect. (Those who would dismiss a 'universalist' reading in light of an alleged relativism in Montaigne might consider the anti-relativist interpretation in M. Conche's *Montaigne et la philosophie* (1987).)

[19] Contemporary philosophers with a passing exposure to Buddhist texts sometimes complain that, while they seem rich in philosophical themes, these texts do not explicitly identify premises and conclusions in ways that would make attributions of philosophical reasoning possible; but insofar as such philosophers are often content to tease out argument structures in (ancient or early modern) *Western* texts – that is, to impose structures of reasoning that are not explicitly there – they should beware of the looming double standard.

seems clear is that Montaigne felt that a more open mind about the possibilities for what an afterlife might – or might not – be like could encourage religious toleration among faiths with divergent conceptions of the afterlife; and a sure route to an open mind, he seems to have been proposing, would be systematic scepticism about our ability to settle such matters. (Having addressed *pre-contact* philosophers such as Montaigne and Hume in this section, I return to other Western 'self-sceptical' reflections in section III below – but some of the philosophers I mention below were in the very different position of having been exposed to Asian philosophy; nonetheless, that section resumes the historical overview, starting with a series of possible 'first contact' episodes.)

Some have wondered whether notions of the afterlife are universal in human cultures; but in light of the above, we might wonder whether *doubts* about an afterlife are similarly pervasive across different *philosophical* cultures, not to mention more radical doubts about the personal narratives that language seems to presuppose in describing our quotidian lives. Meanwhile, if we pause to consider what does – or what should – count as a 'philosophical' culture, we come up against questions about the relationship between the comparative history of ideas and cross-cultural philosophy. Jay Garfield has characterized *cross-cultural* philosophy as a more engaged and innovative approach, in contrast to an older *comparative* paradigm, which, while seeking historical accuracy, ran the risk of painting an overly rigid picture of (e.g.) Buddhist doctrine, losing both accuracy and philosophical vitality at the same time (Garfield 2015, ch. 1). A comparative approach remains feasible nonetheless, and may be required in order to pose the 'meta-problem' of how metaphysical problems have been linked to ethical problems in different philosophical traditions. In any case, one can combine elements of both approaches, allowing, for example, a scholarly assessment of strands in the Western tradition that have harbored deep reservations about the notion of personal identity (and *a fortiori*, the afterlife), as well as re-readings of Western sources in light of Buddhist ideas that were not available to their authors. Philosophy needs to be 'problems-based' as well as 'contextual', even when it takes historic texts as starting points; thus, if that latter kind of re-reading may seem ahistorical, that would not settle the question of its philosophical value. Cross-cultural philosophy, despite being unfamiliar to many, may nonetheless qualify as a paradigm of standard philosophical practice.

1.2   Selflessness in Bodhisattva Ethics

Earlier, I summarized some key Buddhist themes without mentioning the Mahāyāna concept of the *bodhisattva*. It is worth highlighting *bodhisattva* ethics, in part because this is a unique Buddhist innovation, and in part because it fascinatingly explores the possibility of a maximally demanding moral standard – proof it seems, among other things, that advanced Mahāyāna philosophy is not the amoral system that some have taken it to be.[20] Though many formulations of this ideal have generated interpretive disputes, a common way to describe a bodhisattva is as someone who willingly remains in cyclic states of being, and even in varying degrees of suffering, for as long as it takes to assist others to reach enlightenment as well (despite being sufficiently advanced to transcend all this via final liberation).[21] One notable feature of this ideal is that 'others' means 'all others'. Another notable feature is that the bodhisattva recognizes a kind of moral requirement to hold off on the prospect of spiritual perfection – or even nirvana – in order to prioritize the prospects of others; in other words, s/he adapts to the modalities of ordinary life, no matter how unseemly or vulgar, in order to help those who need help (often without assuming the *role* of a helper in anyone's eyes, even her own). The bodhisattva is not portrayed, of course, as entirely quotidian in outlook or entirely burdened with worldly matters. His or her motivation is rooted in *bodhicitta*, a conative and cognitive awakening that involves insight into *anātman*. (S/he recognizes the imperfection of saying "I must help other individuals", proceeding instead with an impersonal moral insight along the lines of "welfare *abroad* matters more than *this* welfare".) On the one hand, then, this is a moral agent who is inspired by insights that are at least partly philosophical in nature. On the other hand, the inspiration is intense, and in our day is notable as an element in social and political movements known collectively as 'Engaged Buddhism' – movements displaying intense moral commitment on the part of their members and advocates (cf. King 2009).

Some critics of Madhyamaka ethics, such as Paul Williams, have been famously sceptical, not so much about the moral ideal of the bodhisattva as about its elaboration in the hands of Śāntideva, who emphasizes a strong form of *anātman* as an instance of a wider 'emptiness' (Williams 1998). This is not the place to analyze or respond to Williams's charges against Śāntideva. But we can counter with a challenge: does any Western tradition of philosophical ethics do better in offering a deep justification for moral self-sacrifice?[22] And if so, then by the time it had done so, was it already under the influence of Buddhist literature? (As in the case of Schopenhauer, and less familiarly, in the case of Bertrand Russell.[23]) Or, if justifications were

---

[20] As Keown (2001) shows, Theravāda ethics is more straightforward, in some ways, than Mahāyāna ethics; but it is also worth mentioning that its Pali Canon contains a long-term moral vision very similar to the bodhisattva's, especially in its famous 'Metta Sutta'.

[21] Cf. Dayal (1999) and Goodman (2009); Williams (1998) takes issue with these interpretations, but I incorporate his qualification in speaking of others 'reaching enlightenment *as well*', the issue being whether a bodhisattva is meant to 'postpone' enlightenment itself. (On this issue, see Davis (2013).)

[22] In praising the bodhisattva ideal, I am assuming – as many 'Engaged Buddhists' do – that "*cyclic existence*" can be reinterpreted so as to cohere with ideals that do not depend on belief in rebirth. Meanwhile, those who would propose an Aristotelian answer to this should consult Keown's (2001) *The Nature of Buddhist Ethics*, which appeals to a hybrid of Buddhist and Aristotelian philosophy, actually finding many of the key aretaic elements of the latter in early Buddhism itself. The question remains whether recourse to the notion of personal identity (such as Sorabji (2006) finds in Aristotle) would end up jeopardizing the prospects for an Aristotelian *justification* for altruism.

[23] As Nalini Ramlakhan shows in her chapter here (Chap. 10).

offered – possibly in the case of Spinoza, for example – were they offered as unequivocally as those inherent in the bodhisattva ideal? Or is it time to acknowledge that a robust rational justification along the lines of Śāntideva's never was articulated in Western philosophy prior to the twentieth century?[24]

Another open question, more substantively philosophical, is whether this rational justification – 'robust' in the sense that it rests on a critical form of metaphysics – is the right kind of justification for any moral altruism that we ought to recognize as normative for us. Perhaps no 'ought' should be expected from an 'is', even a metaphysical 'is' (or even a metaphysical '*is not*', as in '*selfhood is not a factor…*'); and there is always the possibility that the metaphysical view invoked here is making the wrong kind of claim in any case. Moreover, as I hinted at the outset, an approach like Śāntideva's might also fail to be the right kind of justification for a different reason: his *Bodhicāryāvatāra*'s denial of selfhood is deployed alongside a kind of debunking of folk-psychology categories in general, a debunking that may extend to moral values as well, *nolens volens*. These debunkings (if not denials) may well be meant as steps towards realizing 'global emptiness'; and seeing as Śāntideva was a Madhyamika, those steps might just be the intended continuation of his argument from *anātman*. One might wonder whether this ultimately leaves morality behind. Charles Goodman claims that bodhisattvas practise the highest form of altruism when they "operate in a vast field of emptiness" (2009, 109); but as he discusses at length, this opens up many conceptual, philosophical and ethical problems. (One might argue that the point of any 'postponement' (of nirvana) must be rather that bodhisattvas would be more likely to engage effectively with moral considerations if they operate within ordinary life using ordinary concepts, albeit with a kind of moral perception that remains untainted by excessive conceptualization; but I set aside these issues for now.) These are all problems for bodhisattva ethics; but they are fruitful problems that parallel, in some respects, contemporary debates about the role of reductionism in revisionary forms of ethical theorizing.[25]

If any Western philosopher comes close to articulating something like a bodhisattva ideal, it may be the founder of the Academy, none other than Plato, a philosopher who is – perhaps too often – cited by Buddhist writers as a foil or an antithesis. As the next chapter shows (Chap. 2 in this volume), Plato's remarks following the parable of the cave reveal important parallels with accounts of the bod-

---

[24] Schopenhauer bears re-examination in this respect, although his reliance on Indian sources mitigates his claim to originality; another avenue for exploration, outlined briefly below, would be via the works of Friedrich Schelling (1775–1854), who picks up on ideas about selflessness expressed by Schleiermacher (noted at the end of Chap. 5 (Davis & Renaud, in this volume)). It is – intriguingly – unclear, however, what Asian sources Schelling had access to prior to 1804, when he expressed similar ideas (in Schelling 2010).

[25] I would argue that these parallels can be illuminating even if reductionism is ultimately not the right framework for interpreting Madhyamaka emptiness (setting aside, as we must here, the question of whether Madhyamaka could 'ultimately' allow a definitive interpretation, by its own lights). One could explore parallels with at least two kinds of reductionism: metaphysical reductionism (in relation to ethics, see Dancy (1997)) and meta-ethical reductionism (see Nuccetelli and Seay (2012)).

hisattva's vocation, and all this unfolds in the *Republic*, a work that highlights the difficulty of pinning down the notion of individual identity, placing the axiological emphasis elsewhere, in the elusive 'One' (an idea that would later suggest a kind of monism not altogether remote from certain Mahāyānist conceptions in – e.g. Yogācāra – metaphysics). The Western tradition may have lagged behind the Buddhist one on some of these points, due in part to what might be called 'Aristotelian amnesia' about these segments of the *Republic*. And yet, whether Peripatetics and Thomists (and other Aristotelians) had that effect or not, Plato himself seems to have overlooked some possibilities seen clearly by Buddhists, such as the emphasis on the welfare of *all* beings, and the specifically *moral* importance of intensive reflection on the elusiveness of diachronic identity in the phenomenal world.

1.3   Points of Historical Contact Between Western and Asian Philosophical Traditions

The backgrounds of the philosophers discussed in the first few chapters of this vol-ume – namely, Plato, the Pyrrhonist sceptic Sextus Empiricus, and Seneca – raise the question of whether Indian philosophical ideas may have caught the attention of ancient Europeans. Examining this question would require a wide-ranging histori-cal investigation that falls outside of our purview in this volume. Nonetheless, it is worth keeping in mind the possibility that, if some ancient Greek or Roman did outline some sort of anticipation of Śāntideva's argument, that philosopher may in turn have imbibed it from an earlier generation of Buddhists. It will probably never be settled, one way or the other, whether the Pythagoreans who influenced Plato came into contact with Indians; but it is well-known that Plotinus, the great Neoplatonist of the later Roman period, tried to learn more about their 'gymnoso-phist' philosophers by (attempting) a voyage to India. These connections have been explored by Thomas McEvilley (2002), who devotes even more attention to the travels of Pyrrho in India (circa 330 BCE); and recently Christopher Beckwith (2015) has concluded that the influence of Buddhist philosophers on Pyrrho and his followers was decisive. Meanwhile, Richard Sorabji suggests that we may find it hard to explain some of Seneca's proposed methods for reaching *apatheia* – through reflection on the daily change in our identities – without considering the possibility that Buddhist ideas had reached him indirectly, albeit through channels that remain undocumented (Sorabji 2006: 41). Sorabji also mentions similar reflections in Plutarch's essay "On the E at Delphi", about a generation later (around 100 CE).

In any case, these particular passages from Plutarch and Seneca, along with simi-lar ones in Lucretius, were not given much attention until they were incorporated into Montaigne's essays in the sixteenth century. In the meantime, with the slight awareness of these passages that may have persisted here and there, there would have been even less awareness of a possible historical link to the Indian philosophi-cal context. Until well into the Renaissance, the concept of an Indian 'gymnoso-phist' existed, but not the concept of a 'Buddhist'; this gap in the European understanding of Asian philosophies lasted until the eighteenth century. We might wonder if, in the meantime, Western philosophers had perhaps thought of arguments *analogous* to Śāntideva's, or at least thought of the general idea that the fate of normative egoism should be linked to the metaphysics of the ego. It certainly seems possible that a Valla or a Pico della Mirandola,[26] if not Erasmus or More, might have considered these possibilities, without needing inspiration from outside the Christian tradition or its Platonic and Stoic praecursors. Many of these Renaissance scholars must have noticed the passages in Seneca and Plutarch; but for all we know, they would have rested content with the implications for personal *apatheia* or *ataraxia*, rather than considering possible moral implications. (The former, in itself, would have been notable; but we cannot be sure even of that sort of impact.)

Montaigne, for one, certainly did notice the passage that Sorabji highlights in Plutarch: he quotes extensively from it at the end of his "Apology for Raymond Sebond" (de Montaigne 2003, 681–82). Even if Montaigne was unaware of the Buddhist conception of *anātman*, it is not outside the realm of possibility that he may nonetheless have imbibed traces of it second-hand or third-hand – hands stretching across millennia – via Plutarch and/or Seneca. In any case, in contrast with other self-sceptical thinkers such as Nietzsche, the scepticism in Montaigne seems, as we have seen, to combine with an underlying belief in altruism. We have already noted how this combination is evident in his late essay 'On Vanity' (1588). Yet, as we have already observed, Montaigne does not *explicitly* construct an argument leading from a no-self view to a cosmopolitan concern for humanity. Spinoza and Hume come closer to making this explicit, and Schleiermacher and Schelling come even closer.[27] Schopenhauer does make this explicit – but by the time he does, it is hardly surprising, insofar as Schopenhauer had probably gleaned the kernel of such an argument from classical Indian texts.[28]

In some ways a more intriguing case is that of Friedrich Schelling, who had been writing on similar themes for decades before Schopenhauer found inspiration in ancient Indian texts. As far as I know, no evidence has come to light that Schelling was *decisively* influenced by Asian sources in any of his early idealist phases. But what I have called 'post-contact inspiration' was clearly widespread and intense in Germany, following the circulation of passages from the *Bhagavad Gita* at the end of the eighteenth century. In 1802, Schelling praised the "sacred texts of the Indians" in his lectures, presumably alluding to the *Gita*, among others.[29] And in 1804, he wrote *Philosophy and Religion*, in which the monism of his Spinozist-inflected con-

---

[26] Lorenzo Valla (1407–57) or perhaps cousin Giorgio (1447–1500); and if not Giovanni Pico della Mirandola (1463–94) then quite possibly his nephew G. Francesco (1470–1533).

[27] On Hume, see Chap. 6 in this volume; on Spinoza and Schleiermacher, see Chap. 5.

[28] App (2006) argues that the *Gita* was an earlier influence on Schopenhauer than the *Upanisads*, and also points out that he had been exposed to Buddhist ideas well before 1818 (the year of the first edition of *World as Will and Representation*). On his exposure to Buddhism, see App (2006: 58, 62n.) and his own *op. cit.*

[29] Cf. Clarke 1997: 63. As App (2006) notes, a German translation of the *Gita* appeared in 1802.

ception of God also bears the traces of both Neoplatonism and Vedanta. Meanwhile, was the *ethical* dimension of this phase of Schelling's work as impersonal as his metaphysics, or at least, as altruistic as the ethics we find in Montaigne or Schleiermacher? Starting with a tragic narrative about humanity's 'fallen' self-conceptions, Schelling laments that "the soul, which subordinates its infinite part to finitude by apprehending itself in [illusory] selfhood, thereby falls" ([1804] 2010, 40). His aim is to reconcile the idea that morality is the soul's "inclination… to be one with God" and the ideal of a "moral community of rational beings" (42–43). How, he asks, can "mankind restore itself to a more perfect life" (46)? Echoing *anātman*, it would seem, Schelling argues that the envisaged achievement of both morality and beatitude requires abandoning the notions of selfhood and personal immortality: "immortality would only be a continued mortality and an ongoing imprisonment of the soul rather than a liberation… the desire for immortality origi- nates directly out of finitude, and would [offer little to] those who strive to release the soul" (47) – a release whose value, and perhaps even whose *de re* nature, is putatively the same throughout the moral community. Admittedly, Schelling was probably influenced here by a kind of *ātmavada* (via Vedanta texts) rather than Buddhist *anātman*. But what he was picking up on, arguably, were some threads that weave through both of these Indian traditions.[30] It remains an open question whether Schopenhauer still deserves credit for the earliest explicit adaptation of such ideas in Western philosophy, or whether such precedents might rather be found in the writings of Schleiermacher and Schelling.

1.4 Perspectives on Ethics Without Self: Overview of Twelve Cross-Cultural Examinations

Some of the background surveyed above helps to account for aspects of the struc- ture of this volume – in particular, the chronological gap between Hellenistic phi- losophy and Spinoza. After Michael Griffin's account of correspondences between Platonic ethics and Buddhist ethics (Chap. 2), one might wonder about correspon- dences in the case of Neoplatonism (and perhaps about the weakening of their reso- nance among medieval philosophers with Platonic tendencies).[31] After Emily

---

[30] Bilimoria (1997) proposes this rapprochement between the traditions: "insofar as the *ātman* remains a designation for the concept of the immutable, undifferentiated, unconditioned and autonomous principle of existence… the Buddhists were justified in calling into question the *par- ticular* conception [i.e. a *different* conception of *ātman*] in their assertion of the *anātman* or no-self doctrine" (1997: 253, my italics). Bilimoria offers an account of a similarly self-sceptical perspec- tive in Shankara's (Advaita Vedanta) approach.

[31] In his Introduction to a new translation of Olympiodorus, Griffin (2014) addresses related themes in Neoplatonism. There is an older secondary literature comparing Indian philosophy and Neoplatonism, e.g. Radhakrishnan (1939), who, in relation to Buddhism, focuses even more on Gnostic parallels (1939, 207 ff.) – yielding interesting comparisons, whatever one may think of the zealous perennialism underlying them.

McRae's account of parallels between Stoics and Buddhist philosophers (Chap. 3), one might wonder about the legacy of Stoic writings in the Renaissance; and after digesting Ethan Mills's discussion of Nagarjunian scepticism and Pyrrhonist scepticism (Chap. 4), one may wish to compare the former to Montaigne as well and consider his impact on early modern philosophy in that light. However, despite some strictly *comparative* resonances, the traces of Buddhist and other Indian philosophical ideas were apparently buried until after the time of Descartes. The rest of this volume therefore passes over the Renaissance period, and picks up the thread with Spinoza in the late seventeenth century.[32] The chapter on Spinoza, written by Mary D. Renaud and myself, provides a bookend for what we can call the precontact phase with respect to Buddhist philosophy, a phase that includes Hume and Kant. While some syncretistic examples of Asian philosophy had come to the attention of Leibniz, Malebranche and others (see Chap. 5), the specifically Buddhist themes were often not understood as such, and were generally not based on good translations of Buddhist texts until the 1800s, when a more informed – if still imperfect – intercultural contact can be said to have begun (Droit 2003). The chapter on Spinoza, which considers his neglected comments on benevolence in the latter part of his *Ethics* as well as the reactions of some contemporaries (such as Pierre Bayle, who interpreted his monism as 'oriental'), closes with a glance at later figures such as Herder and Schleiermacher, who were not only influenced by both Kant and Spinoza, but had finally made direct acquaintance with ancient Indian texts.

The chapters on Hume and Kant, meanwhile, highlight the connection between ethics and ontology (philosophical psychology in particular) in some similar ways. Jay Garfield suggests that Hume's innovative psychology shaped various features of his ethics, such as the supplanting of would-be categorical imperatives with an affective phenomenology of mutual care and concern. Emer O'Hagan addresses Kant, who entertains a similar pattern of thought, in the form of a conditional: a revisionary psychology of personal (non)identity would, in his view, entail the nonapplicability of categorical imperatives. (What Kant ultimately affirms, of course, is the contrapositive: that because there *are* categorical imperatives, we must postulate immortality, and *a fortiori* must affirm the personal identity of the moral agent). We might hesitate, of course, to characterize Buddhist ethics as rejecting all categorical values, especially insofar as 'categorical' means independent of variable desires – making *nirvana*, arguably, a categorical value in that sense.[33] But in any case, we

---

[32] It may be worth acknowledging here that Descartes, traditionally considered the pivotal figure between the Renaissance and a new phase of modern philosophy, advanced a highly cosmopolitan conception of universal moral concern (see Marquardt 2015). In light of his robustly realist affirmation of the self as a persisting and irreducible entity, this reminds us that theories of altruism cannot be monopolized by those who deny this; and anyway, the Buddhist claim is not that believing in *ātman* entails being a normative egoist (so the Buddhist can acknowledge Descartes's consistency, metaphysical soundness aside), it is rather that *an*-ātman entails *not* being a normative egoist (*salva veritate*). Descartes might be germane to comparisons with Buddhist *ethics*; but the metaphysical gulf between them remains wide.

[33] There are fault-lines, on this point, that divide Theravādins from some Mahāyānists (and perhaps Yogācārins from other Mahāyānists) who understand 'nirvāna' very differently; cf. Huntington

can see here a sort of anticipation of the Buddhist nexus – what I called earlier the *connection between insight and praxis* – which turns out to find echoes in both Hume and Kant.

As these chapters illustrate, not all of the authors in this volume accept reductionist versions of the Śāntideva argument; for that matter, we are not all agreed on the soundness of the 'natural' thought offered in the first line of this introduction. To take only Garfield and O'Hagan as examples for the moment, Garfield avoids a reductionist version of *anātman*, and prefers a Madhyamaka/Humean form of care ethics (translating *karuṇā* as 'care'), rather than a consequentialist version of Mahāyānist anti-egoism. There are thus differences of opinion as to how we should *interpret* non-self and *karuṇā*. For her part, O'Hagan does not accept Śāntideva-style arguments when they are cast in the metaphysical form favoured by Buddhist ethicists such as Charles Goodman. O'Hagan's reading of psychological deconstruction as a 'contemplative strategy' recalls the Buddhist notion of conventional truths that are useful but that do not constitute ultimate truths.[34] Like some Madhyamikas – but for more Kantian reasons – she does not go along with the idea that *anātman* is an ultimate truth (or with the idea that ultimate metaphysical truths must be morally or practically decisive, whatever they may be), whereas some other contributors are more open to the possibility that ultimate truth could be a source of first principles, in ethics as well as in metaphysics. For example, Michael Griffin's sympathies lie with Plato (and certain proto-Buddhist elements therein), and Nalini Ramlakhan's with Russell and his understanding of no-self as what she calls *yatha-bhuta-dassana* (in other words, a *truth* rather than a 'strategy'). Disagreements such as these have added richness to the ongoing debate on these questions, both here and among Buddhist philosophers generally.

In the latter half of this volume, several chapters build on perspectives that do embrace an ethical understanding of Buddhist emptiness – as does, for example, Douglas Berger's critique of Schopenhauer and Nietzsche, albeit from a standpoint closer to Yogācāra than to the Madhyamaka of Śāntideva. Berger argues that, whatever else they learned from Asian sources, both Schopenhauer and Nietzsche dogmatically shut the door to the Buddhist transcendence of desire and ego, despite the sound philosophical reasons for keeping such possibilities open. (Berger nonetheless acknowledges that Schopenhauer developed a robust version of the argument from no-self to compassion, in his *World as Will and Representation*.) In the

---

1989, Makransky 1997: ch. 13, Suzuki 1999 (a sutra that aims to subvert certain earlier notions of *nirvana*), Clayton 2006: 115, & Cowherds 2016.

[34] Debates about conventional and ultimate truth in Buddhism provide one sort of occasion for posing the meta-ethical questions that arose in my second paragraph (in the introduction). Important discussions include Keown's (2001) on the 'transcendency thesis' (the idea that ethical concerns disappear from the ultimate point of view, an idea Keown rightly challenges), and the Cowherds (2016). As some chapters in the latter seem to confirm, global emptiness claims (e.g. of Madhyamaka origin) may risk subverting the notion of moral truth, potentially disqualifying every form of morality that is not merely a 'conventional' morality. Be that as it may, this possibility arises from reflections on *global emptiness*, not from *anātman* or other self-sceptical approaches to ethics.

chapter that follows, by contrast, Sonia Sikka draws on Heidegger who, despite his own sympathies with elements of the Buddhist tradition, rejected the sort of reductionism about selfhood that characterizes some strands of Buddhist doctrine. Sikka suggests that ultimately there may be a greater resonance in Heidegger's work with elements of the Vedānta tradition than with the moral ideals of *bodhicitta* and radically self-sacrificing *karuṇā*.[35]

In their discussions of Nietzsche and Heidegger (respectively), Berger and Sikka address ethical concerns mainly in connection with non-moral value, having to do with the pursuit of 'meaning', for lack of a better word (something along the lines of 'path', as in the Sanskrit term *marga*). Ramlakhan also addresses this issue, with reference to William James's *Varieties of Religious Experience*. But the last four essays of the volume, Ramlakhan's included, shift the focus back to the interpersonal dimension – that is, to how the morality of *altruism* may need to be modified in light of a critical examination of selfhood, and all the more so, perhaps, if that examination reaches similar ontological conclusions in both the Buddhist and the Western contexts.[36] Ramlakhan shows that both James and Russell were sceptical about the ontological basis of personal identity, and that both recognized the ethical implications, which, in James's case, may have included a form of impersonal consequentialism. (She also discusses their awareness of Buddhist moral arguments based on *anātman*, and their having belonged to one of the first generations of Anglo-Americans to come across those arguments in primary sources.) In his chapter, Stephen Harris discusses some recent arguments along similar lines, famously expounded by Derek Parfit in *Reasons and Persons* (1987, first ed. 1984), to the effect that radical altruism, if not impersonal consequentialism, would be supported by a revisionary conception of selfhood – one that Parfit himself considered Buddhist in spirit. Harris also considers how Mark Siderits has utilized Buddhist premises to defend Parfitian moral conclusions, and questions whether Śāntideva provides those premises in the way that Siderits and Charles Goodman have claimed. Ultimately Harris recommends an approach more akin to the virtue-oriented Buddhist ethics defended by Damien Keown (2001), albeit while preserving the Mahāyāna inflections of Śāntideva's perspective.

In his chapter in this volume – the penultimate chapter – Ashwani Peetush transposes the moral issues to the level of normative political philosophy, drawing on the

---

[35] Sikka thereby maintains some critical distance from – *inter alia* – a famous but unsubstantiated story related by William Barrett about Heidegger's reaction to reading work by the Japanese Buddhist philosopher Daisetz Suzuki (mentioned in Barrett 1956); allegedly, Heidegger remarked on a close convergence between his ideas and the Zen perspective of Suzuki. In her fn. 1, Sikka cites studies that trace other ways in which East Asian philosophical works may have influenced Heidegger.

[36] In the case of Ramlakhan's remit, this means the post-idealist generation of James and Russell, to which Henri Bergson could be added (with his *Two Sources of Morality and Religion* expressing a deep affinity with Buddhist axiology); meanwhile the claim of intercultural convergence could be strengthened by looking, as we have not done here, at similar ideas in their idealist predecessors (as the ethical themes here cut across the idealist-realist divide), such as F.H. Bradley (1846–1924) and J.M.E. McTaggart (1866–1925).

work of Charles Taylor to show that consequentialism may not be the only notable alternative to the various forms of liberalism and libertarianism that rely on an onto-logical commitment to individualism. As Taylor's approach also reveals, and as Peetush shows, the sorts of revisions to individualistic conceptions of selfhood that seem warranted need not be of the reductionist kind advanced by Parfit; but even when they are not of that kind, they carry potent ethical implications, as Buddhists and other philosophers in the classical Indian tradition perceived. In a similar spirit, we turn – that is, Pragati Sahni and myself – to the Buddhist-influenced perspectives of Arne Naess and other environmental philosophers, considering the role that revision-ary notions of identity can play both in deep ecology and in competing conceptions of environmental ethics. Some deep ecologists echo the kind of non-reductionist ontol-ogy Peetush discusses; and once again, the approach favoured by Siderits and Goodman provides a fruitful contrast, especially in light of the ethical stakes involved.

Returning to the question posed at the outset above: what if the 'ethical' implica-tions of dispensing with the classical notion of selfhood are more radically subver-sive – to the point of not being *ethical* at all? For example, what if the philosophical implications are of the kinds associated with moral nihilism, or more broadly some form of what was called 'anti-realism' in twentieth-century meta-ethics?[37] Irrealisms of these kinds arose out of existentialism, cultural relativism and empiricist non-cognitivism (each of which tended to promote doubts about personal identity as well). It might seem that the very idea of morality – if not ethics in general – would be subverted, not only by these perspectives, but by Buddhist ontological revisionism as well. To put the question in terms that echo all of these developments: should we consider these ontological paradigm shifts, not as heralds of new moral imperatives, but as insights that would simply reveal the emptiness of morality?[38] Of course, this question has been loaded so as to echo the Buddhist theme of 'emptiness'; but this immediately raises the reverse question: is it fair to assimilate themes in the Buddhist tradition of ethical reflection to themes concerning 'emptiness' in existentialism and its kin (whether we describe these as scepticism, nihilism or non-cognitivism)? A lengthy answer, available only within the scope of a book – perhaps indeed a book like this one – would be that one should be sceptical of this assimilation without rul-ing out assimilations along different philosophical lines. But the short answer, for now, will have to be that further scrutiny of what came after Heidegger and Russell, seen in parallel with Buddhist ideas, would be a welcome supplement to our work

---

[37] This meta-ethical question is raised in some of the chapters here, e.g. in the latter half of Chap. 5; in Emer O'Hagan's discussion of Charles Goodman's ethics of emptiness (Chap. 7); in Nalini Ramlakhan's discussion of William James's pragmatism (Chap. 10); in Stephen Harris's account of Susan Wolf's objections to Parfit's reductionism (Chap. 11); and elsewhere, in Cowherds (2016), cited especially by Jay Garfield (Chap. 6).

[38] Williams (1998) worries about this in connection with a sort of nihilism that certain Buddhist views seem to imply about values – something that he thinks is indeed implied, *nolens volens*. (One can dispute his diagnosis of the problem; but the texts and contexts he cites may show at least that the question is not just a peculiarly modern preoccupation.) Some of the Cowherds (2016) argue that there is no such problem; I have argued that there is a problem, but one incurred else-where, i.e. not as a result of the *anatman* claim that worries Williams (Davis forthcoming).

here. Meanwhile, these questions have also formed an important backdrop to the contemporary debate between Damien Keown and Charles Goodman as to the so-called 'foundations' of Buddhist ethics, and the adjacent debate between them and a host of others who argue that Buddhist ethics neither contains nor permits 'foundations' (see, e.g., Barnhart 2012). Insofar as ethical realism and anti-realism have a bearing on these debates, ontology and/or metaphysics will have a crucial role to play in deepening and refining the various considerations at play.

The works of Damien Keown, Mark Siderits and Charles Goodman are mentioned in several of the chapters that follow in this volume, but it is worth making one further remark on the prominent roles they play in the dialectics pursued in the closing chapters of this volume.[39] These are contemporary figures who exemplify a transition from the post-contact philosophers covered here (from Schopenhauer to Russell) to more recent philosophers, who not only draw inspiration from Buddhist philosophy, but do so with a level of familiarity and fluency that was rarely present – at least among philosophers – until near the turn of the present century. One of the complications in analyzing the traces of Buddhist ideas in such writers as Heidegger and Russell results from their limited knowledge of both primary and (credible) secondary sources, not to mention limited understanding of the languages and cultures of India and elsewhere. Since their passing, this situation has changed, with writers like those mentioned here offering a historic first: the advent of a simultaneous expertise in philosophy and scholarship, where both the philosophy and the scholarship are conducted with deep cross-cultural understanding. With respect to what has often been referred to as an encounter – if not a clash – between so-called 'Western' and 'Eastern' philosophical sensibilities (so-called for a long but perhaps now lapsed period of time), we may hope that a merely 'post-contact' phase has finally graduated to what Siderits calls '*fusion philosophy*'.[40]

References

App, Urs. 2006. Schopenhauer's Initial Encounter with Indian Thought. *Schopenhauer-Jahrbuch* 87: 35–76.

Barnhart, Michael G. 2012. Theory and Comparison in the Discussion of Buddhist Ethics. *Philosophy East and West* 62 (1): 16–43.

Barrett, William. 1956. *"Introduction" to D. Suzuki's Zen Buddhism*. New York: Doubleday.

Beckwith, Christopher. 2015. *Greek Buddha: Pyrrho's Encounter with Early Buddhism in Central Asia*. Princeton: Princeton University Press.

Bergson, Henri. [1932] 1977. *The Two Sources of Morality and Religion*. Trans. R.A. Audra and C. Brereton. Notre Dame: University of Notre Dame Press.

---

[39] These three philosophers are hardly alone in exploring innovative forms of Buddhist ethical theory, and an earlier version of this footnote had included a list of names of others who have advanced the state of the art in this area – however, the list grew too long to fit into a single note. (See Gowans 2015, for both a survey of some of these writers and a detailed assessment of the problems and prospects for their interpretations and positions).

[40] Siderits (2015, 1–5).

Bett, Richard. 2000. *Pyrrho, his Antecedents, and his Legacy*. Oxford: Oxford University Press.

Bilimoria, Purushottama. 1997. On Śankara's Attempted Reconciliation of 'You' and 'I': *Yusmadasmatsamanvaya*. In *Relativism, Suffering and Beyond: Essays in Memory of Bimal Matilal*, ed. P. Bilimoria and J. Mohanty. Delhi: Oxford University Press.

Clarke, J.J. 1997. *Oriental Enlightenment: The Encounter between Asian and Western Thought*. London: Routledge.

Clayton, Barbra. 2006. *Moral Theory in Śāntideva's Śikṣāsamuccaya: Cultivating the Fruits of Virtue*. New York: Routledge.

———. 2009. Sāntideva, Virtue and Consequentialism. In *Destroying Mara Forever: Buddhist Ethics Essays in Honor of Damien Keown*, ed. J. Powers and C.S. Prebish. Snow Lion: Ithaca.

Conche, Marcel. 1987. *Montaigne et la philosophie*, 1st ed, 2nd ed, 1996. Paris: Ed. Mégare.

Cowherds. 2016. *Moonpaths: Emptiness and Ethics*, ed. Cowherds. New York: Oxford University Press.

Dancy, Jonathan, ed. 1997. *Reading Parfit*. Oxford: Blackwell.

Davidson, Herbert. 1992. *Alfarabi, Avicenna and Averroes on Intellect*. Oxford: Oxford University Press.

Davis, Gordon. 2013. Traces of Consequentialism and Non-Consequentialism in Bodhisattva Ethics. *Philosophy East and West* 63: 275–305.

———. forthcoming. The *Atipada* Problem in Buddhist Meta-Ethics. *Journal of Buddhist Ethics*.

Dayal, Har. [1932] 1999. *The Bodhisattva Doctrine in Buddhist Sanskrit Literature*. Delhi: Motilal Banarsidass.

de Montaigne, Michel. 2003. *The Complete Essays*, ed. & trans. M.A. Screech. London: Penguin.

Droit, Roger-Pol. 2003. *The Cult of Nothingness: The Philosophers and the Buddha*. Chapel Hill: University of North Carolina Press.

Garfield, Jay. 2015. *Engaging Buddhism: Why it Matters to Philosophy*. Oxford: Oxford University Press.

Goodman, Charles. 2009. *The Consequences of Compassion: An Interpretation and Defence of Buddhist Ethics*. Oxford: Oxford University Press.

Goodman, Charles, and Sonam Thakchoe. 2016. The Many Voices of Buddhist Ethics. In *Moonpaths: Emptiness and Ethics*, ed. Cowherds, 7–20. New York: Oxford University Press.

Gowans, Christopher W. 2015. *Buddhist Moral Philosophy: An Introduction*. New York: Routledge.

Griffin, Michael (ed.). 2014. *Olympiodorus: Life of Plato and On Plato First Alcibiades 1–9*. Trans. M. Griffin. London: Bloomsbury.

Huntington, C.W. 1989. *The Emptiness of Emptiness: an introduction to early Indian Mādhyamika*. Honolulu: University of Hawaii Press.

Jenkins, Stephen. 2016. Walking into Compassion: The Three *Alambana of Karuṇā*. In *Moonpaths: Emptiness and Ethics*, ed. Cowherds, 97–118. New York: Oxford University Press.

Keown, Damien. 2001. *The Nature of Buddhist Ethics*, rev. ed. New York: Palgrave.

King, Sallie. 2009. *Socially Engaged Buddhism*. Honolulu: University of Hawaii Press.

Long, David. 2012. *Hume and Buddhism: A Comparative Study of Personal Identity, Skepticism and Moral Sentiments*. Saarbrucken: LAP Lambert.

Makransky, John J. 1997. *Buddhahood Embodied: Sources of Controversy in India and Tibet*. Albany: SUNY Press.

Marquardt, Sarah. 2015. The Long Road to Peace: Descartes's Modernization of Generosity in The Passions of the Soul. *History of Political Thought* 36 (1): 53–83.

McEvilley, Thomas. 2002. *The Shape of Ancient Thought: Comparative Studies in Greek and Indian Philosophies*. New York: Allworth Press.

Montaigne, Michel. 2003. *The Complete Essays*, ed. & trans. M.A. Screech. London: Penguin.

Nagel, Thomas. 1986. *The View from Nowhere*. Oxford: Oxford University Press.

Nuccetelli, S., and G. Seay, eds. 2012. *Ethical Naturalism: Current Debates*. Cambridge: Cambridge University Press.

Parfit, Derek. 1984 (rev. ed. 1987). *Reasons and Persons*, rev. ed. Oxford: Clarendon Press.

Plutarch. 1936. The E at Delphi. In *Plutarch: Moralia,* vol. V. Trans. F.C. Babbitt. Cambridge, MA: Harvard University Press.

Radhakrishnan, S.. 1939 (2nd ed. 1940). *Eastern Religions and Western Thought,* 2nd ed. Oxford: Oxford University Press.

Śāntideva. 1995. *The Bodhicaryāvatāra.* Trans. K. Crosby and A. Skilton. Oxford: Oxford University Press.

Schelling, F.W.J. [1804] 2010. *Philosophy and Religion.* Trans. K. Ottmann. Putnam: Spring Publications.

Sextus, Empiricus. 2000. *Outlines of Scepticism.* Ed/Trans. J. Annas and J. Barnes. Cambridge: Cambridge University Press.

Siderits, Mark. 2000. The Reality of Altruism: Reconstructing Śāntideva. *Philosophy East and West* 50 (3): 412–424.

———. 2006. Buddhist Reductionism and the Structure of Buddhist Ethics. In *Indian Ethics: Classical and Contemporary Challenges,* ed. P. Bilimoria, J. Prabhu, and R. Sharma. Aldershot: Ashgate.

———. 2015. *Personal Identity and Buddhist Philosophy: Empty Persons.* 2nd ed. Surrey: Ashgate.

Sorabji, Richard. 2006. *Self: Ancient and Modern Insights about Individuality, Life and Death.* Oxford: Clarendon Press.

Strawson, Galen. 2011. *The Evident Connexion: Hume on Personal Identity.* Oxford: Oxford University Press.

Suzuki, D.T. (trans.). [1932] 1999. *The Lankāvatāra Sutra: A Mahāyāna Text.* Delhi: Motilal Banarsidass.

Taylor, Charles. 1989. *Sources of the Self: The Making of the Modern Identity.* Cambridge, MA: Harvard University Press.

Thiel, Udo. 2011. *The Early Modern Subject: Self-Consciousness and Personal Identity from Descartes to Hume.* Oxford: Oxford University Press.

Williams, Paul. 1998. *Altruism and Reality: Studies in the Philosophy of the Bodhicaryāvatāra.* London: Curzon Press.

Chapter 2
The Ethics of Self-Knowledge in Platonic and Buddhist Philosophy

Michael Griffin

2.1 Introduction

This chapter explores Plato's discussions of self-knowledge, and its ethical implications, in the light of similarly motivated arguments in the Buddhist philosophical tradition. Each section begins with Plato, and concludes with Buddhist parallels or contrasts. Section 2.2 contrasts Plato's early portrayal of Socrates with the Pāli canonical depiction of the Buddha. Socrates and the Buddha diagnose a common misunderstanding of selfhood as the primary cause of human suffering: in particular, both maintain that we are misled into error and unhappiness by identifying our bodies, our social status, or our possessions as self. Both recommend a radical reconceptualization of the self as a necessary step toward their respective ultimate concerns, human well-being (*eudaimonia*) and liberation (*nirvāṇa*). But Socrates endorses a positive view that the Buddha rejects, namely, that one's soul (*psychē*)—a locus of cognitive agency capable of reflexive self-awareness—*is* one's self.

Section 2.3 explores a Buddhist style of objection to this line of argument: the plurality and impermanence of mental states render the soul an implausible candidate for selfhood. Plato would respect this worry: in dialogues like *Republic* and *Phaedrus*, he analyzes the soul as a complex of rational, emotional, and desiderative agencies whose disunity and impermanence are evidently problematic. But Plato's metaphysical theory of Forms or Patterns (*eidē, ideai*) offers resources for a reply: even if a given soul presently lacks synchronic and diachronic coherence,

I would like to record my gratitude to Gordon Davis, Richard Sorabji, Mark McPherran, and Adam Kay, who kindly read and commented on earlier drafts of this chapter. I am, of course, solely responsible for its remaining faults.

M. Griffin (✉)
University of British Columbia, Vancouver, BC, Canada
e-mail: michael.griffin@ubc.ca

© Springer International Publishing AG, part of Springer Nature 2018
G. F. Davis (ed.), *Ethics without Self, Dharma without Atman*, Sophia Studies
in Cross-cultural Philosophy of Traditions and Cultures 24,
https://doi.org/10.1007/978-3-319-67407-0_2

philosophy may strive for the *prescriptive* objective of psychological harmony and unification, guided by reason in its apprehension of Forms.

In Sect. 2.4, I review the relationship of this objective with Plato's ethic of world-transcendence, which is constituted by the reasoning soul's uninhibited contemplation of Forms. I highlight the Platonic and Buddhist traditions' comparable motivations for valuing world-transcendence, grounded in their metaphysical analyses of impermanence. But Plato's analysis of perceptible objects as impermanent processes is again counterbalanced by his theory of Forms, which provide an eternal and satisfying reality to which the soul can fly (*Tht.* 176B). Although this view seems basically opposed to Buddhist ontology, there are interesting parallels with later Buddhist schools of thought, including Yogācāra.

In Sect. 2.5, I explore a tension, shared by both traditions, between an objective of world-transcendence and a genuine concern for embodied, altruistic social virtue. This tension emerges in strikingly similar ethical challenges facing the Platonic Philosopher-King and the Mahāyāna Bodhisattva, whose liberating insight and self-knowledge virtually obliges him or her to return to the "cave" of social service. Their cases are mutually illuminating, as their respective decisions to re-enter the cave or *saṃsāra* are open to similar consequentialist, deontological, and virtue-ethical interpretations; neither, however, is exhaustively explained by any one of these modern meta-ethical accounts.

Section 2.6 is an appendix on themes in the intellectual legacy of Platonism. This discussion focuses on the metaphysics and ethics of Aristotle, who is not otherwise treated in detail in this volume. Despite contrasting views on the nature of being, personhood, and the human good, I suggest that Aristotle, Plato, and Buddhist thinkers may draw similar conclusions about the therapeutic role of the enlightened philosopher in society.

2.2 Socrates: The Therapy of Reason

2.2.1 Socrates

For Socrates, philosophy was a way of life[1]; for his contemporaries, it was a pattern of behavior peculiar to one man, Socrates. In fact, the word "philosophy" (*philosophia, philosophein*) may have developed its familiar sense in fourth-century Greek in

---

[1]The treatment of "ancient philosophy as a way of life" has become increasingly familiar in anglophone scholarship on later Greek philosophy, particularly in the wake of foundational work by Michel Foucault and Pierre Hadot (see Hadot 1995; Hadot and Chase 2004; Chase et al. 2013; Sorabji 2014); this basic concern arguably bridges the Graeco-Roman and Indic philosophical traditions (see for instance Carlisle and Ganeri 2010; Ganeri 2013). For the Socratic origins of philosophy in this sense, see for example Cooper (2012, pp. 24–69). For his influence on the first-generation "Socratics," see Boys-Stones and Rowe (2013). On Plato in general, Fine (2008) is a helpful overview of recent literature, and Cooper and Hutchinson (1997) is now the standard translation in English.

part to label and generalize Socrates' unusual conduct[2]: Socrates did not take himself to be engaged in a pre-existing social practice called philosophy, but to be doing something unique, at least in his community and lifetime.[3] Relying on Plato's *Apology*, chronologically the earliest of the Platonic dialogues, we can reconstruct a brief account of what Plato took this Socratic practice to be. (In this chapter, "Socrates" will name the character in Plato's "earlier" dialogues, unless otherwise noted).[4]

Socrates traced his philosophical career to an oracle delivered by Apollo's priestess at Delphi.[5] She declared him the wisest (*sophōtatos*) of human beings (*Ap.* 20E–21B). Conscious of Apollo's reputation for enigma, Socrates puzzled over the oracle's meaning:

> When I heard of this reply I asked myself: "Whatever does the god mean? What is his riddle? I am very conscious that I am not wise at all; what then does he mean by saying that I am the wisest? For surely he does not lie; it is not legitimate for him to do so." (Plato, *Apology* 21B, tr. Grube)[6]

Characteristically, Socrates put the god to the test. He embarked on an ambitious social experiment (*Apology* 21C–E), deploying a distinctive method of question and answer—the "cross-examination" or *elenchos*[7]—to test contemporaries with a reputation for "wisdom" (*sophia, phronēsis*). (Socrates may take "wisdom" to be a

---

[2] Plato, as several scholars have argued, spent the first half of the fourth century effectively "constructing" the social practice of philosophy as a more broadly applicable lifestyle based on the idiosyncratic life of Socrates, inviting others to follow in Socrates' footsteps (Blondell 2002; Nightingale 2000), and vying with his contemporary Isocrates (cf. *Antidosis* 271) to define the kind of "learning outcome" that *philosophia* offers. Socrates' behavior struck some of his contemporaries as sufficiently peculiar to warrant its own verb (*sōkratein*): see for example Aristophanes, *Birds* 1282.

[3] "You will not easily find another like me—and if you take my advice, you will spare my life" (*Ap.* 31A); "I make you *be* happy (*eudaimōn*)" (*Ap.* 36E). But "You [sentenced me to execution] in the belief that you would avoid giving an account of your life, but… [t]here will be more people to test you, whom I now held back… they will be younger and you will resent them more" (*Ap.* 39C–D).

[4] Since the historical Socrates left no written record, we are dependent on divergent witnesses, especially his pupils Plato and Xenophon and the contemporary comic playwright Aristophanes, for an account of his views—the "Socratic problem" (Blondell 2002; see also Press 2000). In this chapter, we are primarily interested in Plato's depiction of Socrates and the model of philosophy and selfhood that he derived from Socrates. For these purposes, this section will rely primarily on the set of dialogues by Plato generally considered "early," which present a more or less coherent picture of Socratic thought (see for example Irwin 2008).

[5] Socrates' relationship with the gods, and especially with Apollo (whom he repeatedly describes himself as serving), is an interesting and broad-ranging question. See McPherran for a compelling interpretation of the evidence: Socrates is committed to "the value of rational elenctic philosophy" while acknowledging that this commitment "is crucially shaped by—and, reciprocally, also shapes—[his] conception of himself as a divinely guided servant of the gods" (McPherran 1996: 10).

[6] Unless otherwise specified, translations from Plato are taken, sometimes with minor adaptations, from the standard translations in Cooper and Hutchinson (1997).

[7] So named for its resemblance to the cross-examination of a witness in the courtroom. For the procedure of the elenchus, which I treat in general terms below, see Vlastos (1983) and Matthews (2008, pp. 124–25).

kind of comprehensive expertise in human values, demonstrated in the capacity to articulate consistent definitions of the moral and aesthetic terms in which one justifies one's actions and beliefs).[8] Socrates anticipated that he would bring to light a person wiser than himself, disproving at least a literal interpretation of the oracle's claim (*Ap.* 21C). Instead, his cross-examinations proved the oracle provisionally correct. He found a range of public luminaries—poets, priests, politicians, and technical experts—lacking in wisdom.[9] It remains an open question whether Socrates would have passed his own test,[10] but by the age of seventy, he was prepared to conclude that he *did* hold some advantage, which lay in the recognition of his own ignorance: "I am likely to be wiser… to this small extent, that I do not think I know what I do not know" (21D).[11]

Socrates' search for wisdom occupied his life. It became a vocation, a "service to the god". Along the way, Socrates made powerful friends and enemies, developed into a controversial public figure and target for satire, and grew impoverished, by his own report (*Ap.* 23B). He also became a countercultural hero for Athens' younger generation (23C) during the later years of the Peloponnesian War, foreshadowing his eventual prosecution in 399 BCE on charges of impiety and "corrupting the young" (24B).

2.2.2 Socratic Philosophy

During Plato's dramatization of his trial, Socrates uses the verb *philosophein* to name his activity for the Athenian jury, and he goes on to explain what he takes this verb to mean.[12] (In its earlier colloquial sense, *philosophein* evidently denoted a love of knowledge, or a curious disposition).[13] Since Socrates' usage of the term

---

[8] For the nature of Socratic "wisdom," see for example Cooper (2012, p. 48); for the role of definition in his method, see Aristotle *Metaph.* 1.6, Matthews (2008, pp. 123–124). For a vivid depiction of the experience of encountering Socrates, see Plato, *Laches* 187E-188B: "You don't appear to me to know that whoever comes into close contact with Socrates and associates with him in conversation must necessarily, even if he began by conversing about something quite different in the first place, keep on being led about by the man's arguments until he submits to answering questions about himself concerning both his present manner of life and the life he has lived hitherto. And when he does submit to this questioning, you don't realize that Socrates will not let him go before he has well and truly tested every last detail…"

[9] Socrates recognized that the poetic tradition—stretching back to Greece's literary fountainheads, Homer and Hesiod—offered a kind of inspired moral and aesthetic truth (a point stressed at *Apology* 22C, *Ion*, and in *Republic* 2), but the poets that Socrates met were unable to articulate and explain that inspiration on interrogation. Socrates also found that technical experts, like physicians and engineers, were deceived by their domain-specific knowledge into imagining themselves wise in general.

[10] See Vlastos (1983), with replies by Kraut, Brickhouse and Smith, and Polansky.

[11] In Plato's dialogues, Socrates does not explicitly claim to know nothing (or to know one thing, namely, that he knows nothing). See for example Matthews (2008, pp. 117–18).

[12] In this sense, Plato's *Apology* can be read as a "metaphilosophical" text (see Sellars 2014).

[13] LSJ s.v. φιλοσοφέω A.

"philosophy" in this passage is different from our own, this passage is worth quoting in full:

> Men of Athens, I am grateful and I am your friend, but I will obey the god rather than you, and as long as I draw breath and am able, I shall not cease *to practice philosophy*, to exhort you and in my usual way to point out to any one of you whom I happen to meet: "Good Sir, you are an Athenian, a citizen of the greatest city with the greatest reputation for both wisdom and power; are you not ashamed of your eagerness to possess as much wealth, reputation, and honors as possible, while you do not care for nor give thought to wisdom or truth, or the best possible state of your soul?" Then, if one of you disputes this and says he does care, I shall not let him go at once or leave him, but I shall question him, examine him and test him, and if I do not think he has attained the goodness that he says he has, I shall reproach him because he attaches little importance to the most important things and greater importance to inferior things. I shall treat in this way anyone I happen to meet, young and old, citizen and stranger, for this is what the god orders me to do, and I think there is no greater blessing for the city than my service to the god. For I go around doing nothing but persuading both young and old among you to care not for your body or your wealth in preference to or as strongly as for the best possible state of your soul, as I say to you: "Wealth does not bring about excellence (*aretē*), but excellence makes wealth and everything else good for human beings, both individually and collectively." (*Ap.* 29D-30B).

In this passage, Socrates takes *philosophia* to consist in (at least) two fundamental activities[14]:

1. **Exhortation** (*parakeleusis*) to others to value the excellence or virtue (*aretē*) of their soul (*psychē*),[15] especially wisdom (*sophia, phronēsis*),[16] more than possessions, physical attributes, or social status.
2. **Examination** (*exetasis, elenchos*) of those who claim already to possess such excellence of soul, especially wisdom, as well as examination of oneself (*Ap.* 38A).

   - If the subject proves to lack psychological excellence while supposing that they possess it, Socrates will demonstrate their ignorance for their benefit. If the subject proves to possess that excellence (which has not occurred in Socrates' experience), he will learn from them. (The latter point is implicit here, but explicit elsewhere, e.g., *Euthyphro* 5A–B).

---

[14] Socrates reinforces this twofold function elsewhere in the *Apology*, when he glosses his function as a civic gadfly as "persuading (*peithōn*) and reproaching (*oneidizōn*) you all day long" (*Ap.* 31A), and explains his activity as encouraging his contemporaries to "give an account of [their] life," "testing" them, and "reproaching [them] for not living in the right way" (39D).

[15] The "soul," for Socrates, is roughly speaking the locus of cognitive and emotional activity and the seat of free moral choice. The force of the noun *psychē* develops substantially between Homer (eighth century BCE) and the classical period (see for example Sullivan 1995).

[16] The "excellence of the soul" described here includes wisdom, one of the four traditional moral virtues or human excellences (*aretai*). Socrates elsewhere treats wisdom as identical with, or causal of, the other three traditional moral virtues: justice (*dikaiosunē*), courage (*andreia*), and self-control (*sophrosunē*). Socrates may have treated the four virtues as effectively identical with one another and with wisdom. (See for example Brickhouse and Smith 2010, 2015).

Socratic "exhortation" is vividly dramatized by the writers who occupied his inner circle[17]: Socrates enjoins his interlocutors to resist any form of motivation unsupported by reason, including outward pressures of social conformity and authority,[18] and inward pressures of involuntary appetites, aversions, and the drive for status; he aims to make room for a liberated faculty of practical reason.[19] Socratic "examination" (*elenchos, exetasis*) is typically portrayed by Plato as follows. Early in the narrative of a dialogue, Socrates intercedes in an interlocutor's execution of a moral choice. In a series of questions, he tests his interlocutor's capacity to articulate stable and universally consistent definitions of the value terms in which he justifies his action: these are normally virtue terms, like "courage" (*Laches*), "self-control" (*Charmides*), "piety" (*Euthyphro*), "justice" (*Republic* 1), and "wisdom."[20] No character in Plato's "early" dialogues succeeds in articulating a definition of a value term that survives the Socratic *elenchos*,[21] and the interlocutor often finds himself "frozen" (*Meno* 79E-80B) and unable to act at the end of the process. Here is a person who *thought* that they were acting for considered reasons: but those reasons have been revealed as confabulation justifying non-rational motives.[22] Unless the interlocutor is hostile, the conclusion of the examination often also makes the interlocutor available for Socratic exhortation and encouragement.

Socrates later explains that philosophy in this sense has an outcome and goal (cf. *Ap.* 38A), namely, the condition called *eudaimonia*—well-being, flourishing, or "happiness"[23]:

---

[17] For instance, Plato's *Gorgias* is a *tour de force* display of Socrates' capacity to compel hostile interlocutors to grant the value of psychological virtue. Several studies of the "early Socratics" trace the depiction of Socrates by Xenophon, Plato, and contemporaries (see for example Boys-Stones and Rowe 2013; Vander Waerdt 1994).

[18] Socrates aptly diagnoses the influence of conformity and authority in human motivation (Nussbaum 2012, pp. 54–55); in a very loose sense, he can be seen as doing a kind of proto-social-psychological experiment, noting results similar to Asch (1951) and Milgram (1963).

[19] Socrates maintains, it seems, that conformity (or majority opinion alone), authority, involuntary appetite, and status or reputation are all insufficient motivations for action. A crisp statement is *Crito* 46A: "I am the kind of man who listens to nothing within me but the argument that on reflection seems best to me." Against conformity, see *Apology* 32B-33A (in his own practice) and *Crito* 47A-48A and *Gorgias* 471E-476A (in theory); against authority, see *Charmides* 161C, *Apology* 32C–D; against appetites and status as sole motivators, see *Apology* 32B-33A.

[20] For example, when the prophet Euthyphro announces his intention to prosecute his father on the grounds that this is the reverent or pious thing to do, Socrates infers—and Euthyphro agrees (*Euth.* 4E-5A)—that Euthyphro thinks he knows about a virtue called "piety," and that Euthyphro can demonstrate this wisdom by articulating a definition that will capture each and every action that qualifies as "pious" (*Euth.* 6D–E). Socrates also supposes that he himself can learn from such an articulation, and thereby become wiser and improve his prospects as a virtuous moral agent (*Euth.* 5A–B, 9A; cf. *Apology* 26A). In practice, Euthyphro is unable to produce a definition for which Socrates cannot produce a counter-example.

[21] In Plato's later dialogues, however, Socrates himself produces moral definitions that are not explicitly refuted: for example, the definitions of virtue terms in *Republic* 4.

[22] As a classic early study in social psychology showed, this is a common phenomenon (Nisbett and Wilson 1977).

[23] For eudaimonism in ancient Greek thought, see for example Annas (1995).

The Olympian victor makes you *think* yourself happy (*eudaimōn*); I make you *be* happy (*Ap.* 36E-37A).[24]

Philosophical activity is indispensable for achieving *eudaimonia*. Without examination, in fact, a human life is not worth living (*Ap.* 38A). Thus the unconditional acting out of one's examined and rationally justified beliefs constitutes a third component of philosophy:

3. **Living the examined life:** One should act only based on those beliefs that one has subjected to rational examination (*exetasis*), and not on other motivations (such as fear of physical harm or loss of reputation: e.g. *Ap.* 22E-23A, 28B-29B).

   • "[T]he greatest good for a human being [is] to discuss excellence (*aretē*) every day and those other things about which you hear me conversing and testing myself and others, for the unexamined life is not worth living for human beings..." (*Ap.* 38A).

2.2.3   The Socratic Self

Socrates elsewhere diagnoses the specific form of ignorance that he is primarily concerned to isolate and remove. It is *self*-ignorance, a lack of understanding of what one authentically is, and what one's capacities or powers really are.[25] The contrary of self-ignorance is self-knowledge, which Socrates sometimes identifies as virtue or excellence (*aretē*).[26] Only the person who knows herself can care for herself, and only the person who cares for herself can achieve *eudaimonia*. This diagnosis interprets another instruction from Delphi, the famous injunction to "Know Thyself" (*gnōthi seauton*), as Socrates explains in the *Phaedrus*:

> But I have no time for such things [as mythological exegesis and natural philosophy]; and the reason, my friend, is this. I am still unable, as the Delphic inscription orders, to know myself; and it really seems to me ridiculous (*geloion*) to look into other things before I have understood that. This is why I do not concern myself with them. I accept what is generally believed, and, as I was just saying, I look not into them but into my own self: Am I a beast more complicated and savage than [the monster] Typhon, or am I a tamer, simpler animal with a share in a divine and gentle nature? (*Phaedrus* 229E-230A)

---

[24] This sentence alludes to the familiar Platonic distinction between appearance and reality: outer "goods" *appear* to make us happy or well-off, but only wisdom *really* makes us happy.

[25] For the idea in Xenophon that self-knowledge might amount to a knowledge of one's *capacities*, see Johnson (2005a).

[26] On Socratic self-knowledge see for example Johnson (2005a); Moore (2014); Rappe (1995); Tsouna (2001). Key Platonic passages include *Phaedrus* 229E and *Philebus* 48C, both cited below; *Charmides* 164D (where Plato has Socrates state that a traditional Greek virtue, self-control (*sophrosunē*), is in fact identical with self-knowledge), *Protagoras* 343B, and *Rival Lovers* 138A. The *Alcibiades I*, whose authenticity has been doubted, offers an excellent summary account, which is also discussed in §2.2.3.1.

Socrates implies that self-knowledge should be achieved before other knowledge, and elsewhere suggests that self-knowledge is indispensable for happiness. Plato here and elsewhere depicts the ordinary lack of self-knowledge as "ridiculous" or comical (*geloion*).[27] In *Philebus* 48C-49A, a passage that develops a more systematic analysis of the injunction at *Apology* 29D-30B, Socrates enumerates three distinct, and increasingly "ridiculous," grades of self-ignorance: (1) lack of knowledge of one's possessions ("If someone thinks he is richer than he is…"); (2) lack of knowledge of one's physical attributes ("if people think they are taller and handsomer than they are"); and finally—by far the most common, ridiculous, and dangerous—(3) lack of knowledge of one's soul's excellence (to suppose that one possesses wisdom when one does not). Since we do not know what we really are, we do not know what is really good for us, and we cannot possibly act in our own rational self-interest.

This negative account is descriptive for most of society; the Stoic philosopher Chrysippus would memorably capture a similar concern in the dictum "everyone is crazy" (*pantes mainontai*).[28] But Socrates also offers a positive, prescriptive account of self-knowledge. It begins from the recognition that one is not identical with one's possessions or body (*sōma*), but with one's soul (*psychē*), a view that would resonate through the later Platonic tradition (see Sorabji 2006, ch. 6). The Socratic psychē appears to self-reflection as the subject active in first-personal awareness, something like the phenomenological experience that Dan Zahavi describes as "an invariant dimension of first-personal givenness throughout the multitude of changing experiences" (2005, p. 132); but the special accent for Socrates lies on the active experience of *agency* or 'putting things to uses', especially in cognitive agency (e.g., *Alc.* 127E-130D).

A very personal version of the Socratic distinction between the soul and the body is offered in the *Phaedo*, as Socrates comforts his friends in the face of his impending execution:

> I can't persuade Crito that *I* am this Socrates here who is talking to you now and marshalling all the arguments; he thinks that *I* am the corpse whom he will see presently lying dead…
> (*Phaedo* 115C-D, tr. Tarrant & Tredennick)

Socrates' use of the first-person pronoun in this passage is also interesting as implying that Plato regards, not only soul "in general," but the individual *Socrates* as an immortal soul. (This raises the question whether a soul, or more precisely an intellect or even a locus of first-personal experience, can be properly individual[29]; to

---

[27] The same observation occurs in the *Philebus*, generally thought to be a late dialogue (48C): "The ridiculous (*geloion*) is… among all the vices, the one with a character that stands in direct opposition to the one recommended by the famous inscription in Delphi. — You mean the one that says "Know thyself," Socrates? — I do. The opposite recommendation would obviously be that we not know ourselves at all."

[28] Chrysippus at Plutarch, *De stoic. Rep.* 1048E, perhaps reflecting the ubiquity of irrationality.

[29] For the question, perhaps closely related, whether a stream of consciousness is 'egological' or 'nonegological', see Thompson (2011, §3).

this, some later Platonists like Plotinus appear to answer in the affirmative).[30] This identification of self with soul evidently originated with the historical Socrates, and is not an invention of Plato's. Thus Xenophon, another disciple of Socrates and a valuable independent source, reports:

> [Socrates] would say this: that as soon as the soul (*psychē*) – in which alone is wisdom (*phronēsis*) – has departed from a man, even though he be our nearest and dearest, we carry out his body (*sōma*) and hide it in the tomb. Moreover, he said that each person, even when he is alive, loves himself most of all (*hekastos heautou... ho pantōn malista philei*): he removes or lets another remove from his body (*sōma*) whatever is useless and unprofitable (*anōpheles*). He removes his own nails, hair, corns; he lets the surgeon cut and cauterize him, and, aches and pains notwithstanding, feels bound to thank and pay him for it. He spits out the saliva from his mouth as far away as he can, because to retain it doesn't help him, but harms him... [Socrates] meant to show that unreason was worthless (*aphron atimon*), and was urging that one care for (*epimeleisthai*) what is most wise (*phronimōtaton*) and useful (*ophelimōtaton*)... (Xenophon, *Memorabilia* 53–55)

For Socrates, the argument turns on what we value. It is crucial that the soul can and does reflect on itself *as* self, as the locus of a "first-person stance" toward psychological states like thinking, feeling, and desiring, with the accent falling on conscious reasoning.[31] Socrates argues that the familiar experience of self-specification as a *cognitive agent*[32] is valuable and valid to a greater degree than other acts of self-specification, for example, as a locus of bodily sensation. In particular, Socrates highlights the value of self-recognition as a reflective *moral* agent.

The value of the soul's self-recognition lies in the direct ethical consequences of a soul's authentic and self-reflexive self-knowledge: when I grasp that I am a soul (*psychē*) and not a body (*sōma*), it follows (from Socrates' further view that everybody acts in their own perceived best interest)[33] that I will do only what is good for my soul, even if that conflicts with my physical or social best interests. Courage on the battlefield might conflict with my body's short-term health; a strong sense of social justice might reduce my opportunities to profit from others' misfortune. But the person who recognizes herself as a soul, and not body or possessions, will consistently choose virtue in these cases, because it is good for the soul. Plato would maintain this view throughout his literary career.[34] For Socrates, the soul possesses several kinds of excellence, which we call the "virtues" (*aretai*), perhaps picking

---

[30] See below, §2.4.1.1, and Sorabji 2006, pp. 115–17. The *Alcibiades I*, if it is by Plato, may contrast the self (*auto to auto*) with *each* self (*auto hekaston*) at 130D, but the vocabulary is difficult to interpret.

[31] For the argument that the soul must be self-reflexive, see Gerson (2003, p. 31).

[32] For the notion of self-specification as a cognitive agent in modern psychology, see Christoff et al. (2011).

[33] On Socrates' "denial of weakness of will" and intellectualism, see for example Devereux (2008, pp. 144–150).

[34] It occurs clearly in Plato's chronologically latest dialogue, the *Laws*: "As in other matters it is right to trust the lawgiver (*nomothetēs*), so too we must believe him when he asserts that the soul is separated from [or "better than"] the body in every respect, and that in actual life (*autōi tōi biōi*) what makes each of us (*hēmōn hekaston*) to be what he is is nothing else than the soul, while the body is a semblance (*indallomenon*) which attends on each of us..." (Plato, Laws 12, 959A–B).

out different situational aspects of the same thing.[35] Socrates argues at length that all the capacities of both soul and body—wealth, reputation, strength, beauty, courage, self-control,[36] and intelligence, for example—are morally indifferent without one capstone virtue: wisdom (cf. *Meno* 87E-89A). In a refrain that resonates with Buddhist ethics (cp. Majjhima Nikaya 9), wisdom is the root virtue, and ignorance the root vice. Plato develops this view, for instance, in the *Euthydemus* (278E-281E) and *Meno* (87E-89A). Socrates also argues that all of the virtues are somehow identical with, or forms of, wisdom.[37] Without wisdom, one cannot be happy or well-off (*eudaimōn*).[38]

2.2.3.1   Compendium: The First Alcibiades

The *Alcibiades I* attributed to Plato in antiquity (whose authorship is disputed today)[39] offers a useful compendium of these basic points: since we are ignorant (and worse, ignorant of our ignorance), we are liable to harm ourselves and our communities (*poleis*): therefore, we should improve ourselves by practicing self-cultivation until we achieve excellence (*aretē*) (*Alc.* 119A, 124B, 127D-128A). In order to cultivate ourselves, we must first discover what we are (127E-128E). We are not identical with our possessions or our bodies, but with the *user* or controller of our body, namely soul or *psychē* (127E-130D)[40]; this is presented as a phenomeno-logical intuition, not as a decisive conclusion, which would require a full under-standing of selfhood (*auto to auto*). Only by knowing and cultivating ourselves as *psychē* can we consistently benefit ourselves and our communities (133C-134B).

2.2.4   Socratic Ethics and Intellectualism

According to the Socratic position represented in Plato's "early" dialogues, genuinely excellent actions arise from the judgement of a unified, rational soul. No one errs intentionally (so error is a matter of ignorance, not wrong-doing), and no one in her right mind ever fails to do what she considers best on reflection, so long

---

[35] For the thesis of the "unity of the virtues," see *Laches* 199D–E, Devereux (2008, p. 150).

[36] In this list, capacities like "courage" and "self-control" only become virtues when wisdom is added: without it, the name "courage" could simply describe recklessness. The doctrine that only virtue is good, and everything else indifferent, becomes an essential view of the later Stoic school.

[37] See Devereux (2008, p. 150).

[38] Socrates' argument does not establish with certainty whether wisdom is one and the same as *eudaimonia*, or an (essential) component of *eudaimonia* (*Euthydemus* 282A–B). See Parry (2004).

[39] For a recent overview of the debate, see for example Smith (2004).

[40] Compare Parfit (1984) on "non-reductionist" and "reductionist" accounts of selfhood; as Sorabji (2006) argues, the Greek tradition is largely committed to various forms of a non-reductionist view; but see further on Plato below, §2.3, and compare also Gill (2009).

as it is in her power (the denial of incontinence, or *akrasia*: *Protagoras* 358D).[41] This view was later elaborated by Zeno of Citium, and became the core of early Stoic ethics,[42] although Stoics do allow for emotion – as a kind of "fluttering" or oscillation of reason – to overwhelm good judgement and cause ethical incontinence.[43] Human excellence necessarily entails the acquisition of ethical beliefs that are true, which can then be pinned down and made unshakeable and actionable in the permanent form of knowledge (*epistēmē*). Crucially, the later Stoics (and possibly some earlier Stoics) argue that *personhood* is really just such a capacity for rational choice, or *prohairesis*.[44] The Stoics grant that we are often motivated by *seemingly* non-rational impulses that are excessive and unreasonable[45]: these they call "affections" or "feelings" (*pathē*). But even these affections inevitably involve a value judgment – a false one: for example, the judgment that something other than virtue or excellence (*aretē*) is good for me.

Once an agent's false beliefs are uprooted for good, virtuous action can be guaranteed: the person who has *no* false beliefs—the Stoic sage (*sophos*)—will always do the right thing.[46] The sage in this sense was intended to reflect an idealized Socratic philosopher[47]: she has obtained wisdom and eliminated desire and aversion, experiencing no affections (*apatheia*) whatsoever; she has emotions, but only good emotions (*eupatheiai*), including joy, will, and rational caution.[48] This Stoic archetype of sagehood has genuine support in the "early" Socratic dialogues.

2.2.5 Buddhist Parallels: Self-Knowledge and Self-Ignorance

The early Socratic dialogues and early Buddhist suttas portray their protagonists as dialecticians engaged in exchanges of question and answer, often with historical contemporaries.[49] In an analogy common to both traditions, Socrates and the

---

[41] In addition to his debate with Protagoras, Socrates argues the case in detail in *Meno* 77–78. For an account of the tradition of denial of acrasia in Greek philosophy, with its Socratic roots, see Bobonich and Destrée (2007); for a brief overview of Socrates' own theory, see Matthews (2008).

[42] See for example Inwood (1985), and the chapter on Stoicism in this volume (McRae).

[43] See Sorabji (2000, pp. 56, 64–65).

[44] See for example Epictetus *Disc.* 1.1.23 (see also Sorabji 2006, pp. 181–200).

[45] See Arius Didymus 65.

[46] See Cooper (2012, p. 13).

[47] For Socrates as Stoic role model, see DL 7.23, Sellars (2006, p. 4), with index s.v. Socrates.

[48] The Stoics countenance "positive emotions" (*eupatheiai*), and they also recognize unavoidable "first movements" or instinctive reactions. See Sorabji (2000) for a detailed discussion.

[49] For Socrates, see for example Plato, *Symp.* 172A-173E and Boys-Stones and Rowe (Boys-Stones and Rowe 2013); for the early Buddhist tradition, see Gombrich (2009, pp. 161–79) and Harvey (2012, pp. 29–31). For similarities in the practice of the Socratic and early Buddhist traditions, see Carpenter (2014, pp. 20–47).

Buddha represent themselves as "physicians" of the psyche[50]: they offer their contemporaries a kind of therapy (*therapeia*) designed to relieve a psychological illness and pave a path to authentic well-being (*eudaimonia*) or release from suffering (*nibbāna*).[51] Both protagonists diagnose a particular psychological ailment that others have failed to notice—absurdly, considering its urgency (cf. *Philebus* 48C-49A, Majjhima Nikaya 63). They locate the cause of human discontent in an attachment to impermanent possessions, sensory experiences, and social status,[52] rooted in ignorance. The resolution of discontent lies at least partly in the abandonment of that attachment and the correction of that ignorance,[53] and the means to this resolution lies at least partly in commitment to a new set of beliefs about virtue and value, which must be endorsed both intellectually and practically. Both Socrates and the Buddha argue that suffering is rooted in ignorance, and conversely that the root of authentic happiness is wisdom.

In both traditions, the specific kind of wisdom that we seek is self-knowledge, and the kind of ignorance that we aim to root out is self-ignorance (see §2.2.3). In Socrates' designation of *self*-ignorance as especially "absurd" (*geloion, Phaedrus* 229E, *Philebus* 48C), we might identify a particularly rich vein of comparison with contemporary Buddhist thought.[54] Like Socrates, the Buddha proposes that ignorance of *what we really are* – ignorance about selfhood – primarily conditions our suffering (e.g., Samyutta Nikaya 22:82; 22:45). Both traditions agree that body is

---

[50] For Socrates, see Vlastos (1991); for Plato and the later Hellenistic tradition, see Nussbaum (2013, pp. 13–77), with *Gorgias* 464B-465D; cf. Gorgias, *Helen* 14, Democritus B51, Isocrates, *Peace* 39. For the Buddhist tradition, see for instance the "poisoned arrow" simile of Majjhima Nikaya 63; at least since Hendrick Kern in 1882 and 1884, medical metaphors have been popular in Western scholarship for interpreting the four nobletruths, although they have also been overplayed (see Anderson 2013, p. 189). For a discussion of the use of medical analogies in both Buddhist and Greco-Roman traditions, see Gowans 2010.

[51] A rich comparison of *eudaimonia* and *nirvāṇa* has been developed by Keown (1992, ch. 8), who influentially articulates Aristotelian virtue ethics as a framework analogous to Buddhist ethics. See also §4 and §5 below.

[52] Early Buddhist critiques of acquisition, loss, praise, blame, pleasure and pain as human motivations (e.g., AN 8:6) can be profitably compared with Socrates' views. "These eight worldly conditions keep the world turning around (*anuparivattanti*)… gain and loss, fame and disrepute, praise and blame, pleasure and pain." For a general comparison of Socrates' mission with Buddhist practice, see Carpenter (2014, p. 3).

[53] Although Socrates does not explicitly articulate a *list* of (something like) three *kleśas*, Plato comes close. Approaching his argument for the tripartition of the soul (*Rep.* 4; see §2.3 below), Plato suggests that happiness arises from (1) self-control (*sophrosunē*) applied to appetite (*epithumia*), preventing involuntary desires; (2) courage (*andreia*) applied to temper (*thumos*), preventing involuntary aversion; and (3) wisdom (*sophia*) applied to reason, preventing ignorance; and the just cooperation of all three in practice.

[54] The Buddha also teases out the apparent absurdity of pursuing abstract philosophical or cosmological concerns when we have no idea how to cure ourselves from the "poisoned arrow" of suffering (Majjhima Nikaya 63), the cure which is his teaching; similarly, the Buddha claims to teach *only* this lesson, although he also differs from the dramatic Socrates in claiming to possess a much wider range of knowledge (SN 56.31).

not self. Some[55] of Socrates' argumentative moves (cf. Xenophon, *Mem.* 53–55) would be familiar to early Buddhist writers, who developed comparable arguments. For instance, both traditions argue along the following lines: (a) a candidate for the self must be wholly subject to one's voluntary choice; (b) one's body is not wholly subject to one's voluntary choice (one cannot say "let my body be thus; let my body not be thus," Samyutta Nikaya 22:59); therefore, (c) one's body is not a viable candidate for one's self. Underlying this argument, perhaps, is the assumption that the self just *is* the subject of first-person experience and agency.[56] (Similar arguments develop today from the tension perceived between the first-person stance and naturalism, although as Ganeri has stressed, Indic philosophical systems can offer room for both perspectives).[57] But there is a deeper divergence between the early Socratic and Buddhist analyses: Socrates recognizes the soul (*psychē*) as a non-reductionistic self, meaning by "soul" (as discussed above) something like the seat of personal identity and the first-personal *owner* or agent involved in volitions and cognitive experience, while the Buddhist analysis proceeds to eliminate not only body (*rūpa*) but also the mental aggregates (feeling, perception, volition, and consciousness) as candidates for selfhood (e.g. *Milindapañha* 25–28), concluding that liberation (*nirvāṇa*) lies at least partially in release from *all* "identifying as self" (*ahaṇkāra*).[58] In general, this statement is accepted throughout Buddhist philosophy, although some later Buddhists regard the view of "no-self" not as a doctrine that is true or false, but as a useful "medicine" which is eventually to be expelled together with the poison it cures.[59] In the wider Indian context, certainly, Socrates comes closer to āstika schools like the Nyāya-Vaiśeṣika in endorsing the discovery of a true or authentic self, genuine *ahaṇkāra*, as a valid and healthy pursuit.[60]

Methodologically, Socrates and the Buddha—as dramatic characters in their respective traditions—are lively questioners who advocate the rejection of tradition (*anussavena*) and oral persuasion (*bhabbarūpatāya*) as moral criteria, as long as these disagree with one's own reasoning and conscience (e.g., Anguttara Nikaya 3:65; Plato, *Crito* 46A)[61]; but there are also differences in their dialectical techniques

---

[55] As a matter of style, Socrates perhaps places heavier weight on dialectical arguments from social consensus and common practice (*endoxa*); here, he plays up the idea that we are all prepared to lose harmful or useless parts of our body, or suffer bodily pain, for our greater good.

[56] For the self as "owner" of the person in antiquity, see Sorabji 2006, and on Plato on the self as first-personal in particular see Gerson 2003; for a modern view of the self as subject of first-person experience, see Zahavi 2005.

[57] Ganeri (2012).

[58] One sutta even suggests that it can be *especially* damaging to identify with the fleeting and impermanent contents of the mind (SN 12:61).

[59] For instance, Nāgārjuna *Vigrahavyāvartanī* 22, 27, and 29, with Candrakīrti *Prasannapadā* 248–49, cited in Sorabji (2006, pp. 288–89).

[60] See Edelglass and Garfield (2009, pp. 298–304). For a comparison with Nyāya thought, see also below, §2.3.3.

[61] Compare for example the often-cited Kālāma Sutta (AN 3:65), which illustrates both the Buddha's method of question and answer, and the idea that the interlocutor should "get to know for themselves" (*attanāva jāneyyātha*); see Edelglass & Garfield (2009, pp. 175–78).

and self-fashioning.[62] For example, the early Socratic schools maintain that reason or intellectual insight is capable of motivating action, and that reason alone may be sufficient to motivate at least some actions (see e.g. Frede 2002, pp. 7–8; Bobonich and Destrée 2007; Cooper 2012, pp. 11–13), but the Hellenistic schools (or at any rate their Roman descendants) also stress daily exercises for concentration (Hadot 1995). This methodological distinction might be profitably compared to the division drawn in different Buddhist practice lineages between a path of "bare insight" (*suddha-vipassana*) and a path of "meditative absorption" (*jhana*), which stresses mental, emotional, and physical exercises alongside knowledge.

In spite of the divergences between the Socratic and Buddhist analysis of the self, their prescription for social practice as virtuous action[63] is in many respects similar.[64] In the Socratic (and Stoic) sage's achievement of freedom from desire and aversion, there is a counterpart to the early Buddhist ideal of the arahant, calm, wise, and free from the taints of desire and aversion,[65] although there is a crucial difference: if we bracket the "later" dialogues, the Socrates of Plato's "early" dialogues does not yet argue that a philosopher could and should *escape the world*, as the arahant seeks to do. But this is also a difference between the early "Socrates" and the later Platonist and Academic traditions. Plato will offer a view that is more evidently resonant with the early Buddhist ideal (as his Socrates will assert, "we must escape from here": see *Theaetetus* 176B and below, §2.4.2), although even this is not yet an argument for escape from cyclic existence and rebirth *tout court*, but rather an exhortation to escape to a better state of being (see §2.5 below). There are some suggestions in the direction of thorough escape from cyclic existence in the Platonic tradition, as we will see below; Plato himself may come closest to such an exhortation in the *Phaedrus* and *Republic* 10.

---

[62] Socrates repeatedly disclaims wisdom, in a move that appears diametrically opposed to the Buddha's assertion of general knowledge (although both interestingly restrict their *teachable* expertise to self-knowledge and happiness; see below, §1.3); and Socrates appears to embrace the efficacy of inferential reasoning, about which the Buddha is more cautious.

[63] For the "practice" of non-self, see Carpenter (2014, pp. 31–32), who profitably compares Epictetus' "Socratic" view (in this case, identifying reasoned voluntary choice, *prohairesis*, as self) with Buddhist praxis.

[64] There are, of course, exceptions, primarily arising from Socrates' value for virtuous social action. For example, Socrates thinks it is right to obey the laws of his state and fight in battle, anticipating the Platonic and Aristotelian view that *thumos* (temper, spirit) can be useful in defense of family or loved ones or community. This also presages the tension between purely "contemplative" virtue, mostly withdrawn from social action, and "social" virtue, which might even engage in public affairs; see §3.2.

[65] In the standard formulaic description (e.g. SN 3:3), the arahant has destroyed the taints (*āsavas*), lived the holy life, done what had to be done, laid down the burden, reached their own goal, utterly destroyed the fetters of existence, and are completely liberated through final knowledge.

2.3   Plato: The Therapy of the Complex Soul

2.3.1   Actualizing Excellence (aretē)

Later generations of philosophers in the Socratic tradition, including Plato, Aristotle, and Zeno (the founder of the Stoic school), sought to systematize and codify Socrates' general account. Aristotle maintained that virtues or excellences (*aretai*) are states or dispositions of the soul (cf. *Nic. Eth.* 2.5, 1105b19–28), which depend on the exercise of reason (*logos*), and are voluntary (1114b29–30); when a virtuous disposition is realized and put into practice (*ergon*), the resulting activity constitutes or produces well-being (*Nic. Eth.* 1.7). This argument is based in a broader teleological position, generally shared by Plato (e.g., *Republic* 1, 352D-354C), that organic beings (including human beings) and artefacts have essential, natural functions, the idealized performance of which is called *excellence*.[66] Aristotle maintains, then, that human beings have an essential function: namely, *eudaimonia*, which consists in the actualization of a human potential for excellence, a voluntary disposition for *reasoned or wise action* (*Nic. Eth.* 1.7; notably, this kind of action may be strictly contemplative).

Several core intuitions drive this perspective: human beings seem (Aristotle thinks) to locate our *selves* in or near our capacity for reason (*dianoia*, cf. *Nic. Eth.* 9.4, 1166a16–17) and voluntary choice (*prohairesis*, *Nic. Eth.* 6.2),[67] and in some important sense we *constitute* ourselves by actualizing this capacity for reasoned, voluntary choice.[68] As for Socrates, we ought to recognize our selves in our capacity for cognitive agency, and then focus on enacting this capacity *well*, with excellence or virtue (*aretē*). This view may be grounded in (or at least related to)[69] one of Aristotle's most influential metaphysical doctrines, namely, his treatment of capacity or power (*dunamis*)[70]: naturally occurring entities possess *capacities* (*dunameis*) that can be *actualized* (as *energeiai*) by factors internal or external to themselves, and a being's process of *self-actualization* tends toward what is good for that being.

---

[66] For example, *this wood-and-iron* is an artefact, *hammer*, because it has the capacity to *pound nails*; if its structure changes in such a way that it can no longer pound nails, it ceases to be a hammer *as such*, though it may be made of the same stuff as it was; if it pounds nails especially efficiently, it is an *excellent* hammer. *This muscular tissue* is an organ, *heart*, because it *pumps blood and supplies oxygen*; if it ceases to do so, it is no longer a heart *as such*, and if it does so very well, it is an *excellent heart*. And *this flesh-and-bone* is an animal, *human*, because… well, why? For essences in Aristotle, see for example Chiba (2012). For Aristotelian teleology, see for example Johnson (2005b).

[67] On *prohairesis* in Aristotle's concept of selfhood, and 'self as practical reason' in general, see Sorabji (2006, pp. 181–200).

[68] For this interpretation of "self-constitution" in Aristotle, see Korsgaard (2009). In Griffin (2014a), I tentatively explored its application to ancient Neoplatonic psychology.

[69] The independence of Aristotle's ethics from his metaphysics is an open question.

[70] See *Metaphysics* Θ, Cohen (2016).

2.3.2   The Tripartite Soul: Logos, Thumos, and Epithumia

In comparison to the unyielding rationalism of Socrates in the "early" dialogues and the Stoics (§2.2, above), Plato appears to have elaborated a more complex—and on some views, more pragmatic—account of the psychology of motivation.[71] According to this view, excellent actions do not arise *solely* from the rational behavior of a fully rational soul. The soul also has multiple irreducibly non-rational motivations, including emotional and desiderative agencies. These agencies may sometimes be *felt* to be at odds; human excellence entails cultivating their harmony. (It is important to note that both the rational and non-rational elements of the soul are conceived as having beliefs; see for example Sorabji 2002: 21). Various techniques, on the Platonic view, may be required for the therapy of those rational and non-rational dispositions that lead to harmful action.[72] This is an important step, as it invited later philosophers to do more than simply "argue and assume" that a persuasive argument will yield behavioural change, but demand that philosophy cultivate a suite of therapeutic methods, both rational and non-rational, including music, narrative, habituation, and general features of childhood upbringing.[73]

One argument for this alternative position develops in the first book of Plato's *Republic*. (The *Republic* is generally considered a "middle-period" dialogue, primarily representative of Plato's own creative elaboration of Socrates' ideas).[74] In Book 2, Plato develops a pervasive analogy between individual souls, on the one hand, and human communities, on the other hand.[75] Just as communities perform their functions well or poorly depending on their capacity for cooperation or "justice" among their citizens, each soul functions as a multiplicity that will perform well (excellently) or poorly depending on its capacity for cooperation or justice: justice makes complexes healthy and efficacious, while injustice ruins them (1, 351C-352B). Socrates then leads his interlocutor to the conclusion that justice (as a kind of psychological health or inner unity) conduces to a good life for a soul (352D-354C). But if the soul is a community of sorts, whose happiness depends on the realization of its characteristic excellence through cooperation, then who are its (hopefully cooperative) members? In Book 4, Plato answers this question in terms of a celebrated "tripartition" of the human soul, clustering around three distinct and

---

[71] On Plato's psychology, see for example Lorenz (2008); for a recent contrast with the rationalism espoused by the Stoics (which shares some features with Socrates' rationalism), see Cooper (2012, pp. 158–166).

[72] For the notion of these methods as analogous to medical "therapy" see Nussbaum (2013) and Ganeri and Carlisle (2010).

[73] Ranging from (1) simple social habituation from an early age (Aristotle, *Nicomachean Ethics*) to (2) "spiritual exercises" undertaken to cultivate concentration or moral virtue (see Hadot 1995 and §5.2 below) to (3) visualization exercises and analytical arguments aiming for insight (e.g., Plotinus *Enn.* 1.6.9, 5.3.9). See Burnyeat 1999. Functionally, these eventually play a role similar to the interlocking function of *sīla, samadhi, and paññā* in Buddhist pedagogy.

[74] See Irwin (2008).

[75] *Rep.* 2, 368C-369A; on the analogy, see for example Ferrari (2003).

sometimes competing loci of motivation (436A–B).[76] He offers a lively argument, based on a prototype of the "Principle of Non-Contradiction," that the soul must contain at least three *distinct* seats of motivation (in some sense), since we sometimes experience directly opposed attitudes about one and the same thing at the same time.[77] These three seats are (very loosely translated):

(1) **reason** (*logos*), the seat of rational reflection and speech, motivated by argument;
(2) **temper** (*thumos*), the seat of anger, pride, and self-esteem, motivated for status;
(3) **desire** (*epithumia*), the seat of myriad sensory appetites, motivated for pleasure.

(1) The first locus of motivation (*logos*) is rational, moved by argument and reflection, and calculates or plans (439D). The latter two are non-rational. (2) *Thumos* is moved by concerns of status, for example, facilitating an angry response when it is wrongly demeaned, engaging in competition, or enacting behavior that cultivates social status and reputation (440E). (3) *Epithumia* is moved by any kind of desire or appetite, particularly appetites for sense-experiences (*aisthēta*); hunger and thirst are paradigmatic examples (439B). Plato suggests that in our ordinary state, *thumos* sometimes allies with *logos* against *epithumia* (440E) for example, when *logos* counsels against the indulgence of a strong appetite, *thumos* helps to resist the appetite, because its indulgence might lead to a reduction of social status and reputation.

2.3.2.1 Self as Soul: A Challenge of Mereology

Plato offers a number of colourful metaphors to illustrate the inward struggle, or "civil war," that can arise between the parts of a soul. In the *Phaedrus*, another "middle-period" dialogue, Plato portrays the soul as a winged chariot, with its three parts respectively portrayed as charioteer (*logos*), noble horse (*thumos*), and ignoble horse (*epithumia*) (246A-254E). Later in the *Republic* (Book 9) he offers a memorable simile of *logos* as an "inner man," *thumos* as an inner lion, and *epithumia* as a many-headed beast (due to the competing multiplicity of desires and appetites in any individual) (9, 588B-589B). While Plato allows such a plurality, I think it is important to notice that his "split person" is rather different from the kind of "split person" considered by Parfit, for example (Parfit 1984, pp. 254–73): Plato is identifying real, first-personal attitudes that appear to the third-person observer as

---

[76] On these three "clusters of motivation," see Cooper (1984).
[77] This experience is a "phenomenological datum" for Plato (Shields 2013). As Socrates puts it here, "the same thing will not be willing to do or undergo opposites in the same respect, in relation to the same thing, at the same time" (*Rep.* 436B8–9). See Brown (2003§2.1). Compare Aristotle, *Metaphysics* 4(Γ)0.3, 1005b19–20.

one, but can be seen from the first-person standpoint as multiple loci of experience "wrapped" (*periplason*) in a single *apparent* individual (588D). And Plato is not evidently drawn to reductionism about the person. But which of these three "parts" of the soul qualify as "self," if any? After all, Plato's argument for the partition of the soul depends on a phenomenological experience of three *different*, and sometimes simultaneously *contrary*, constellations of attitudes or motivations. As we noticed above, Plato generally insists that the "real self" ("what each of us really is")[78] is the soul. If the soul is complex, is the *self* also a mereological sum of some kind, comprised of (at least) three parts? If so, what kind of sum is it? In the passage just cited, Plato writes as if one of these parts alone—our capacity for reason (*logos*)—is the true "inner human" (589A).[79]

Plato's view seems to have been that our capacity for reason is truly voluntary (or "up to us"), and that our capacity for reason acts in our best interest as a whole; if we put reason into practice in our practical choices, then our social action is also voluntary and in our best interest. By contrast, the other two "parts" of the soul do not (always) act voluntarily—we might feel that we act unwillingly on an appetite, or on an angry temper—and they sometimes work against our best interests. There are resonances here of an argument that also appealed to early Buddhist thinkers: if some factor is not wholly subject to voluntary control, or if it tends to harm us, it is disqualified from candidacy as "self" (e.g., Samyutta Nikaya 22:59).

Still, how can Plato allow for "self" to pick out both the multiplicity of clusters of motivation in a person *and* their singular capacity for reason? This struck interpreters in the later Platonic tradition as a genuine tension that needed resolving. Later Neoplatonists, like Plotinus and Proclus, sought a coherent solution that embraced the tension: our ordinary (descriptive) experience of selfhood *really is* plural, but we can strive (prescriptively) to constitute ourselves as a unity by identifying with our capacity for pure and practical reason,[80] and cultivating the cooperation of our non-rational capacities under the guidance of reason. This, Plotinus thinks, is roughly what Plato means by recommending a "cooperative society" of the soul, in which reason is a beneficent ruler acting for the genuine benefit of the whole.

Plato himself may take a similar view. Thus, as Christopher Shields has argued, while Plato's three seats may be loosely called "parts" (*merē*), they are probably not to be conceived as homunculi or as "parts" in a compositional sense at all; rather, they constitute "distinct motivational streams" upon which a single soul can draw in preparing to act.[81] The soul that is doing the acting is, in *essence*, uniform.[82] Certainly

---

[78] *Ton de onta hēmōn hekaston ontōs*, Laws 959B.

[79] See Sorabji 2006: 116–17.

[80] See Korsgaard (2009). I offer some tentative reflections on the theme of "self-constitution" in later ancient Platonism in Griffin (2014a).

[81] Shields 2013: 167–8.

[82] This, again, is the argument of Shields 2013.

we cannot deny the phenomenological experience of psychological disunity, of competing attitudes to one and the same object, and we may, with Plato in *Republic* 1, recognize the outward, social harm that can follow from inner inconsistency and disharmony: but this situation is not a necessity. It may be possible to overcome this disunity and *achieve* psychic harmony.

Indeed, this is what Plato appears to suggest in *Republic* 4. A happy and excellent soul will be a cooperative soul, in which the three parts each "do their own work" in a harmony: this constitutes psychological justice. It is true that the soul may initially seem disunified, but it is up to us to unify it, so that all of our capacities *are* voluntary and *are* working in our best interest. This is a kind of virtuous achievement—true justice:

> And in truth justice is, it seems, something of this sort [i.e., each person "doing his own work"]. However, it isn't concerned with someone's doing his own externally, but with what is inside him, with what is truly himself and his own. One who is just does not allow any part of himself to do the work of another part or allow the various classes within him to meddle with each other. He regulates well what is really his own and rules himself. He puts himself in order, is his own friend, and harmonizes the three parts of himself [i.e., *logos*, *thumos*, and *epithumia*] like three limiting notes in a musical scale—high, low, and middle. He binds together those parts and any others there may be in between, and from having been many things he becomes entirely one, moderate and harmonious. Only then does he act. And when he does anything, whether acquiring wealth, taking care of his body, engaging in politics, or in private contracts—in all of these, he believes that the action is just and fine that preserves this inner harmony and helps achieve it, and calls it so, and regards as wisdom the knowledge that oversees such actions. And he believes that the action that destroys this harmony is unjust, and calls it so, and regards the belief that oversees it as ignorance. (*Republic* 4, 443C-E.)

The soul that possesses the resulting condition of *inner* justice will also act justly and cooperatively on the *outside*—the inside and the outside will be in harmony.[83] Moreover, this soul will act in a way that is self-controlled, courageous, and wise (the other three traditional kinds or forms of excellence) because self-control amounts to the appropriate control of *epithumia*, courage involves the correct application of *thumos*, and wisdom involves the right activity of *logos*.

Securing such an inner "community" is a matter, in part, of shaping reason (*logos*) by rooting out false beliefs and cultivating true beliefs. Like the later Stoics, Plato places a strong constraint on this factor of development: only *knowledge* (*epistēmē*) qualifies as a cognitive state that will guarantee right action. As for Socrates, "knowledge" can be demonstrated by the successful articulation of consistent definitions of the terms in which we justify our choices. True beliefs (which will not pass such a test) might generate good behavior *by accident*, but not reliably. This appears to have been a substantial difference between Plato and his contemporary Isocrates, whose philosophical school likely competed with the Academy for students; whereas Isocrates maintained that philosophy entailed the cultivation of true beliefs (*Antidosis* 271), Plato insisted that only knowledge could guarantee virtue,

---

[83] Something like this might be the sense of the famous "closing prayer" of Plato's *Phaedrus*.

for those without knowledge lack a clear model for action in their souls (e.g., *Rep.* 6, 484C–D; 7, 506C, 520C).

Perhaps Plato envisions the entirety of the harmonious soul as "merged into the course" of uniform reason, like tributaries to a river.[84] But there is evidence that the just soul is still conceived like a city or community, with both non-rational and rational (aspectual) parts continuing independently to act in harmony.[85] In addition to shaping reason to cultivate knowledge, the curriculum prescribed by Plato in *Republic* 7 shows that other techniques are also necessary.[86] The non-rational components of the soul need to be cultivated by non-rational methods: for instance, *thumos* can be improved by music that stirs the spirit, and storytelling that offers salutary moral examples.[87] Plato also accepts that some affections or passions (*pathē*) are irreducible features of human experience, or at any rate of embodied human experience. As the later Peripatetic tradition interpreted this view, drawing on Aristotle, the goal of ethical cultivation is not *apatheia* or the state of being without affections (as the Stoics maintained); rather, it is *metriopatheia*, the moderation of affections in such a way that they are permitted to determine action only when and as appropriate and suitable to the particular case. For example, anger could be characterized as an outburst of *thumos* with an irreducibly irrational component, but for the *metriopatheia*-theorist, such an outburst is sometimes useful (for example, in defending one's loved ones or community). The Stoics would later deny this.

2.3.2.2   Self as Soul: A Challenge of Continuity

In addition to this challenge of psychological disunity, Plato recognizes a challenge of psychological impermanence. In *Symposium*, his protagonist, Diotima, stresses that our mortal nature "seeks so far as possible to live forever and be immortal," (207D), and argues that this is possible only through renewal[88]:

> Even while each living being is said to be alive and to be the same—as a person is said to be the same from childhood till he turns into an old man—even then he never consists of the same things, though he is called the same, but he is always being renewed and in other respects passing away, in his hair and flesh and bones and blood and his entire body. And it's not just in his body, but in his soul, too, for none of his manners, customs, opinions, desires, pleasures, pains, or fears ever remains the same, but some are coming to be in him while others are passing away... And in that way everything mortal is preserved, not, like the divine, by always being the same in every way, but because what is departing and aging leaves behind something new, something such as it had been... (207D-208A)

---

[84] A metaphor used artfully and helpfully by Shields 2013: 168.

[85] For the "constitutive" model of the soul as a plural citizenry of motivational forces that need harmonization, contrasted with a Humean "combat" model in which either passion or reason would have to conquer (if reason were a force of motivation at all), see Korsgaard 2009: 133–35.

[86] See Burnyeat 1999.

[87] *Republic* 4.

[88] On this passage and its interpretation in later Greek philosophy, see Sorabji (2006, pp. 64–65).

This passage comes close to treating a human being as a causal chain of psychological and physical processes, a treatment that would resonate with the characteristically Buddhist analysis of a human person as collections of impermanent but causally related factors, mental (*nāma*) and physical (*rūpa*). Even as he acknowledges this kind of insight, however, Plato elsewhere stresses the definitional necessity of the individual soul's permanence, unchangeability, and immortality (*Phaedo*). These apparently contradictory views can be found in nearly contemporary Platonic dialogues. One approach to their resolution would be to treat individual psychological continuity through time as a virtue that must be *achieved*, much as synchronic unity of the tripartite soul is not given, but must be cultivated under the guidance of reason (above, §2.3.2.1). Hence, slightly later in the *Symposium* (211A-212B), Plato has Diotima describe genuine immortality and permanence as features that a person can *earn* by proceeding toward the understanding of, and likeness to, a Form or Pattern. The underlying metaphysical theories will be further discussed below (§2.4).

2.3.3   Buddhist Parallels: The Complex Soul

As we noted above, Socrates agreed with the Buddhist tradition in disavowing body (*rūpa*) as self (*ātman*), but disagrees by positively locating self somewhere, from the Buddhist viewpoint, among the mental factors (*nāma*). Plato and his successors developed sophisticated phenomenological analyses of the parts (or, for some schools, capacities) of the soul, allowing that there were many: Aristotle's inventory, for instance, includes nutrition, perception, and mind, and perhaps imagination and desire.[89] Plato's tripartite analysis in *Republic* 4 in terms of reason, temper, and desire marks one step in such a development. Although the comparison should remain loose,[90] it is interesting to contrast Plato's psychology with the Buddhist analysis of the *nāma*-factors. Once Plato has allowed complexity into the soul's first-person experience, a Buddhist analyst could reply just as Nāgasena replied to the Greco-Bactrian king Milinda[91]: the constituent *parts* of a soul might be valid objects of phenomenological acquaintance, as the reins, pole, axle, and wheels of a chariot[92] are valid objects of vision; but where is the "soul" or "chariot" *separate* from these parts?

---

[89] See Aristotle, *DA* 2–3.

[90] In the Greek tradition, accounts of personhood in terms of psychophysical holism or interdependence, analogous to Buddhist *nāma-rūpa* analysis, will not develop explicitly until the Hellenistic period. For that development, see Gill (2009).

[91] *Milindapañha* 25–28 (Edelglass and Garfield 2009, pp. 272–74). It is interesting, of course, that this dialogue represents a conversation between a Buddhist monk and a Greek-speaking king conversant with Greek philosophy; Milinda's initial response to Nāgasena might suggest a typical Greek response to the Buddhist analysis, that it was an impractical form of nihilism or nominalism.

[92] As we have seen, Plato also makes use of the chariot analogy for the soul; this may have been coincidence or a cross-cultural commonplace, going back at least as far as the Kaṭha Upaniṣad in the Indian tradition.

Plato faces this problem of composition more or less squarely in the *Republic*, as we have seen above (§2.3.2). He acknowledges that the soul is disunified. While he accepts this analysis descriptively, however, his next move is to offer a prescriptive alternative: the soul *ought* to be unified, and this will take effort on the part of the person. Building on considerations common to the Socratic and Buddhist traditions (§2.2.5), he recognizes that what is involuntary is not self, and what disrupts well-being is not self. Therefore temper and appetite are not self. But he stops at reason (*logos, dianoia*) and perhaps more fundamentally but less explicitly, our basic awareness of cognitive processes and objects (*nous*); from a first-person standpoint, reason *does* feel voluntary, and from a practical standpoint, acting rationally *does* seem to be "good for us."

But there are further metaphysical concerns that drive the Buddhist analysis, including concerns about diachronic unity, as we have also seen (above, §2.2.3). How can Plato license his inference from constellations of first-person perceptual and cognitive events—including feelings, perceptions, volitional formations, and awareness—to an "owner" of those events (cp. Samyutta Nikaya 1:135), especially when those events are diachronically dispersed over time, and synchronically often opposed or in competition, as Plato himself accepts in *Republic* 4? Plato was familiar with similar concerns in (his interpretation of) the "flux" doctrine that he attributes to the Presocratic philosopher Heraclitus, according to which there are no stable *things*, but only continuous series of events, "ever flowing." Does Plato himself endorse this Heraclitean analysis? According to one popular line of interpretation, which I shall adopt below,[93] he does so, at least for the deliverances of sensory perception and for some contents of cognition. Does he also entertain the reduction of *persons* to streams of causally connected psychophysical events, in the spirit of Derek Parfit and the Buddhist tradition?[94] Passages such as *Symp.* 207D-208A may imply that he does, at least at some stages in the development of his ideas; but as I have briefly suggested above (§2.2.3), here too Plato insists that the human soul *can* achieve genuine diachronic and synchronic unity and stability ("immortality"), and *ought* so to do. Indeed, the soul's very capacity for understanding the Forms, displayed in the use of reason, implies its potential for unity in and through time: like later Nyāya respondents to the Buddhist no-self theory,[95] Plato appeals to the viability of language and communication as a proof that *some* entities must be stable, including the subject who thinks and understands.[96] The motivation for Plato's view is the celebrated "theory of Forms," a structuring key for Platonic

---

[93] See the pithy summary in Burnyeat and Levett (1990, pp. 8–9). In the following sections, I will adopt an interpretation of psychological synchronic and diachronic unity as a virtue to be achieved, although I will only be able to touch briefly on the broad questions of metaphysics and epistemology implied by this reading.

[94] See Siderits (2003).

[95] See Jayanta Bhaṭṭa, extract from *Nyaymanjari*, translated by Chakrabarti (1982, p. 225), and excerpted in Sorabji (2006: 295–96), with discussion on those pages by Sorabji.

[96] As an example of Plato's appeal to language and understanding as a ground for the necessity of Forms, see perhaps *Parmenides* 135B–D (though the interpretation of this passage is difficult).

metaphysics and epistemology. To trace the steps in Plato's reasoning, we turn next to the importance of contemplation and a new contemplative ethos that develops in a series of central Platonic dialogues.

2.4 Plato: The Therapy of Contemplation

2.4.1 Plato's Forms

To this point, the "Socratic" and "Platonic" treatments of wise practical action share a common purpose: both regard human excellence and *eudaimonia* as a matter of an embodied soul acting with intentional, rational virtue in the world, based on consciously cultivated *knowledge* or wisdom. While it is essential for Socratic philosophy that the soul be recognized as self, in preference to body and possessions, the "output" of this philosophical outlook is still *embodied action in a social community*, rather than transcendence or renunciation of that activity.

According to a "developmental" reading of the dialogues (see Irwin 2008), Plato, later in his philosophical career, worked out an alternative (or perhaps complementary) account of human excellence and happiness. According to Aristotle (*Metaph.* 1.6, 987a29-b13),[97] in developing this view, Plato was motivated not only by the ethical and logical views of Socrates, but also by earlier ("pre-Socratic") philosophical thought, particularly his disctinctive interpretations of the epistemological and metaphysical views of the Ionian philosopher Heraclitus (c. 535–475 BCE) and the Italian philosopher Parmenides (c. 515–460 BCE). As Aristotle reports (*Metaph.* 1.6, 987a29-b13), Plato developed a basic worry about the feasibility of the Socratic project, as he interpreted it. Socrates had maintained that human excellence entails knowledge about the way things really are (specifically, souls and their virtues). This knowledge could be demonstrated by articulating general definitions that remained stable, or consistent, across multiple cases. But Heraclitus (as Plato thought) had argued that apparently stable facts about things in the world are really "in flux." The resulting metaphysical doctrine was epitomized by Heraclitus' pupil Cratylus (cf. Plato, *Cratylus* 402A) in a simple phrase: *panta rhei*, "everything flows," or in a popular English paraphrase, "change is the only constant." The historical and philosophical implications of Aristotle's interpretation are notoriously difficult to untangle, and it is not at all clear what in it is Aristotle's speculation, what Plato really thought (as far as the dialogues can show), and what Plato's "Heraclitus" has to do with the historical Heraclitus. Still, it is possible to say something about several kinds of "Heraclitean flux" that interested Plato, and may

---

[97] The value of Aristotle's testimony has been extensively debated, especially since Harold Cherniss' seminal work (Gerson 2014). For the applicability of this passage to the "flux" doctrine especially, see Irwin (1977).

have helped to motivate the introduction of Forms as basic entities in ontology, objects of knowledge in epistemology, and normative paradigms in ethics.[98]

In the *Theaetetus*, Plato notes several motivations for the Protagorean relativist thesis that "man is the measure of all things" (151E-152A), and credits two deeper, explanatory theories to Heraclitus. Here we can only trace these in outline, leaving aside a number of questions with a large independent literature.[99]

1. Diachronic flux: "One cannot step in the same river twice" (Heraclitus B12 DK). Each sensory object constantly undergoes local movement and qualitative change over time (Plato, *Theaetetus* 181B-182C), gaining properties it previously lacked and losing properties it previously had. "What is really true," on this view, "is this: the things of which we naturally say that they 'are', are in the process of coming-to-be, as the result of movement and change and blending with one another. We are wrong when we say they 'are', since nothing ever is, but everything is coming to be.... Let us take it as a fact that all the wise men of the past, with the exception of Parmenides, stand together [on this point.]" (*Theaetetus* 152E).

   • For example, during the past year, Socrates has become continually shorter relative to Theaetetus (who is a growing boy) (*Tht.* 155B–C); anticipating the "ship of Theseus" problem (Plutarch, *Life of Theseus* 22–23), is it possible to truly predicate "tall" or "short" of Socrates when he is constantly shrinking in some aspect, yet undergoing no substantial change?[100]

2. Synchronic flux, or the *compresence of opposites*: "The road up and the road down are one and the same" (Heraclitus B59–61 DK). Each sensory object with a feature F simultaneously has the opposite feature not-F, in a different aspect or relative to something else. As Owen and Colvin (Colvin 2007, p. 762) point out, Plato marks these cases with the word *hama* ("at the same time").

   • For example, Socrates is "short" relative to Simmias and "tall" relative to Phaedo (*Phaedo* 102B–C), so it is possible to say truly that Socrates is short or tall?

Plato might have found the "flux doctrine" problematic for an ethically pragmatic reason. At face value, it rendered the Socratic moral project infeasible: stable or

---

[98] This account is indebted to Colvin and Irwin (Colvin 2007; Irwin 1977).

[99] In particular, (1) whether both properly qualify as "flux" for Plato: As Colvin (2007, p. 761) points out, it is not clear that the compresence of opposites is considered by Plato to be "Heraclitean flux"; for the view that it could be, see Fine (1992, p. 55); and (2) how they cut across the differentiation between substantial and merely relative change, on which see Irwin (1977). Evidently diachronic flux could be substantial (I *really do* get shorter) or only relative (I get shorter *relative to* the growing Theaetetus); but perhaps synchronic flux must be relative (I am short relative to Simmias and tall relative to Phaedo).

[100] This is ordinarily viewed as a "succession of properties in the same subject over time," where the change is not merely relative but substantial; but it can also be relative change. The language of *s-change* is adapted from Irwin (1977, p. 4). I follow Irwin in treating both self-change and aspect-change as kinds of flux).

consistent definitions of moral values could not exist if there *were* no stable moral values to be defined. (Plato thinks that Protagoras adopts such a meta-ethical interpretation of Heraclitus' metaphysics when he claims that "man is the measure of all things," or "things just are as they seem to the perceiver.")[101] Plato finds this result explanatorily unsatisfying: it fails to explain, for example, why a sick man should consult experts (like physicians), rather than his own guesswork (*Tht.* 178C).

But Plato also had deeper, epistemological and semantical reasons to worry about the "Heraclitean" metaphysical position. This basic concern is visible when he reflects that the Heraclitean position makes for a world comprised not of stable *things* but of perceptual *events* or *comings-to-be* (182A–C) involving a passive and active element, perceiving and being-perceived. Perhaps, then, we should say not that *Socrates is pale*, but that this *perception becomes palely*. But we cannot even say that much:

> Since not even this abides, that what flows flows pale, but rather it is in the process of change, so that there is flux of this very thing also, the paleness, and it is passing over into another colour, lest it be convicted of standing still in this respect—since that is so, is it possible to give any name to a colour which will properly apply to it? —I don't see how one could, Socrates; nor yet surely to anything else of that kind, if, being in flux, it is always quietly slipping out (*hupexerchetai*) from under your words. —And what about any particular kind of perception; for example, seeing or hearing? Does it ever abide, and remain seeing or hearing? —It ought not to, certainly, if all things are in motion. (*Tht.* 182C-E)

Nothing, then, is stable on this view; language and predication simply fail to apply to reality (and rather, things "slip out from under" our words, as Theodorus puts it here; Plato suggests a similar outcome at *Cratylus* 439C–440D). One could embrace this conclusion and arrive at the view that words are basically without content. But Plato was motivated by a different school of thought, especially by the Eleatic metaphysician Parmenides, to insist that meaningful language, rational discourse, and knowledge depend on the fact that words and thoughts refer in a stable way to real beings, and sentences refer in a stable way to real states of affairs. Terms and thoughts must pick out *something* unitary and objective in the world if they are to have meaning[102]:

> Is each of the thoughts one, but a thought of nothing? —No, that's impossible, he said. —Of something, rather? —Yes. —Of something that is, or something that is not? —Of something that is. (Plato, *Parmenides* 132B-C)

According to this view, if the world contains *no* stable, unitary, real objects, then language, discourse, and knowledge cannot exist or be trusted (cf. *Parm.* 135B–C, *Tht.* 183C–E, *Crat.* 439C–440D). The historical Parmenides was perhaps prepared to accept such a paradoxical conclusion in part: conventional language, he thought, articulated only *illusory* beliefs, like the belief that there are many things and they

---

[101] *Tht.* 151E-152A.

[102] As the historical Parmenides put it in one of the most exegetically contested fragments we have, "Thinking and being are the same" (B3 DK). Compare also the Nyāya response to Buddhist no-self theorists (above §2.3.3).

are capable of change. Only one statement, *esti* ("[it] is"), picked out a truth. But this radical conclusion had a price that Plato was unwilling to pay.

Plato resolved the dilemma, perhaps to his own satisfaction,[103] as follows. He may[104] have acknowledged that Heraclitus' analysis of sensory reality is correct: sense-objects have no stability, the sensory "world" is comprised of events rather than stable objects, and if a predicate (for instance, "beautiful") applies to a sense-object, it only *seems* in a conventional sense to apply relative to this observer at this point in time. But the success of philosophical discourse implies that the world includes other, more stable and "real" items, not available to sensation or belief.[105] Plato calls these *ideai* or *eidē* (traditionally rendered "Forms" in English, by way of the Latin *forma*, though "patterns" may be a more intuitive translation in modern English). Forms are those patterns or recognizably recurring features across cases of virtue of which "for each thing there is a character that is always the same," as Plato has Parmenides say. (The word "form" had already been used in this sense by Socrates in Plato's early dialogues, to pick out how one virtue can be instantiated in many different actions: cf. *Euthyphro* 6D–E).

> If someone… won't allow that there are forms for things and won't mark off a form for each one, he won't have anywhere to turn his thought, since *he doesn't allow that for each thing there is a character that is always the same.* In this way he will destroy the power of *dialegesthai* ["dialectic," "conversation"] entirely. (*Parm.* 135B-C)

The Forms serve as the genuine, unitary, stable, and unchanging targets of semantic reference and knowledge. When I use the word "beautiful," I really pick out a pattern, "Beauty," that is always just what it is. This pattern cannot be available to sensation, since, as the "Heracliteans" stressed, sensory objects are always in "flux." It is only in virtue of reference to the Form that assertions about sensible objects have meaning. I might *seem* to predicate beauty of the handsome Alcibiades. But according to Plato's "Parmenidean" theory of reference, the term only successfully refers if it picks out something stable and objective. Alcibiades' beauty fails to meet those criteria: it is diachronically unstable (Alcibiades may not be physically attractive in fifty years, and he wasn't around to be physically attractive fifty years ago), and his beauty is only present relative to something else, or for that matter for the observer (Agathon may consider Alcibiades beautiful, while Socrates may not; for that matter, Agathon at t_1 may consider Alcibiades beautiful, but Agathon at t_2 may not). Moreover, no one can effectively *define* Alcibiades' beauty in a consistent way. Nonetheless, when I use the word "beautiful," we all seem to *know* what I mean. There must really *be* some single, stable object, Beauty, that I do successfully pick out, and which *can* be defined. This will be the Form, Beauty (*to kalon*).

---

[103] Whether Plato was satisfied with any final "version" of a theory of Forms is an open question; see for example Peterson (2008).

[104] This is much debated; for the evidence from the *Theaetetus*, see discussion in Burnyeat and Levett (1990, pp. 8–9).

[105] For their role in Plato's theory of perception, see the "simile of the divided line" in *Republic* 6, 509D-511E.

This solution places Socrates' ethical project on firmer metaphysical and epistemological foundations: the virtue-terms for which Socrates seeks definitions, like justice, wisdom, courage and self-control, do successfully pick out real beings in the world, namely, Forms. But Plato's solution also supports an ambitious project: it is possible to examine reality scientifically, because *in general*, most definable terms that we use in ordinary language, once hardened by philosophical dialectic, can and do pick out Forms. The Socratic search for definitions can be applied not only to moral and value terms, but perhaps even to nature (*phusis*) as a whole, and special subjects like arithmetic, geometry, astronomy, and biology, all fields of research that Plato would patronize in the Academy. Reality is also now open to a two-level analysis: there is the "conventional" reality of sensory experience, to which language and philosophical discourse do not (strictly speaking) apply; and there is the "ultimate" reality of philosophy, comprising Forms.

One of the most famous descriptions of a Form, which was deeply influential in the later Platonic tradition, is Diotima's account in Plato's *Symposium*. Here Plato picks up Socrates' famous, but mysterious, claim to "erotic" expertise, to explain how the philosopher is literally a "lover" of wisdom, of a Form that never changes, remains "itself by itself with itself," and is the same from every perspective (*Symp.* 210E-211D).[106]

> [O]ne goes always upward for the sake of this Beauty, starting out from beautiful things and using them like rising stairs: from one body to two and from two to all beautiful bodies, then from beautiful bodies to beautiful ways of life (*nomoi*), and from ways of life to learning beautiful things, and from these lessons he arrives in the end at this lesson, which is learning of this very Beauty, so that in the end he comes to know just what it is to be beautiful. And there in life... if anywhere should a person live his life, beholding that Beauty. (*Symp.* 211B-D)

Plato's theory of Forms—and the "Heraclitean" worries that motivate it—open a range of new questions, many of which he recognizes in the dialogues.[107] For our purposes, questions about who we are and how we ought to live are particularly salient.

---

[106] In various "early" dialogues, including *Lysis*, Socrates professes a kind of expertise in "erotics"; this may be partly a tongue-in-cheek claim pointing to a pun (*erōs*, "love"; *erotan*, "ask questions"; cf. *Cratylus* 398C–E), but Socrates is also represented as a lover in the romantic sense (*erōtikos, erastēs*) by many characters, and Plato develops a powerful account of Socrates' erotic "love" as applying to Beauty and Wisdom here in the *Symposium*.

[107] One, which Aristotle stresses in *Metaph.* 1.6 and elsewhere, is the nature of "participation." Surely the proposition that "Alcibiades is beautiful" has meaning, but how does (the body of) Alcibiades, a spatiotemporal object of sense-perception, participate in a timeless, unchanging Form? (This question is explored partly in *Timaeus*). Do Forms participate in themselves, or in each other? (This question is explored partly in the *Sophist*).

2.4.1.1   Self as Soul: A Challenge of Flux

If "we" are souls, are we, like sensory objects, not really *there* in any stable sense? Are we subject to diachronic flux, so that we cannot be "pinned down" as real in any salient way?[108] Are we subject to synchronic flux, so that we contain opposite properties at one and the same time? (As we noticed above, Plato does posit a multiplicity of parts of the soul in *Republic* 4 on the grounds that we simultaneously experience opposite attitudes or motivations about the same object).

Plato begins from the basic assumption that *we know Forms*—after all, Forms are posited partly *in order to be* the proper objects of knowledge. Now Forms are stable and constant (diachronically and synchronically); if we were unstable and inconstant, how could we know about them?[109] This line of inquiry leads Plato to the conclusion that the soul itself is fundamentally *like* a Form: stable, eternal, and immortal (*Phaedo* 79A–E), and that the soul employs a non-sensory form of perception, *nous* ("intuitive awareness," "attention") to apprehend Forms (see below). Thus Plato talks in many contexts, most vividly in the *Phaedo*, as if the soul and self are really unitary and unchanging.

The apparent tension between accounts like *Republic* (where Plato's psychology is driven by by a phenomenology of the soul's differing motivations and change over time) and *Phaedo* (where Plato's psychology is driven by the soul's similarity to, and apprehension of, unchanging and unitary Forms) would play a significant role in later Platonist thought, as Neoplatonists, including Plotinus, strove to develop a single coherent account that embraced both perspectives. For instance, if my soul is a Form or at least Form-like, and if Forms are necessarily universals predicated of many particulars, then how can I be a unique individual?[110] Many ancient Platonists and some Aristotelians maintained that Platonic Forms are *not* universals.[111] The Neoplatonist Plotinus appears to add that there are Forms of individuals: my intellect (*nous*) is, from a certain point of view, the Form of my individuality actively contemplating itself and all of the Forms.[112] Indeed, for Plotinus, I discover my self in encountering

---

[108] See Plutarch, *Life of Theseus* 22–23: "The ship wherein Theseus and the youth of Athens returned had thirty oars, and was preserved by the Athenians down even to the time of Demetrius Phalereus, for they took away the old planks as they decayed, putting in new and stronger timber in their place, insomuch that this ship became a standing example among the philosophers, for the logical question of things that grow; one side holding that the ship remained the same, and the other contending that it was not the same."

[109] This *reductio* relies on the assumption, already familiar in Presocratic Greek philosophy, that "like knows like": I cannot apprehend something from which I am utterly dissimilar (e.g., Empedocles B109 DK).

[110] See Sorabji (2006, pp. 34–35 and 115–17).

[111] See Gerson (2004) for a modern argument that Platonic Forms are not universals. For the ancient tradition, see the papers collected in Chiaradonna and Galluzzo (2013).

[112] For interpretations of Plotinus' interesting view, already much discussed in antiquity, see Rist (1963), Kalligas (1997), and Sikkema (2009). For difficulties with Plotinus' view introduced in connection with the Greek view of reincarnation (in contrast with the Indic view), see also Sorabji (2006, pp. 122–23) and Sorabji (2012).

my own irreducible individuality, which is paradoxically one and the same with the principle of individuation (*to hen*) that grounds the Forms and reality.[113]

The view that the soul is Form-like has important ethical and phenomenological consequences, given the basic tenets of the Socratic project. If *I* am properly speaking my soul, and my soul is like a Form, what is the best way to cultivate myself? The answer that appeals to Plato is a new one, which will also appeal to Aristotle and later ancient Platonists. According to this view, the ideal method of self-cultivation, as an entity that transcends the sensory world, may lie in a world-transcending activity, contemplation or witnessing (*theōria*) of the Forms.[114]

2.4.2   A Contemplative Ethic

During a famous interlude in the *Theaetetus,* Socrates offers a classic statement of the ethos that happiness lies *beyond* the sensory world:

> But it is not possible, Theodorus, that troubles (*kaka*) should be destroyed—for there must always be something opposed to the good; nor is it possible that troubles should have their seat in heaven. But they must inevitably haunt human life, and prowl about this earth. That is why one should make all haste to escape from earth to heaven; and escape means *becoming like a god* as much as possible; and a man becomes like a god when he becomes just and reverent, with wisdom (*phronēsis*). (*Tht.* 176A-B)

The soul's "ascent to heaven" is portrayed in different dialogues using different similes. But Plato seems to have in mind a kind of contemplative practice undertaken by the embodied soul, gradually shifting away from valuing sense-perceptions (including desire for the pleasant, and aversion to the unpleasant), to valuing direct insight into Forms – a "path" from sensation to pure insight (*Phd.* 65D-66E). The soul that departs from the body, as Socrates and his friends decide in the *Phaedo,* will naturally develop "direct" access to the contemplation of Forms, without the mediation of sense-perception (*Phd.* 64C-66E). Plato develops the same idea in the *Phaedrus,* where the soul is envisaged as a chariot that flies to heaven to "feast" on the contemplative image of the Forms. (Plato makes explicit that this is a simile; he does not *literally* mean that the Forms are physically beyond the canopy of the stars)[115]:

---

[113] See Plotinus, *Enn.* 6.9.10, and Sikkema (2009); for the later Neoplatonist identification of gods with individualities, see also Butler (2005).

[114] See discussion below. The fundamental value of contemplation is clear for ancient Platonists: see for example Cooper 2012, ch. 6, Sorabji, 2004, 17(a). It is a debatable but viable interpretation of the fundamental texts for Aristotle, including especially *NE* 10.7: see for example Ackrill, 1975; Kraut 1989; Sorabji 2006, p. 35.

[115] The tension between these cosmological metaphors and the insistence on the non-spatiality and non-temporality of the intelligible world (*noētos topos*) was developed in later Platonism; for a very helpful explanation of Plotinus' treatment of this point, see Wilberding (2005).

Of that place beyond the starry sky none of our earthly poets has yet sung, and none shall sing worthily. But this is the manner of it, for assuredly we must be bold to speak what's true… It is there that True Being lives, without color or shape, that cannot be touched; reason alone, the soul's pilot, can see it, and all true knowledge is knowledge thereof. Now even as the mind of a god is nourished by reason and knowledge, so also is it with every soul that wants to receive her true food; then, when at last she has seen Being, she is content, and contemplating truth she is nourished and glad, until the revolution of the heaven brings her back again full circle. And while she is borne around she sees Justice, its very self, and likewise Self-Control (*sophrosyne*), and Knowledge… and when she has contemplated and feasted… she descends again within the heavens and comes back home. (*Phaedrus* 247C)

During embodied life, too, the soul possesses the means to "ascend." In *Republic* 6–7, Plato famously describes the ascent as an escape from an allegorical "cave," where sensory experiences are portrayed as shadows playing on the wall, mere imitations of the realities outside (*Rep.* 7, 514A-520A). The allegory represents an ontological, epistemological, and value hierarchy that Plato has offered in *Republic* 6, ascending from sensation through reasoning to knowledge to the source of knowledge (the Good) (505E–513E).

1. First, we imagine human beings constrained in such a way that they can only perceive—and have only *ever* perceived—shadows or reflections, cast by firelight and puppets that they cannot see. Such human beings would think that realities were simply shadows (7, 514A-515C).
2. Second, we imagine that these artificial constraints could be loosened, and a human being could ascend, first to see the puppets and the fire, and ultimately to see the realities of "our" real world, including the sun. Their eyes would take time to adjust, and it would be a difficult path (515C-516C).
3. Third, we imagine that such a person returned to his former fellow prisoners. He would meet with a hostile reception, particularly if he tried to aid and educate them; but he would do so for the greater good (cf. 520A–D) (516C-517A).

In the allegory, as Plato explains (517B–C) the shadows are visible objects; the fire is the visible sun; the world above is the intelligible world of the Forms; and the true sun is the Form of the Good, which makes real beings real, knowable, and good. This closing account of the Form of the Good, which generates or provides insight or intelligence (*nous*) and provides being and knowability to Forms (509A–C), was especially influential in later ancient Platonism. Subsequent Platonists, perhaps following Plato himself,[116] identified the Good with the One (*to hen*) described in Plato's *Parmenides*, as Dodds (1928) showed.

In the *Symposium*, Socrates (recalling a lesson that is attributed to the prophetess Diotima) describes a "ladder" of steps, from a single sensory beauty to many, then to psychological beauty, then to the beauty of cultures and customs, branches of knowledge, and finally the Form itself (*Symp.* 210E-212B, quoted above). While Aristotle differs from Plato about the metaphysical status of Forms, he argues in the

---

[116] cf. Aristoxenus, *Harmonica*, 2.30, Dillon (2003).

tenth book of the *Nicomachean Ethics* that this contemplative ideal of happiness—
the activity of *nous*—is a plausible description of the *highest* human well-being[117]:

> If happiness is activity in accordance with excellence, it is reasonable that it should be in
> accordance with the highest excellence; and this will be that of the best thing in us... [T]he
> activity of intellect, which is contemplative, seems both to be superior in worth and to aim
> at no end beyond itself, and to have its pleasure proper to itself (and this augments the
> activity), and the self-sufficiency, leisureliness, unweariedness (so far as this is possible for
> man), and all the other attributes ascribed to the blessed man are evidently those connected
> with this activity, it follows that this will be the complete happiness of man, if it be allowed
> a complete term of life (for none of the attributes of happiness is incomplete). (*Nic. Eth.*
> 10.7)

Plato, then, appears to offer two distinct approaches toward human flourishing.
First, in the dialogues that we designate "early," he argues that wisdom in social
actions, arising from examination, conduces to happiness. But in the dialogues that
we assign to his "middle period," Plato adds that wisdom in the sense of contemplation
and understanding of Forms constitutes happiness. Since this contemplation is not
identical with socially virtuous activity, and could conceivably even *conflict* with
socially virtuous activity, Plato bequeaths an apparent tension to interpreters. In
Plato's case, this tension might be resolved by resorting to the developmental
hypothesis: Plato simply changed his mind between composing the "early" dialogues
and (say) the *Phaedo*. But a similar tension occurs in the *Nicomachean Ethics*,
where Aristotle's endorsement of contemplation as the highest form of happiness in
Book 10 appears to conflict with his endorsement of social virtues earlier in the
treatise; since this tension appears within a single text (although the *Ethics* was
certainly not composed as a unity), many scholars have been motivated to resolve it
exegetically, either embracing the contemplativist conclusion as authoritative
(Nagel 1972) or explaining the compatibility of the two accounts (Ackrill 1974).
Later ancient Platonists, similarly committed to the assumption that Plato's corpus
represented a single, unified, and coherent philosophical outlook, were moved to
similar exegetical efforts; these culminated in the Neoplatonic doctrine of a "ladder
of virtues," comparable in some respects to later Indo-Tibetan lam rim literature.

2.4.3   Buddhist Parallels: Metaphysics

2.4.3.1   Metaphysics of Flux and Forms

The analysis of reality as flux, as Plato portrays it in the *Theaetetus*, is framed in a
way that early Buddhist thinkers might have found relatively accurate to the mark of
reality as impermanent (*anitya, anicca*): even the metaphor of the flowing river is
common to both traditions (e.g., Anguttara Nikaya 7:70). Beyond the intuitions that

---

[117] Unless Aristotle intends later in the book to restrict such a fully contemplative life to gods; see
Sorabji 2006, p. 35. The implications of Aristotle's purely 'contemplative' happiness in *NE* 10 has
been extensively debated: see for example Ackrill 1975, Kraut 1989.

the stream of perceived reality is diachronically unstable and synchronically self-contradictory, there are two more deeply interesting parallels:

1. The "Heracliteans" insist that "reality" is really composed of a sequence of perceptual events or processes, not things (*Tht.* 182A–E); a similar view is important in early Buddhism (e.g., Samyutta Nikaya 5:10), and develops into the "dhamma theory" of the early Abhidhamma theorists (Bodhi et al. 1993, pp. 3–4).
2. The "Heracliteans" allow that these events "slip out from under" our words (*Tht.* 182C–E, *Crat.* 439C-440D), with the apparent consequence (according to Plato) that the evident semantic power of language and thought to designate beings is misleading at best. Plato finds this consequence especially problematic, since it appears self-refuting and radically sceptical: one uses language to draw inferential conclusions that undermine the capacity of language to draw inferential conclusions (*Parm.* 135B–C).[118]

Plato believes that he stands "in the middle" (180E-181A) between two horns of a dilemma, represented respectively by the "Heraclitean" flux doctrine and the "Parmenidean" view that "the same thing is for thinking and for being" (B3 DK). Arguably, Plato treads what he regards as a middle path: he accepts Heraclitus' analysis so far as it goes, but restricts its scope to sense-data, avoiding its destructive consequences for dialectic; and he accepts Parmenides' analysis so far as it goes, but restricts its scope to Forms, avoiding the counterintuitive conclusion that change is illusory. And he applies this conclusion to the nature of soul as self: soul is Form-like and characterized by intuitive knowledge of Forms (*noēsis*), but embodied in a sensory system. He does not treat the realm of Forms as a separate "world" (despite the occasional opposition of a *noētos* and *aisthētos topos*), but as a reality whose conventional image or reflection is produced by the opinions that we derive from sensation and ordinary language; the development of this idea in later Neoplatonic philosophy of language and logic[119] is arguably comparable to the Prasaṅgika treatment of the "two truths".[120] The phenomenological implications of Plato's view will be drawn out extensively in the Neoplatonist tradition.

A Platonist might have seen the tradition of Buddhist metaphysics and epistemology as electing for the "Heraclitean" horn of the dilemma, embracing the implications of impermanence (*anitya*), and abandoning the "Parmenidean" intuition that semantic reference *must succeed* in picking out some metaphysical reality, possessing the character that the phenomenology of thought and reference implies: namely, reality, unity, and mind-independence (*Parm.* 132B–C). Such a Platonist might also see in the later Madhyamaka dialectic of Nāgārjuna, with its assertion that a mental episode has no real object whatsoever (*MMK* 1:8), the necessary (and undesirable) consequences of this line of thought; it would entail a profoundly

---

[118] He teasingly criticizes the "Heraclitean" school as difficult to talk to, since they're too flexible with their definitions to play the dialectical game properly (*Tht.* 170E-180C). Aristotle expresses exasperation with radical scepticism in similar terms (*Metaph.* 4.5).

[119] For this idea in later Platonism, see for example Griffin (2014b).

[120] See Jinpa (2002, pp. 148–51).

sceptical philosophical practice (Garfield 2002, pp. 3–23), which Plato recognized as a seed of Protagorean relativism in ethics (*Tht.* 152A), leading to a kind of nihilistic nominalism.

The Madhyamaka dialectician, in turn, might critique Plato's supposed "middle ground" as an excessive concession to the Parmenidean (or eternalist) horn of the dilemma, a "grasping for existence" and an admission of permanent personhood.[121] Plato's endorsement of Forms as essentially real and permanent could certainly be seen by the Madhyamaka dialectician as a kind of eternalism (cf. *MMK* 15.7–11): instead, the assertion "it is" should be abandoned, as should the whole assertion "it is not"; a true middle ground will recognize that *all* conditioned beings are empty (*śūnya*) of inherent existence (*svabhāva*), but this "emptiness" does not constitute non-existence, instead pointing the way toward the realization of dependent origination.

Despite their basic differences, the exegetical traditions that stem from these sources converge on important points. (Of course, both traditions are exceptionally long, spanning more than a millennium and multiple cultures and languages; it will be easy to find a diversity of conclusions in either). For example: the later hypotheses of Plato's *Parmenides* have puzzled Western interpreters since antiquity,[122] but according to the interpretation that prevailed in ancient Neoplatonism (cf. Plotinus *Enn.* 6.9),[123] these hypotheses elaborate a metaphysical analysis of the essential unity (*to hen*) of things—identical with the Good of *Republic* 6—as neither (1) existing nor (2) not existing, nor (3) both-existing-and-not-existing, nor (4) neither-existing-nor-not-existing (137C-166C), a dialectical conclusion that pointed the way to the Neoplatonic first principle, the only truly unconditioned being. Interpreted according to this Neoplatonic hermeneutic, the *Parmenides*, including its critique of a "naïve" theory of Forms (130A-134E), is practically a "Platonist *Mūlamadhyamakakārikā*," with "unity" (*to hen*) playing a part not unlike emptiness. Meanwhile, some later Neoplatonists, such as Plotinus, might agree provisionally with Candrakīrti that at the *ultimate* level of analysis even Forms are not "intrinsically" or "independently" subsistent, because they do depend on causes and conditions (cf. *Prasannapadā* 15.11) (see Thakchoë 2015, pp. 99–100), namely, on unity or individuation (*to hen*). This view could be translated into the Indo-Tibetan context if the Neoplatonist principle of "unity" is recognized phenomenologically as a kind of pure *vijñāna* or "witnessing consciousness" (cf. Albahari 2009), functioning as a ground of experience beyond reification or the construction of self or being in the Yogācāra sense (Carpenter 2014, pp. 140–41).

---

[121] See for example Siderits (2003, ch. 2).

[122] See for example Proclus *in Parm.* (Morrow and Dillon 1992).

[123] See Dodds (1928).

2.4.3.2   World-Transcendence

More important than these metaphysical and phenomenological details, however, is a basic development toward a "world-transcending" ethos in Platonism, represented in later dialogues including the *Phaedo* and *Theaetetus*. Plato offers a normative case that the human soul *ought to* recognize the impermanence (e.g., *Tht.* 182D–E), dissatisfactoriness (e.g., *Tht.* 176A–B, *Phaedrus* 248A–B), and non-reality (e.g., *Timaeus* 27D-28A) of sensory experience, then seek assimilation to the Forms in a kind of contemplative "ascent" toward permanence and unity. Plato does not (at least explicitly) represent this ascent as a path toward complete and lasting escape from the cycle of birth and death, but there are interesting similarities between this portrayal of the fruits of the philosophical path and the Buddhist portrayal of release (see below, §2.5).

2.4.3.3   Implications: Metempsychosis and Incarnation

If the human soul is unitary and permanent like a Form, why is it subject to mortality in the "cave" of embodiment? How does sensible experience arise for a fundamentally super-sensible soul? Plato explores this question from two perspectives: a theory of metempsychosis, which may draw on Pythagorean sources, and an account of the "creation" of the sensible world from a super-sensible paradigm.

2.4.4   *Metempsychosis*

Plato adopts a theory of metempsychosis, perhaps drawing on earlier Pythagorean sources.[124] On the view that Plato presents—which may be partially a mythical "analogy" or "simile," like the Allegory of the Cave, for a philosophical truth that he considers difficult to express in writing[125]—the human soul, after contemplated the Forms "in heaven" during a period of disembodiment, may subsequently animate an animal or human body, and then return to an intermediate location for a kind of "judgement" or "purification" before ascending to a (temporary) heavenly existence, or descending to a (temporary) corrective sub-chthonic existence.[126] A soul does not *ordinarily* "remember" its past lives, but it *is* capable of being reminded of its

---

[124] On early Pythagorean theories of metempsychosis, see for example Burkert (1972).

[125] "To describe what the soul actually *is* would require a very long account, altogether a task for a god in every way… but to say what it is *like* is humanly possible…" (*Phaedrus* 246A); the philosopher "won't be serious about writing… with words that are as incapable of speaking in their own defense as they are of teaching the truth adequately" (*Phaedrus* 276C); "there is no writing of mine about these matters, nor will there ever be one" (*Letter* VII B-C, if authentic). For the celebrated problem of Plato's "unwritten doctrines," see recently Gerson (2014).

[126] See in particular the "Myth of Er" (*Republic* 10, 614a–621d), the myth of judgement (*Gorgias* 523a–527a) and the myth of the "winged soul" (*Phaedrus* 246a–249d).

sojourn in heaven among the Forms.[127] Once a soul figuratively loses her "wings" and "falls" from the heavens, she enters a human body (248A–C). (Animal incarnation is only entertained later, following human incarnation). She enters a hierarchy of human incarnation that Plato develops in the *Phaedrus*, contingent on the quality of a soul's memory of the Forms.

> [A] soul that has seen the most will be planted in the seed of a man who will become a lover of wisdom or of beauty, or who will be cultivated in the arts and prone to erotic love. The second sort of soul will be put into someone who will be a lawful king or warlike commander; the third, a statesman, a manager of a household, or a financier; the fourth will be a trainer who loves exercise or a doctor who cures the body; the fifth will lead the life of a prophet or priest of the mysteries. To the sixth the life of a poet or some other representational artist is properly assigned; to the seventh the life of a manual laborer or farmer; to the eighth the career of a sophist or demagogue, and to the ninth a tyrant. Of all these, any who have led their lives with justice will change to a better fate, and any who have led theirs with injustice, to a worse one. (*Phaedrus* 248C-249A)

But Plato also maintains, in a passage that became famous in antiquity,[128] that the selection of a life is ultimately a soul's own choice and responsibility: "responsibility lies with the one who makes the choice; the god has none" (*Rep.* 10, 617D–E).

2.4.5 The Demiurge and the Nature of the Sensory World

How does sensible reality—the "shadows" on the wall of the cave—come into being in imitation of the Forms? In the *Timaeus*,[129] Plato has a protagonist, the Pythagorean Timaeus, explain that a divine "craftsman" or Demiurge (*dēmiourgos*) has moulded this world in space and time, in imitation of the eternal Forms, which are without place or time. The Demiurge does not impose the Forms and create the world *ex nihilo*, but out of a pre-existing substrate, the "Receptacle," which functions as the pure potentiality-for-being-something, like Aristotelian matter (*hulē*). The story of the Demiurge was puzzling in the later tradition, and the identity of the Demiurge was extensively debated; according to an answer that became standard, the Demiurge stands for the mind (*nous*), as it creates the sensory world in imitation of its true apprehension of the Forms (cf. *Republic* 10, 596C–E).

---

[127] E.g. *Meno* 80D-81A, *Phaedo* 73C.

[128] An ancient bust of Plato, inscribed with the phrases "all soul is immortal" (*Phaedrus* 245C) and "the responsibility is the chooser's: god is not responsible [or: to blame]" (*Rep.* 10, 617E), may point toward the Platonic ideas that especially captured popular imagination in antiquity (Miller 2009). For the influence of this passage in late ancient philosophical theories of the "choice of lives," see recently Wilberding (2016).

[129] See Johansen (2008).

2.4.5.1 Buddhist Parallels: The Demiurge

In the early centuries CE, Gnostic thinkers equated Plato's Demiurge with the God of the Hebrew Bible, and argued for the existence of a world "beyond" the Demiurge, answering to Plato's Forms. This Gnostic Demiurge is in error when he claims that he is the only god, and there is nothing above or beyond him.[130] The story of the Gnostic Demiurge is strikingly similar to the Buddhist narrative of a Brahma who is the first to be reborn from the luminous Ābhassara plane into a new world, and upon arrival, wishes for company, and finding that new beings are reborn there, considers himself their creator (Digha Nikaya 1; compare Digha Nikaya 11, which portrays a Great Brahma who has recognized his own ignorance, and Digha Nikaya 27).

2.5 Platonic Bodhisattvas?

In *Republic* 6, Plato has Socrates describe philosophers as follows. These people enjoy making an exact study of what is "always the same" (484B, 485A): that is, the non-contingent, invariable, and general truths (moral, aesthetic, or natural) that are available for contemplative investigation.[131] Their understanding (*epistēmē*) of these truths furnishes them with the capacity to recognize policies or conventions (*nomoi*) in public life that would correspond to these true standards (484C–D), although such policies are rarely found in force in the constitutions of the world (cf. 496A-497C). Temperamentally, philosophers are lovers of wisdom (seekers after all truth: 485D), self-controlled (free from motivation by pleasure: 485D), brave (free from aversion to pain or death: 486B), just and gentle (unharmful to others)[132] (486B), quick to learn (486C–D), and measured and graceful (*eucharis*) in thought (486D; see also 487D): their nature is defined by curiosity, a kind of tolerance for ambiguity, and freedom from outward or inward motivations that conflict with their considered values. They have developed such a disposition in their present life thanks to a certain momentum or *torque* imparted by their prior activity: by their vivid impression and memory of Forms perceived directly by the soul (cf. *Phaedrus* 248C-249A), which can occur when the soul is "turned" in an act of metanoia to the Good (*Rep.* 518C); and by a consistent pattern of virtuous activity enacted through the habituation of the non-rational soul and body (*Phaedrus* 256A-257A). The life

---

[130] For a general overview of the Gnostic movement, see for example Pagels (2004) and King (2005).

[131] Plato refers to an *enarges en tēi psychēi paradeigma*, a "vivid pattern in the soul", which philosophers recognize eternal truths.

[132] Here and elsewhere, Plato develops the distinction between someone who is "gentle" or "tame" (here, *hēmeros*) and someone who is "wild" or savage; compare also the savagery "like wild animals" of ordinary "political" life at 496D, and the question at the opening of the *Phaedrus* whether the self is gentle like a god or savage like a monster. The tame person is governed by reason and does no harm to others; in fact, as Socrates stresses in the *Gorgias*, the philosopher would rather be harmed than do harm, though he would prefer to avoid both (*Gorg.* 469C).

situation that allows for these acts of mental and moral self-expression, as Plato suggests in *Republic* 10 (617E), follow from the individual's free choice: for the conditions of a life, "responsibility lies with the one who chooses; the god is not responsible" (*aitia helomenou: theos anaitios*).

In all their actions, philosophers are distinguished by acting only according to *knowledge*, and not according to *belief* (cf. 506C).[133] Knowledge derives from the philosopher's direct acquaintance with truths, or Forms. That direct acquaintance, on Plato's view, is always available for a person to access, but for most people it is accessed rarely[134]; it may be triggered by logical reasoning from hypotheses, but it is not identical with the conclusions of valid arguments (510C-511A). The ultimate object of experience is "the Good" (*to agathon*), a kind of value-object that lies before being (509B) and furnishes knowability and reality to beings. As Socrates explains in the next book's allegory of the cave (*Rep.* 7), a suitably disposed person might be led from (a) perceiving and acting in the "ordinary" world constituted by beliefs about unpredictable sense-impressions, to (b) a world constituted by stable arguments about predictable, generalizable laws or patterns, to (c) direct contemplation of the Forms that constitute those patterns, and finally (d) the Good.

Philosophers who arrive at such a contemplation of the Good experience their life in such a positive way that they say they believe they have reached "the isles of the blessed" (519C). If they dwell in a social constitution that is unsuitable to them, it is best for them to remain in this separate contemplation, and to adopt a quietist attitude to their society (496A–E): they "take refuge behind a little wall (*teikhion*)," lead a quiet and virtuous life, and mind their own business, striving to act well and contemplate reality without interfering in wider public life. Piecing this passage together with Plato's suggestions in the *Phaedo* and *Phaedrus*, the philosopher who contemplates in this way might reasonably look forward to a perpetual joy, circling with the stars, the gods, in a recurring contemplation of the meadow of truth (*Phaedr.* 248A), winning the "Olympic contest" of human happiness (*Phaedr.* 256B, *Rep.* 10, 621B–D).

If, however, the external conditions are fairer – if philosophers dwell in a constitution where they may be able to do good for the polity by engaging in public affairs and advocating for better policy based upon their knowledge of general facts – then they ought to be *compelled for the common good* to reach comprehensive insight into the Good, then become active in public life as advocates for collectively beneficial conventions and policies (519C–E). These philosophers, acting always for the common good and from full awareness of moral truths, will advise and govern "as people who are awake, rather than dreaming" (520C–D). But, as Socrates' interlocutor protests, why should philosophers agree to serve in this way

---

[133] Knowledge that *p*, according to one definition mooted in *Meno* 98A, is true belief that *p* accompanied by understanding of the reason (*aitia*) why *p* is so; but a similar account of knowledge as "justified true belief" is rejected in the *Theaetetus*.

[134] Loosely, in Ned Block's terminology, real knowledge is always available to "access consciousness" (Block 1995).

(519D), apparently to relinquish their own highest happiness? Aristotle, in his analysis of Plato's constitution, raises the same puzzle (*Politics* 2.5, 1264b1–1264b26).

Socrates justifies his proposal as follows: the philosophers will agree to ascend to the Good and then to return to help others in the "cave" because "we'll be giving just instructions to just people" (*dikaia gar dē dikaiois epitaxomen*, 520E). The passage suggests that the *character* of the philosophers is central; they will return from blissful contemplation to help others precisely *because* they are just, or have a disposition to just actions like this one.[135] Socrates' justification has been interpreted in various ways. Perhaps the philosophers simply refuse to break the founders' law, because it is unjust to break a just law.[136] Perhaps – on one radical suggestion – the philosophers of *Republic* 7 are not so unselfish as they seem, and *need* to be compelled to act for the greater good, unlike the truly unselfish philosophers of *Republic* 6.[137] More likely, perhaps, the philosopher's direct experience of the Form of the Good produces a wish to benefit others, a kind of altruistic motivation[138]: the philosopher's good lies in establishing and maintaining an ethically active relationship with the Good or the Forms, "a relationship that is strained or ruptured when one fails to do one's fair share in a just community."[139]

Socrates proceeds to advocate a graded path of study for men and women to reach this goal (cf. 540C) to cultivate such a philosophical nature and hence to benefit their societies: in childhood (before the age of 20), a person of suitable disposition should study music, poetry, and physical exercise (521D-3); subsequently, between twenty and thirty, they should study arithmetic, plane geometry, solid geometry, astronomy, and harmonics (536D); then, from thirty to thirty-five, dialectic (539E); then from thirty-five to fifty, the philosopher should engage in political life in the "cave" of public affairs, before, at fifty, those who have demonstrated the relevant aptitude and ability should be encouraged to contemplate the Good itself, and take turns in legislative and political work as advisors and governors. Socrates then reminds his interlocutors of the metaphorical nature of the discussion: we are speaking here of philosopher-kings who come to power in a community or *state* (*polis*), as a metaphor for the reason that comes to power in an individual *psychē* (541B). (It is an open question just how literally Socrates means his talk of a *state* in *Rep.* 2–9: the central argument of the *Republic* is applied to the inward organization of an individual *psychē*, not to a literal *polis*.[140] But Socrates does seem to suppose that inward justice or harmony will produce outward or social justice).[141]

---

[135] Crucially, Socrates makes clear that the policy is just *only* because in *this* constitution the philosophers have been intentionally nurtured to serve the common good, and therefore they owe some support to the common interest; in other constitutions, where philosophers arise "spontaneously", they are at liberty to do as they will.

[136] So Brown (2004).

[137] So Weiss (2012).

[138] See for example Kraut (2000), Mahoney (1992).

[139] Kraut (2000, p. 214).

[140] See for example Annas (1999), ch. 2.

[141] See Kraut (2000, p. 213).

There are a number of interesting points of comparison here with Buddhist ethics, and especially with mature Mahāyāna thought. For the Mahāyānist in the Indo-Tibetan tradition, for instance, a person of "lesser" capacity, possessing *only* the ability to pursue a beneficial lifestyle and accrue positive *karma*, should do that much, minimizing their suffering and yielding better rebirths in the future. The person of "middling" capacity, who can apprehend the truth and achieve awakening and liberation from cyclic existence, ought to pursue *nirvāṇa* and escape altogether from cyclic existence governed by *karma*. But the person of "great" capacity, the potential *bodhisattva*, should seek awakening and *nirvāṇa* with a specifically altruistic motivation, the "awakened mind" (*bodhicitta*) that strives to prevent "all present and future suffering and depression" for all living beings,[142] and ultimately to rescue *all* sentient beings from the depths of cyclic existence.[143] Where the "saint" or *arhat* of "middling" capacity aims just at their own liberation, which is challenging enough, the *bodhisattva* aims to achieve awakening, arrive at the highest good of *nirvāṇa*, and then return into cyclic existence to benefit others, willingly contributing their own happiness, karmic merit, and freedom to others (e.g., Śāntideva, *Introduction* 3.32–33).

Several scholars, notably Charles Goodman, have argued strongly that from the early Mahāyāna tradition forward the ethics of the bodhisattva can be analyzed as a kind of consequentialism, perhaps a form of rule utilitarianism (Goodman 2009, p. 75). The bodhisattva, certainly for Śāntideva, commits to a thoroughgoing self-sacrifice for the good of all sentient beings (Goodman 2009, p. 90). A fully enlightened Buddha, who has attained *nirvāṇa*, willingly strives to help others trapped in the cycle of becoming, or *saṃsāra*; in fact, the enlightened person who remains in cyclic existence *as long as possible* is the best of all (Goodman 2009, pp. 105–106). Particularly in light of Damien Keown's analysis of *nirvāṇa* as the good (Keown 1992; see ch. 8), the parallelism with the Platonic philosopher's return to the cave is striking: only the very *best* philosophers will "witness the Good" and, relinquishing their own immediate self-interest, proceed to help others in the cave (*Rep.* 7, 540A–D).

The parallelism may be illuminating for the exegetical debate about the cause of the philosophers' return to the cave in *Republic* 7. Goodman argues that the bodhisattva is motivated by consequentialist and specifically *utilitarian* considerations to help beings in *saṃsāra*: the good of the many, of all sentient beings, outweighs her own imminent self-interest. Gordon Davis has highlighted an attractive alternative: Buddhist sources emphasise not only the *benefits* of actions, but the intrinsic quality of actions and actors, resonating in some respects with Kant's "kingdom of ends" (Davis 2013, pp. 290–293). Again, Damien Keown has emphasized the role of virtue in Buddhist ethics (Keown 1992): from this vantage point, perhaps the bodhisattva performs an action not *primarily* because of its beneficial consequences (the liberation of all sentient beings), nor *primarily* because of the action's intrinsic quality or rationality or any particular duty incumbent on the actor

---

[142] See for example Śāntideva's *Compendium* (Śāntideva 1971, p. 15), translated by Goodman (2009, pp. 89–90).

[143] See for example Śāntideva's *Introduction* (Śāntideva 1998), 10.55.

(because it is incumbent, say, upon *any* liberated being to help others), but because this kind of action is in keeping with the character of the bodhisattva, whose virtue entails the salvation of sentient beings.

We might consider the Platonic passage with these alternatives in view. (1) The philosopher will return to the cave because one must not "make any one class [e.g., philosophers] outstandingly happy, but contrive to spread happiness *throughout* the community (*en holēi tēi polei*)" (519E); this motivation looks at least superficially utilitarian, maximizing happiness for the greatest number. But again, (2) the philosophers must act on others' behalf because they owe a kind of "debt" or obligation (*opheilon*) to the community that made their education and ascent possible (520B); this motivation looks superficially deontological. And finally, when Socrates is pressed for a fundamental reason why the philosophers will not "disobey" the injunction to descend into the cave, he explains that (3) "it is because we'll be giving just orders to just people" (*dikaia gar dē dikaiois epitaxomen*, 520E), and therefore – *because* of their just character – they will choose to help. This motivation intuitively fits a virtue-ethical framework. While we can hardly to justice to the passage's complexity here, there is arguably good textual evidence for all three readings: the philosopher will act because it will benefit the entire community; because she owes a kind of duty to her community; *and* because her innate character dictates just behaviour. But the third explanation – the explanation from character – appears to play a privileged role. Strictly speaking, (1) the "utilitarian" or consequentialist argument for the philosopher's descent at 519E is not offered to explain the philosopher's *motivation*, but why, from the constitutional founder's perspective, the philosopher's descent is *good*. (2) The deontological argument at 520B again does not explain the philosopher's motivation, but why they *ought* to descend into the cave as the founders and laws ask them to. Only (3) the argument from the *character* of the philosopher is offered to explain their *choice* to obey that law: it is *because they are just* that they choose to agree. Perhaps a similar argument can apply to the ethics of the bodhisattva: consequentialist considerations may show that it is *good* for the bodhisattva to remain in *saṃsāra* to help sentient beings; deontological considerations may show that the bodhisattva *ought* to do so, and that it is rational for them to do so; but it is considerations that relate to the excellent *character* of the bodhisattva (rooted in the cultivation of the *paramīta*s and *bodhicitta*) that specially function to explain why the bodhisattva chooses freely to perform this action.

2.6   Appendix: Aristotle and the Platonic Legacy

The present chapter closes with a brief sample of Plato's intellectual legacy in the following generation, concentrating on the views of his pupil Aristotle, who is not discussed in detail elsewhere in this volume.[144] (The following chapters deal at

---

[144] See Dillon (2003) for the "heirs of Plato," and Gerson (2006 and 2013) for a view of Aristotle in the context of ancient Platonism. The Platonic dialogues served subsequent philosophers as an "inexhaustible mine of suggestion" (Whitehead 1979, 39)—a reservoir of fundamental questions

length with later Hellenistic schools that do draw inspiration from Plato, namely the Stoa and the Skeptical Academy).[145]

Like Plato, Aristotle developed theoretically rich accounts of human personhood, and derived normative and ethical insights from these analyses.[146] He describes the nature of the human *psychē* as "one of the most difficult [questions] there is" (*DA* 1.1, 402a10). It is beyond the scope of this appendix to survey Aristotle's views comprehensively.[147] Here, I just aim to sketch several intuitions that arguably motivated his analysis of biological organisms in general and human beings in particular, and several conclusions that he may have found persuasive. These are: (1) that human persons are *beings*; (2) that human persons, like other beings, are what they are not in virtue of their matter (*hylē*), but primarily in virtue of their *form* (*eidos*), the structuring pattern that is the "soul" (*psychē*) of the person; (3) that human souls strive toward teleological ends determined by this structure (namely, *eudaimonia*, or the complete realization of our capacities as a rational, social being), determining the "virtues," patterns of excellence (*aretē*) in habit and thought than provide normativity to human life; and (4) that human souls possess a further, god-like and immortal capacity for contemplative awareness (*nous*), in virtue of which we might arrive at a higher form of human good, although—like the Platonic philosopher returning to the "cave," or the Buddhist *bodhisattva*—Aristotle's contemplative philosopher will nevertheless "descend" from that divine state in order to better her community as well as herself.

Following this line of interpretation, Aristotle's ultimate concern is the fulfilment or perfection of an essential human nature through the cultivation of the virtues or forms of human excellence (*aretai*), which are fostered in their turn by a faculty for making consistently wise choices. As Damien Keown has argued, such an account of Aristotelian "virtue ethics" may provide a promising structural analogue to Buddhist ethics.[148]

---

and tentative methods. Plato's perceived comprehensiveness and pedagogical flexibility contributed to his enduring appeal, especially in later antiquity. See Boys-Stones (2001), chs. 6–7, for a rich theory of Plato's value in antiquity, and Dillon (1996) for the development of Platonism following Plato.

[145] See Mills (on Skepticism) and McRae (on Stoicism).

[146] It remains an open question whether Aristotle's account of the human good is really grounded in his metaphysics and theory of human nature. Some (e.g., Hursthouse 1999; Foot 2001) have argued positively; others (e.g., MacIntyre 1984; McDowell 1998b) have denied it. I do assume a positive answer here (cf. Irwin 1980). For an excellent and detailed study of later twentieth-century and early twenty-first-century views on this problem, see Berryman forthcoming.

[147] For fuller discussions of the issues discussed below, good starting points are Shields 2012 and 2016; Kraut 2014; Cohen 2016.

[148] See Keown 1992, especially ch. 8. Others such as Goodman 2009 (see also above, §2.5) have favoured a kind of consequentialism, such as character consequentialism, as a more promising framework for interpreting Buddhist ethics.

2.6.1 What Is a "Being"? Linguistic and Metaphysical Intuitions

Clarity about "how we should speak," Aristotle suggests, can help to illuminate "how things really are" (see *Metaphysics* 7.4, 1030a27–28). Aristotle attended closely to the use of ordinary language as well as the formalized dialectical practices of the Platonic Academy.[149] In fact, one intuitive entry-point into Aristotle's metaphysics is the simple Greek demonstrative term *tode,* which roughly means "*this here*".[150] *Tode* might plausibly seem to have meaning insofar as it has a real extension: that is, for my utterance "this here" to refer successfully, I must be "pointing"[151] (verbally, visually, mentally, or otherwise) toward some *thing* that strikes me and my audience as *real* and *distinguishable* from other things.[152] Aristotle can be understood as drawing special attention to such ontological implications of demonstrative speech. When he tables the question "what is being?", he twice settles the answer using the following criterion: what counts most as *some* "*this*"[153]

---

[149] For the development of dialectical practice in the Academy, see recently Fink 2012. Irwin 1988 offers one influential account of the relationship between earlier Academic dialectic and Aristotle's science of demonstration. Martha Nussbaum has emphasized Aristotle's attention to the appearances or *phainomena* in terms of ordinary beliefs and assertions Nussbaum (1986: ch. 8), although it is continually debated whether Aristotle had a definite *method* of analyzing widely held opinions (*endoxa*) in quite this way (e.g., Frede 2012; Reinhardt 2015). Aristotle also played a role in inspiring the twentieth century turn toward "ordinary language" philosophy in English—philosophy that attends especially to "what we do or do not say or, more strongly… what we can or cannot say" (Ryle 1953: 67)—although most current scholars of Aristotle would not consider him an "ordinary language" philosopher in that sense. It is also interesting, as a separate but related question, to consider the influence of the subject-predicate structure of Greek on Aristotle's ontology; see for example Mann 2000: 7–8.

[150] LSJ s.v. *hode.* See also below, n. 151.

[151] The intuition is captured in the literal force of the Greek verb for "mean" (*sēmainein,* literally "point out"); later Greek philosophers explicitly emphasized this function of demonstrative language (see for example Porphyry, *in Cat.* 56,9; the speaker might have been literally envisaged as "pointing with the finger" metaphorically, as Ammonius puts it at *in Cat.* 10,2. Augustine's famous theory of imposition (e.g., *Conf.* 1.8.13) has roots in this literature on the *Categories*). We might also compare Kaplan's earlier notion of the true demonstrative (1989a; see also his revised view in 1989b).

[152] Consider Aristotle's criteria of separability and "this-ness" for being-ness (*ousia*) or substantiality at *Metaphysics* 7.1, and the assumption that a real being is both a "this" and a numerical unity (*Cat.* 3b10–13). (Plato, too, stresses that if a thought successfully refers, it refers to something real and unitary: *Parmenides* 132B–D). What Aristotle means by either of these criteria is another scholarly crux; on separability, see (just for instance) Fine 1984, Morrison 1985; on the "this," see Gill 1989: 31–4, and Irwin 1988, e.g. 90 and 211–213. A fuller and current discussion

[153] Like Irwin 1988: 211–213 (see his 558 n. 34), I take *tode* to be the demonstrative and *ti* the indefinite article, and the whole phrase *tode ti* to mean "some *this*." This is one among many possible interpretations (see for instance Gill 2006: 355 with notes), which can in turn be fundamental for the analysis of Aristotle's criteria for substancehood.

(*tode ti*)? In the *Categories*,[154] individual substances (*ousiai*) turn out to be more *real* than their properties (such as their qualities and quantities and relations) precisely because substances better satisfy the *tode ti* criterion.[155] In *Metaphysics Z*, form (*eidos*) turns out to be causally and explanatorily prior to matter (*hulē*), because form better explains why beings show up as "some *this*" (*tode ti*) (see *Metaphysics* 7.3, 1029a27–33). The *Categories* and *Metaphysics* may represent different phases in Aristotle's metaphysical thought, but they are strikingly similar in the fundamental role they assign to this underlying intuition.

In supposing that linguistic structure may illuminate ontology (to some restricted degree),[156] Aristotle differs from most Buddhist positions. It is an early and persistent feature of Buddhist metaphysics to restrict the scope of ordinary language to "conventional" truth, as opposed to "absolute" truth; and Buddhist philosophers are at pains to dismantle the apparent semantic force of demonstrative or deictic gestures (like "this chariot here").[157] In the strictest sense, most "conventional" indexicals and demonstratives fail to pick out anything at all in the world—although the positions of Buddhist schools are subtle and vary widely.[158] It is also striking that Aristotle employs "separability" (perhaps meaning something like "independent existence") as a criterion for real being[159]; this appears to run counter to the pervasive Buddhist account of "dependent origination." Thus, it seems reasonable to assert that the Buddhist tradition is deeply skeptical about several of the basic intuitions

---

[154] On the role of the *Categories* in Aristotle's philosophy, see for example the excellent introduction to Bodéus 2001and chapters in Bruun and Corti 2005. Frede 1985: chs. 2–3 provides an excellent introduction to its place in the Aristotelian corpus. Wedin 2000 is an example of a careful *metaphysical* reading of the *Categories,* while Menn 1995 argues that the treatise should be viewed as a handbook for *Topics*-style debate, and Morison 2005 develops a compelling case for the *Categories* as an introduction to logic. Compare Ackrill (1963, 78–9), who suggests that the dialectician of the *Categories* might point out some particular entity—say, Socrates or Bucephalus—and try to answer the question "What is it?" (*ti esti?*)—perhaps for the sake of dialectical exercise, debate, and philosophical insight.

[155] "Every substance (*ousia*) seems to signify a certain *this*" (*Cat.* 3b10–23). Aristotle goes on to make a finer-grained distinction between primary *ousiai* (like Socrates), which seem to have this feature primarily, and others. The metaphysics of the *Categories*—if indeed it is meant to be a metaphysical treatise—is notoriously tricky to pin down; a relatively comprehensive analysis that attempts a reconciliation with the *Metaphysics* is Wedin 2000. See also Mann 2000 for a fuller discussion of the context and history of the work.

[156] Aristotle is certainly sensitive to the conventional nature of language; a locus classicus is *De Int.* 1.1. Aristotle points out a specific example of ordinary Greek usage coming apart from logical meaning at *Cat.* 10a28-b13 (there is no Greek adjective *aretaios* meaning "virtuous" from the noun *aretē*, "virtue"; instead Greek uses *spoudaios*).

[157] "I can discover no chariot. 'Chariot' is a mere empty sound" (*Questions of King Milinda* 3.1.1).

[158] See Garfield 2002: ch. 1 for a detailed comparison of some forms of Buddhist "skepticism" about semantic reference with Western philosophy. The Cowherds (2011) offer a lively, cross-cultural study of the doctrine of the "two truths" in Buddhism.

[159] There are a wide range of readings of what Aristotle might mean by "separable"; see again Fine 1984, Morrison 1985, and for a brief survey, Miller 2012, 307–9.

that ground Aristotle's metaphysics (while Buddhists also recognize their appeal, and spend time attempting to challenge it); these underlying differences are interesting and substantive, and would be worthwhile to explore in more detail.

2.6.2   Human Beings Are Primarily Form and "Soul" (psychē)

Aristotle's metaphysics also underpin his analysis of natural organisms, and hence of human persons. He takes it as granted that there *are* persons—that the individual human being (*ho tis anthrōpos*) is a substantial reality (*ousia*), which exhibits unity in number, form, and function.[160] After all, a human person seems to be *par excellence* "some *this*" in a common-sense way.[161] Now, all organisms are compounds of form (*eidos*) and matter (*hylē*) (*Physics* 2.1)—in this sense, adopting a derivation of Aristotle's technical terminology, we are all "hylemorphic compounds". But Aristotle also asserts that the evident "*this*-ness" of organisms is creditable more to their structure or pattern (*eidos*) than to the medium in which that pattern is instantiated.[162] For instance, when we point to a statue of Hermes, its "some *this*-ness" is creditable more to its form *as Hermes* than to its medium *of bronze*[163]; if I point to Michelangelo's David and say "this," then I don't likely mean to refer to it just as a body of raw marble, but as marble organized *thus*; and similarly, when I point out Socrates, I am concerned to point to his form as a human being, more than to his flesh and bone.

For Aristotle, the soul (*psychē*) of an animal, on the whole, is the *form* of the body of the animal, as a whole; more specifically, it "is a first actuality of a natural body which has life in potentiality" (*De Anima* 2.1, 412a27–8). The primary functional *potential* that is thus *actualized* is life: indeed, in ordinary Greek, a living being is called *empsychos* ("ensouled").[164] But in addition to this core function of living, the *psychē* has multiple more specific capacities. Chief among these, for Aristotle, are the capacity for nourishment (shared by plants, animals, and human beings); the capacity for perception (shared by animals and human beings); the capacity for certain higher forms of thought (peculiar to human beings); and several other capacities, notably desire. Much of the treatise *On the Soul (De Anima)* is devoted to the analysis of these functional capacities or potentials of the soul.

---

[160] Thus ὁ τις ἄνθρωπος ἢ ὁ τις ἵππος can be used as examples of individual οὐσίαι (*Cat.* 3, 1b4–5), as individuals that are 'one in respect of number' as well as form (*Metaph.* 5, 1016b31–3), and exist naturally (*Phys.* 2.1, 192b9–11). See for example Charlton 1994. Modern metaphysicians sympathetic to Aristotle (such as Fine 1994 and Koslicki 2010) tend to treat the unity of organisms as a central target for any promising explanation of composition.

[161] Common-sense realism about personhood is arguably a common feature of ancient Greek thought (for an overview, see Sorabji 2006); there were exceptions, such as Democritus (fr. 68 b9).

[162] See for example *Metaph.* H.3, 1043a35-1043b5; *Metaph.* Z.11, 1037a5–11; *DA* 412a6–9.

[163] See for example *Physics* 191a8–12.

[164] LSJ s.v. *empsychos*.

2.6.3 The Separability of nous

Most of these capacities of the soul are actualizations of some bodily potential—thus, they do not happen without a properly disposed bodily organ (cf. *DA* 2.1, 413a3–5): I do not become hungry for nourishment without a digestive system; I do not see without a physical visual system. But Aristotle proposes that a certain subset of mental states might be an exception: perhaps I can *think* or be aware (*noein*) without an appropriately disposed physical apparatus. Thus Aristotle introduces a certain kind of thinking or awareness (*nous*),[165] namely *active* or "creative" *nous*, at *De Anima* 3.5. This *nous poiētikos*, he explains, is "separate (*khōristos*), unaffected (*apathēs*), unmixed (*amigēs*), in its essence actuality (*tēi ousiāi energeia*) (*DA* 3.5, 430a17-18), and it is "immortal and everlasting" (*athanaton kai aidion*, *DA* 3.5, 430a23). What Aristotle means here has been the subject of a tremendous industry of commentary since antiquity. Two traditionally popular alternatives are still quite viable today: that Aristotle is speaking of (in some sense) the mind of God; or that Aristotle is speaking of a divine and immortal mind of each individual. Some version of the first position has been taken, for example, by Averroes; the second by Aquinas.[166]

This is all, again, interestingly different from the Buddhist analysis of the person. Like the Buddhist, Aristotle recognizes the human person as a kind of psychophysical compound (*nāma-rūpa*) and distinguishes the psychological or phenomenological elements from the material ones. Some of Aristotle's subdivisions of the soul's capacities—distinguishing perception and desire from pure thought or awareness, for example—may also be usefully compared to the Buddhist five-aggregate analysis of the person as an apparent or conventional compound of body, feeling, perception, mental formations and consciousness. Aristotle also recognizes that it is problematic to determine whether the person is the person in virtue of the soul or body or both.[167] But he comes down firmly on the position that the soul *is* the person. And he does not seriously challenge the view that there *is* a divine and immortal element in the human soul, although his characterization of that element here remains compressed and mysterious. Moreover, Aristotle is prepared to treat this element as "separable," independent, unconditioned, and immortal—descriptors that most Buddhist thinkers reserve solely for *Nibbāna* or *Nirvāṇa*.[168] In this respect, it is possible Aristotle's active *nous* might be profitably compared with basic awareness or witnessing consciousness as it is understood in orthodox schools of Indian philosophy, as well as some interpretations of the phenomenology of *Nirvāṇa*.[169]

---

[165] The more common translations of *nous* as "mind" and *noein* as "think", in a philosophical context, can mask some of their more ordinary and non-cognitive force; cf. LSJ s.v. *noeō* A.2 "*perceive by the mind, apprehend… take notice… art aware…*".

[166] Miller 2012: 333 n. 47 offers a brief summary of modern and historical positions. On the implications of this idea for Aristotle's notion of selfhood, see Sorabji 2006.

[167] E.g., *Metaphysics* Z.11.

[168] See for example Dhp 277–79 and MN 26 (*Ariyapariyesana Sutta*).

[169] For Indian positions on selfhood and witness consciousness, in both historical and modern perspective, see Siderits, Thompson, and Zahavi 2011. For one perspective on the Pāli canonical notion of *Nibbāna* as a kind of consciousness, see Harvey 1995.

2.6.4   Ethical Implications

Aristotle, as we have seen, defines the human person chiefly as the *form* or species of humanity. Therefore,[170] he concludes in his ethical works (most famously, at *Nicomachean Ethics* 1.7) that the goal of human life involves the actualization of just that form of life—for a human being, flourishing (*eudaimonia*) by realizing in practice the best capacity of the human soul.[171] This picture of human well-being as flourishing, unhindered maturation might be represented by the popular analogy of an acorn flourishing as an oak tree, but it is also more complex: whereas an oak tree has primarily to realize the *nutritive* capacity or potential of its soul, a human being has also to realize (like other animals) its *perceptive* and *locomotive* capacities, and (uniquely) its capacity for reasoned and reflective *thought*. To realize these human capacities *well* is to realize them according to the standard of excellence or virtue (*aretē*). Certain human excellences belong to our character (*ēthikai aretai*) and are cultivated by habit (*ethos*): examples include generosity and self-control. Other human excellences belong to our intellect (*dianoia*) and are cultivated by reflection: examples include insight, understanding, and practical wisdom. (See *Nicomachean Ethics* 1.13–2.1, 1102b13–1103a18).

Moreover, the human being possesses a still higher capacity for contemplation (*theōria*), employing the separate and divine faculty of *nous* (as described above); and in some places, particularly later in the tenth book of the *Nicomachean Ethics*, Aristotle stresses that this contemplative activity is truly the highest life for a human being.[172] He echoes certain interpretations of Plato in stressing the value of pure contemplation, which resonates with both Buddhist and Platonic expressions of longing for world-transcendence (see §2.4 above). Like Plato in *Republic* 7, however,

---

[170] This "therefore" represents a debatable but likely interpretation; for the debate, see above (n. 145), and again Berryman forthcoming.

[171] *Nic. Eth.* 1.7, frequently referred to as the "function argument," is another major locus classicus of Aristotelian scholarship. See Kraut 2014: §2 for a brief overview.

[172] According to one reading of *Nic. Eth.* 10.7–8. There is a famously difficult question here. Aristotle offers a fairly broad account of human happiness in *Nic. Eth.* 1.7 (*eudaimonia* is the activity of *psychē* according to its best *aretē*), and proceeds to spend much of this particular treatise analyzing and defining virtues of character and intellect. But in the tenth book, he seems to restrict the highest happiness just to theoretical or contemplative wisdom. Readers have often wondered whether this more restrictive account is compatible with the preceding books of the treatise, and whether it is really plausible (what about the human need for food and basic external goods, as Aristotle himself observes at 1178b33–35)? Many different solutions have been offered: Ackrill (1974) defends a fairly comprehensive and pluralist reading of the treatise, but is challenged by Kenny (1992) and Kraut (1989); and there are helpful recent contributions. See Irwin 2012 for a helpful summary of key issues, and a tentative endorsement of a moderate and pluralist account of *Nic. Eth.* 10, including both contemplative and practical virtue.

Aristotle may suppose that at least some philosophers will necessarily "return" from pure contemplation to benefit the community (*polis*) and the lives of its citizens.[173]

Despite the abstract premises that divide Buddhist, Platonist, and Aristotelian philosophers, their practical conclusions are arguably similar. The philosopher should pursue a fulfilling life of insight (*sophia, paññā*) into the nature of reality, especially one's own nature as a human person, and put that insight into practice in order to better the quality of others' lives as well as one's own. The Delphic injunction to "know thyself" (*gnōthi seauton*) is indispensable to the good life[174]: as the Platonist commentator Proclus points out, I must discern *what I am* in order to discern *what is good for me* (*On the Alcibiades* 1,3–7). That foundation holds whether the content of this self-knowledge is Plato's experience of the true human person as a conscious, reasoning agent; Aristotle's understanding that human nature is a set of essential potentials seeking fulfilment; the later Neo-Platonist's recognition of personhood as irreducible individuality and unity (*to hen*: Plotinus, *Enn.* 6.9.10; see above, §2.4.1.1); or the Buddha's observation that insight (*paññā*), wherever it glances, perceives that 'this is not mine; I am not this; this is not my self' (*netaṃ mama, nesohamasmi, na meso attā, SN* 22.45). The practical outcome of these apparently diverse self-experiences is comparable: the excellent human being is just, brave, self-controlled, generous, and wise.

References

Ackrill, J.L. 1963. *Aristotle's Categories and De Interpretatione*. Oxford: Clarendon Press.
———. 1974. Aristotle on Eudaimonia. *Proceedings of the British Academy* 60: 339–359, repr. in A. Rorty (ed.), *Essays on Aristotle's Ethics* (Berkeley, 1980): 15–33.
Albahari, M. 2009. Witness Consciousness: Its Definition, Appearance, and Reality. *Journal of Consciousness Studies* 16 (1): 62–84.
Almog, J., J. Perry, and H.K. Wettstein. 1989. *Themes from Kaplan*. New York: Oxford University Press.
Anderson, C. 2013. *Pain and Its Ending: The Four Noble Truths in the Theravada Buddhist Canon*. New York: Routledge.
Annas, J. 1995. *The Morality of Happiness*. Oxford: Oxford University Press.
———. 1999. *Platonic Ethics, Old and New*. New York: Cornell University Press.
Asch, S.E. 1951. Effects of Group Pressure on the Modification and Distortion of Judgments. In *Groups, Leadership, and Men*, ed. Asch, 177–190. Pittsburgh: Carnegie Press.
Berryman, S. Forthcoming. Aristotle in the Ethics Wars. *Review of Metaphysics*.

---

[173] Aristotle suggests, interestingly, that the psychological state (*hexis*) of practical wisdom (*phronēsis*) which guides individually virtuous decisions is identical with the state of political expertise that guides collectively virtuous decisions (*Nic. Eth.* 6.8). See Cooper 2012: ch. 3 for one depiction of how practically wise and politically active philosophers might structure a just community which allows others to pursue pure contemplation (138–40).

[174] Compare Plato, *Phaedrus* 229E, *Philebus* 48C, Samyutta Nikaya 22:82; 22:45.

Block, N. 1995. On a Confusion About a Function of Consciousness. *The Behavioural and Brain Sciences* 18 (2): 227–247.

Blondell, R. 2002. *The Play of Character in Plato's Dialogues*. Cambridge: Cambridge University Press.

Bobonich, C., and P. Destrée. 2007. *Akrasia in Greek Philosophy: From Socrates to Plotinus*. Leiden: Brill.

Bodéüs, R. 2001. *Catégories—Aristote: texte établi et traduit par Richard Bodéüs*. Paris: Belles Lettres.

Bodhi, B., Anuruddha, & B. Bhikkhu. 1993. *A Comprehensive Manual of Abhidhamma.*. Pariyatti.

Boys-Stones, G. 2001. *Post-Hellenistic Philosophy*. Oxford.

Boys-Stones, G., and C. Rowe. 2013. *The Circle of Socrates*. Indianapolis: Hackett Publishing.

Brickhouse, T.C., and N.D. Smith. 2010. *Socratic Moral Psychology*. Cambridge: Cambridge University Press.

———. 2015. Socrates and the Unity of the Virtues. *Journal of Ethics* 1 (4): 311–324.

Brown, E. 2003. Plato's Ethics and Politics in The Republic. ed. E.N. Zalta. *Stanford Encyclopedia of Philosophy*. http://plato.stanford.edu/entries/plato-ethics-politics.

———. 2004. Minding the Gap in Plato's 'Republic'. *Philosophical Studies: An International Journal for Philosophy in the Analytic Tradition* 117.1 (2): 275–302.

Bruun, O., and L. Corti, eds. 2005. *Les Catégories et leur histoire*. Paris: Vrin.

Burkert, W. 1972. *Lore and Science in Ancient Pythagoreanism*. Cambridge, MA: Harvard University Press.

Burnyeat, M.F. 1999. Culture and Society in Plato's Republic. *Tanner Lectures on Human Values* 20 (1999): 215–324.

Burnyeat, M.F., and M.J. Levett. 1990. *The Theaetetus of Plato*. Indianapolis: Hackett.

Butler, E.P. 2005. Polytheism and Individuality in the Henadic Manifold. *Dionysius* 23: 83–104.

Carlisle, C., and J. Ganeri, eds. 2010. *Philosophy as Therapeia*. Cambridge: Cambridge University Press.

Carpenter, A. 2014. *Indian Buddhist Philosophy*. Routledge.

Chakrabarti, A. 1982. The Nyaya Proofs for the Existence of the Soul. *Journal of Indian Philosophy* 10: 211–238.

Charlton, W. 1994. Aristotle on Identity. In Scaltsas, Charle and Gill 1994: 41–53.

Chase, M., S.R.L. Clark, and M. McGhee, eds. 2013. *Philosophy as a Way of Life: Ancients and Moderns – Essays in Honor of Pierre Hadot*. Hoboken: Wiley.

Chiaradonna, R., and G. Galluzzo, eds. 2013. *Universals in Ancient Philosophy*. Pisa: Edizioni della Normale.

Chiba, K. 2012. Aristotle on Heuristic Inquiry and Demonstration of What it is. In *The Oxford Handbook of Aristotle*, ed. C. Shields, 171–201. Oxford: Oxford University Press.

Christoff, K., D. Cosmelli, D. Legrand, and E. Thompson. 2011. Specifying the Self for Cognitive Neuroscience. *Trends in Cognitive Sciences* 15 (3): 104–112.

Cohen, S.M. 2016. Aristotle's Metaphysics. *Stanford Encyclopedia of Philosophy*. http://plato.stanford.edu/entries/aristotle-metaphysics/.

Colvin, M. 2007. Heraclitean Flux and Unity of Opposites in Plato's *Theaetetus* and *Cratylus*. *Classical Quarterly* 57 (2): 759–769.

Cooper, J.M. 1984. Plato's Theory of Human Motivation. *History of Philosophy Quarterly* 1 (1): 3–21.

———. 2012. *Pursuits of Wisdom: Six Ways of Life in Ancient Philosophy from Socrates to Plotinus*. Princeton: Princeton University Press.

Cooper, J.M., and D.S. Hutchinson. 1997. *Plato: Complete Works*. Indianapolis: Hackett.

Cowherds, The. 2011. *Moonshadows: Conventional Truth in Buddhist Philosophy*. Oxford: Oxford University Press.

Davis, G. 2013. Traces of Consequentialism and Non-Consequentialism in Bodhisattva Ethics. *Philosophy East and West* 63 (2): 275–305.

Devereux, D. 2008. Socratic Ethics and Moral Psychology. In *The Oxford Handbook of Plato*, ed. G. Fine, 139–164. Oxford: Oxford University Press.

Dillon, J.M. 1996. *The Middle Platonists: 80 BC to AD 220*. Cornell UP. Reprint of 1977 original, with revisions and new afterword.

———. 2003. *The Heirs of Plato*. Oxford: Oxford University Press.

Dodds, E.R. 1928. The Parmenides of Plato and the Origin of the Neoplatonic "One.". *Classical Quarterly* 22.3 (4): 129–142.

Edelglass, W., and J.L. Garfield. 2009. *Buddhist Philosophy: Essential Readings*. Oxford: Oxford University Press.

Ferrari, G.R.F. 2003. *City and Soul in Plato's Republic*. Chicago: University of Chicago Press.

Fine, G. 1992. *On Ideas: Aristotle's Criticism of Plato's Theory of Forms*. Oxford: Oxford University Press.

———. 1994. A Puzzle Concerning Matter and Form. In Scaltsas, Charles and Gill 1994: 13–40.

———. 2008. *The Oxford Handbook of Plato*. Oxford: Oxford University Press.

Fink, J. 2012. *The Development of Dialectic from Plato to Aristotle*. Cambridge: Cambridge University Press.

Foot, Philippa. 2001. *Natural Goodness*. Oxford: Oxford University Press.

Frede, M. 2002. Introduction. In *Rationality in Greek Thought*, ed. M. Frede and G. Striker, 1–28. Oxford: Clarendon Press.

Frede, D. 2012. The *Endoxon* Mystique: What *Endoxa* Are and What They Are Not. *Oxford Studies in Ancient Philosophy* 43: 185–215.

Ganeri, Jonardon, and Clare Carlisle. 2010. *Philosophy as Therapeia. Royal Institute of Philosophy Supplement: 66*. Cambridge: Cambridge University Press.

Ganeri, J. 2012. *The Self: Naturalism, Consciousness, and the First-Person Stance*. Oxford: Clarendon Press.

———. 2013. Philosophy as a Way of Life: Spiritual Exercises from the Buddha to Tagore. In Chase, Clark, and McGhee, 116–31.

Garfield, J.L. 2002. *Empty Words: Buddhist Philosophy and Cross-Cultural Interpretation*. Oxford: Oxford University Press.

Gerson, L.P. 2003. *Knowing Persons: A Study in Plato*. Oxford: Oxford University Press.

———. 2004. Platonism and the Invention of the Problem of Universals. *Archiv für Geschichte der Philosophie* 86: 233–256.

———. 2006. *Aristotle and Other Platonists*. Cornell University Press.

———. 2013. *From Plato to Platonism*. Cornell University Press.

———. 2014. Harold Cherniss and the Study of Plato Today. *Journal of the History of Philosophy* 52 (3): 397–409. https://doi.org/10.1353/hph.2014.0059.

Gill, C. 2009. *The Structured Self in Hellenistic and Roman Thought*. Oxford: Oxford University Press.

Gombrich, R.F. 2009. *What the Buddha thought*. London: Equinox.

Goodman, C. 2009. *Consequences of Compassion: An Interpretation and Defense of Buddhist Ethics*. Oxford: Oxford University Press.

Gowans, C.W. 2010. Medical analogies in Buddhist and Hellenistic thought: Tranquility and Anger. *In Carlisle and Ganeri* 2010: 11–34.

Griffin, M.J. 2014a. Proclus on the Ethics of Self-Constitution. In *Causation and Creation in Late Antiquity*, ed. A. Marmodoro and B.D. Prince, 202–219. Cambridge: Cambridge University Press.

———. 2014b. Universals, Education, and Philosophical Methodology in Later Neoplatonism. In *Universals in Ancient Philosophy*, ed. R. Chiaradonna and G. Galluzzo, 353–380. Pisa: Edizioni della Scuola Normale.

Hadot, P. 1995. *Philosophy as a Way of Life*. Hoboken: Wiley-Blackwell.

Hadot, P., and M. Chase. 2004. *What is Ancient Philosophy?* Cambridge, MA: Harvard University Press.

Harvey, P. 1995. *The Selfless Mind: Personality, Consciousness, and Nirvana in Early Buddhism.* Routledge.

———. 2012. *An Introduction to Buddhism.* Cambridge: Cambridge University Press.

Hursthouse, Rosalind. 1999. *On Virtue Ethics.* Oxford: Oxford University Press.

Inwood, B. 1985. *Ethics and Human Action in Early Stoicism*, 1985. Oxford: Clarendon Press.

Irwin, Terry. 1980. The metaphysical and psychological basis of Aristotle's ethics. In *Essays on Aristotle's ethics*, ed. Amélie Oksenberg Rorty, 35–53. Berkeley: University of California Press.

Irwin, T. 1977. Plato's Heracliteanism. *The Philosophical Quarterly* 27: 1–13.

———. 1988. *Aristotle's First Principles.* Oxford: Oxford University Press.

———. 2008. The Platonic Corpus. In *The Oxford Handbook of Plato*, ed. G. Fine, 63–87. Oxford: Oxford University Press.

———. 2012. Conceptions of Happiness in the *Nicomachean Ethics*. In *Shields* 2012: 495–528.

Jinpa, T. 2002. *Self, Reality and Reason in Tibetan Philosophy.* London: Routledge.

Johansen, T.K. 2008. The Timaeus on the Principles of Cosmology. In *The Oxford Handbook of Plato*, ed. G. Fine, 463–483. Oxford: Oxford University Press.

Johnson, D.M. 2005a. Xenophon at his Most Socratic (*Memorabilia* 4.2). *Oxford Studies in Ancient Philosophy* 29: 39–73.

Johnson, M.R. 2005b. *Aristotle on Teleology.* Oxford: Oxford University Press.

Kalligas, P. 1997. Forms of Individuals in Plotinus: A Re-examination. *Phronesis* 42 (2): 206–227.

Kaplan, D. 1989a. Demonstratives. In Almog, Perry, and Wettstein 1989: 481–563.

———. 1989b. Afterthoughts. In Almog, Perry, and Wettstein 1989: 565–614.

Keown, D. 1992. *The Nature of Buddhist Ethics.* London: Palgrave Macmillan.

King, K.L. 2005. *What is Gnosticism?* Cambridge, MA: Harvard University Press.

Korsgaard, C.M. 2009. *Self-Constitution: Agency, Identity, and Integrity.* Oxford: Oxford University Press.

Koslicki, K. 2010. *The Structure of Objects.* Oxford: Oxford University Press.

Kraut, R. 1989. *Aristotle on the Human Good.* Princeton: Princeton University Press.

———. 2000. The Defense of Justice in Plato's Republic. In *Plato's Republic*, ed. R. Kraut, 197–221. Lanham: Rowman & Littlefield.

———. 2014. Aristotle's ethics. In ed. E.N. Zalta, *Stanford Encyclopedia of Philosophy* (Summer 2017 ed.) https://plato.stanford.edu/archives/sum2017/entries/aristotle-ethics.

Lorenz, H. 2008. Plato on the Soul. In *The Oxford Handbook of Plato*, ed. G. Fine, 243–266. Oxford: Oxford University Press.

MacIntyre, Alasdair. 1984. *After Virtue: A Study in Moral Theory.* 2nd ed. Notre Dame: University of Notre Dame Press.

Mahoney, T.A. 1992. Do Plato's Philosopher-Rulers Sacrifice Self-Interest to Justice? *Phronesis* 37 (3): 265–282.

Mann, W.R. 2000. *The Discovery of Things: Aristotle's Categories and Their Context.* Princeton University Press: Princeton.

Martha, Nussbaum. 1986. *The fragility of goodness. Luck and ethics in Greek tragedy and philosophy*, Revised edn. Cambridge: Cambridge University Press, 2001.

Matthews, G.B. 2008. The Epistemology and Metaphysics of Socrates. In *The Oxford Handbook of Plato*, ed. G. Fine, 114–138. Oxford: Oxford University Press.

McDowell, John. 1998a. *Mind, Value, and Reality.* Harvard: Harvard University Press.

———. 1998b. Two Sorts of Naturalism. In McDowell 1998a: 167–197.

McPherran, Mark. 1996. *The Religion of Socrates.* University Park: Pennsylvania University Press.

———. 2013. *Plato's Republic: A Critical Guide.* Cambridge: Cambridge University Press.

Menn, S. 1995. Metaphysics, Dialectic, and the *Categories*. Revue de Métaphysique et de Morale, 100e Année, no. 3: 311–337.

Milgram, S. 1963. Behavioural Study of Obedience. *Journal of Abnormal and Social Psychology* 67 (4): 371–378.

Miller, S.G. 2009. *The Berkeley Plato.* Berkeley: University of California Press.

Miller, F.D. 2012. Aristotle on the Separability of Mind. In Shields (2012): 306–339.
Moore, C. 2014. How to "Know Thyself" in Plato's Phaedrus. *Apeiron* 47 (3): 390–418.
Morison, B. 2005. Les *Catégories* d'Aristote comme introduction à la logique. *In Bruun & Corti* 2005: 103–120.
Morrow, G.R., and J.M. Dillon. 1992. *Proclus' Commentary on Plato's Parmenides*. Princeton: Princeton University Press.
Nagel, T. 1972. Aristotle on eudaimonia. *Phronesis* 17 (3): 252–259.
Nightingale, A.W. 2000. *Genres in Dialogue: Plato and the Construct of Philosophy*. Cambridge: Cambridge University Press.
Nisbett, R.E., and T.D. Wilson. 1977. Telling More Than We Can Know: Verbal Reports on Mental Processes. *Psychological Review* 84 (3): 231–259.
Nussbaum, M.C. 2012. *Not for Profit: Why Democracy Needs the Humanities*. Princeton: Princeton University Press.
———. 2013. *The Therapy of Desire*. Princeton: Princeton University Press.
Pagels, E. 2004. *The Gnostic Gospels*. NY: Random House.
Parfit, D. 1984. *Reasons and Persons*. Oxford: Oxford University Press.
Parry, R. 2004. Ancient Ethical Theory. In E.N. Zalta, ed. *Stanford Encyclopedia of Philosophy*. http://plato.stanford.edu/archives/fall2014/entries/ethics-ancient.
Peterson, S. 2008. The Parmenides. In *The Oxford Handbook of Plato*, ed. G. Fine, 383–410. Oxford: Oxford University Press.
Press, G.A. 2000. *Who Speaks for Plato?* Lanham: Rowman & Littlefield.
Rappe, S.L. 1995. Socrates and Self-Knowledge. *Apeiron* 28 (1): 1–24.
Reinhardt, T. 2015. On *Endoxa* in Aristotle's *Topics*. *RhM* 158: 225–246.
Rist, J.M. 1963. Forms of Individuals in Plotinus. *Classical Quarterly* n.s. 13.2: 223–231.
Śāntideva. 1971. *Śikṣā-samuccaya: A compendium of Buddhist doctrine*. Trans. C. Bendall and W.H.D. Rouse. Delhi: Motilal Banarsidass.
———. 1998. *The Bodhicaryāvatāra*. Oxford: Oxford University Press.
Scaltsas, T., D. Charles, and M.L. Gill, eds. 1994. *Unity, Identity and Explanation in Aristotle's Metaphysics*. Oxford: Clarendon Press.
Sellars, J. 2006. *Stoicism*. New York: Acumen.
———. 2014. Plato's Apology of Socrates: A Metaphilosophical Text. *Philosophy and Literature* 38 (2): 433–445.
Shields, Christopher. 2012. *The Oxford Handbook of Aristotle*. Oxford: Oxford University Press.
———. 2013. Plato's Divided Soul. In McPherran (2013): 147–170.
———. 2016. Aristotle's Psychology. In ed. E.N. Zalta, *Stanford Encyclopedia of Philosophy*. Winter 2016 ed. https://plato.stanford.edu/archives/win2016/entries/aristotle-psychology.
Siderits, M. 2003. *Personal Identity and Buddhist Philosophy: Empty Persons*. Aldershot: Ashgate.
Siderits, M., E. Thompson, and D. Zahavi. 2011. *Self, No Self? Perspectives from Analytical, Phenomenological, and Indian Traditions*. Oxford: Oxford University Press.
Sikkema, J. 2009. On The Necessity of Individual Forms in Plotinus. *International Journal of the Platonic Tradition* 3: 138–153.
Smith, N.D. 2004. Did Plato Write the "Alcibiades I?". *Apeiron* 37 (2): 93–108.
Sorabji, R. 2000. *Emotion and Peace of Mind*. Oxford: Oxford University Press.
———. 2006. *Self: Ancient and Modern Theories about Individuality, Life, and Death*. Chicago: University of Chicago Press.
———. 2012. Self and Morality: Cross-Cultural Perspectives. In *Self-Knowledge and Agency*, ed. M. Sen, 52–62. New Delhi: Decent Books.
———. 2014. Philosophy and Life in Ancient Greek and Roman Philosophy: Three Aspects. *Royal Institute of Philosophy Supplement* 74: 45–74.
———., ed. 2016a. *Aristotle Transformed: The Ancient Commentators and Their Influence*. 2nd ed. London: Bloomsbury.
———., ed. 2016b. *Aristotle Re-Interpreted : New Findings on Seven Hundred Years of the Ancient Commentators*. London: Bloomsbury.

Sullivan, S.D. 1995. *Psychological and Ethical Ideas: What Ancient Greeks Say*. Leiden: Brill.

Ryle, Gilbert. 1953. Ordinary language. *The philosophical review* 62.2: 167–186.

Thakchoë, S. 2015. Reification and Nihilism? The Three-Nature Theory and Its Implications. In *Madhyamaka and Yogacara*, ed. J.L. Garfield and J. Westerhoff, 72–110. Oxford: Oxford University Press.

Thompson, E. 2011. Self-No-Self? Memory and Reflexive Awareness. In *Self, No Self? Perspectives from Analytical, Phenomenological, and Indian* Traditions, ed. M. Siderits, E. Thompson, and D. Zahavi, 157–175. Oxford: Oxford University Press.

Tsouna, V. 2001. Socrate et la connaissance de soi: quelques interprétations. In *Figures de Socrate: Philosophie Antique*, vol. 1, ed. M. Narcy, 37–64.

Vander Waerdt, P., ed. 1994. *The Socratic Movement*. New York: Cornell University Press.

Vlastos, G. 1983. The Socratic Elenchus. *Oxford Studies in Ancient Philosophy* 1: 27–58.

———. 1991. *Socrates, Ironist and Moral Philosopher*. New York: Cornell University Press.

Weiss, R. 2012. *Philosophers in the "Republic"*. New York: Cornell University Press.

Whitehead, A.N. 1979. *Process and Reality*. 1929. Reprinted with corrections, ed. D.R. Griffin and D.W. Sherburne. Free Press.

Wilberding, J. 2005. "Creeping Spatiality": The Location of Nous in Plotinus' Universe. *Phronesis* 50 (4): 315–334.

———. 2016. The Neoplatonic Commentators on 'Spontaneous' Generation. In Sorabji (2016b): 211–230.

Zahavi, D. 2005. *Subjectivity and Selfhood: Investigating the First-Person Perspective*. Cambridge, MA: MIT Press.

Chapter 3
Detachment in Buddhist and Stoic Ethics: *Ataraxia* and *Apatheia* and Equanimity

Emily McRae

3.1 Introduction

Reading Buddhist ethics in relation to Stoic ethics highlights a central issue in understanding emotional-ethical life: the value of attachment to those that we love. Attachments create some obvious moral problems, such as unjustifiable partiality, and less obvious ones, such as intense emotional upheaval at the loss of a loved one or even at a loved one's disappointment, scorn, or contempt.[1] In addition to these kinds of problems, sometimes our attachment to others makes us treat them *worse* and not better, for instance harping on loved ones' flaws, smothering them, or punishing them out of jealousy or spite when they hurt us. Attachment, even when it is going well (that is, when the object of our attachment is not lost or threatened), is not always conducive to love, compassion, or other generally positive modes of emotional engagement.

Both Stoic and Buddhist ethics are deeply concerned with the ethical dangers of attachment, which is not to say that they do not tolerate or accommodate attachments (as I will argue below). Rather, their ethical perspectives reveal some of the more problematic aspects of attachment. Three dangers stand out: (1) the destructive consequences of overwhelming emotionality, brought on by attachment, both for oneself and others; (2) the dangers to one's agency posed by strongly held, but ultimately unstable, attachments; and (3) the threat to virtuous emotional engagement with others caused by one's own attachment to them.

The first two kinds of moral danger – overwhelming emotionality and threatened agency – have informed Stoic models of detachment. I follow David Wong (2006) in distinguishing two interpretations of Stoic detachment: detachment as freedom

---

[1] I will not focus on the danger of unjustifiable partiality here. For more on this topic, see McRae (2013).

E. McRae (✉)
University of New Mexico, Albuquerque, NM, USA
e-mail: emcrae@unm.edu

© Springer International Publishing AG, part of Springer Nature 2018
G. F. Davis (ed.), *Ethics without Self, Dharma without Atman*, Sophia Studies in Cross-cultural Philosophy of Traditions and Cultures 24, https://doi.org/10.1007/978-3-319-67407-0_3

73

from emotionality (or, at least, strong, afflictive emotionality), articulated in Stoic discussions of *apatheia*, and detachment as resilience to the vicissitudes of the strongly felt, unstable attachments that threaten one's agency, articulated in Stoic discussions of value of *ataraxia* (freedom from disturbance). In this paper I draw on Buddhist texts to present a third model of detachment, which responds primarily to the third moral danger of attachment, the danger of not loving well. On this model, detachment enables and enhances proper love and compassion and is conceived of as a tool for virtuous emotional engagement. This model challenges some influential interpretations of Buddhist conceptions of detachment that reduce them to one of the Stoic models, either the extirpation of emotions or resilience to threat to agency.

3.2   Detachment As Freedom from Emotion: *Apatheia* As an Ethical Ideal

One interpretation of the Stoic model of detachment is as freedom from emotion (*pathe*), or *apatheia*. Cicero tells us, approvingly, of the Stoic sage who, after hearing that his son had died, calmly remarked, "I knew that I had begotten a mortal" (TD 3.30). Even the grief of losing a child is extirpated in the heart of the Stoic sage. "It is often asked whether it is better to have moderate passions or none," Seneca writes. "Our people drive out the passions altogether" (Ep. 116.1). In ancient Hellenistic schools, *apatheia*, the freedom from or absence of emotion, was contrasted to a more moderate approach to emotionality, *metriopatheia*, the moderation of emotion. This ideal found expression in Aristotle's ethics, which defines as virtuous certain ways of feeling and acting that are neither excessive nor deficient, and was defended by many of his followers (Sorabji 2000, 196). Although several attempts were made to unite these two ideals, by for instance seeing *metriopatheia* as a stage one achieves before *apatheia*[2] or as seeing these ideals as appropriate for different kinds of people,[3] in the ancient Hellenistic world the dispute between these ideals was nevertheless substantive, as Seneca's quotation makes clear (Sorabji 2000, 206–210).

Early Stoics, however, differed with regard to how devoid of affect the ideal of *apatheia* really is. Chrysippus, for example, maintained that the Stoic sage, while free from the passions (*pathe*), retains a narrow set of positive affective states, *eupatheiai*, which include joy (*khara*), caution (*eulabeia*) and reasonable wishing (*boulêsis*).[4] Seneca conceded that the Stoic sage may feel "hints and shadows" of the passions, even though she is "free from the passions themselves" (De Ira 1.16.7). Nevertheless, all Stoic philosophers agree that the *apatheia* requires a robust

---

[2] See Plotinus I.2.2 (13–18); I.2.3(20), I.2.6 (25–27); Sorabji (2000, 197)

[3] See discussion of Philo of Alexandria and Maimonides in Richard Sorabji, *Emotions and Peace of Mind* (New York: Oxford University Press, 2000, Chapter 25).

[4] Graver, p.51; Sorabji (2000), p. 47–51; Diogenes Laertius *Lives* 7.116; Cicero *Tusc.* 4.12–13.

freedom from the disturbances that we (and they) would typically characterize as emotional states, including anger, compassion, envy, love, and intense joy (Nussbaum 1994, chapter 10).

There are two main styles of Stoic argument for the extirpation of emotion: arguments based on recognizing proper indifference to externals and arguments from the phenomenology of emotion. Arguments of the first kind take the following form: (1) The good or virtuous life is self-sufficient. It does not depend on external objects, such as wealth, status, prestige or fame (or even friendship), health or reasonably good fortune. (2) We should, then, not attach importance to such "externals" since they have no significant place in virtuous living. (3) Emotions are judgments that affirm, wrongly, the value of such externals. Anger wrongly affirms the appearance that others can take something of real value from you against your will. Grief wrongly affirms the delusional hope for the immorality of loved ones. (4) Therefore emotions only serve to mislead us, do not support virtue, and can become a major obstacle in the achievement of virtue. For this reason, the wise person works to extirpate her emotions.

The first premise, about the self-sufficiency of happiness (or good, virtuous living), is a central Stoic claim.[5] It is complicated by the fact that the some Stoic philosophers also admit that some externals, particularly friendship, health, and political engagements are also good in the sense that they can be chosen over other options (for example, choosing health over sickness), should one be in the position to choose.[6] But these external "goods" do not in any way constitute the final good, or virtue. As Epictetus puts it, you should choose them as you choose appetizers at a party: should the tray come your way, we can "reach out your hand and take some," but we do not pursue the tray (or actively avoid it) (*Handbook,* Chapter 15). For the above argument to work as a stoic argument, however, we only need the claim (uncontroversial for Stoics) that the good life is self-sufficient (and whether that claim is consistent with the qualified values of externals is a thorny issue in Stoic ethics that we can happily avoid in this discussion). The second premise follows from the self-sufficiency of virtue: since happy living is virtuous living, and virtuous living is self-sufficient, to live virtuously (and, so, happily) we must actively and vigilantly reject the tenacious appearance, that nearly all of us have, that externals are part of happy living.

The third premise rests entirely on the Stoic view of emotions as judgments or beliefs about appearances.[7] An emotion is an assent to an appearance, that is, the belief that the way something strikes one upon encountering it is the way it truly is.

---

[5] Consider, for one example, Epictetus opening remarks to *The Encheiridion* that happiness is entirely in our control, so long as we use our reason well (Ch. 1). For more on this aspect of Stoic conceptions of the good life, see Irwin ("Virtue, Praise and Success: Stoic Responses to Aristotle" (1990)).

[6] Also see Epictetus *Discourses* §2. See Nussbaum's discussion (1998), Chapter 10.

[7] See Martha Nussbaum, *Upheavals of Thought* (New York: Cambridge University Press, 2001) and Martha Nussbaum, *Therapy of Desire: Theory and Practice in Hellenistic Ethics* (Princeton, NJ: Princeton University Press, 1994), especially Chapter 10; Margaret Graver, *Stoicism and Emotion* (Chicago: University of Chicago Press, 2007).

For example, upon experiencing the death of a loved one it may appear to me that something of irreplaceable value is forever gone from my life. My grief is my assent to that appearance. Because my emotions judge externals to be a significant part of my happiness, emotions are, on the Stoic view, false beliefs or irrational judgments. It is for this reason that the wise person extirpates them.

The second style of Stoic argument for the extirpation of emotion relies less on points of Stoic doctrine – the self-sufficiency of happiness, the Stoic theory of emotions – than the first argument. This kind of argument instead draws on the phenomenology of emotional life, something that is accessible to the Stoic and non-Stoic alike. It also more directly addresses the way that the extirpation of emotion is a model of *detachment* rather than an implication of human rationality (that is, that full human rationality requires the extirpation of the emotions). There are two basic kinds of arguments from the phenomenology of emotion, one that focuses on the disruption of one's peace of mind and one that focuses on the destructive consequences of emotionality for others.

Argument for Preserving Peace of Mind (1) Emotions are, by their nature, disruptive to tranquility. Their physical symptoms disrupt the equilibrium of the body; their compulsive energy destroys the tranquility of the mind. Consider Seneca's discussion of the everyday symptoms of strong emotionality:

> Some people have burst blood vessels in their excessive ardor, and spit up blood from shouting louder than their strength could bear, and blurred their vision when weeping forced water into their eyes too vigorously, and relapsed into illness when they were sick. No path leads more quickly to insanity: many, accordingly, have prolonged anger's frenzy and never regained the capacity for thought once they let it go…Angry people curse their children with death, themselves with poverty, their households with ruin, and they deny they're angry just as madmen deny they're insane (De Ira II.36.4–5).

But, (2) the wise person, on the Stoic view, is free from such violent disturbances, which Seneca later calls "disgusting and horrifying sight[s] of swelling and distortion"(I.1.3–5). And so, (3) the wise person works to extirpate emotions, now conceived not only as irrational judgments, but as violent disturbances to one's peace of mind. Positive emotions, too, can be violent disturbances, for instance exhilarating joy may distract or disorient. For Seneca, the Stoic sage does not completely lack feelings of gladness and joy, but "they do not fill the breast, they simply relax the brow" (Epistles, 23.3).

Argument from the Destructive Consequences to Others Like the previous argument, this argument rests on observable facts about the phenomenology and psychology of emotionality. (1) Strong emotions – especially anger, hatred, envy, resentment and spite – can have disastrous effects on the objects of such emotions and even bystanders. Seneca gives examples of the damaging effects of anger for the public moral order during his own lifetime:

> Consider the cities of vast renown whose foundation stones can now hardly be made out: anger cast these cities down. Consider the wastelands, deserted, without an inhabitant for many miles: anger emptied them. Consider the many leaders known to history as examples of grim destiny: anger ran one through in his bed, struck another dead (sacrilege!) at the dinner table, tore another limb from limb in full view of the crowded forum, the very bosom of the law (De Ira I.2.2).

But the damaging effects of rage and other strong emotional states is not controversial. For this to be an argument for the extirpation of emotion, rather than simply the moderation of emotion, the Stoic needs the following claim: (2) Emotional reactions, once begun, are very difficult, or even impossible, to stop. Once we have begun a particular emotional trajectory, we are subject to the consequences of that trajectory, just as "people who have jumped off a cliff retain no independent judgment and cannot offer resistance or slow the descent of their bodies in freefall" (De Ira I.7.4). As Seneca puts it, "…once the mind has submitted to anger, love, and the other passions, it's not allowed to check its onrush: its own weight and the downward-tending nature of vices must – must – carry it along and drive it down to the depths" (I.7.4). For this reason, (3) we are better off extirpating emotions rather than trying (futilely) to manage them, contra Aristotle (De Ira I.7.2).[8] Again, Seneca:

> Aristotle says that some passions, if used well, serve as weapons. That would be true if, like the arms of war, they could be taken up and put off at the judgment of the one who dons them. But these weapons that Aristotle gives to virtue fight all on their own; they don't wait for the hand that wields them, they're not possessed, they do the possessing" (De Ira I.17.1)

The damaging consequences, then, of strong emotionality cannot be countered simply by its moderation, but only through its extirpation.

3.3 Detachment As Freedom from Disturbances: *Ataraxia* and the Protection of Ethical Agency

Some Stoic sources, however, suggest that detachment is not about just avoiding the badness of emotionality (either its irrationality or destructive consequences) but is rather about preserving one's agency, which often entails the extirpation of emotions. The early Stoic Zeno, for example, claimed that *apatheia* is the freedom from the influence of emotion that results in disobedience to reason.[9] This suggests that he

---

[8] See Nussbaum's discussion of the "argument from excess" in *Therapy* (1994) p. 396–398. It also possible for the Stoic to challenge Aristotelian moderation of emotion using the concept of no-self: If self is an illusion, then what sense can we make of the Aristotelian approach of cultivating the self through the moderation of emotion? There is some evidence that Seneca, in particular, may have had access to some Buddhist texts, or at least Buddhist ideas, particularly no-self (See Richard Sorabji, *Self: Ancient and Modern Insights about Individuality, Life and Death* (Chicago: University of Chicago Press, 2006), p. 41). I doubt this will turn out to be a successful line of argument for the Stoic, but it does reveal intriguing historical connections between Roman Stoic and Indian Buddhist thinkers (connections that I cannot, unfortunately, pursue here).

[9] See Galen PHP 4.2.12,24; 4.4.21, 23; 5.4.14; Sorabji (2000), Chapter 3.

saw the threat to one's rationality as the main cause of concern; emotionality is only problematic insofar as it contributes to that threat.

Consider Epictetus's advice to a distraught father whose anxiety would not allow him to remain by the side of his sick daughter. When Epictetus asked the father if he thought he had acted correctly, the man replied that he had acted naturally: "It's what all we fathers go through."

> 'I don't dispute that reactions like yours occur,' Epictetus said. 'The point at issue is whether they ought to….So show me how, exactly, you acted in accordance with nature.' [When the father admits that he cannot, Epictetus responds:]
> 'No, to leave your child's side when she is sick, and go away, is not a rational act, and I don't suppose that even you will argue otherwise. But we still have to consider whether it is consistent with family affection…Was it right for you, being affectionately disposed toward your child, to go off and leave her? Let's take her mother. Doesn't she feel affection for her daughter?'
> 'Of course she does.'
> 'Then she should, too, have left her?'
> 'No.'…
> 'In fact, it is unfair and illogical to say that people whose affection is the equal of yours should not be permitted to do what you claim was justified in your case owing to this very great affection you profess…would you want to be so loved by [your family] that, because of their love, you would always suffer sickness in isolation? Isn't that more like the affection you pray your enemies would show you, that they should go away and leave you be? And if so, the inescapable conclusion is that what you did was no act of affection at all" (Discourses, I.11.1–26).

Epictetus is not arguing that familial affection is not rational, but rather that the father's extreme reaction is not an act of affection, not natural and, what amounts to the same thing for Epictetus, not rational. The problem with the father's anxiety is that it threatens his agency, causing him to act in way that he would not otherwise choose. In this case, the strong emotional response is actually inhibiting the father from properly tending to his loved ones. His extreme anxiety threatens his ability to act in accordance with affection for family. Interestingly, the feeling of affection for family is not challenged here, nor does Epictetus suggest that it should, like the father's anxiety, be extirpated.

Lawrence Becker (1998) has argued against the claim that Stoic detachment is the ideal of the extirpation of emotion. It is better understood as a kind of resilience to the threats to agency that strong emotionality poses. The value (and necessity) of detachment, he argues, follows from the fact of the vulnerability of human agency. The problem is not emotional engagement in itself, or even the destructive consequences that it can cause; the problem is that some emotional engagements, especially strong ones, threaten one's agency, as the father's anxiety made him unable to choose to remain with his sick daughter. Attachments are acceptable, even desirable, as long as they remain "encapsulated," that is, they do not extend beyond their proper boundaries in ways that diminish one's agency. According to Becker, the typical Stoic views, such as the indifference to external goods and the self-sufficiency of virtue and the need to extirpate emotions are simply "efforts to immunize ourselves against bad fortune" (Becker 1998, 156). The detachments the

Stoics encourage should not be read as ideal or universal goods, but rather as necessary step to full agency. "We do not want to *be* detached; we want to be *able* to detach ourselves when that is necessary to preserve our agency" (156).

This interpretation of Stoic detachment relies on the Stoic (and broadly Hellenistic) ideal of *ataraxia,* the freedom from disturbances, including worry, apprehension, fear, anger, and even unpleasant physical sensations such as hunger and thirst. "Distress never befalls [the sage]," Seneca tells us. "[His] soul is serene, and nothing can happen that would cloud it" (Seneca Clem. 2.5.4). *Ataraxia* connotes a pervasive calmness and tranquility, even in the face of external threats that would normally disturb us. Although it is highly valued, no Hellenistic school holds it as a final end or equivalent to *eudaimonia*.[10] For the Stoics, the final end of human life is virtue, which they understand as living in accordance with reason; tranquility, or *ataraxia*, is the consequence of virtuous living.[11] On Becker's model of detachment, *ataraxia* can be understood as the tranquility that comes from knowing that one can detach when it is appropriate to do so, that is, when attachments threaten to undermine one's agency. It is the confidence and moral stability that arises from knowing that one can encapsulate one's attachments.

3.4 Detachment in Buddhist Ethics and the *Bodhisattva* Ideal

Both conceptions of detachment – as extirpation and as resilience – are present to some extent in Buddhist ethics. The fourteenth-century Tibetan philosopher Tsongkhapa, for example, recommends "uprooting" negative emotional responses, such as anger, by "destroying them at the root" (Tsongkhapa 2000, 155–156).[12] Only the complete extirpation of such emotions, rather than their careful management or moderation, will be enough to reach the ideal of enlightenment. One reason is that for many Buddhist thinkers, including Tsongkhapa, anger is an unjustified response to being wronged because it fails to acknowledge core truths about the way the world is, particularly the facts of interdependent arising, impermanence and no-self (Tsongkhapa 2000, 160–6).[13] Like Seneca, Tsongkhapa also recognizes the destructive consequences of anger and uses them to motivate training the mind to uproot anger:

---

[10] The possible exception here is the Pyrrhonian school, or Pyrrhonist tradition, of skepticism.

[11] See Gisela Striker, "Ataraxia: Happiness as Tranquility," *The Monist* 73, no. 1 (1990): 97–111.

[12] See Daniel Cozort, ""Cutting the Roots of Virtue:" Tsongkhapa on the Results of Anger," *Journal of Buddhist Ethics* 2 (1195): 83–104.

[13] Tsongkhapa, and other Tibetan Buddhist philosophers, rely on the doctrine of the two truths – conventional and ultimate – in order to assert, for example, that there is no independently existing self while at the same time continue to speak meaningfully about the self, its cultivation, its ethical obligations, and its relationships with others. For more on the relationship between the two truths, see Cowherds (2011), Garfield (2010), Duckworth (2010), Spackman (2014).

The faults of anger visible in this lifetime are that you do not experience a peaceful and good mind; the joy and happiness that you had previously perish, and you cannot regain them; you cannot sleep well; and you weaken the stability wherein your mind stays calm. When you have great hatred, even those for whom you formerly cared forget your kindness and kill you; even friends and relatives will get annoyed and leave you; although you gather others with your generosity, they will not stay (157–8).

Tsongkhapa is not alone among Buddhist thinkers in advocating for the extirpation of negative emotionality based on their irrationality and destructive consequences for self and others. These are key features the analysis of emotional-ethical life of two other very influential Buddhist moral philosophers, the eighth-century Indian philosopher, Santideva, and the fifth-century scholar of the Pali canon, Buddhaghosa.[14]

The resilience that comes from detachment is also valued in Buddhist ethics, as we can see in Tsongkhapa's discussion of the importance of self-control when one is on the verge of being overwhelmed by negative emotionality.[15] Those who become angry or hateful and end up hurting others "have become like servants of their afflictions, because they are under the control of others, i.e., their afflictions" (161). When morally accomplished person is hurt by others out of anger or hatred they refrain from indulging in these negative feelings, thinking "They do this because the demons of the afflictions have eliminated their ability to control themselves" (161). Becoming free from destructive emotionality is understood, at least partially, in terms of self-control (Tibetan: *rang dbang*) and maintaining one's ability to make wise choices.

Given these similarities, some scholars have equated Buddhist detachment with some form of Stoic detachment.[16] In his discussion of the Buddha's statement that "Delusion alone ties one person to another," David Wong writes, "Note that the way in which the Buddhist poem urges detachment to family is quite similar to the Stoic argument that one should not attach to that which the external world can takeaway. Do not attach to anything or anyone that can be taken away at any moment" (Wong 2006, 208). But this explanation is far more Stoic than Buddhist. It is not the threat of loss and the frightening sense of vulnerability it inspires that is especially problematic in Buddhist ethics; it is rather the delusional assumptions that ground many interpersonal relationships including familial ones, such as a false sense of ownership of others and the projection of security and permanence in what is

---

[14] See Shantideva, *A Guide to the Bodhisattva's Way of Life*, trans. Alan Wallace (Ithaca, NY: Snow Lion, 1997); Buddhaghosa, *The Path of Purification*, trans. Bhikku Nanamoli (Colombo, Ceylon: R. Semage, 1956).

[15] This is a tricky point in Buddhist contexts, since there are obviously aspects of what we might call agency that are systematically challenged. See the discussion of moral agency in Jay Garfield, "What is it Like to be a Bodhisattva? Moral Phenomenology in Śāntideva's Bodhicaryāvatāra," *Smith Philosophy Department*, February 8, 2011, http://www.smith.edu/philosophy/docs/garfield_bodhisattva.pdf (accessed October 20, 2014) and Emily McRae, "Emotions and Choice: Lessons From Tsongkhapa," *Journal of Buddhist Ethics*, April 2012.

[16] See Joel Marks, "Dispassion as an Ethical Ideal," in *Emotions in Asian Thought*, ed. Joel Marks, Roger Ames and Robert Solomon, 139–159 (Albany, NY: SUNY Press, 1995); David Wong, "The Meaning of Detachment in Daoism, Buddhism, and Stoicism," *Dao: A Journal of Comparative Philosophy* V, no. 2 (2006): 207–219.

actually an ever-changing dynamic between ever-changing people. These assumptions are based in confusion, yet they provide the context for much of our interpersonal emotional life.

Many Stoics would no doubt agree that certain kinds of emotional attachments to others are problematic because such attachments are based in ignorance, or, at least, poor reasoning, and not only because they lead to an unacceptable vulnerability and suffering. To use Epictetus' example, we get angry when our lamp is stolen because we mistakenly take the lamp to have value for us, to contribute to our final end. When we realize that this is not true – that only virtue can truly matter to us, and that is under our control – we cease to be angry about the theft of the lamp. We have correctly characterized it as an "indifferent" (Discourses I.18). Once our faulty reasoning has been corrected, we cease to have such problematic attachments.

But in Buddhist ethics, part of the release from ignorance and the suffering ignorance causes is through deep, and sometimes intense, emotional engagement with others. It is for this reason that I do not think that Buddhist ethics – especially Tibetan Buddhist ethics – shares the Stoic priority on making oneself invulnerable to upset, distress, or disturbance.[17] Freedom from confusion and, we will see, boundless love and compassion, are the general priorities in Tibetan Buddhist ethics; invulnerability to suffering caused by ignorance, hatred and attachment is the welcome consequence of achieving these.

To understand Buddhist detachment only in terms of extirpation and resilience – as we have understood Stoic detachment – would risk ignoring a foundational aspect of Buddhist (especially Mahayana) ethics: the *bodhicitta* orientation and the related primacy of love and compassion. Jay Garfield defines *bodhicitta* as "a standing motivational state with conative and affective dimensions… [that] centrally involves an altruistic aspiration, grounded in compassion, to cultivate oneself as a moral agent for the benefit of all beings" (Garfield 2011, 2).[18] *Bodhicitta* includes both the aspiration to relieve the suffering of others (*aspirational bodhicitta*) and acting on that aspiration (*engaged bodhicitta*) by practicing the six *paramitas* (perfections) of generosity, ethical discipline, patience, joyful diligence, meditative concentration, and wisdom (Santideva). *Bodhicitta* is cultivated not only by engaging in virtuous action, but also through training the emotions, actively challenging confused systems of beliefs, and by developing one's skills of moral perception and receptivity.[19]

---

[17] See Epictetus, *Handbook* ch.1

[18] There are some similarities between *bodhicitta* – the commitment to benefitting all members of the moral community – and the Stoic ideal of the *cosmopolis*, which, at least on some interpretations, includes the idea that our moral obligations are to all members of the moral community and not just members of our community or nation-state. There are important differences between the two concepts, however, such as who counts as a member of the moral community (all sentient beings or all rational beings?) and what the role of love and compassion is in achieving these ideals.

[19] See Garfield (2011) and Emily McRae, "Buddhist Therapies of the Emotions and the Psychology of Moral Improvement," *History of Philosophy Quarterly* 32, no. 1 (April 2015).

The eradication of afflictive mental states (*nyon mongs, kleshas*), including negative emotionality, is understood in the context of cultivating *bodhicitta*. Even the sternest command to eradicate negative emotionality is often accompanied by an ardent appeal to cultivate positive emotionality, particularly love, compassion, and sympathetic joy. In fact, for Tibetan Buddhist thinkers, one of the main problems with negative emotionality is the way that it can obstruct, obscure, or prevent more positive emotionality. For this reason, many of the meditative techniques that specifically deal with working with, or even eradicating, the negative emotions can be found in discussions of cultivating positive emotionality.[20] The above quotations from Tsongkhapa, for example, are found in a section of text devoted to cultivating patience and compassion. Discussions of the evils of envy are often found in larger tributes to the virtues of sympathetic joy.[21] The idea is that, while earnestly cultivating sympathetic joy at the success of others, one may confront the obstacle of envy and will need meditative techniques for taking on such a formidable obstacle.

This focus on the earnest, dedicated, and sometimes intensely passionate, cultivation of positive emotionality marks a significant difference between Stoic and (at least Tibetan) Buddhist conceptions of virtuous emotional-ethical life. Although some Stoics do allow for the sage to experience *eupatheia*, as noted earlier, these "emotions," by definition, are not experienced intensely or passionately and do not threaten the sage's *ataraxia*. Note, too, that compassion and love are not even included on the list of *eupatheia*. Epictetus, for example, only gives a begrudging acceptance of compassion if it is one's only way to avoid becoming angry (Discourses I. 18). In Tibetan Buddhist ethics, however, intense, passionate experiences of certain emotions, especially love and compassion, are highly valued and many texts offer meditative practices specifically designed to elicit them. Patrul Rinpoche's text *The Words of My Perfect Teacher* (written in the nineteenth century) encourages the reader to "...meditate with such unbearable compassion that your eyes fill with tears" (202). By vividly imagining the suffering of other sentient beings, one "cannot but feel intense and unbearable compassion" (204–205).[22] Consider the following meditation designed to elicit compassion for animals (particularly animals that might be under one's care):

> Imagine yourself as an old yak, your back weighed down with a load far too heavy, a rope pulling you by the nostrils, your flanks whipped, your ribs bruised by the stirrups. In front, behind and on both sides, you feel only burning pain. Without a second's rest, you go up long slopes, down steep descents, you cross wide rivers and broad pains. With no chance to swallow even a mouthful of food, you are driven on against your will from the early dawn until late in the evening when the last glimmers of the setting sun have disappeared. Reflect

---

[20] This is very common in Buddhist ethical texts. For one example, see the discussion of love and resentment in Buddhaghosa, *The Path of Purification*, trans. Bhikku Nanamoli (Colombo, Ceylon: R. Semage, 1956).

[21] See Rinpoche Patrul, *The Words of My Perfect Teacher*, trans. Padmakara Translation Group (San Francisco, CA: Harper Collins, 1994), p. 213.

[22] See Emily McRae, "A Passionate Buddhist Life," *Journal of Religious Ethics* 40, no. 1 (March 2012): 99–121.

on how difficult and exhausting it would be, what pain, hunger and thirst you would experience, and then take that suffering on yourself. You cannot but feel intense and unbearable compassion (204–205).

The compassion that Patrul Rinpoche is recommending here is visceral – "intense and unbearable" – rather than abstract, "vague or intellectual" (203). It is not, to borrow Hume's phrase, a "calm" passion. This passage is included in a section of the text devoted to methods to help one arouse *bodhicitta*. To effectively integrate *bodhicitta*, Patrul Rinpoche argues, one must be capable of strong and unbearable emotional investments.

Given this core commitment to the *bodhisattva* ideal and the conviction that compassion is the means for and expression of such an ideal, Buddhist detachment cannot be only the extirpation of strong emotional ties, nor can it be only the resilience to demanding situations – particularly interpersonal relationships – that might otherwise threaten one's agency. Such understandings of detachment either eliminate or reduce the overall scope and intensity of one's emotional engagement with others and seriously challenge the moral value of interpersonal relationships. This implication is unacceptable in a *bodhicitta* ethic. In Buddhist ethics, the question is not *how much* emotional engagement is acceptable but rather *what kinds* of emotional engagement should we cultivate (and intensify), and which should we give up? Given that there are emotional engagements that we should not only cultivate but also intensify, any sense of detachment in the *bodhicitta* context must accommodate this emotionally intense engagement with others. Because compassion and love are directed at specific others and not held only in some abstract sense (e.g. "love of humanity"), an acceptable understanding of detachment in the Tibetan Buddhist context must allow for certain kinds of deep, emotionally charged relationships.[23]

3.5 Equanimity and Detachment

Perhaps the closest concept of detachment in Tibetan Buddhist ethics to either *ataraxia* or *apatheia* is equanimity (*btang snyoms*). In general, equanimity in Buddhist ethics is understood as one of four main moral affective states, the other three of which are love (*byampa*), compassion (*snying rje*) and sympathetic joy (*dga' ba*). These four moral affective states are common to all Buddhist (and some non-Buddhist) traditions and are sometimes referred as the Four Brahmaviharas (the "abodes of Brahma") or, in Mahayana Buddhist traditions including the Tibetan tradition, the Four Immeasurable Qualities (*tshad med bzhi*). They are called

---

[23] See Patrul Rinpoche (202–203) and Kamalasila's discussion of equanimity in *Stages of Meditation* (Ithaca, NY: Snow Lion Press, 2001). Note that at a certain point in one's meditation practice, one cultivates "objectless compassion" in which one's compassion has no object because one is no longer bound by subject/object duality. This is different than taking an abstract object, such as "humanity," as an object.

immeasurable because, with practice, one can cultivate to encompass increasingly more members of the moral community. Like the other immeasurable qualities, equanimity is itself an affective state, which is marked by feelings of tranquility and calmness, rather than the absence of affective states. In this way, equanimity is similar to *ataraxia*: it is a freedom from (certain) disturbances and its expression is tranquility..[24]

In *The Words of My Perfect Teacher*, Patrul Rinpoche gives a standard (for the Tibetan philosophical tradition) definition of equanimity: "Equanimity (*btang snyoms*) means giving up (*btang*) our hatred for enemies and infatuation with friends, and having an even-minded (*snyoms*) attitude towards all beings, free of attachment to those close to us and aversion for those who are distant" (196). Even from this short definition we can see the dual focus of equanimity on (i) the mental states (desires, motivations, feelings, etc.) of the one who feels it ("giving up hatred and infatuation") and (ii) the ways it informs our relationships with others (our "friends" and "enemies").

Unlike the other affective attitudes (immeasurable qualities) with which it is always grouped – love, compassion and sympathetic joy – equanimity does not take another directly as its object, but rather the proper object is the craving and aversion one feels about another. In his commentary on Patrul Rinpoche's text, the early twentieth-century Tibetan scholar Khenpo Ngawang Pelzang notes that "...the object on which we focus [in equanimity practice] is both the attachment and aversion in our own mind"(137). Although a certain person or group of people may trigger the reactions of craving and aversion, equanimity practices focus on the reactions themselves, as they occur in one's own mind.[25]

This is important because it prevents one from developing an attitude of indifference towards others, a danger that Patrul Rinpoche is keen to warn us against. Again, *The Words of My Perfect Teacher*: "[I]t is no substitute for boundless equanimity just to think of everybody, friends and enemies, as the same, without any particular feeling of compassion, hatred or whatever. That is mindless [or ignorant] equanimity (Tibetan: *gti mug btang snyoms pa*) and brings neither benefit or harm" (198). We often think that detachment from certain kinds of affective experiences just means (or, at least, implies) detachment from interpersonal relationships. If one is not craving a loved one's attention or is not averse to her absence, then, we may reason, one is not just detached from one's craving and aversion, but also detached from the person who no longer elicits them. Patrul Rinpoche is challenging this assumption. We can detach from (that is, reduce and eventually eliminate) craving and aversion towards a particular person *without*

---

[24] See Maria Heim, "Buddhism on the Emotions," in *Oxford Handbook of Religion and Emotion*, 190–210? (New York: Oxford University Press, 2008) and Emily McRae, "Equanimity and Intimacy: A Buddhist-feminist Approach to the Elimination of Bias," *Sophia* 52, no. 3 (2013): 447–462.

[25] Khenpo Ngawang Pelzang also adds "and the attachment and aversion in others' minds"but this does not seem to actually factor into the discussion that follows. See Khenpo Ngawang Pelzang, *A Guide to the Words of My Teacher*, trans. Padmakara Translation Group (Boston: Shambala, 2004), p.132.

emotionally detaching from the person herself. Detaching from the relationship or from the other person is "mindless," emotionally lazy, indifferent. The type of equanimity lauded in Patrul Rinpoche's texts, and in Tibetan Buddhist ethical texts more generally, is boundless – and not mindless – equanimity.

Equanimity practices are designed to tackle craving and aversion without doing damage to our relationships with those we love. In fact, by reducing craving and aversion, the aim of equanimity practices is to allow one to engage with others in better ways, namely though love, compassion and joy (the other immeasurable qualities). Patrul Rinpoche compares this kind of equanimity to a great sage giving a banquet who "invite[s] everyone, high or low, powerful or weak, good or bad, exceptional or ordinary, without making any distinction whatsoever." Our attitude towards others, likewise, "should be a vast feeling of compassion, encompassing them all equally" (198). It is equanimity that allows one's compassion to be vast.

3.6   Detachment As Enabling Emotional Engagement: Loving Through Equanimity

Tibetan conceptions of equanimity (especially Patrul Rinpoche's) suggest another model for understanding detachment in the context of personal relationships: detachment as *enabling* virtuous emotional engagement with others. On this model, detachment is not aimed at extirpating emotions that destroy peace of mind or protecting one's agency (although these may be consequences); it is about skillfully removing obstacles to the virtuous emotional engagement with other members of the moral community. Feelings of craving and aversion present serious challenges to emotionally engaging with others in virtuous ways. I will briefly consider two main challenges: the challenge of partiality and the afflictive emotionality of relating to others as "enemies," and the challenge of intimacy and the afflictive emotionality that arises in the context of loving relationships.

In Patrul Rinpoche's discussion of equanimity, he is particularly concerned with using equanimity to counter unjustified partialities and biases. He even changes the traditional order of presentation of the four immeasurable qualities – usually presented as love, compassion, sympathetic joy and equanimity – and suggests beginning one's practice with equanimity precisely to deal with problems of partiality. If we do not start with equanimity, he warns, "whatever love, compassion and sympathetic joy we generate will tend to be one-sided and not completely pure" (195). The typical prejudices that we have – "infatuation with friends and hatred for enemies" – are specifically targeted here, and are included in the very definition of equanimity.

Such prejudices create the conditions for morally problematic bias, stereotyping, and the inability to empathize, which in turn can lead to injustice, discord, and violence. As such, they present a major obstacle to the foundational Buddhist value of extending one's love and compassion to every member of the moral community.

Reducing, and eventually giving up, feelings of aversion and craving allow one to connect with members of the moral community – especially those who one perceives as enemies or obstacles to one's happiness – in more virtuous ways.[26]

There is a strong tendency, both philosophically and psychologically, to dichotomize attachment, love, cherishing, emotional investment, and care, on the one hand, and detachment, distance, coldness, and indifference, on the other. The Tibetan Buddhist ideal of loving through equanimity challenges these associations, not just by arguing the moral harms of partiality with regard to strangers and "enemies," but also by uncovering the harms of attachment for those that we love. Put simply, attachment can impede our ability to love our "loved ones."

One way that attachment inhibits love is by maintaining and reinforcing negative emotionality that makes loving actions difficult to perform. Epictetus' case of the anxious father is a vivid example. On a Buddhist view, the anxiety would be understood as arising from attachment that, unlike love, is not grounded in a profound investment in another's wellbeing, but rather in one's own desires and expectations. In addition to debilitating anxiety, attachments to loved ones can create other negative emotional habits such as jealousy or possessiveness, "smothering" or trying to control the loved one, and excessive anger and disappointment with the loved one's failures.

Another way that attachment can hinder loving well is by becoming attached to narratives about our loved ones – and ourselves in relation to our loved ones – that are morally problematic, limiting or just outdated. One might, for example, be attached to the narrative of oneself as the provider for one's child. But, eventually, this narrative will become outdated and, if one continues to insist on it, may result in one's child feeling excessively sheltered and smothered. It may also prevent the possibility of allowing the child to provide for the parent, which is not only bad for the parent but bad for the child, since she is discouraged from expressing her concern and practicing her skills of taking care of others.

The above is an example of becoming attached to a narrative about oneself and one's loved ones that is outdated. But sometimes we can become attached to narratives that limit oneself and others in morally problematic ways, not because they are outdated but because they are incomplete or overly narrow. For example, one may become attached to the narrative, perhaps even based in evidence, that constructs the loved one as selfish, lazy, or shallow. But this narrative can make moral change and improvement difficult for the loved one, especially if held rigidly. If your family members or friends see you as selfish, lazy or shallow, it may be difficult to construct a new, morally improved identity, since identities are largely socially constructed; we rely on the feedback of loved ones to construct our self-narratives, and to change them. Even less negative narratives about a loved one, for example that she is carefree, fun-loving, and free-spirited, if held too tightly, can prevent her from expressing or developing other, morally significant, aspects of her

---

[26] For more on the role of equanimity in cultivating impartiality, see McRae (2013).

character, such as moral seriousness, responsibility and discipline, at least in the context of the relationship. In these cases, attachments to narratives about our loved ones and ourselves in relation to our loved ones actually inhibit our ability to love them well.

3.7 Conclusion

To conclude, I will briefly summarize what I take to be the main benefits of thinking about the detachment as enabling virtuous emotional engagement. First, like the extirpation model, this model of detachment recognizes the dangers of strong negative emotionality, both in one's interactions with enemies and with loved ones. But it maintains a robust role for the presence and even cultivation of strong positive emotionality. Because the Buddhist model of detachment does not rest on the assumption – as the Stoic models do – that emotions are essentially irrational judgments, these Buddhist thinkers are not philosophically committed to the extirpation of all emotionality.[27] Rather, they are committed to uprooting emotionality (and beliefs, desires, attitudes, etc.) that promotes suffering, is based in confusion, and is "afflictive," that is, experienced as being outside of one's control. But, on a Buddhist view, not all emotionality is suffering-promoting, confused, or afflictive. The emotionality of love, compassion, and sympathetic joy, promote the alleviation of suffering (both for self and others), are trainable (and so are not outside one's control), and help increase one's moral knowledge and insight. Such emotions are not confused because they recognize the moral urgency of suffering and the interdependent nature of members of the moral community.

Second, the Buddhist model of detachment attempts to preserve moral agency, and so shares that aim with the Stoic philosophers analyzed here. But part of cultivating moral agency on the Buddhist view is developing the capacity to feel vast compassion and love, and not just mildly, but strongly and passionately. Feeling love and compassion enable one to respond to what on Buddhist views is the core moral challenge: the profound suffering of self and others. And detachment, on this view, enables one to feel – and cultivate – love and compassion with less bias and more discernment.

---

[27] Strictly speaking, there may be no category of "emotion" in Buddhist philosophy of mind. See George Dreyfus, "Is Compassion an Emotion," in *Visions of Compassion*, ed. Richard Davidson and Anne Harrington (New York: Oxford University Press, 1994); Maria Heim, "Buddhism on the Emotions," in *Oxford Handbook of Religion and Emotion*, (New York: Oxford University Press, 2008); Emily McRae, "Buddhist Therapies of the Emotions and the Psychology of Moral Improvement," *History of Philosophy Quarterly* 32, no. 1 (April 2015), forthcoming.

References

Aristotle. 2002. *Nicomachean Ethics*. Trans. Sarah Broadie and Christopher Rowe. Oxford: Oxford University Press.

Becker, Lawrence. 1998. *A New Stoicism*. Princeton: Princeton University Press.

Buddhaghosa. 1956. *The Path of Purification*. Trans. Bhikkhu Nanamoli. Colombo: R. Semage.

Cicero. 1971. *Tuscan Disputations*. Loeb Classical Library. Trans. J.E. King. Cambridge: Harvard University Press.

Cowherds. 2011. *Moonshadows: Conventional Truth in Buddhist Philosophy*. New York: Oxford University Press.

Cozort, Daniel. 1995. 'Cutting the Roots of Virtue': Tsongkhapa on the Results of Anger. *Journal of Buddhist Ethics* 2 (1995): 83–104.

Dreyfus, George. 1994. Is Compassion an Emotion. In *Visions of Compassion*, ed. Richard Davidson and Anne Harrington. New York: Oxford University Press.

Duckworth, Douglas. 2010. Two Models of the Two Truths: Ontological and Phenomenological Approaches. *Journal of Indian Philosophy* 38:5: 519–527.

Epictetus. 1983. *Handbook*. Trans. Nicholas White. Indianapolis: Hackett.

———. 1998. *Discourses*. Trans. Robert Dobbin. New York: Clarendon Press.

Garfield, Jay. 2010. Taking Conventional Truth Seriously: Authority Regarding Deceptive Reality. *Philosophy East and West* 60 (3): 341–354.

———. 2011. What is it Like to be a Bodhisattva? Moral Phenomenology in Śāntideva's Bodhicaryāvatāra. *Smith Philosophy Department*. 2011-8-February. http://www.smith.edu/philosophy/docs/garfield_bodhisattva.pdf. Accessed 20 Oct 2014.

Graver, Margaret. 2007. *Stoicism and Emotion*. Chicago: University of Chicago Press.

Heim, Maria. 2008. Buddhism on the Emotions. In *Oxford Handbook of Religion and Emotion*, 190–210. New York: Oxford University Press.

Kamalasila. 2001. *Stages of Meditation*. Ithaca: Snow Lion Press.

Marks, Joel. 1995. Dispassion as an Ethical Ideal. In *Emotions in Asian Thought*, ed. Joel Marks, Roger Ames, and Robert Solomon, 139–159. Albany: SUNY Press.

McRae, Emily. 2012a. A Passionate Buddhist Life. *Journal of Religious Ethics* 40 (1): 99–121.

———. 2012b. Emotions and Choice: Lessons From Tsongkhapa. *Journal of Buddhist Ethics*, April 2012.

———. 2013. Equanimity and Intimacy: A Buddhist-feminist Approach to the Elimination of Bias. *Sophia* 52 (3): 447–462.

———. 2015. Buddhist Therapies of the Emotions and the Psychology of Moral Improvement. *History of Philosophy Quarterly* 32: 1.

Nussbaum, Martha. 1994. *Therapy of Desire: Theory and Practice in Hellenistic Ethics*. Princeton: Princeton University Press.

———. 2001. *Upheavals of Thought*. New York: Cambridge University Press.

Patrul, Rinpoche. 1994. *The Words of My Perfect Teacher*. Trans. Padmakara Translation Group. San Francisco: Harper Collins.

Pelzang, Khenpo Ngawang. 2004. *A Guide to the Words of My Teacher*. Trans. Padmakara Translation Group. Boston: Shambala.

Seneca. 2010a. On Anger. In *Anger, Mercy, Revenge*, ed. Martha Nussbaum. Trans. Robert Kastor, 1–97. Chicago: University of Chicago Press.

———. 2010b. On Clemency. In *Anger, Mercy, Revenge*, ed. Martha Nussbaum. Chicago: Chicago University Press.

———. 1917–1925. Lucius Annaeus. *Moral Epistles*. The Loeb Classical Library, 3 vols. Cambridge: Harvard University Press.

Shantideva. 1997. *A Guide to the Bodhisattva's Way of Life*. Trans. Alan Wallace. Ithaca: Snow Lion.

Sorabji, Richard. 2000. *Emotions and Peace of Mind*. New York: Oxford University Press.

————. 2006. *Self: Ancient and Modern Insights about Individuality, Life and Death*. Chicago: University of Chicago Press.

Spackman, John. 2014. Between Nihilism and Anti-Essentialism: A Conceptualist Interpretation of Nagarjuna. *Philosophy East and West* 64 (1): 151–173.

Striker, Gisela. 1990. Ataraxia: Happiness as Tranquility. *The Monist* 73 (1): 97–111.

Tsongkhapa. 2000. *The Great Treatise of the Stages of the Path to Enlightenment*. Ithaca: Snow Lion.

Wong, David. 2006. The Meaning of Detachment in Daoism, Buddhism, and Stoicism. *Dao: A Journal of Comparative Philosophy V* 2: 207–219.

Chapter 4
Skepticism and Religious Practice in Sextus and Nāgārjuna

Ethan Mills

Abbreviations

M   *Pros Mathēmatikous* (*Against the Professors*) (Sextus 2012)
MMK   *Mūlamadhyamakakārikā.* (*Root Verses on the Middle Way*) (Nāgārjuna 1997)
PH   *Pyrrhōneioi Hypotypōseis.* (*Outlines of Pyrrhonism*) (Sextus 2000)
VV   *Vighrahavyāvartanī.* (*Overturning the Objections*) (Nāgārjuna 1994)

In the contemporary world, skepticism and religious practice are usually thought of as incompatible, if not entirely antithetical. The reason for this is obvious if we assume that religious practice requires *beliefs* concerning religious matters and that skepticism often consists of *doubts* concerning such beliefs. My aim here is to show how two ancient philosophers give reasons to question the assumption that skepticism is incompatible with religious practice; in doing so these skeptics reveal a unique category of religiosity without belief that merits further attention from philosophers of religion. The Pyrrhonian skeptic, Sextus Empiricus (c. 200 CE), says that piety toward the gods is compatible with the Pyrrhonian way of life. The founder of Madhyamaka Buddhist philosophy, Nāgārjuna (c. 150–200 CE), embodies a skeptical practice as the pursuit of the goal of non-attachment in intellectual matters. While Sextus shows that skepticism and religious practice could be *compatible*, Nāgārjuna suggests that skepticism might *constitute* a type of religious practice.

After some preliminary remarks on the relevance of this chapter to ethics and *anatta* (non-self), I will give an overview of the issue of skepticism and religious

The author would like to thank Gordon Davis and Stephen Harris for reading earlier drafts of this chapter. The author also benefitted from comments by audiences who heard versions of this chapter at the University of Tennessee at Chattanooga (2014), the Chattanooga Institute for Noetic Sciences (2015), and the Canadian Philosophical Association Annual Congress (2013).

E. Mills (✉)
University of Tennessee at Chattanooga, Chattanooga, TN, USA
e-mail: ethan-mills@utc.edu

© Springer International Publishing AG, part of Springer Nature 2018   91
G. F. Davis (ed.), *Ethics without Self, Dharma without Atman*, Sophia Studies
in Cross-cultural Philosophy of Traditions and Cultures 24,
https://doi.org/10.1007/978-3-319-67407-0_4

practice in the texts of Sextus and Nāgārjuna. Then I will show how Sextus and Nāgārjuna represent a kind of religiosity without belief that is in contrast both to conventional views about the relation between belief and religious practice as well as some contemporary views in philosophy of religion concerning belief and faith. After considering some objections to my claim that Sextus and Nāgārjuna represent a distinct category of religiosity, I will end with some reflections on what the study of Sextus and Nāgārjuna could add to contemporary philosophy of religion.

Several scholars have argued in favor of historical hypotheses there were philosophical interactions between Greek and Indian traditions in ancient times and that these interactions explain the similarities between Pyrrhonian skepticism and some forms of Buddhism.[1] Such studies often begin with the intriguing report of Diogenes Laertius that Pyrrho traveled in Alexander's entourage to India where he met with "gymnosophists."[2] While these historical hypotheses are extremely interesting, nothing I discuss in the present chapter rests on resolving these historical issues. The skeptical religiosity of Sextus and Nāgārjuna might be explained by historical interaction, sheer coincidence, or a kind of "convergent evolution" in which, just as eyesight has evolved along different branches of the phylogenetic tree, two traditions might develop similar ideas from unconnected sources in response to similar philosophical pressures. This is not something I can resolve here. Thus, I shall – appropriately enough – suspend judgment about the question of whether historical interaction between ancient Pyrrhonian and Buddhist philosophers provides the best explanation for similarities between Sextus and Nāgārjuna.

4.1   Skepticism, Religious Practice, Ethics, and *Anatta*

Here I will not be discussing ethics in the sense of other-regarding principles for interaction between moral agents or for moral agents' treatment of non-moral agents, but rather in the sense of how individuals might live their lives, which includes one's attitudes toward belief and religious practice. My concern here is less with ethics in the modern sense of inquiry into rules for the treatment of others and more with the ancient Greek sense of *ethos* as a concern for one's character and one's way of life. Of course, there may be some overlap between these two senses,

---

[1] Among scholars proffering hypotheses of historical interaction, the main disagreement is whether the direction of influence was primarily from India to Greece or *vice versa*. Flintoff (1980) argues that Pyrrho was directly influenced by Buddhist philosophy, making the direction of influence from India to Greece. McEvilley (2002, Ch. 18) argues in favor of a complex interaction in which India influenced Greece several centuries before Pyrrho's lifetime; according to McEvilley, when Pyrrho brought his ideas to India, he then influenced the subsequent development of Buddhism, particularly Madhyamaka. Kuzminski (2008, Ch. 2) agrees with Flintoff on the direction of influence and opposes McEvilley's view. Beckwith (2015) argues that the primary influence was from India (or central Asia) to Greece such that Pyrrho's system is based on an early, pre-canonical, form of Buddhism.

[2] See Diogenes Laertius 9.61 (in Inwood and Gerson 1997, 285).

for instance in Aristotle's idea that moral virtues such as justice and friendship are necessary for the attainment of the highest intellectual virtues or in the Buddhist arguments that reflecting on non-self will make one more compassionate toward others (see the chapters on Śāntideva in this volume). However, the two senses need not be related; for instance, Sextus describes Pyrrhonian skepticism as a way of life (*agōgē*) rather than as a philosophical system that might include the articulation and defense of ethical principles (PH 1.8).

Contemporary examples of similar distinctions have been proposed by Julia Annas, Charles Taylor, and Christine Korsgaard. According to Annas, Plato's concept of justice in the *Republic* is an agent-centered notion of virtue rather than an act-centered notion; common justice is about what we owe to others while Platonic justice concerns harmony within one's soul (Annas 1995, 190). My concern here is much more in line with this notion of agent-centered virtue; while followers of Sextus or Nāgārjuna may well act in certain ways toward others, the focus of each philosopher is much more on an individual's effort to live non-dogmatically or to become unattached to views.[3]

Charles Taylor discusses one major issue of personal identity in terms of "our orientation in relation to the good" (Taylor 1989, 42). Taylor's thought is quite complex, but the point I'm using here is that ethics could be discussed purely in terms of how one situates oneself toward some good.[4] The Platonic Philosopher, for instance, takes this seriously with regard to the Form of the Good. There is a similar idea at work when Sextus describes the intellectual life of Pyrrhonian skeptics who strive for the good of freedom from disturbance (*ataraxia*) or when Nāgārjuna utilizes arguments in favor of emptiness to lead to the cessation of conceptual proliferation (*prapañcopaśama*), which in turn leads to the Buddhist good of *nirvāṇa*.

Korsgaard discusses "the principle of prudence, which is sometimes identified with self-interest. This principle concerns the ways in which we harmonize the pursuit of our various ends" (Korsgaard 1997, 216).[5] The principle of prudence comes into play after one has decided on one's ends; for instance, Sextus and Nāgārjuna (at least in the texts I will discuss here) begin after one has decided to commit oneself to a Pyrrhonian or Buddhist practice, or in Taylor's terms, after one has situated one's life in relation to some good. If you want to be a Pyrrhonian or a Buddhist, then Sextus and Nāgārjuna have something for you. If you're still deciding whether you want to pursue Pyrrhonism or Buddhism, then you will find little in the way of normative arguments in favor of engaging in these practices.[6]

---

[3] According to Annas, "For us, this type of agent-centered morality is most familiar in religious versions, notions such as that to the pure in heart all things are permitted, or that if you love God you may do as you like" (Annas 1995, 193). Likewise, many Buddhists claim that an enlightened person will automatically act in the morally correct manner.

[4] I am drawing this account from Taylor 1989, Chs. 2 and 3.

[5] Another helpful distinction is Thomas Nagel's distinction between the principle of prudence and the principle of altruism (Nagel 1970, 19).

[6] One interpretive debate about Sextus is whether he is offering a normative argument in favor of Pyrrhonism or a descriptive account of what a Pyrrhonian does (Thorsrud 2009, Ch. 7). I favor the descriptive interpretation, since this gives Sextus a better response to the objection that skepticism

Even if there is a normative account stated or implied, the vast majority of Sextus's work seems to consist of descriptions of Pyrrhonian argumentative practices. Likewise, while it may initially appear that Nāgārjuna is giving normative arguments in favor of Buddhist doctrines such as emptiness, which in turn may be an implicit endorsement of Mahāyāna Buddhist practices, at the end of the *Mūlamadhymakakārikā* he says that the purpose of Buddhism is "the abandoning of all views" (MMK 27.30). Sextus and Nāgārjuna tell us *how* to be a Pyrrhonian or a Buddhist, not *why* to be a Pyrrhonian or a Buddhist.[7] In any case, neither Sextus nor Nāgārjuna are primarily concerned with ethics in the sense of arguing for normative conclusions about one's other-regarding behavior. Their concern is to help readers to undergo the internal intellectual transformation from being a person who is prone to dogmatism or attachment to views to being a person who experiences freedom from mental disturbance (*ataraxia*) or the cessation of conceptual proliferation (*prapañcopaśama*).

From a Buddhist perspective, the distinction between normative, other-regarding ethics and agent-centered virtue or the principle of prudence must be qualified in light of the other major topic of this volume: *anatta* (non-self). Nāgārjuna cannot, in the final analysis, be concerned with the harmony of one's soul (like Plato) or with self-interest. Śāntideva and other Buddhists argue that there is no ultimate distinction between self and other because there is no self that stands apart from the other, although there are differing streams (*santāna*) of impersonal aggregates (*skandhas*). The distinction between me and you may be useful as a conventional truth, but it is most often one of the principal sources of suffering. As I see it, Nāgārjuna's main goal is to lessen one's attachments to beliefs (even Buddhist beliefs), since grasping at and identifying with *my* views or *my* philosophical theories serves to reify my self in opposition to others.[8]

---

is inconsistent, which has been one of the most pervasive objections to Academic and Pyrrhonian skepticism. One version of the objection says that it is inconsistent to use arguments to conclude that arguments are not powerful enough to offer rational support for their conclusions. On the descriptive interpretation, Sextus avoids this problem because he is simply not interested in giving an argument to support the conclusion that one ought to be a Pyrrhonian; he is merely describing what Pyrrhonian skeptics do, which means the objection rests on a category mistake.

[7] Still, one might wonder if Sextus and Nāgārjuna are giving any normative account of the adaptation of means and ends. In other words, one might wonder if they have a sense of the normativity of instrumental reason in the sense Korsgaard (1997) describes. My inclination is to say that they do not have any such account. For Sextus, such an account would contradict his careful denial that Pyrrhonian skeptics have beliefs (at least about philosophical matters – see PH 1.7). Nāgārjuna may well agree with Korsgaard when she claims, "There is no position from which you can reject the government of instrumental reason: if you reject it, there is no you" (Korsgaard 1997, 254; a similar constitutive note is struck in Taylor 1989, 27). The difference, of course, is that as a Buddhist, Nāgārjuna would take connection between this rejection of normativity and a loss of a sense of self to be a good thing!

[8] Support for this reading comes from MMK 18, especially verses five and nine. There Nāgārjuna makes connections between non-self, emptiness, imagination (*vikalpa*) and the destruction of conceptual proliferation (*prapañca*), all of which lead to liberation (*mokṣa*).

There is an interesting similarity between Sextus and Nāgārjuna on this point. M. F. Burnyeat has argued that Pyrrhonism is psychologically impossible, since practicing Pyrrhonists must radically dissociate themselves from their own mental states (Burnyeat and Frede 1997, Ch. 2). Aside from the problem of attempting to judge what is possible for a thoroughly committed Pyrrhonist from our (presumably dogmatic) position,[9] I suspect this sort of dissociation and indifference is part of what gives rise to freedom from disturbance, since a great deal of the disturbance comes from the feeling that one must defend *one's own* views and attack those of others.

4.2 Sextus Empiricus

Sextus Empiricus is the author of the most complete sources available on Pyrrhonian skepticism, a school of Hellenistic philosophy that traces its roots to Pyrrho (c. 365–275 BCE).[10] I won't discuss the historical details of ways in which Sextus might differ from other Pyrrhonians; instead I'll take his texts as representative of at least one brand of Pyrrhonism. Sextus tells us that Pyrrhonian skepticism is a method of achieving tranquility (*ataraxia*) by means of suspension of judgment (*epochē*). Unlike modern skepticism, which is a theoretical position about whether we can or do have knowledge in some or all domains, Pyrrhonism is a kind of intellectual therapy for those whose mental tranquility is disrupted by philosophical speculation. Pyrrhonian skeptics react to philosophical disputes by suspending judgment without believing either that knowledge is or is not possible, but representatives of the other major branch of Hellenistic skepticism, Academic skeptics, are often thought to make the claim that knowledge is impossible.[11] Sextus says that Academic skeptics "have asserted that things cannot be apprehended" while Pyrrhonian skeptics "are still investigating" (PH 1.3); elsewhere he says, "we [Pyrrhonian skeptics] say that appearances are equal in convincingness and lack of convincingness (so far as the argument goes), while they [Academic skeptics] say that some are plausible and others implausible" (PH 1.227).

I'll stress two main points about Sextus. First, Sextus's target is belief rather than knowledge. Second, Sextus's Pyrrhonism is entirely practical, having no theoretical commitments whatsoever. Given these points, one might expect that the prospects for a Pyrrhonian religious practice are slim, if not entirely ruled out; however, this

---

[9] For more on this point, see Hankinson 1995, 286.

[10] For a collection of fragments and excerpts on Pyrrhonism and Academic skepticism, see Inwood and Gerson 1997.

[11] It should be noted that at least one Academic, Carneades, might have had a more nuanced approach in simply claiming that he had a persuasive impression that knowledge is impossible rather than knowing that knowledge is impossible (Thorsrud 2009, Ch. 4). See also Cicero's discussion of Carneades in *Academica*, 2.99–111 (Cicero 2006, 58–65).

is not what Sextus says. Sextus begins his discussion of the gods in the *Outlines of Pyrrhonism* (PH) by pointing out that Pyrrhonians do engage in religious practice.

> Since the majority have asserted that god is a most active cause, let us first consider god, remarking by way of preface that, following ordinary life without opinions, we say that there are gods and we are pious toward gods and say they are provident: it is against the rashness of the Dogmatists that we make the following points. (PH 3.2)

The parallel section of *Against the Professors* gives more details.

> Since not everything that is conceived also shares in reality, but something can be conceived but not be real, like a Hippocentaur or Scylla, it will be necessary after our investigation of the conception of the gods to inquire also into their reality. For perhaps the sceptic will be found to be safer than those who do philosophy in another way; in line with his ancestral customs and laws, he says that there are gods and does everything that tends to worship of and reverence towards them, but as far as philosophical investigation is concerned, he makes no rash moves. (M 9.49)

But how can Pyrrhonian skeptics possibly engage in pious worship and reverence toward the gods if they have no *beliefs* about the existence or nature of the gods? Wouldn't such a practice be a hollow sham? Wouldn't it be, as Harald Thorsrud puts it, an "unintentional parody of the genuine article" (Thorsrud 2009, 189)? Perhaps we shouldn't take Sextus seriously when he claims that Pyrrhonians can engage in genuine religious practice.

There are a few possible responses to the claim that Pyrrhonians would be insufficiently religious. First, one might suggest, like Thorsrud, that for Pyrrhonian skeptics "piety is … reduced to certain kinds of conventional behaviour along with the relevant dispositions. Belief or lack of belief is no longer essential" (Thorsrud 2009, 190). Second, one might suggest, as does Julia Annas, that Pyrrhonian religious practice makes more sense in the context of ancient pagan religions. Annas distinguishes between "religious beliefs" and "theological beliefs": religious beliefs are "culturally specific beliefs about Athena, Mithras, Isis, about animal sacrifice, vows, dedication, temples, and so on" while theological beliefs are "beliefs about the gods, God, or the divine … where this is taken to be something universal and cross-cultural" (Annas 2011, 76). Annas suggests that Pyrrhonians might have culturally specific religious beliefs while avoiding cross-cultural theological beliefs (Annas 2011, 78, 82).[12] I would note that this interpretation seems to require what is called the "some belief" or "urbane" interpretation of Pyrrhonism, whereas Thorsrud's interpretation is more in line with the "no belief" or "rustic" interpretation.[13]

I think Thorsrud's interpretation is preferable, since – whatever the virtues of the some belief interpretation of Pyrrhonism might have elsewhere – in the passages quoted above Sextus never says that a skeptic will have *beliefs* (*doxa*) about the gods

---

[12] Annas asks, "What has he [i.e., a Pyrrhonian] lost that he originally had before becoming interested in theology? He cannot now commit himself to any universal, cross-cultural claim about the existence and nature of God. But this is not something he did in the first place" (Annas 2011, 82).

[13] Two good places to start on this interpretive debate are Burnyeat and Frede 1997 and Thorsrud 2009, Ch. 9. Also, "some belief" and "urbane" do not necessarily name precisely the same interpretation, but there's enough overlap for my purposes here.

(whether religious or theological). He simply reports that Pyrrhonians will *say* that there are gods and *perform* certain pious actions, both of which could be done without any beliefs about the gods.

4.3 Nāgārjuna

Nāgārjuna (c. 150–200 CE) is usually regarded as the founder of the Madhyamaka school of Buddhist philosophy. Here I'm not going to delve into the vast ocean of Nāgārjuna interpretation,[14] nor will I offer a detailed argument in favor my own version of a skeptical interpretation.

On my interpretation, Nāgārjuna – especially in the *Mūlamadhyamakakārikā* and *Vigrahavyavartanī* – has two general phases in his philosophical procedure, corresponding to his two main kinds of statements: those statements that support the philosophical position of emptiness and those statements that seem to deny that he has any position at all. The first phase is that of offering arguments for emptiness and against essence *(svabhāva)*; this first phase would look like a form of global anti-realism if Nāgārjuna stopped with these statements, but he goes on. The second phase is that of demonstrating that this idea of emptiness has the peculiar property of undermining not only all other philosophical views, but even itself, thus leaving a thorough Mādhyamika without any views, theses, or positions whatsoever. As I mentioned earlier, doing so has the effect of eliminating attachment to one's own views and thus to the false idea of the self. This second phase is what mystical interpreters claim is a step to a further ineffable realization, but on my interpretation it represents nothing but the purging of philosophical impulses, the end of philosophy itself; in other words, Nāgārjuna is a radical skeptic, who, much like his Pyrrhonian counterparts, ultimately takes no philosophical positions of his own.

I don't mean that Nāgārjuna's texts are a steady march from phase one into phase two. His texts freely move between these phases, injecting emptiness wherever needed. Still, a general tendency to move toward the second phase can be detected in the *Mūlamadhyamakakārikā* (hereafter, MMK) from the fact that the verses most amenable to phase two are found in the dedication *(mangalam)*, at the end of several chapters, and especially at the end of the text.[15] The MMK ends by saying, "I bow to him, Gautama, who, by means of compassion, taught the true Dharma for the purpose of abandoning all views" (MMK 27.30).[16] Of course, there is a long-standing debate about whether "all views" *(sarvadṛṣṭi)* here means all views what-

---

[14] Two currently popular varieties of interpretations of Nāgārjuna are anti-realist interpretations (e.g., Siderits 2000 and Westerhoff 2009) and mystical interpretations (e.g., Murti 1955 and Taber 1998).

[15] The end of chapter verses are 5.8, 13.8, 25.24, and 27.30. Other verses suggestive of phase two are 18.5, 21.17, and 24.7.

[16] *sarvadṛṣṭiprahānāya yaḥ saddharmam adeśyat/*
   anukampām upādāya taṃ namasyāmi gautamaṃ// MMK 27.30.

soever, or all *false* views, as is commonly interpreted by many Indian, Tibetan, and Western commentators.[17] I think we should take Nāgārjuna at his word.[18] While I can't solve the dispute here, I will say that one strength of my interpretation is that we can take Nāgārjuna at his word in both phases; we need not ignore or downplay the significance of either.

If my skeptical interpretation is correct, we have a puzzle about skepticism and religious practice. How can Nāgārjuna be a *Buddhist* if he is also a skeptic? Don't Buddhists need to *believe* certain propositions such as the Four Noble Truths? Isn't Right View one component of the Eightfold Path? Don't many Mahāyāna Buddhists claim that knowledge of emptiness is required for liberation? Thus, a major objection to my skeptical interpretation is that no Buddhist can be a skeptic of this sort since a Buddhist must aim for some kind of liberating knowledge.

Unlike Sextus, Nāgārjuna never explicitly discusses this issue. However, I think we could respond to this problem on Nāgārjuna's behalf by first noting that the two phases of Nāgārjuna's philosophical practice are representations of two tendencies that have been present in Buddhist philosophy from the very beginning. As Steven Collins points out, "One approach to the attainment of the 'emptiness' of *nibbāna*, naturally, was a direct assault on any form of conceptualization, any view whatsoever ... The other approach ... was to proceed through an analysis of what does have conceptual content, in order to classify it into known categories; the ability to classify any experience or concept into a known, non-valued impersonal category was held to be a technique for avoiding desire for the object thus classified" (Collins 1982, 113).[19] This second tendency is the more popular one in which the purpose of Buddhism is to decrease desire through insight into the true nature of reality. The other tendency is what Collins calls "Quietism," which is "an attitude which empha-

---

[17] Proponents of the "false views" translation note that *dṛṣṭi* often has a negative connotation of "a wrong view" (Monier-Williams 1994, 492). While it's possible that Nāgārjuna meant "wrong views," it is also possible he meant views in general. The same Sanskrit word is used for the element of the Eightfold Path known as "right view" (*samyag-dṛṣṭi*), which has a positive connotation. In any case, an appeal to the text cannot solve this debate. My point is that if we want to take "*dṛṣṭi*" as meaning all views, it is possible to do so in a way that makes sense of the text. In favor of my translation, though, I would point out that a major reason in favor of the "false views" translation – that the text cannot make sense otherwise – is simply not the case.

[18] In this I agree with Garfield in his agreement with Ngog and the Nying-ma school (Garfield 2002, 46–68). Patsab Nyimadrak and Khedrupjey's opponent in the *Great Digest* are others who take MMK 27.30 at face value.

[19] For another example of Early Buddhist quietism, see the following line from the *Sutta Nipāta*: "(only) when a man renounces all opinions, does he make no quarrel with the world" (Collins 1982, 130). Also, Richard Hayes has identified a kind of skepticism within the Buddhist tradition from the Nikāyas up until at least Dignāga; Hayes calls this "skeptical rationalism ... according to which there is no knowledge aside from that which meets the test of logical consistency, and moreover very few of our beliefs meet this test" (Hayes 1988, 41). Hayes also claims that Nāgārjuna exemplified this type of skepticism (Hayes 1988, 52–62).

sizes passivity in religious practice, and which seeks to attain as its final goal a state of beatific 'inner quiet'" (Collins 1982, 139).[20]

My skeptical interpretation shows Nāgārjuna's innovation in bringing these two tendencies together. Nāgārjuna transforms this uneasy dichotomy into a cohesive dialectical practice: he tries to show that the practice of analysis, when pursued all the way to the emptiness of emptiness, can be used as a means to the practice of making an assault on conceptualization itself. Thus, Nāgārjuna is, while a reformer and innovator, working quite entirely within Buddhist parameters by synchronizing two seemingly disparate strands of Buddhist philosophy. A skeptical interpretation of Nāgārjuna shows that the radical program of purging oneself of philosophical views is a path to the goal of non-attachment, perhaps just the remedy needed for intellectuals prone to grasping at theories, which in turn reinforces the idea of the self.

A skeptical Mādhyamika might even participate in Buddhist religious rituals without any beliefs about merit, karma, and so forth. Nāgārjuna's religiosity without belief may not work for religions such as many forms of contemporary Christianity that are tied explicitly to acceptance of a creed, but it could work for forms of Buddhism amenable to skeptical or quietist expressions. Unlike fideist skeptics such as Montaigne,[21] Nāgārjuna is not "… annihilating his intellect to make room for faith" (Montaigne 1987, 74), but rather he engages in philosophical destruction to bring about mental quietude, which is the absence of any faith or belief.

Thus, for both Sextus and Nāgārjuna, skepticism and religious practice are entirely compatible. And Nāgārjuna takes this compatibility one step further to show how his skeptical practice could even *constitute* a kind of religious practice.

4.4 Religiosity Without Belief

In the remainder of this chapter I'd like to think about ways in which these ancient skeptics might contribute to discussions in contemporary philosophy of religion concerning the relation between religious belief and religious practice. After a

---

[20] Similarly, Paul Fuller suggests that there are two main ways of understanding the role of views (*diṭṭhi*) in early Buddhism: the opposition understanding, in which right views are opposed to wrong views, and the no-view understanding, in which the goal is to avoid all views whatsoever (Fuller 2005, 1). Fuller's concern is more with modern interpretations that the early Buddhist tradition has a single attitude toward views rather than Collins's and my understanding that the tradition contains both attitudes. Also, Fuller argues against both the opposition and no-view understandings: "the opposition understanding is challenged because there is not an opposition between wrong-view and right-view as incorrect and correct truth claims but an opposition between craving and the cessation of craving. … the rejection of all views is not being advised, but the abandoning of craving and attachment to views … The early texts do not reject knowledge, but attachment to knowledge" (Fuller 2005, 8). Fuller argues in favor of what he calls the "transcendence of views," which is a "different order of seeing" in which right view "apprehends how things are *and* is a remedy for craving" (Fuller 2005, 157).

[21] Whether Montaigne is a fideist remains a matter of interpretive dispute, but I think it makes sense of the *Apology*. See Hartle 2005 and M. A. Screech's introduction in Montaigne 1987.

clarification of what it is that I'm claiming Sextus and Nāgārjuna are denying, I'll structure this section as an assessment of conceivable objections to my contentions that Sextus and Nāgārjuna give examples of practices that are both skeptical and genuinely religious and that such practices constitute a unique category of religiosity that philosophers of religion ought to acknowledge.

At this point it would help to clarify what I mean by religious belief. A recent definition given by J. L. Schellenberg gives a clear account of what it is that I'm claiming Sextus and Nāgārjuna lack. According to Schellenberg, some subject S's having a religious belief requires that "S is disposed to apprehend the state of affairs reported by a certain disposition *p*, when that state of affairs comes to mind, under the concept *reality*" (Schellenberg 2005, 81). Sextus explicitly brings up this issue when he says that we can discuss the gods without positing their reality, just as people discuss mythological creatures without taking them to be real. For Nāgārjuna, it is precisely taking one's views to represent reality that causes the kind of attachment his skeptical practice is meant to dissipate.

Perhaps the most obvious objection to my claim would be that the skepticism of Sextus and Nāgārjuna is not in fact compatible with religious practice. What they give us is at best a shadowy simulacrum of genuine religious practice. While defining religion and religious practice is extremely difficult, one might think that this kind of skepticism definitely crosses the line. A recent primer in philosophy of religion says that.

> religion is constituted by a set of beliefs, actions, and experiences, both personal and collective, organized around a concept of Ultimate Reality that inspires or requires devotion, worship, or a focused life orientation (Peterson et al. 2013, 7).

Obviously if belief and the other parts of this definition are jointly sufficient for calling something a religion, then a practice must include belief or somehow be related to one's holding a belief in order to be deemed religious. Hence, skeptical religiosity without belief is not a genuine form of religious practice.

The centrality of something like belief is also present in definitions of religion that don't make explicit mention of belief. According to Schellenberg,

> 'S is religious (or exhibits religion)' should be viewed as synonymous with the conjunction of the following propositions:
>
> S takes there to be a reality that is ultimate, in relation to which an ultimate good can be attained.
> S's ultimate commitment is to the cultivation of dispositions appropriate to this state of affairs. (Schellenberg 2005, 23)

Schellenberg doesn't think belief is required for religious practice; however, the phrases "S takes there to be a reality that is ultimate" and "S's ultimate commitment" already involve something much closer to belief than either Sextus or Nāgārjuna would endorse. For Sextus, such taking to be or ultimate commitment is too close to dogmatic belief and goes far beyond nondogmatically living in accordance with appearances. For Nāgārjuna, Schellenberg's definition would lead to a dangerous kind of attachment to religious views. Nonetheless, a proponent of definitions like Schellenberg's might object that Sextus and Nāgārjuna lack the proper attitude or commitment necessary for religious practice.

My response to these sorts of objections is that the concepts of religion and derivative concepts such as religious practice may not be susceptible to precise definition. Many scholars have suggested that religion is a Wittgensteinian family-resemblance term, and thus the kind of religiosity without belief we find in Sextus and Nāgārjuna adds one more member to the family, even if this member is the odd uncle or distant cousin of the bunch. While it does not include one feature – the presence of belief – that is central to many varieties of religious practice, it still shares enough similarities – such as the performance of rituals or the pursuit of some good such as inner peace – that we are warranted in calling it a form of religious practice.[22] Another approach would be to admit that Sextus and Nāgārjuna don't fit the typical definition of religion, but to induct their version of religious practice as an honorary member of the club on account of the other features they do share. This is the approach Daniel Dennett uses to claim that Buddhism could be considered an honorary religion even though most forms of Buddhism don't involve seeking the approval of supernatural agents; his analogy is that some people consider octopi and other cephalopods to be "honorary vertebrates" on account of their intelligence (Dennett 2006, 7–12). I can't offer full arguments in favor of these approaches here, but I do think they suggest that there's something hasty, if not closed-minded, about simply denying that Sextus and Nāgārjuna may be describing a genuinely religious practice, especially concerning a category as broad and fuzzy as religion.

Another objection might come from recent work in philosophy of religion claiming that religious practice requires faith and that faith is not necessarily a kind of belief. Two proponents of the view that faith may be nondoxastic are Robert Audi (1992) and J. L. Schellenberg (2005). Audi and Schellenberg concentrate on propositional faith, or faith-that, as opposed to attitudinal faith, or faith-in. The basic idea is that it is possible to have faith that a state of affairs is the case without having a *belief* that this state of affairs is in fact the case. This kind of faith also occurs in non-religious contexts, such as a runner's faith that he will finish the race or someone's faith that a friend will overcome an illness (Schellenberg 2005, 129–130; Audi 1992, 58).[23] In these non-religious cases, one does not quite *believe* that a state of affairs obtains or will obtain in the future, but one nonetheless has some sort of positive cognitive attitude toward this state of affairs. Thus, someone might object that while it is true that Sextus and Nāgārjuna do not have religious *beliefs*, they do nonetheless have a kind of religious *faith*.

Nonetheless, I still think Sextus and Nāgārjuna give us a distinct category of religious practice that contains neither beliefs nor propositional, nondoxastic faith.

---

[22] For a detailed discussion and criticism of family-resemblance views, see Schellenberg 2005, Ch. 1.

[23] None of this should be taken to imply that Audi's and Schellenberg's positions on nondoxastic faith are identical. For instance, Audi thinks that faith is incompatible with doubt, whereas Schellenberg thinks faith in some circumstances requires doubt in the form of religious skepticism (Audi 1992, 59; Schellenberg 2005, 132). See also Schellenberg 2007 and 2009. Draper 2011 gives a helpful overview of Schellenberg 2005, 2007, and 2009 while Smith 2010 is a critique of Schellenberg's religious skepticism.

This can be seen with regard to Schellenberg's definition of propositional faith, especially the following parts:

> ... S considers the state of affairs reported by *p* [some religious proposition] to be good or desirable. ... S tenaciously and persistently represents the world to herself as including that state of affairs. ... S voluntarily and committedly adopts a policy of assent toward that representation – or, more broadly, toward *p*. (Schellenberg 2005, 139)

One problem for Sextus would be that taking anything to be good or desirable by nature is a form of dogmatism, one that he spends a great deal of time attempting to avoid (e.g., PH 3.168–238). For both Sextus and Nāgārjuna, "tenaciously and persistently representing the world" is really the whole problem with belief and the very disease their philosophical therapies are designed to cure. On this count, non-doxastic faith might even be *more* problematic in so far as it might be less susceptible to being dislodged by skeptical argumentative strategies – how could *arguments* work against a cognitive state that may be unresponsive to evidence? Lastly, adopting a "policy of assent," even if Schellenberg is right that this is not merely a form of weak belief, would be quite close to belief in terms of its psychological effects concerning mental disruption and attachment.[24]

Nonrealist or Wittgensteinian approaches in philosophy of religion might suggest another objection that Sextus and Nāgārjuna *do* have religious beliefs once we correctly understand what it means to hold a religious belief. According to nonrealism, religious beliefs do not refer to non-observable phenomena (God, *karma*, etc.), but instead are expressions of attitudes or part of rituals. D. Z. Phillips, a prominent representative of Wittgensteinian philosophy of religion, claims that careful attention to the grammar of religious beliefs rules out both realism and nonrealism – realism because it neglects the larger context and effects of religious beliefs and nonrealism because it neglects that part of the context of religious beliefs is that such beliefs are *about* something (Phillips 1993, Ch. 4).[25] In so far as Sextus and Nāgārjuna emphasize the practical, active aspects of religious practice, perhaps they are in fact a lot closer to the real meaning of religious belief than it first appears.

In response, I would note that nonrealist and Wittgensteinian approaches concern the meaning of religious beliefs; these approaches attempt to make sense of what's going on when people sincerely hold and express religious beliefs. Sextus and Nāgārjuna, on the other hand, are offering a critique of holding religious beliefs; they simply wouldn't be interested in offering any alternative philosophical account of belief. Hence, they can't be so easily included in the nonrealist or Wittgensteinian fold.[26]

---

[24] For recent critical responses to Schellenberg's account of non-doxastic faith, see Chignell 2013, Dole 2013, and Howard-Snyder 2013.

[25] See also Mulhall 2001 for an overview of Wittgensteinian philosophy of religion. Another issue to consider is Wittgenstein's own relationship with Pyrrhonism, an issue taken up in Fogelin 1994, 205–222.

[26] Furthermore, while it's hard to know what ancient philosophers would think about contemporary developments, I think Sextus and Nāgārjuna may well critique nonrealist and Wittgensteinian notions of belief (whether Wittgenstein himself can be more favorably compared is a different

4.5 Conclusion

What I've been trying to show is that the kind of skeptical religious practice represented in the work of Sextus and Nāgārjuna constitutes a unique category of religiosity. As I mentioned earlier, this is relevant to ethics in the sense of an agent-centered, prudential concern for situating oneself toward some good. Furthermore, Nāgārjuna's skeptical therapy has an important place in lessening one's attachment to the idea of self, which is in line with the Buddhist emphasis on *anatta* (non-self); this also accords well with the type of dissociation from philosophical belief described by Sextus.

There are a number of reasons that the skeptical category of religious practice exemplified by Sextus and Nāgārjuna has been overlooked in contemporary philosophy of religion. The first is the relative neglect of Hellenistic and Indian philosophy among most contemporary North American philosophers and in particular a general lack of understanding of ancient – as opposed to modern – skepticism. Another major factor is the predominance of Abrahamic monotheism (especially Christianity), which still largely sets the agenda for contemporary philosophy of religion.

What are some of the lessons Sextus and Nāgārjuna might teach philosophers of religion today? First, skepticism about religion is generally seen by contemporary philosophers of religion as a threat; if we are unable to know or rationally believe anything about topics such as whether God exists or whether there's an afterlife, religion is thought to be imperiled. Rather than argue against skepticism about religion, Nāgārjuna might say that a Buddhist could embrace skepticism insofar as it can destroy dogmatic attachment; Sextus would say that religious practice is not at all imperiled by Pyrrhonism. Contemporary philosophers of religion often attempt to answer religious skepticism by showing that we could have genuine religious knowledge, or at least rational belief or faith (e.g., Alston 1992, Audi 1992, Smith 2010, etc.). Sextus and Nāgārjuna, on the other hand, do not need to engage in such philosophical enterprises for the simple reason that their philosophical and religious practice does not rest on knowledge-claims, beliefs, or even nondoxastic faith.[27]

---

issue). According to Sextus, a Pyrrhonian is concerned to avoid mental disturbance, and it seems to me that nonrealist or Wittgensteinian beliefs could provoke mental disturbance just as easily as their realist counterparts. Nāgārjuna's point is that beliefs of a philosophical or religious nature often involve harmful psychological attachments that can't be eliminated simply by another definition of what it means to hold a belief – the tendency toward belief itself should be eliminated.

[27] The study of Sextus and Nāgārjuna could be useful in pursuing what Andrew Chignell, echoing a suggestion from Nicholas Wolterstorff, has called "liturgical philosophy." This idea "involves de-emphasizing ideal cases of justified bare theistic belief in favour of the philosophically significant features of actual religious adherence *as modelled in various liturgical contexts*. In other words, it would turn to real-world religious practice – especially the sort that goes on in ritual *leitourgia* – as a guide for philosophical reflection concerning the attitudes and doctrines involved in religion generally (Chignell 2013, 197.

Furthermore, even those philosophers who accept some form of religious skepticism most often do so in line with modern, as opposed to ancient, skepticism. For ancient skeptics such as Sextus and Nāgārjuna, skepticism is an intellectual therapy leading to a peaceful state of mind, whereas for modern skepticism from Descartes and Hume up to the present day, skepticism is usually seen as an epistemological position about whether knowledge is possible or actual.[28] A recent defense of religious skepticism can be found in the work of J. L. Schellenberg, who consciously differentiates his position from Sextus on account of what he sees as Sextus's lack of concern for truth-seeking (Schellenberg 2007, xi-xiii). It's not my place here to recommend ancient over modern skepticism, but merely to point out that the ancient piece of the skeptical puzzle often goes missing in contemporary discussions.

Lastly, I think the kind of religiosity without belief that I've been discussing here gives a good demonstration of the benefits of doing philosophy of religion in a way that's not unduly centered on Christian theology. After all, if we mean to engage in something called "philosophy of *religion*" as opposed to something called "philosophy of Christian theism," then we ought to consider modes of religiosity that fall outside the purview of Abrahamic monotheism. If I'm right that the form of skeptical religiosity exhibited by Sextus and Nāgārjuna is a unique category worthy of further inquiry, then I've done just that.

What I haven't done is to delve into further details of this category of religiosity without belief. Is it parasitic on forms of religiosity that do include belief? How would it deal with charges of inconsistency or self-refutation faced by many forms of skepticism? Aside from a lack of belief, is there a list of features shared by most or all tokens of this type of religiosity? Could questions of rationality and justification apply to it? Would it be a meaningful form of religious expression for people in the contemporary world?[29] At this point I find it fitting to follow the Pyrrhonians and say that I will keep investigating.

References

Alston, William P. 1992. Knowledge of God. In *Faith, Reason and Skepticism*, ed. Marcus Hester, 6–49. Philadelphia: Temple University Press.
Annas, Julia. 1995. Plato and Common Morality. In *Plato's Ethics*, ed. Terence Irwin, 183–197. New York: Garland Publishing.

---

[28] See Ribeiro 2009 for an argument that there is a great deal of continuity between ancient and modern skepticism; interestingly, Ribeiro argues that Sextus and Montaigne are similarly committed to religious practice as a part of local tradition.

[29] Annas (2011) suggests that, at least with Sextus, the answer to this question is "no," given the gulf between the ancient pagan context and the context of monotheism today, although she does admit that she isn't considering polytheistic religions such as Hinduism (Annas 2011, 83). It may be promising to consider these issues in light of the pluralism and syncretism of many contemporary forms of Hinduism, especially those influenced by Neo-Vedānta.

———. 2011. Ancient scepticism and ancient religion. In *Episteme, Etc.: Essays in Honour of Jonathan Barnes*, ed. Benjamin Morison and Katerina Ierodiakonou, 74–89. New York: Oxford University Press.

Audi, Robert. 1992. Rationality and Religious Commitment. In *Faith, Reason, and Skepticism*, ed. Marcus Hester, 50–97. Philadelphia: Temple University Press.

Beckwith, Christopher I. 2015. *Greek Buddha: Pyrrho's Encounter with Early Buddhism in Central Asia*. Princeton: Princeton University Press.

Burnyeat, Myles, and Michael Frede, eds. 1997. *The Original Sceptics: A Controversy*. Indianapolis: Hackett.

Cicero. 2006. *On Academic Scepticism*. Trans. Charles Brittain. Indianapolis: Hackett.

Chignell, Andrew. 2013. Prolegomena to any non-doxastic religion. *Religious Studies* 49 (2): 195–207.

Collins, Steven. 1982. *Selfless Persons: Imagery and Thought in* Theravāda *Buddhism*. Cambridge: Cambridge University Press.

Dennett, Daniel. 2006. *Breaking the Spell: Religion as a Natural Phenomenon*. New York: Penguin.

Dole, Andrew. 2013. Is Sceptical Religion Adequate as a Religion? *Religious Studies* 49 (2): 235–238.

Draper, Paul. 2011. Faith Without God: An Introduction to Schellenberg's Trilogy. *Philo* 14 (1): 59–65.

Flintoff, Everard. 1980. Pyrrho and India. *Phronesis* 25 (1): 88–108.

Fogelin, Robert J. 1994. *Pyrrhonian Reflections on Knowledge and Justification*. Oxford: Oxford University Press.

Fuller, Paul. 2005. *The Notion of Diṭṭhi in Theravāda Buddhism: The Point of View*. New York: Routledge Curzon.

Garfield, Jay. 2002. *Empty Words: Buddhist Philosophy and Cross Cultural Interpretation*. New York: Oxford University Press.

Hankinson, R.J. 1995. *The Sceptics*. New York: Routledge.

Hartle, Ann. 2005. Montaigne and skepticism. In *The Cambridge Companion to Montaigne*, ed. Ullrich Langer, 183–206. Cambridge: Cambridge University Press.

Hayes, Richard. 1988. *Dignāga on the Interpretation of Signs*. Boston: Kluwer.

Howard-Snyder, Daniel. 2013. Schellenberg on Propositional Faith. *Religious Studies* 49 (2): 189–194.

Inwood, Brad, and L.P. Gerson, eds. 1997. *Hellenistic Philosophy: Introductory Readings*. 2nd ed. Indianapolis: Hackett Publishing.

Korsgaard, Christine. 1997. The Normativity of Instrumental Reason. In *Ethics and Practical Reason*, ed. Garrett Cullity and Berys Gaut, 215–254. Oxford: Oxford University Press.

Kuzminski, Adrian. 2008. *Pyrrhonism: How the Ancient Greeks Reinvented Buddhism*. Boulder: Lexington Books.

McEvilley, Thomas. 2002. *The Shape of Ancient Thought: Comparative Studies in Greek and Indian Philosophies*. New York: Allworth Press.

Monier-Williams, M. 1994. *Sanskrit-English Dictionary*. New Delhi: Munshiram Manoharlal.

Montaigne, Michel. 1987. *Apology for Raymond Sebond*. Trans. and Ed. M.A. Screech. New York: Penguin Books.

Mulhall, Stephen. 2001. Wittgenstein and the Philosophy of Religion. In *Philosophy of Religion in the 21st Century*, ed. D.Z. Phillips and Timothy Tessin, 95–118. New York: Palgrave.

Murti, T.R.V. 1955. *The Central Philosophy of Buddhism: A Study of the Mādhyamika System*. London: Unwin.

Nāgārjuna. 1994. In *Nāgārjunian Disputations: A Philosophical Journey Through an Indian Looking-Glass*. Ed. and Trans. Thomas L. Wood, 307–322. Honolulu: University of Hawaii Press.

———. 1997. In *Nāgārjuna and the Philosophy of Openness*. Ed. and Trans. Nancy McGagney. New York: Rowman and Littlefield.

Nagel, Thomas. 1970. *The Possibility of Altruism*. Princeton: Princeton University Press.

Peterson, Michael, William Hasker, Bruce Reichenbach, and David Basinger. 2013. *Reason and Religious Belief: An Introduction to the Philosophy of Religion*. 5th ed. New York: Oxford University Press.

Phillips, D.Z. 1993. *Wittgenstein and Religion*. New York: St. Martin's Press.

Ribeiro, Brian. 2009. Sextus, Montaigne, Hume: Exercises in Skeptical Cartography. *The Modern Schoolman* 87 (1): 7–34.

Schellenberg, J.L. 2005. *Prolegomena to a Philosophy of Religion*. Ithaca: Cornell University Press.

———. 2007. *The Wisdom to Doubt: A Justification of Religious Skepticism*. Ithaca: Cornell University Press.

———. 2009. *The Will to Imagine: A Justification of Skeptical Religion*. Ithaca: Cornell University Press.

Sextus, Empiricus. 2000. *Outlines of Scepticism*. Translated by Julia Annas and Jonathan Barnes. Cambridge: Cambridge University Press.

———. 2012. *Against the Physicists*. Trans. Richard Bett. Cambridge: Cambridge University Press.

Siderits, Mark. 2000. Nāgārjuna as Anti-Realist. In *Indian Philosophy: A Collection of Readings: Epistemology*, ed. Roy Perrett, 11–15. New York: Garland Publishing.

Smith, Patrick T. 2010. The Enduring Challenge of Religious Skepticism: An Evaluation of a Recent Model. *Philosophia Christi* 12 (2): 419–428.

Taber, John. 1998. On Nāgārjuna's So-Called Fallacies: A Comparative Approach. *Indo-Iranian Journal* 41: 213–244.

Taylor, Charles. 1989. *Sources of the Self: The Making of Modern Identity*. Cambridge, MA: Harvard University Press.

Thorsrud, Harald. 2009. *Ancient Scepticism*. Berkeley: University of California Press.

Westerhoff, Jan. 2009. *Nāgārjuna's Madhyamaka: A Philosophical Introduction*. Oxford: Oxford University Press.

Chapter 5
Spinoza Through the Prism of Later 'East-West' Exchanges: Analogues of Buddhist Themes in the *Ethics* and the Works of Early Spinozists

Gordon F. Davis and Mary D. Renaud

In the late seventeenth century and early eighteenth century, one sees the first significant contact between European philosophers and the world of Buddhist and other Asian philosophical traditions. As we shall see, however, this contact was limited in many ways, especially during the lifetime of Baruch Spinoza (1632–77), our main focus in this chapter. Our chapter falls into the 'pre-contact' part of this volume, because for almost all the figures we discuss here, the *primary* sources of Asian philosophy – and especially Buddhism – remained largely unavailable. The sort of direct inspiration for which Schopenhauer is famous was still a long way off, whether we are speaking of Spinoza's own time and place, or of those, almost a century later, who began to see the putatively 'Asiatic' resonance of his philosophy as a positive rather than a negative feature. Our aim here is not merely historical, though. Besides noting such episodes as the 'Chinese Rites Controversy' in Spinoza's time, we will approach Spinoza on his own terms, before asking how his ideas compare to those of Buddhist ethics. And in addition to considering Chinese forms of Buddhism, we consider the Indo-Tibetan ones (and some Hindu themes) that came to be familiar only in the late eighteenth century – the time when Spinozist ideas were taken more seriously than ever before, albeit newly inflected with currents of thought deriving partly from Asian sources.

We wish to thank both the anonymous referees for their comments, and the following people for helpful correspondence and conversations: Charles Goodman, Sandy Hinzelin, Simon Kow, Mitia Rioux-Beaulne, Mark Siderits, Erik Stephenson, Angela Sumegi and all of our fellow contributors to this volume.

G. F. Davis (✉)
Department of Philosophy, Carleton University, Ottawa, ON, Canada
e-mail: Gordon.Davis@carleton.ca

M. D. Renaud
Brown University, Providence, RI, USA
e-mail: mary_renaud@brown.edu

© Springer International Publishing AG, part of Springer Nature 2018
G. F. Davis (ed.), *Ethics without Self, Dharma without Atman*, Sophia Studies in Cross-cultural Philosophy of Traditions and Cultures 24,
https://doi.org/10.1007/978-3-319-67407-0_5

Some Spinoza scholars might still be intrigued by the suggestion Lewis Maverick made many years ago, to the effect that Spinoza himself may have been influenced by early reports of Chinese philosophical ideas, those relayed by Jesuits in the early 1600s.[1] Other Spinoza scholars might dismiss such speculation, and refrain from direct comparisons, and might instead scrutinize the motivations and biases of writers who have explored such comparisons, bolstering a scepticism about the various books that have trumpeted a convergence of Spinozist and Buddhist thought, ranging from Melamed's *Spinoza and Buddha* (1933) to kindred explorations by Jon Wetlesen (1979) and Arne Naess (2008).[2] We will not be pursuing either of those historical investigations here. Rather, our concern is to reconsider the question that these writers were asking in the first place, the question of how much of Spinoza's thought was prefigured in Buddhist doctrine. To that extent, we ourselves risk getting entangled in something akin to an 'Orientalizing' tendency, which is one way to describe the early modern interest in Asian philosophy, with its widespread use of the term 'oriental' in European languages, and its risk of imposing additional distorting lenses where an initial hermeneutic prism is already *ipso facto* present.[3] Be that as it may, another of our aims, occupying the second half of the chapter, is to chart the development of a Spinozist ethic that inspired a few French and German writers who were also open to the insights of Asian philosophical traditions. In light of this, we consider, finally, the impact of this ethic on the social and political context of both rationalist and romantic phases of the European Enlightenment.

Following our examination of Spinoza's ethical system, we will encounter an odd cast of characters: Pierre Bayle, Nicolas Malebranche, Denis Diderot, J.G. Herder, Goethe and some other early 'Romantic' figures. Only the latter among these were Spinozists. Bayle and Malebranche were certainly not – but they had a decisive influence on a tendency to assimilate Spinoza's philosophy to that of Buddhist and other Asian traditions (leaning initially towards an unfavourable assessment of both). Their interventions came without first-hand knowledge of Buddhist texts. But towards the end of Herder's life, the first translations from Sanskrit texts were having an impact, not only on him but also on the young romantic philosophers under his influence. Historians of philosophy are generally aware of this new factor in the post-Kantian context; but they rarely appreciate the extent to which the impact was felt in the areas of moral, social and political philosophy. The sources of inspiration were by then not exclusively Buddhist (perhaps in contrast to some earlier phases of interest in Chinese philosophy); but in any case, we

---

[1] Maverick (1939) speculates about Spinoza's access to one such report, a 1615 account by Nicholas Trigault, re-published in Amsterdam during his most formative philosophical period (1649–50); see also Lai (1985, 152n.).

[2] Other works in this vein include Hessing (1977) and Wienpahl (1979).

[3] Perhaps any risk of 'Orientalism', meanwhile, can be mitigated in proportion to the number of primary sources that one is able and willing to consider (charitably, but also critically, in context). The lack of such sources prior to Herder's time is one thing that makes something like 'Orientalism', ill-defined though it may be, a factor in the period we cover here.

will address this impact more fully, and give both Spinoza and the role of Asian philosophy due recognition for fostering a new understanding of ethical altruism, one that stands in contrast to both Christian sentimentalism and Kantian rationalism.[4]

5.1 Varieties of the Personal, the Impersonal and the Altruistic

In the next section, we offer an interpretation of the relevant aspects of Spinoza's *Ethics* – those bearing on personal identity on the one hand, and altruism on the other. Before doing that, some general remarks about each of these topics may help to clarify what is at stake, not only for Spinozists, but within contemporary philosophy as well. One thing that is at stake in contemporary Buddhist philosophy is how best to characterize the impersonal perspective that would or should supplant the personal one; and this is also of great interest to utilitarian moral theorists, as well as metaphysicians who contrast reductionism in philosophy of mind with non-reductionist accounts of 'extended mind'. As Mark Siderits puts it in his book *Personal Identity and Buddhist Philosophy*, prominent alternatives to non-reductionist realism about selfhood (and to his own two-level treatment) include (1) a 'punctualist' model ("the view that the experiencing subject is not an enduring person but rather an ephemeral person-stage"[5]), and (2) a '*Weltgeist*' model (asserting each person's "identification... [with the] aggregation" of all beings[6]). Put simply, and without attempting a non-circular formulation, persons or 'selves' may disappear from ontology, either because (1) only the temporal parts of persons are real, or (2) only the collectivity of all mental phenomena is real, and only in a form that lacks interpersonal dividing lines.

Siderits's own proposal goes beyond this dichotomy, partly because he introduces his own innovations, albeit based on materials from the Buddhist tradition. But these two basic approaches figure prominently in classical Buddhist literature. There are endless examples of the *Weltgeist* model, especially in Mahāyāna texts;

---

[4] For that matter, it is an altruism that contrasts with classical Greek and Hellenistic models as well. We will not consider the alleged Stoic roots of Spinoza's ethics; but implicitly, our interpretation does cast doubt on (the role of) a eudaimonistic approach, which was common to almost all of Hellenistic ethics.

[5] Siderits 2003, 37. Siderits sometimes treats these models as optional frameworks for practical or moral deliberation; but we consider them here as ontologies.

[6] Siderits, 42. The medieval Muslim philosopher Averroes was notorious for similar ideas, amounting to variations on so-called 'monopsychism', which already encompassed two different claims: that minds *can* fuse (at least in the afterlife) vs. that the one and only primeval mind never underwent fission in the first place. In relation to both Buddhism and Spinoza, it is the latter idea that seems in play. (We note Spinoza's familiarity with Averroes below.) Montaigne ([1580] 2003, 497) cites Virgil to express a similar idea; and Bayle (1697), in note (A) to his "Spinoza" article, relates the "âme du monde" idea to both Stoic and Indianphilosophies (see n. 23 below, regarding Bayle's sources on India).

and its association with 'non-duality' is strengthened in the Yogācāra tradition in particular (where mind is not set over against an external world, but rather constitutes all of reality).[7] For example, the *Lankāvatāra Sutra* defends non-violence by asking, "how can [one] who desires to approach all living beings as if they were himself... [kill] living being[s] that [are] of the same nature as himself?" (Suzuki 1932, 212). And Vasubandhu argues that we must act "[to benefit] all sentient beings without any interruption... with the confidence that 'self' and 'others' are really the same" (Anacker 257).[8]

Śāntideva, the eighth-century Madhyamaka moralist, is often seen as relying on a punctualist model, at least in some of his arguments for universal altruism. For instance, he says, "The notion 'it is the same me [in the future]' is a false construction... The continuum of consciousnesses, like a queue, and the combination of constituents, like an army, are not real. The person who experiences suffering does not exist. To whom will that suffering belong?" (BCA 8: 98, 101).[9] But there are also echoes of the *Weltgeist* conception, for instance in verse 91, just prior to that passage: "Just as the body, with its many parts... should be protected as a single entity, so too should this entire world which is divided, but undivided in its nature to suffer and be happy." Elsewhere, Śāntideva speaks of 'oceans of misery' which are in reality 'oceans of virtue' (cf. 8: 113, 9: 102–103, 9: 157–158).[10] Shifting between the two conceptions, he says, "I should dispel the suffering of others because it is suffering like my own suffering. I should help others too because of their nature as beings, which is like my own being" (8: 94), and "in order to allay my own suffering and to allay the suffering of others, I devote myself to others and accept them as myself... resolve [to say] 'I am bound to others'! From now on you must have no other concern than the welfare of all beings" (8: 136–137).[11]

As evidenced in various social movements falling under the umbrella of 'Engaged Buddhism', an activist guided by these injunctions could quite naturally find herself at home among those in – for example – the global human rights movement. But altruism, or even the ideal of impartial benevolence, could be either more limited or less limited than that. It could be more limited, if applied only within the bounds of some community or nation (not an approach that Engaged Buddhists would encourage). Or it could shed all limitations, and override the notion of basic rights, thus

---

[7] The Yogācāra school can be said to go beyond monopsychism, embracing panpsychism as well (as reflected in the 'Citta-matra' (*mind-only*) label that has traditionally been attached to it).

[8] Vasubandhu makes this remark in Part V of his *Madhyānta-Vibhāga-Bhāṣya* (here cited in the Anacker translation), i.e. in his Yogācāra works, not his earlier works.

[9] The moral conclusion follows in the next verse (8:102): Suffering "must be warded off simply because [it is] suffering. Why is any limitation put on this?" ('BCA' abbreviates *Bodhicaryāvatāra*, translated in Śāntideva (1995).)

[10] One might ask: is there any evidence of a move from 'oceans' to a single, all-encompassing 'ocean'? Śāntideva is aware of this option, and perhaps leaves it to the Yogācārin after all, as his dialogue with a Citta-matra exponent suggests (9: 11–34).

[11] Although he uses the phrase "*you* must have...", verse 137 addresses itself impersonally to 'Mind', suggesting that the resolve is constructed in personal terms but mandated by an impersonal source.

removing a potential obstacle to maximizing overall welfare. The refrain at BCA 8: 102, "why is any limitation put on [reducing suffering]?" seems to propose a move in that direction. And Śāntideva's analogy with the body might also favour the kind of moral consequentialism that subordinates human rights to a welfarist goal (insofar as a person can justifiably sacrifice a limb for their own greater good). In his book *Consequences of Compassion*, Charles Goodman (2009) tries to show that early Mahāyāna ethics tended to move in this consequentialist direction; and it is important for ethical theorists to be aware of such evidence of cross-cultural convergence with respect to over-arching principles such as that of universal perfectionist consequentialism.[12] But we mention it here, because less extreme forms of altruism will interest us as well – and they will interest us, to the extent that they are inspired by, or inferred from, impersonal *ontologies*. In the case of Spinoza, it will be sufficiently important to track the grounds and consequences of any retreat from egoism; but once egoism is abandoned or superseded, the range of available altruistic frameworks may appear quite open. Of course, it might be a matter of historical record, as to which paradigms of altruistic activism found expression (for instance, in the writings of French revolutionaries inspired by Spinozists); but philosophically, and at the level of extrapolating from Spinoza's arguments, the options remain open-ended.

5.2 Spinoza's Ethics: Mind, Substance and the Collective Highest Good

Spinoza claims that all persons, and all minds and bodies in general, have "finite and… determinate existence" (*Ethics*, Part II, D7), though even in this "singular" form, their boundaries can shift or merge.[13] Persons are not substances, as Descartes had claimed in texts that occupied Spinoza's attention in his early years. Descartes holds that there are two kinds of substance – thinking substance(s) and extended substance(s) – whereas Spinoza recognizes only one impersonal substance. Already we can glimpse this broad parallel: Spinoza's move from dualism to monism resembles the Mahāyāna Buddhist shift to a principle of 'non-duality'. But before we explore this parallel, it will help to flesh out a little more of the Cartesian system, in terms of which – and against which – Spinoza framed his own.

For Descartes, thinking substances are divided into infinite and finite substances. The single infinite thinking substance, God, depends on nothing whatsoever for its

---

[12] That is, this is an important issue in ethical *theory*, even if the idea of sacrificing human rights in the name of consequentialism should be deemed unwise (or worse) in *practical* ethics.

[13] Pt II D7 adds: "if a number of Individuals so concur in one action that together they are all the cause of one effect, I consider them all, to that extent, as one singular thing." It is perhaps not clear whether this lends itself to a 'Weltgeist' approach; but in any case, we see below that Spinoza sees continuity of memory as relevant to the concept of personal identity, which leaves this notion of 'singularity' – insofar as it applies to bodies – of uncertain significance with regard to personal identity. (All further quotations from Spinoza are from his *Ethics* (Curley trans. in Spinoza [1677] (1985).)

existence, while the many finite thinking substances, individual minds, or souls, depend on nothing other than God's concurrence for their existence. Extended substances, such as human bodies, are, like souls, finite substances that depend on God's concurrence. Although a human is a combination of a finite thinking substance (*res cogitans*) and a finite extended substance (*res extensa*) – a combination of a soul and a body – the *self* (*ego*) is a purely mental being. Descartes' two substances can be conceived as existing independently of one another, and this sustains his notion of an afterlife: the soul, the essence of selfhood on this view, can subsist after the body's death, complete in itself.

Spinoza rejects almost all of this. According to Spinoza, there is but one kind of substance. In fact, there is but one substance: the infinite substance. There are no finite substances in his metaphysics. For Spinoza, as for Descartes, the infinite substance is God. Thought and extension are not separate substances; they are separate attributes of the infinite substance. These attributes are neither separable, nor divisible; they are ways in which substances can be conceived, rather than separate substances unto themselves (IIP7Schol).

This rejection of Cartesian dualism has implications for Spinoza's view of persons and the self. While Spinoza tells us that a human "consists of a Mind and a Body", and that "the human Mind is united to the Body", this is envisioned in a radically different way from that of Descartes' union of mind and body (IIP13Cor, IIP13Schol). A human person can no longer be the coupling of a soul and a body as separate, finite substances, since there are no such finite substances in Spinoza's ontology. The mind and the body are the same singular thing conceived under different attributes, under the attributes of either thought or extension, respectively (IIP21Schol). Bodies are modes of the attribute of extension, and minds are modes of the attribute of thought. What distinguishes an individual body from another is the specific ratio of motion and rest shared by its constituent parts, and a mind is merely the idea of a particular body (IIP21Schol, IIL1, IIL5). This ratio of motion and rest is maintained by the body's *conatus*, which is "the striving by which each thing strives to persevere in its being" (IIIP7). It is crucial, however, that this "striving" not be thought of as a conscious endeavour. As Genevieve Lloyd tells us, "for Spinoza this striving is not to be construed as something the individual does. Strictly, there is no agent here, no subject identifiable independent of the striving" (Lloyd 1994, 5). Nevertheless this, the *conatus* of a thing, is its essence; it is that which differentiates it from other singular things.

Within this framework, where does one locate the self? Or to borrow Roger Scruton's words to express the same query: "Whether conceived as mind or body, [if] I am no more than a finite mode of the divine substance; in what, then, does my individuality consist?" (Scruton 1999, 24). Lloyd remarks, "The treatment of 'all that we know as the world,' in Hegel's phrase, as modes of the one substance, seems to leave little room for individual existence. As mere modes within the totality of thought, our minds would appear to have little scope for autonomous selfhood" (Lloyd 6–7).

Without the Cartesian soul that can exist after death and that is identified with the self in Descartes' framework, Spinoza indeed appears not only to do without an eternal soul, but perhaps without a self altogether. This is the conclusion Scruton arrives at, interpreting Spinoza to be denying the "identity, separateness, and self-sufficiency of the person" (Scruton 1986, 53).

There are in fact two trains of thought in Spinoza's *Ethics* that can support this conclusion. One is akin to the 'punctualist' approach outlined above. There are phases in each person's life (though variations on them unfold differently for different people – or so presumably Spinoza would admit); and their succession puts numerical identity in question. As Spinoza says, "Sometimes a man undergoes such changes that I should hardly have said he was the same man" (IV, P39Schol.). Although he is not explicit about there being a different individual at each moment, he does suggest that time, alone, is enough to alter us to the point of no longer being the same individual: "A man of advanced years believes [an infant's] nature to be so different from his own that he could not be persuaded that he was ever an infant, if he did not make this conjecture concerning himself from [the example of] others" (ibid.). The other, and more pervasive, line of thought is akin to the *Weltgeist* conception. Spinoza appears to offer a view of persons as merely segments of the complete infinite substance: "if we proceed [consistently], we shall easily conceive that the whole of nature is one Individual" (II P13 L7Schol.).[14]

Despite these apparent challenges to the notion of an 'ego', Spinoza has often been interpreted, especially in recent years, as both a psychological and an ethical egoist. Spinoza seems to argue, at least in certain segments of the *Ethics*, that human beings behave in a fundamentally self-interested way. Some commentators emphasize statements implying that we are motivated by the positive and negative effects we believe something will have on our striving for self-preservation (Nadler 2014, 44). We seek or avoid things that will help or hinder us in the pursuit of this aim and that will bring about the related affective states – or so the story goes. Joy is felt when external things increase the power with which we strive for our own preservation, and we experience sadness when external things decrease the power with which we strive for this preservation.

Both the scope of this 'we', and the possible subordination of these emotions to a higher normative standard, are reconsidered by Spinoza in Part V; and at the end of this section we will note the apparent qualifications he makes there, to his '*conatus*' doctrine. But let us first see how the story continues, as (theoretical-cum-exegetical) egoists would have it.

Not only does each thing strive for its own preservation, but this striving is each thing's "actual essence". At the heart of Spinoza's psychological and moral theories, lies this *conatus* doctrine, laid out in the propositions at III P6 and III P7: "Each thing, as far as it can by its own power, strives to persevere in its being" and "The striving by which each thing strives to persevere in its being is nothing but the actual

---

[14] To avoid prematurely placing Spinoza in the *Weltgeist* camp, we should note that he is here using the term "Individual" in the sense of a singular thing, as opposed to the sense of a person. Nonetheless, his claim amounts to a kindred sort of monism.

essence of the thing." In addition, it is not that we strive for the things that we desire, but rather that we desire things as a result of our striving. Desire is experienced by humans when they are *conscious* of their striving as it is related to both the mind and body together (in other words, when they are conscious of appetite; III P9Schol). Support for Spinoza's psychological egoism and desire-based account of human motivation can be found throughout the *Ethics*, but psychological egoism is a thesis about our motivation to act, not about what justifies our actions or what makes them right or wrong.

In presenting his account of right action, Spinoza makes a number of claims that make him appear to be a kind of moral relativist. He tells us, for instance,

> As far as good and evil are concerned, they also indicate nothing positive in things, considered in themselves, nor are they anything other than modes of thinking, or notions we form because we compare things to one another. For one and the same thing can, at the same time, be good, and bad, and also indifferent. For example, Music is good for one who is Melancholy, bad for one who is mourning, and neither good nor bad to one who is deaf. (IV Pref, II/208).

Passages such as these make it appear as though the truth-status of claims about what is good or bad are relative to individual perspective(s). Adrian Moore argues that Spinoza escapes relativism thanks to his claim that there is a perspective shared by all humans, one that is structured in terms of an ideal of human nature we strive towards, an ideal that is naturally desired by all humans. In light of this, Moore thinks that "Spinoza is able to cut through the relativization" and provide a non-relativized ground for evaluations of 'good' and 'bad' (Moore 54–55).[15]

Even if the criteria for *what makes things good or bad* are not relative to each person, however, it might still be that *what it is right or wrong for each person to do* is fixed in relation to their particular interests. Such is the case with ethical egoism and, according to a number of authors, Spinoza is not only a psychological egoist, but an ethical egoist as well. Nadler, for example, asserts that Spinoza's moral philosophy is one of "unadulterated and exceptionless egoism" (Nadler 2014, 42). On this egoist interpretation of his ethics, Spinoza is seen as claiming that actions can only be right or wrong in light of the interests of the agent, and that what justifies moral prescriptions and proscriptions, even those prescribing that we act to benefit others, is ultimately self-interest.

According to Spinoza's *conatus* doctrine, all of one's actions are strivings to increase one's power. Actions that increase one's power are good, and those that decrease one's power are bad. Agents are more or less perfect to the degree that they are powerful with regard to this striving that is their nature: "For the perfection of things is to be judged solely from their nature and power; things are not more or less perfect because they please or offend men's senses, [but] because they are of use to,

---

[15] Even these considerations might be subordinate to the more robust normative framework that emerges in Part V – which raises the question whether correct evaluations are (at best) determined by non-relative desire, or are subject to *non-relative determination* (independent of desire in any usual sense). We address the key ideas of 'eternal mind' and 'love of God', at the end of this section.

or are incompatible with, human nature." (I preface, II/83). One might also see the early sections of Part IV as confirming that Spinoza considers all actions that serve the agent's interest to be right, and to be right *because* they serve her interests. "Since reason demands nothing contrary to nature," Spinoza says, "it demands that everyone love himself, seek his own advantage, what is really useful to him, want what will really lead man to a greater perfection, and absolutely, that everyone should strive to preserve his own being as far as he can" (IV P18Schol). And indeed virtue is nothing other than acting, in accordance with reason, by "acting from the laws of one's own nature," for the sake of preserving one's being.

Such passages seem, indeed, to be strong support for an egoist interpretation. Nevertheless, this is an unusual egoism, as it appears to be an egoism without any ego to speak of, given Spinoza's apparent reductionist or eliminativist view of the self. This peculiarity is one of the factors that leads some to question this egoist interpretation of Spinoza's ethical foundation and to favour an altruist interpretation instead.

Some defenders of an altruist interpretation cite Spinoza's argument from IV P30 to IV P37. This section states that things that are like us in nature are good for us, and things that are contrary to our nature are evil for us (IV P30 & P31). Persons must agree in nature with one another to the degree that they "live according to the guidance of reason" (IV P35). The "greatest good of those who seek virtue", is common to all, and can be enjoyed equally by all. This good sought by everyone who lives according to reason, the good towards which reason strives, is *understanding* (IV P36 and P37Dem). We are, therefore, better for others, and they for us, the more we increase our ability to live in accordance with reason or help others increase theirs. Consequently, doing either is a way of acting for the benefit of others, and "[t]he good which everyone who seeks virtue wants for himself, he also desires for other men." (IV P37).

Our common human nature, which allows us to enjoy increases in one another's ability to live in accordance with reason, necessitates that whenever I act in my own best interests, I am also acting in the best interests of others, and vice versa. However, that it *turns out* that what is good for me also happens to be that which is good for others of the same nature is not enough to disqualify ethical egoism (nor to disqualify it as an interpretation of Spinoza, if he offers only an account of prudential reciprocity). Although when we act in our own best interests, our actions are in the best interest of others as well, that they coincide is merely incidental, from the point of view of ethical theory, if it remains the case that what *justifies* an action or makes an action right is that *it is good for me*.

In a novel interpretation, Matthew Kisner claims that there is an additional way that reason justifies altruism in Spinoza's framework. He contends that reason requires that we act impartially; it does not, ultimately, involve strategizing in terms of individual interests, as these are tied to limited perspectives, perspectives that are sub-rational (Kisner 2009, 552; 559). Kisner suggests that Spinoza holds that reason is blind to spatial and temporal properties and that it is, therefore, not guided by considerations that are of interest only from the particular perspective of a given individual (Kisner 552). Reason takes note of only our essential properties, which are common to all, and takes no notice of the spatial and temporal properties on which one's individual perspective rests (Kisner 560).

Reason's neutrality with respect to spatial and temporal properties is most evident, Kisner thinks, in the case of temporal properties, as Spinoza claims that things "must be conceived without any relation to time, but under a certain species of eternity" (II P44 Cor2 Dem; Kisner 560). Furthermore, in the case of spatial properties, reason understands individual things as no more than "modes of the single indivisible substance" (Kisner 562). If reason does not understand individual things as being separate from one another spatially or temporally, there are no rational grounds for taking a partial perspective. Because reason demands that we take an impartial perspective, there would seem to be no justification for prioritizing our own interests over those of others. It would, therefore, be irrational to give preference to oneself, one's own desires, or one's own needs. Instead, we are to act from universal principles that apply to all equally (Kisner 561, 562 note 26).

Consequently, reason demands that we act on behalf of others as readily as on our own behalf, as it requires that we act through a disinterested and selfless concern, guided by an evaluation of the good from an objective and impartial perspective (Kisner 552). In other words, acting in light of reason demands that we give equal priority to acting for the benefit of others and acting for our own benefit, and so it will require us, at least at times, to be guided by impartial benevolence. Morality, for Spinoza, is "[t]he Desire to do good generated in us by our living according to the guidance of reason" (IV P37Schol.1).

Though we would not endorse every detail of Kisner's reading, its appeal to a monistic ontological basis could be reinforced by considering how Spinoza entertains versions of both the punctualist and *Weltgeist* analyses outlined above. Moreover, Kisner's interpretation of Spinoza bears some resemblance to a natural way of reading Śāntideva's recourse to the no-self premise, and if one were to align it – even more closely – with the ego-eliminativist interpretations of Lloyd and Scruton, we begin to see a striking degree of overlap.

Meanwhile, at the level of moral reflection, recall how Śāntideva's argument leads to the conclusion that we should want for others the same good that we want for ourselves. He tells us that "If [suffering] must be prevented, then all of it must be" and that if we think there is no reason to prevent suffering, "then this goes for oneself as for everyone" (Śāntideva 8: 103). As we have seen, Spinoza reaches a similar conclusion: "The good which everyone who seeks virtue wants for himself, he also desires for other men" (IV P37)[16].

---

[16] For the record, Spinoza could not possibly have read any works by Śāntideva – who was first translated into French in the late 1800s, and into English in the early twentieth century. Apart from the travel reports of Jesuits, in fact, he could not have been exposed to *any* Buddhist writings. But as Jay Garfield points out in his chapter, the medieval sources available to seventeenth-century philosophers reflected a wide range of ancient authors. Not only might some Greeks and Romans have read Buddhist sources (see also Emily McRae's remarks on Seneca); there would also have been a wealth of information about India in medieval Spain, where Averroes lived. Spinoza knew of Averroes' ideas via Elijah Delmedigo (Fraenkel 2012, 205 ff.).

But we might wonder: despite the impression Spinoza gives, of presenting each new proposition as a *conclusion*, is that particular proposition (IV P37) in fact a preview of a new claim – and one that calls for further explanation? Philosophically, at least, it seems unsupported by Spinoza's previous remarks about the *conatus*, and so we are led to seek an explanation in the final sections of the *Ethics*. Interestingly, the part of the *Ethics* that seems to have had the biggest impact on the German Romantics is its last, fifth part – the section that is arguably the most neglected among contemporary philosophical commentators. That last point might help to explain why Kisner finds himself outnumbered by those who try to incorporate the *conatus* doctrine into some form of egoism, because it is in this neglected final stretch of the *Ethics* that Spinoza appears to add a level of normative reflection that runs in the opposite direction – away, that is, from ethical egoism.

The first place where Spinoza resumes the line of thought expressed at IV, P37 is at V, P20: "Love toward God cannot be tainted by an affect of Envy or Jealousy: instead, the more men we imagine to be joined to God by the same bond of Love, the more it is encouraged."[17] Why does the joining *of others* to God matter to 'my' mind's love of God? A prudential answer seems implied in that proposition; but a deeper answer emerges, one that dispenses with the first-person. "The Mind's intellectual love of God… is part of the infinite Love by which God loves himself" (V, P36). Since the 'self-understanding' that comes with this re-orientation is outside of space and time, it cannot have anything to do with – and cannot retain any notion of – personal identity. And Spinoza admits that all this must qualify his earlier statements: "[T]he method of living rightly [as argued earlier] is the seeking of our own advantage. But to determine what reason prescribes as useful, we took no account of the eternity of the Mind, which we only came to know in the Fifth Part" (V, P41, Dem.). The most ethically relevant 'identity' now comes to the fore, with *conatus* either fading in importance or at least appearing less individualized, *sub specie aeternitatis*. "Insofar as our Mind knows itself," Spinoza says, "under a species of eternity, it necessarily has knowledge of God, and knows that it is in God and is conceived through God" (P30). Spinoza seems, at this point in Part V, to be reducing the appearance(s) of the personal to the reality of the impersonal. And this reality determines Spinoza's ultimate normative ideal: "Blessedness consists in Love of God" (P42) – or as he also describes it, *intellectual liberation*. Even if 'good' and 'bad' must be defined relativistically,[18] the blessedness or liberation inherent in impersonal awareness is a non-relative perfection, and *ipso facto* is something that it is desirable for all to attain.

---

[17] Spinoza appeals to IV P37 in the Demonstration that follows this proposition.

[18] A stipulation that a Spinozist (even a Spinozist guided mainly by Part V) can let stand, perhaps; although it seems infelicitous. 'Good' is such a paradigmatically thin normative term, that it would surely be better to allow that perfection or blessedness are good in a non-relative sense – indeed, as in 'highest good'.

Jon Wetlesen argues that "[i]f a person clearly and distinctly sees [as Spinoza urges] that his perceptions of things and egos… are projections of his own imagination, he will develop what the Buddhists call… insight into… the unsubstantiality of egos (*anatta*). Thereby he overcomes the ignorance… which was a necessary condition for his bondage under the passions… and attains freedom instead" (Wetlesen 1979, 198).[19] Even if Wetlesen is right to see this unfolding in Spinoza's own reflections, however, we should be cautious about tracing a similar convergence with respect to views on what moral altruism requires of us. Spinoza himself does not seem to connect the dots as explicitly as Śāntideva does.[20] (As we shall see, some of the early German Romantics come much closer to doing so, with help from both traditions.) And there is a very different motivation for caution here: perhaps both Buddhist ethics and Spinoza's ethics risk running into a similar pitfall. Perhaps they each take a step too far, an *atipada*,[21] into an ontology so remote from common sense that it loses contact with the very idea of moral engagement.[22] In fact, this was Pierre Bayle's assessment, expressed in an article on Spinoza that was widely read in the early 1700s and beyond – an assessment we now turn to consider in detail.

---

[19] A full assessment of this interpretation (in terms of projections of imagination) might require addressing the notion of *adequacy* of ideas, something we do not have space for here. It must be admitted, in any case, that Wetlesen seems to be assuming something along the lines of the *subjectivist* reading of (the account of attributes in) Spinoza, a reading proposed by Hegel, and later, with greater attention to Spinoza's texts, by Wolfson (1934). Many interpreters have rejected this reading, but it has received more favourable treatment in recent years; see e.g. Newlands (2011) and Della Rocca (2012). Even if one is inclined to dismiss this reading, however, it is historically relevant here nonetheless, since, as we shall see, German idealists (with a tendency to read Spinoza in the same way Hegel did) played a key role in combining Spinozist metaphysics with ethical ideas that they claimed to find echoes of in 'Eastern' mysticism.

[20] A complaint along these lines is voiced even by Schopenhauer, an admirer of Spinoza's: "[T]he ethics in Spinoza's philosophy does not… proceed from the inner nature of his teaching… though in itself it is praiseworthy and fine" (Schopenhauer 1969, 284). Our position on Spinoza is the inverse: we think that at least one aspect of his ethics (his defence of benevolence) may well follow from his core metaphysics; but unlike Schopenhauer, we suspend judgment on both elements of his philosophy.

[21] *Atipada* is Sanskrit for *step-too-far*. As Davis (2018) proposes, it could be used to refer to a particular pitfall in some kinds of anti-realist philosophy, where an anti-realist about certain categories of entity wishes to deploy this anti-realism in the service of ethics while also extending the scope of the anti-realism in such a way that they – inadvertently – debunk the very notion(s) of normativity that their (or perhaps any) ethics would seem to require. It need not be the departure from common sense that causes the problem, of course; the self-defeating move might instead result from a departure from some deep meta-ethical presupposition of moral discourse.

[22] Beyond counselling 'caution', we will not attempt here to resolve either this question, or the similarly pointed question of whether Spinoza has an ontology that is so reductive that it cannot accommodate truths about intrinsic value or inherently moral obligation (which could be worrying even for some who are not concerned to safeguard 'moral engagement'). To do so would be to confront large issues about monism and its compatibility with distinctions between normative and descriptive properties, the latter issue being perhaps anachronistic in this context. Nonetheless, these issues are not entirely out of place here: see the discussion of Malebranche below.

5.3 Critics of the 'Asiatic' Spinoza: Bayle and Malebranche

Many consider Spinoza to be not only a sort of apologist for egoism, but also a materialist and a rationalist; such people will approach any Buddhist reading with a great deal of scepticism. Even more careful scholars, who hesitate to attribute materialist theses to Spinoza, and who qualify his 'rationalism' in light of his ideas about intuitive knowledge, may find close comparisons with Buddhist philosophy fanciful, not to mention anachronistic. However, one thing that suggests that the comparison is not fanciful is the fact that, in one important respect, the comparison is not so anachronistic – or at least, was not considered to be in Spinoza's own time. One of the first famous expositions of Spinoza's philosophy, Pierre Bayle's "Spinoza" article in his 1697 *Dictionnaire historique et critique*, draws close parallels between Spinoza's impersonal monism and the Chinese sect of 'Fo' – which seems to involve a nebulous amalgam of Chinese Buddhist beliefs, whether amalgamated by Bayle or by some real Chinese sect of the period (and in fact, it seems, a bit of both, according to Lai 1985). Bayle appears unconcerned by his lack of information about the precise identity of this 'sect' and its historical background – for better or worse (after all, his aim in that context is not to achieve historical accuracy, except, to some extent, about *Spinoza*).[23] But the reason for his settling for broad brush strokes is significant: it is apparently because he mainly wishes to *use* these parallels to cast doubt on Spinoza's philosophy.

On one hand, Bayle treats Chinese Buddhists as more extreme than Spinoza, saying, "[i]f it is monstrous to maintain that plants, animals, men are really the same thing [i.e. modifications of the one substance]... it is still more monstrous to assert that [substance] has no thought, no power, no virtue" (291) – having in mind, in the latter case, Fo's (Mahāyāna) doctrine of emptiness.[24] On the other hand, Bayle implies that something like Fo's 'monstrous' framework of praxis is in effect the bullet that a consistent Spinozist will have no choice but to bite. He says of these Buddhists that "they make no use of their intellect, but, by a complete insensibility, sink into the rest and inaction of the first principle, which is the true means of perfectly resembling it and partaking of happiness" (291). Bayle's point, of course, is not that Spinoza actually *endorses* quietism or fatalism; his point is rather that Spinoza has no legitimate way of ruling out these ways of embracing monism.[25] For

---

[23] Bayle (1697) did show an interest in Asian culture and religion for its own sake, in at least two other articles, "Brachmanes" (about India) and "Japon" – which connects a few dots with Chinese religion and philosophy, but like others at the time, he seems not to have traced the specifically Buddhist thread back to its origins. (See also Kow 2016, with respect to Bayle and Chinese texts.) One of Bayle's sources was François Bernier's *Suite des Mémoires sur l'Empire du grand Mogol* ([1671] 2008), who links the idea of an "âme du monde" to Hindus, Sufis and Stoics (2008, 341 & 358).

[24] One of the 'monstrous' results Bayle illustrates is the 'Eleatic' implication that there can be no such thing as *change* (or *a fortiori, improvement*) if this assertion is true.

[25] Bayle does not make the fallacious claim that determinism entails fatalism; rather, he argues that a Spinozist has no way of showing fatalists and quietists to be mistaken (and no right to cite such a fallacy).

example, Spinoza can find no grounds, we are told, for seeking out truths instead of falsehoods; after all, "has he any right to say there *are* errors?" (313, our emph.). Pursuing a *reductio ad absurdum*, Bayle asks about all doctrines: "… [*inter alia*] those of Jews, and those of Christians [including those incompatible with Spinoza's monism], are they not modes of the infinite being, as much as those of his *Ethics*? Are they not realities that are as necessary to the perfection of the universe as all his speculations?... How then can he dare to claim that there is something to rectify?" (313–314).[26] "A man like Spinoza would sit absolutely still if he reasoned logically" (314) – or, presumably Bayle would add, insofar as he *does* engage in reasoning and writing, then by his own lights, the results could never be any more 'perfect' (or perhaps, any more *justified*) than those flowing from the pen of a putatively less rational writer. Spinoza may not be a quietist *de facto*; but in principle, Bayle argues, he must be considered as much a quietist as the emptiness-seeking Buddhists.

Philosophically, various questions arise at this point: Should Bayle's critique of Spinoza be a cause for concern among epistemologically-informed Spinozists? Should a critique of this kind compel Mahāyāna Buddhists to reconsider their understanding of emptiness? Does Bayle's critique of what he *attributes* to Mahāyāna Buddhism warrant critical attention among Buddhist philosophers (whether or not it's actually a traditional Chinese view)?[27] These are important questions for the purposes of an overall philosophical assessment. However, our purposes here are more limited. As far as Bayle is concerned, we acknowledge only that a meta-philosophical problem of the kind he poses here may indeed be a problem for certain extreme forms of anti-realism (a problem we called the '*atipada*' problem above), and that it may have some moral implications. In the present context, we can only illustrate the general nature of the problem, and will do so by outlining the morally divergent paths of Herder and Goethe, on the basis of a shared metaphysical Spinozism. If there are dangers of fatalism, nihilism or relativism, however – resulting from these considerations – we may find that they haunt certain Spinozists in ways that perhaps need not concern Buddhists to the same degree.[28]

---

[26] It is in using the word 'rectify' that Bayle perhaps achieves real traction here. After all, there could be a difference between true and false beliefs in such a universe; but what may indeed seem threatened is the *normativity* of truth (e.g. among other things, any '*duty to rectify*' errors).

[27] Lai (1985) tries to trace the origins of the sect that came to Bayle's attention under the 'Fo' label, identifying one of the Neo-Confucian variations on Buddhist metaphysics as the main source.

[28] As always, this depends on which strand of Buddhist philosophy is in question. But one thing seems worth emphasizing: a denial of personal identity does not *per se* entail the sorts of nihilism and relativism that flirt with incoherence (due to the familiar risk of self-refutation, whatever other dangers they may pose). Or at least, this would seem to hold when the *anatta* claim is distinguished from claims about global emptiness. Philosophers will disagree about what constitutes an *atipada*, but one clear sign that most will agree on is that which indicates that a view is self-refuting. Whereas relativism must use the concept of truth (which is problematic for it, yet apparently unavoidable), an *anatta* ontology need not use the first-person voice; so it would seem that the latter is less likely to be self-refuting.

Meanwhile Spinozism, at least, was considered beyond the pale in most seventeenth-century circles, and apparently even in the eyes of the otherwise liberal Bayle. Nonetheless, we come away from the *Dictionnaire* with the sense that he would extend to Chinese philosophers at least the one courtesy he extended to Spinoza: the concession that he, and they, may well have been as morally upright as many writers had claimed (and no less so on account of being 'atheist'). In fact, the praise for Chinese moral attitudes had already become standard lore, partly due to the image popularized by Leibniz (Perkins 2004). Leibniz sided with the Jesuits, during the 'Chinese Rites Controversy', in arguing that newly converted Chinese Christians could retain both the beliefs and practices of their ancient traditions, which in his view did not contradict Christian doctrine. Leibniz did not accept, then, that the Chinese were atheists, as others had claimed.[29] What is interesting about Bayle, on the other hand, is that he conceded that many or most Chinese literati must be atheist, without casting any doubt on their moral refinement. Malebranche echoed this hybrid image; or rather, he acknowledged that *Li* (or '*Ly*') functioned conceptually in certain ways like 'God', but that ultimately the Chinese beliefs were so remote from 'les vraies' that instead of counting as theists, the Chinese approximated "l'impie systeme de Spinoza", despite being pious in certain respects.[30] Despite their own differences, Bayle and Malebranche together contributed greatly, in their time, to suspicion of both Spinoza on the one hand, and of Asian philosophy on the other.

In fact, Malebranche's ultimate judgment was not only that there were troubling deficiencies in Chinese religion, but also that their general philosophical orientation (towards a form of monism that would soon be called 'pantheism') carried its own *moral* dangers. This echoes his verdict on Spinoza. If "God is the infinitely perfect being" (as Malebranche acknowledges Spinoza to have held), "how could he believe that all created beings are but parts or modifications of the divinity? Is it a perfection to be unjust in one's parts, unhappy in one's modifications, ignorant, demented, impious? There are more sinners than good people" – which, on Spinoza's conception, must leave God "necessarily hated, blasphemed, scorned..." A "God who punishes or exacts vengeance on Himself," though putatively "an infinitely perfect being," would contradictorily "compris[e] all the disorders of the universe" ([1688] 1997, 150). As a Christian, of course, Malebranche allowed that 'disordered' individuals could receive God's grace, and that all humans are eligible for it; but in contrast to his way of interpreting the Spinozist position, grace and redemption are

---

[29] Interestingly, while scholars then and now see Spinoza as *unwittingly* (if at all) echoing Chinese ideas, many have argued that Leibniz knowingly incorporated Chinese themes, in ways that are claimed to have had a great impact on Western philosophy and science (Needham (1954), and Jay Garfield, Chap. 6, in this volume).

[30] Malebranche [1708] 1992b, 1074; also see the passages from pages omitted in this edition, quoted in part at p. 1367. Although Malebranche is here focusing on Confucian beliefs, the ones he was discussing were of course *Neo*-Confucian, in this period, and thus greatly influenced by Buddhist metaphysics, which long before had been invoked to fill certain gaps within the more socially oriented Confucian teachings (though Malebranche was probably not aware of this Chinese historical background).

not unconditional – and thus, for him, direct moral concern for all beings is not
unconditional. He sees it as not only philosophically paradoxical, but also a source
of moral corruption, to take steps in the opposite direction, as Spinoza and Mahāyāna
Buddhism had done, towards a kind of unconditional extension of moral esteem.
True to his quest for orthodoxy, Malebranche expresses this without acknowledging
any possibility that expanding the scope of moral esteem in this way might constitute a salutary (or at least novel) ethical vision in its own right.

The question that had not yet been seriously considered, then, was not whether
atheistic Chinese philosophers *could* be morally upright, but rather, whether a perspective like theirs might be *more* moral, at least in certain theoretical respects.
(Notice that an 'unconditional extension of moral esteem' would be among the
more robust alternatives to ethical egoism discussed above, in our first section;
and it would be a short step from there to Charles Goodman's Mahāyānist universalist consequentialism, if the 'disorders' Malebranche mentions came to be
seen as deserving not only compassion but also moral appreciation insofar as
they may indirectly advance the overall welfare of all beings (Goodman 2009).) It
would be left to philosophers in the late eighteenth century to consider this latter
possibility seriously.

We close this section by noting two ironies in Malebranche: (1) despite his aspiration to orthodoxy, he planted some important doubts about personal identity (as
Montaigne had, a century before[31]), or at least about the scope for knowledge of
personal identity; and (2) he introduced a notion of *'volonté générale'* ('General
Will'), which potentially implied a distributive axiology that might seem egalitarian
in some respects. Unwittingly, he would on both counts contribute to a more pro-
gressive – or at any rate less narrowly Christian – perspective, through his impact on
eighteenth-century 'Encyclopedists'. And in Diderot's work, this was combined
both with Spinozism and with a renewed respect for the Chinese philosophical tradition. Through his close familiarity with Bayle and his legacy, on the one hand,
Diderot would certainly have been aware of the presumed parallels between
Spinozism and Buddhism (and with some plausible reading between the
Encyclopedia's lines, we can now notice a tendency to see them as emerging *favour-
ably* from their association in his mind). Through his close familiarity with
Malebranche, on the other hand, he was able to promote a concept – the 'general
will' ideal so important to his friend Rousseau – that would have a decisive impact
on the social and political context of early Romantic inspirations, some of which
came *via* the first genuine European contact with Indo-Tibetan philosophy.

---

[31] Malebranche does this in relation to the epistemology of the *cogito* rather than as an ontological
proposal, in his 1688 *Dialogues* ([1688] 1997, III: vii). In his *Essais*, Montaigne had entertained
both a 'Weltgeist' conception of the soul ([1580] 2003a, 615), and perhaps more seriously, a punctualist conception, in "On Vanity" ([1588] 2003b, pp. 1091; 1106; 1133; and cf. p. 681, in the
"Apology for Raymond Sebond").

5.4   Neo-Spinozists with a Shared Moral Vision: French Rationalists and German Romantics in the Late Eighteenth Century

We have not discussed the 'pantheist' interpretation of Spinoza's philosophy, even though historically it has been bound up with other alleged elements of his philosophy, such as quietism and fatalism.[32] After entering the philosophical lexicon in the 1700s, 'pantheism' quickly became a term of abuse, and remained so until quite recently – though it almost put that usage behind it, so to speak, in the aftermath of an extended debate that was called the *Pantheismusstreit* in Germany in the 1780s and 1790s. We will bring our historical narrative to an end at that point; but before we consider the revival of Spinoza's philosophy in the midst of German idealism, we pause here to consider the role that Diderot and the Encyclopedists played in ensuring that variations on pantheism – including Asian ones – were taken more seriously than they had been by an earlier and perhaps more prejudiced generation of French philosophes.

In relation to Diderot, it is worth reflecting that in addition to the ethical ideas *in* Spinoza, there is also the ethical impact *of his legacy* to consider – that is, the impact on the course of social and political events in modern Europe, albeit channelled through other writers and activists. As part of his celebrated narrative of the trajectory from Enlightenment to French Revolution, Jonathan Israel has emphasized the influence of Spinoza on Diderot, and the influence of Diderot on the most idealistic of the French revolutionaries (Israel 2001, 712). Insofar as one side of the Revolution was ethically idealistic – whatever one may think of its actual moral successes and failings – Diderot's works could accordingly be placed alongside Rousseau's as being among its moral inspirations. Admittedly, Israel does not draw attention to the apparent role of no-self reasoning in Spinoza (whether in Diderot's appropriation or in Spinoza's own writing);[33] but he does emphasize the ontological monism of what we are calling the 'Weltgeist' conception, as inherited by Diderot, and he also mentions Diderot's concept of the General Will, which is at least one ideological item that certainly did impact the Revolution, especially through Rousseau's appropriation of it.[34]

---

[32] Unlike the latter terms, 'pantheism' had not been coined until after Spinoza's time; and while this does not render it useless as an accessory to interpreting the *Ethics*, it does leave one uncertain where, for example, Spinoza would stand on the merits of pantheism versus pan*en*theism.

[33] Citton (2006) does highlight this, though, and its apparent impact on Diderot (Citton 2006, 145).

[34] The *locus classicus* that tackles the enigma(s) and the apparent complexity of Spinoza's influence on Diderot is Vernière (1954). In connection with the contemporary French context, it is also worth mentioning a few other Spinoza commentators who write in French. André Comte-Sponville has often compared themes from Spinoza with themes in Asian philosophical traditions (e.g. regarding Buddhism, see his 2006, pp. 172–80 & 202–04); and Marcel Conche explores similar terrain, albeit with a different assessment, extending his scope from the ethical to the moral (see his 2016, *inter alia*, and the discussion of his 1987 in Comte-Sponville's "Marcel Conche avec et contre Nietzsche" in Comte-Sponville 2015; see also the latter's "Un anachorète malade", e.g. the

As mentioned, however, Diderot's phrase 'General Will' came to him through his reading of Malebranche, rather than through Spinoza. Moreover, it would seem to be a normative rather than an ontological notion, and a political one at that – perhaps echoing certain elements in Spinoza's democratic political theory, but in any case not likely based on it. There are two points worth noticing, though: (1) unlike Rousseau, Diderot treats the General Will as a binding force among and throughout humanity, prior to and independent of any political manifestation (Diderot 1751, "Droit Naturel"); (2) in that role as binding force in humanity, it bears a striking resemblance to the notion of a 'Universal Soul' (*âme universelle*), which Diderot invokes to describe the key premise of certain Japanese philosophers (in the 1765 *Encyclopédie* article "Japonois, Philosophie de"). There are further complications, but they are tantalizing. Diderot is there describing the Confucian sect in Japan, but notice two further points: (3) without his knowing all the background, he was in fact referring to a *Neo*-Confucian sect, and hence one that was heavily influenced by Buddhist philosophy, especially in its metaphysical conception of the place of mind in nature; (4) this is the one strand of Japanese philosophy that Diderot singles out for praise, and for its potential to inspire non-theistic and non-superstitious conceptions of human solidarity, suitable for guiding reformist political liberalism in Europe.

This synthesis of ideas appears to stand Bayle's verdict on its head: Diderot seems to maintain the notion of an 'Oriental' side to Spinoza, since in his view Spinozism is indeed akin to certain strands of Asian philosophy; but rather than sweeping both into the same dustheap, Diderot seems to vindicate both. Meanwhile, there were also connections to Indian philosophy, in particular, that would not have been lost on Diderot. Bayle, who was naturally one of Diderot's favourite authors (despite these differences), had drawn parallels between Japanese beliefs and the beliefs of what he called 'Brachmanes', a term which appears to refer to Indian philosophers in general, in Bayle's usage. Diderot, and others, would have noticed Bayle's highlighting of this alleged affinity – and yet again, with a more welcoming embrace. In any case, it was not until after Diderot's time that Pali and Sanskrit works were available in translation, and before these were to have any impact on moral philosophy in the European context, the so-called *counter*-enlightenment was to intervene (for better *and* for worse, as we shall see).

The term 'counter-enlightenment' is contested, but with respect to one paradigm of enlightenment philosophy – Kant's – there was a clear divide when it came to attitudes to Spinozism. During the German 'Pantheismusstreit' in the 1780s and 1790s, Kant defended his ideal of progress by rejecting Spinozist monism. Coming to the defence of both Spinoza and monism were such figures as Herder, Goethe,

---

claim that Pyrrhonism represents an "orientalisation de la Grèce" and Spinoza an "occidentalisation de l'Orient" (2015, 327).) However, these writers have rarely scrutinized the diachronic dimension of personal identity, and at any rate not with close reference to Spinoza. One recent book that addresses implications for personal identity is William Néria's *Plotin, Shankara, Spinoza* (2014), though the comparison there is with Shankara (in the Vedanta tradition), rather than with Buddhist philosophy.

Schleiermacher and Schelling (see Forster and Melamed 2012, *passim*). And, like Diderot, these figures accepted Bayle's premise that Spinozism echoed Asian philosophy, thereby signalling an openness to Asian philosophy. However, it was not until Schopenhauer's time that Buddhism came to the fore. The enthusiasm of these earlier German figures had been focused rather on Hindu texts; but what is worth emphasizing here is that *texts* were now involved. Bayle and Malebranche had been going on hearsay, but some translations from Sanskrit became available in the 1780s; and meanwhile some were reading Sanskrit in the original, such as Schleiermacher's friend and collaborator, Friedrich Schlegel. For present purposes, we shall briefly mention only Herder, Goethe and Schleiermacher (figures that emerge again in the final chapter of this volume).

Fairly early in his career, in his *Ideas for a Philosophy of the History of Mankind*, Herder expressed a particular veneration for classical Indian philosophy; but we will quote here only from his most explicitly Spinozist work, *God: Some Conversations*.[35] Calling it "the most hallowed and... divine law," Herder has his protagonist articulate a 'law' according to which: "All things that love one another, become assimilated the one to the other." He continues: "All goodness... has the nature of God, who could do nothing else but impart Himself... The laws of beauty urge themselves upon us... and this is precisely the secret of the universally connected, active, self-existent creation. The friendly intercourse of human souls makes them similar to one another" (Herder, 183–84). When this was published in 1787, Herder may or may not have read such works as the *Bhagavad Gita*; but by 1800, he certainly would have done so, and although the following passage cites Spinoza (from the second edition of 1800), it strongly resonates with the *Gita*: "Spinoza determined the excellences and qualities of the human body, the capacities of the human mind, and conducted everything back to Him, through whom all live, in whom we live... let us awaken our true self... He alone in whom all is, who comprehends and sustains all, can say: 'I am the Self'..." (213). There would seem to be some kind of *Weltgeist* conception of metaphysics here; and moreover, that last statement implies a denial of *individual* selfhood. (Herder's claim – easy to miss – is that *only* the divine cosmos ("He alone...") is a 'Self'). The ethical upshot is apparent in the previous passage, which suggests that Herder's vision is one of 'friendly intercourse' among *all* 'human souls' – an '*all*' that seems to involve union in a single being.

We see three elements here, which already arose in our discussion of Spinoza: metaphysical monism, a prudential ideal (the blessedness of wisdom) and, thirdly, a moral ideal, possibly echoing what Kisner described as Spinoza's 'rationality of benevolence', and which Herder might call the *assimilating* power of benevolence (which in turn reprises the theme of monism).[36] Do we see the same three elements in other German 'Romantics', such as Goethe and Schleiermacher? One reason for mentioning Goethe at this juncture is to sound a note of moral caution. Goethe

---

[35] For more detail on this, and also on Herder's moral philosophy, see Sikka (2011).

[36] Sikka (2011) stresses that this could not be the *Kantian* notion of rationality (if indeed that is an apt term at all here), but meanwhile also stresses the role of benevolence in Herder's ethics.

accepted Spinozist monism – or at any rate a view inspired by Spinoza – and was enchanted by the monist metaphysics of Indian literature; however, his legacy raises the risk of '*atipada*', which we mentioned at the end of section II. The risk noted there was that *some* kinds of monism might be pushed so far as to erase all norma-tive distinctions; and in this case, the first element above, a radical ontological monism, might threaten the other two elements, which are *ideals* – and which imply that the evils they combat, though no less *real*, are less *good* per se than what the ideals strive to achieve. (In other words, they presuppose real moral distinctions.) It is an interesting question whether Goethe, in the process of yielding to a kind of monistic resignation, shared this tendency to downgrade what is distinctive about an *ideal*, in the process of yielding ultimately to some kind of monistic resignation. Michael Mack, for one, considers how his Spinozist monism had the effect of hard-ening him to the apparent evils of colonialism in particular.[37] (Mack speaks of "Goethe's refusal to spell out moral judgments," in this or in other areas; moreover, he says, "Goethe reads Spinoza's discussion of good and evil as part of a descrip-tion of nature as being fluid [such that good and evil are categories we 'impose' on a more fluid reality]… [t]he fluidity that marks nature in its entirety calls for inde-cision" (Mack 2010, 170; 161).) Now, Herder was by contrast a critic of colonial-ism, but the case of his friend Goethe raises a troubling question: on what grounds could a Spinozist – such as Herder – be a robust moral critic of that kind and sustain philosophical confidence in such criticisms (insofar as monism may remove the normative basis for *any* true moral judgments)?

It is also an interesting question, then, whether a sound form of metaphysical monism could be reconciled to a meta-normative view that is adequately realist, e.g. for a Buddhist ethicist's purposes (given that anti-realism might follow from some monists' reductionism about moral distinctions); in others words, the question is whether a sound monism could be reconciled to a moral view that avoids an *atipada* of the above kind. And it is yet another interesting question which sub-traditions of Indian or Buddhist philosophy manage to avoid this. The final irony, with which we close, is that it may have been the Christian philosophers, like Bayle and Schleiermacher,[38] who retained enough moral realism to stop short of this *atipada*. This way of putting it is not meant as any endorsement of Christian doctrine or

---

[37] We have left it open whether any 'Weltgeist' monism of the kind endorsed by thinkers such as Goethe could accurately be attributed to Spinoza; we also left it open, in section II, whether Spinoza's metaphysics can rightly be seen as resulting in some sort of anti-realism about individu-als (debunking diachronic identity in particular). In n. 19, we noted the 'subjectivist' interpretation of Spinoza, which is anti-realist about distinctions between attributes, but could be extended to an anti-realism about finite modes (including individual persons). By exploring post-Kantian ideal-ism, we can now see the significance of that interpretation; i.e. even if it did not fit everything Spinoza wrote, it nonetheless became an important variety of *Spinozism* in this period, when Buddhist and other Indian forms of monism were also vindicated, on both 'Spinozist' and separate ethical grounds.

[38] We acknowledge that categorizing Bayle as Christian is somewhat problematic (especially where his philosophy is concerned); meanwhile we follow Todd Ryan (2009) in calling him a moral real-ist, even though this is a problematic interpretation as well.

Christian legacy; on the contrary, figures such as Schleiermacher hold a particular interest partly because, more than Bayle, they challenge the traditional (e.g. Augustinian and Thomist) metaphysics of personal identity. As Michael Forster has recently shown, Schleiermacher was inspired by Spinoza to reframe the notion of individual identity;[39] and we find a striking expression of the moral upshot of this in his 1799 work *On Religion*, a work clearly inflected with the enthusiasm that he and Schlegel were then feeling for such texts as the *Bhagavad Gita*. At one point he says, "[t]o find the universe on the path of the most abstract self-contemplation was the business of ancient oriental mysticism, which, with admirable boldness, joined the infinitely great directly to the infinitely small and found everything bordering on nothingness" (68). Just prior to that point in the text is one of the most remarkable echoes of Śāntideva in early modern philosophy (keeping in mind the resonance between 'nothingness' and the 'annihilation' invoked here):

> [A] limitation of power... prepares... the way to the infinite... and reopens the community that was obstructed for so long. A person who has intuited and known much, and can... further some individual thing for its own sake with all his power, can do nothing else than acknowledge that other things are also supposed to be there and be done for their own sake, because otherwise he would contradict himself. And when such a person has gone as far as he can with what he chose, it will scarcely escape him at the peak of perfection that the object of his choice is nothing without the rest. This acknowledgment of another realm and the annihilation of what is one's own... are not possible without a dim presentiment of the universe and must necessarily precipitate a... more definite longing for the infinite, for the one in the all. (67)

The fact that Schleiermacher stresses the 'annihilation of what is one's own' (elsewhere translated as 'annihilation *of the personal*') seems to indicate both an acceptance of a no-self premise, and a moral reading of the rest of the passage. This phrase suggests that when he says "the object of [one's] choice is nothing without the rest", he does not mean that fulfilment of an agent's goal requires fulfilment of *that* agent's other goals. The things that are 'to be done' for their own sake include the great many things that have final or intrinsic value, on this view, for other beings (or just for being[40]), and thus have as much value as anything that concerns the agent directly, and with a kind of value that nonetheless calls on the agent's moral attention.

As we saw, Spinoza's own language is less moralistic than this, and less moralistic than many Buddhist texts. But for that reason, it may not be Spinoza himself, but instead the Spinozists of the late eighteenth century, who represent the most striking convergence with Buddhist altruism or with Buddhist impartial compassion. Schleiermacher's adoption of the hypothetical/categorical distinction in morality, which came to him via Kant, may seem to distance his approach from that of Buddhist ethicists. But if nothing else, it indicates a possible immunity to the *atipada* problem; and with greater scrutiny of that problem and related concerns, we

---

[39] Forster (2010, 324 ff.); Karl Ameriks has gone further, suggesting that Schleiermacher basically *rejected* claims about individuality (Ameriks 2012, 44–49).

[40] As some deep ecologists might say (see Chapter 13 for contemporary views in ecology with either Spinozist premises – somewhat akin to Schleiermacher's – and/or Buddhist premises).

may see an opportunity for Buddhist ethicists to gain insight from a cross-cultural exchange which, in the historical phases considered here, had ethical insight flowing mainly in the other direction.

We had said our last task would be to show that historians of philosophy 'rarely appreciate' the extent to which the impact of what Schleiermacher calls 'oriental mysticism' was felt in the areas of moral, social and political philosophy, in the nineteenth century. Of course, they appreciate the role of Schopenhauer; although he is not best remembered for social and political philosophy.[41] And historians are aware of Schlegel's role in early nineteenth-century philosophy, though there is a familiar anticlimax: Schlegel turned to Catholicism after his 'orientalizing' romantic phase, and exchanged his revolutionary liberal political theory for a moribund conservativism. Post-revolutionary narratives along those lines tend to obscure the impact that other orientalizing Spinozists had. Through the intermediary of Coleridge, John Stuart Mill developed a romantically inflected form of impartial altruism; Rudolf Steiner invoked Goethe and others while developing one of the earliest forms of environmental ethics in the West; and Schleiermacher paved the way for various forms of liberal idealism that were universalist (both in terms of cultural bases and the scope of moral concern) without being either narrowly Kantian or narrowly utilitarian. A thorough account of how both Hindu and Buddhist ideas informed these developments has yet to be told; but we hope to have shown that when it is told, it will have to highlight multiple sources rather than only Asian sources, and that, in addition to the crucial Spinozist impetus, there were inherently interesting receptions and modulations of Asian sources, such as those that infused the modern period *grace à* Bayle and Diderot, who were themselves agents of Spinoza's legacy.

References

Ameriks, Karl. 2012. 'The Question is Whether a Purely Apparent Person is Possible'. In *Spinoza and German Idealism,* ed. E. Forster and Y.Y. Melamed. Cambridge: Cambridge University Press.

Anacker, Stephan, ed. 1984. *Seven Works of Vasubandhu.* Delhi: Motilal Banarsidass.

Bayle, Pierre. 1697. *Dictionnaire historique et critique* (8th ed., with 1702 revisions). Reproduced at http://artfl-project.uchicago.edu/content/dictionnaire-de-bayle (ed. ARTFL Project at University of Chicago).

———. [1697] 1965. *Historical and Critical Dictionary: Selections.* Trans. Richard H. Popkin. New York: Bobbs-Merrill.

Bernier, François. [1671] 2008. Suite des Mémoires sur l'Empire du grand Mogol. In *Un Libertin dans l'Inde Moghole: Les Voyages de François Bernier,* ed. F. Tinguely. Paris: Chandeigne.

Citton, Yves. 2006. *L'Envers de la Liberté: L'Invention d'un imaginaire spinoziste dans la France des Lumières.* Paris: Éditions Amsterdam.

Comte-Sponville, André. 2006. *L'esprit de l'athéisme: Introduction à une spiritualité sans Dieu.* Paris: Albin Michel.

---

[41] As for his ethics, though, see the chapter in this volume by Douglas Berger (Chap. 8).

————. 2015. *Du tragique au matérialisme (et retour)*. Paris: Presses Universitaires de France.

Conche, Marcel. 1987/1997. *Nietzsche et le bouddhisme*. Paris: Encre Marine.

————. 2016. *Penser encore: Sur Spinoza et autres sujets*. Paris: Encre Marine.

Davis, Gordon. 2018. The *Atipada* Problem in Buddhist Metaethics. *Journal of Buddhist Ethics (forthcoming)*.

de Montaigne, Michel. [1580] 2003a. An Apology for Raymond Sebond. In *The Complete Essays*. Trans. M.A. Screech. London: Penguin.

————. [1588] 2003b. On Vanity. In *The Complete Essays*. Trans. M.A. Screech. London: Penguin.

de Spinoza, Benedictus. [1677] 1985. *The Collected Works of Spinoza*, vol. 1. Trans. Edwin M. Curley. Princeton: Princeton University Press.

Della Rocca, Michael. 2012. Rationalism, Idealism, Monism, and Beyond. In *Spinoza and German Idealism*, ed. E. Forster & Y.Y Melamed. Cambridge: Cambridge University Press.

Deprun, Jean. 1996. Diderot, Malebranche, Leibniz: 'Volonté Générale', 'Miroirs Vivants'. In *Ici et ailleurs: le dix-huitième siècle au présent*, ed. H. Nakagawa, S. Ichikawa, Y. Sumi, and J. Okami. Tokyo: Le Comité Coordinateur des mélanges J. Proust.

Diderot, Denis. 1753. Chinois, Philosophie des. In *Encyclopédie ou dictionnaire raisonné des sciences, des arts et des* métiers, vol. III, ed. Diderot. Paris: Le Breton et al. Reproduced at https://encyclopedie.uchicago.edu (ARTFL Encyclopedie Project, ed. R. Morrissey).

————. 1765. Japonois, Philosophie des. In *Encyclopedié ou dictionnaire raisonné des sciences, des arts et des metiers*, vol. VIII, ed. Diderot. Paris/Neuchatel: Le Breton et al. Reproduced at https://encyclopedie.uchicago.edu (ARTFL Encyclopédie Project, ed. R. Morrissey).

———— [1751–] 2002. *Encyclopédie: Âme, Beau, Certitude, Droit Naturel*. ed. P. Dupouey. Saint-German-du-Puy: Nathan.

Forster, Michael N. 2010. *After Herder: Philosophy of Language in the German Tradition*. Oxford: Oxford University Press.

————. 2012. Herder and Spinoza. In *Spinoza and German Idealism*, ed. E. Forster and Y.Y Melamed. Cambridge: Cambridge University Press.

Forster, E., and Y.Y. Melamed, eds. 2012. *Spinoza and German Idealism*. Cambridge: Cambridge University Press.

Fraenkel, Carlos. 2012. *Philosophical Religions from Plato to Spinoza: Reason, Religion and Autonomy*. Cambridge: Cambridge University Press.

Goethe, J. [1811–] 1920. *Poetry and Truth*. Trans. J. Oxenford. Chicago: J.H. Moore.

Goodman, Charles. 2009. *Consequences of Compassion: An Interpretation and Defense of Buddhist Ethics*. Oxford: Oxford University Press.

Herder, J.G. [1787/1800] 1940. *God: Some Conversations*. Trans. F.H. Burkhardt. New York: Veritas Press.

Hessing, Siegfried, ed. 1977. *Speculum Spinozanum 1677–1977*. London: Routledge.

Israel, Jonathan I. 2001. *Radical Enlightenment*. Oxford: Oxford University Press.

————. 2011. *Democratic Enlightenment: Philosophy, Revolution and Human Rights 1750–1790*. Oxford: Oxford University Press.

Kisner, Matthew J. 2009. Spinoza's Benevolence: The Rational Basis for Acting to the Benefit of Others. *Journal of the History of Philosophy* 47 (4): 549–567.

Kow, Simon. 2016. *China in Early Enlightenment Political Thought*. New York: Routledge.

Lai, Yuen-Ting. 1985. The Linking of Spinoza to Chinese Thought by Bayle and Malebranche. *Journal of the History of Philosophy* 23 (2): 151–178.

Lloyd, Genevieve. 1994. *Part of Nature: Self-knowledge in Spinoza's Ethics*. Ithaca: Cornell University Press.

Mack, Michael. 2010. *Spinoza and the Specters of Modernity*. London: Continuum.

Malebranche, Nicolas. [1680] 1992a.. *Traité de la nature et de la grâce*. In Malebranche, *Œuvres*, v. II, ed. G. Rodis-Lewis. Paris: Gallimard.

————. [1708] 1992b. *Entretien d'un philosophe chrétien, et d'un philosophe chinois*. In Malebranche, *Œuvres*, v. II, ed. G. Rodis-Lewis. Paris: Gallimard.

———. [1688] 1997. *Dialogues on Metaphysics and on Religion*. Trans. D. Scott, Ed. N. Jolley. Cambridge: Cambridge University Press.

Maverick, Lewis. 1939. A Possible Chinese Source of Spinoza's Doctrine. *Revue de littérature comparée* 19: 417–428.

Melamed, S.M. 1933. *Spinoza and Buddha: Visions of a Dead God*. Chicago: University of Chicago Press.

Montaigne, Michel. [1580] 2003a. An Apology for Raymond Sebond. In *The Complete Essays*. Trans. M.A. Screech. London: Penguin.

———. [1588] 2003b. On Vanity. In *The Complete Essays*. Trans. M.A. Screech. London: Penguin.

Moore, Adrian W. 2012. *The Evolution of Modern Metaphysics: Making Sense of Things*. New York: Cambridge University Press.

Nadler, Steven. 2014. The Lives of Others: Spinoza on Benevolence as a Rational Virtue. In *Essays on Spinoza's Ethical Theory*, ed. Matthew J. Kisner and Andrew Youpa, 41–56. Oxford: Oxford University Press.

Naess, Arne. 2008. Through Spinoza to Mahayana Buddhism, or Through Mahayana Buddhism to Spinoza? Reprinted in A. Naess, *The Ecology of Wisdom* (ed. A. Drengson and B. Devall). Berkeley: Counterpoint.

Needham, Joseph. 1954–. *Science and Civilization in China*. Cambridge: Cambridge University Press.

Néria, William. 2014. *Plotin, Shankara, Spinoza: Le Dépassement de la raison et l'expérience de l'absolu*. Paris: Les Deux Océans.

Newlands, Samuel. 2011. Hegel's Idealist Reading of Spinoza. *Philosophy Compass* 6 (2): 100–108.

Perkins, Franklin. 2004. *Leibniz and China: A Commerce of Light*. Cambridge: Cambridge University Press.

Ryan, Todd. 2009. *Pierre Bayle's Cartesian Metaphysics: Rediscovering Early Modern Philosophy*. New York: Routledge.

Śāntideva. 1995. *The Bodhicaryāvatāra*. Trans. Kate Crosby and Andrew Skilton. Oxford: Oxford University Press.

Schleiermacher, F. [1800] 1988. *On Religion: Speeches to Its Cultured Despisers*. Trans. R. Crouter. Cambridge: Cambridge University Press.

Schopenhauer, A. [1818] 1969. *The World as Will and Representation*, vol. 1. Trans. E.F.J. Payne. New York: Dover.

Scruton, Roger. 1986. *Spinoza*. Oxford: Oxford University Press.

———. 1999. *Spinoza*. New York: Routledge.

Siderits, Mark. 2003. *Personal Identity and Buddhist Philosophy: Empty Persons*. Aldershot: Ashgate.

Sikka, Sonia. 2011. *Herder on Humanity and Cultural Difference: Enlightened Relativism*. Cambridge: Cambridge University Press.

Spinoza, Benedictus. [1677] 1985. *The Collected Works of Spinoza*, vol. 1. Trans. Edwin M. Curley. Princeton: Princeton University Press.

Suzuki, D. T. (trans.). 1932. *The Lankavatara Sutra: A Mahāyāna Text*. London: Routledge & Kegan Paul.

Vasubandhu. 1984. *Madhyānta-Vibhāga-Bhāṣya*. Trans. S. Anacker. In S. Anacker (ed./trans.) *Seven Works of Vasubandhu*. Delhi: Motilal Banarsidass.

Vernière, Paul. 1954. *Spinoza et la pensée française avant la Révolution*. Paris: Presses universitaires de France.

Wetlesen, Jon. 1979. *The Sage and the Way: Spinoza's Ethics of Freedom*. Assen: Van Gorcum.

Wienpahl, Paul. 1979. *The Radical Spinoza*. New York: New York University Press.

Willson, A. Leslie. 1964. *A Mythical Image: The Ideal of India in German Romanticism*. Durham: Duke University Press.

Wolfson, H.A. (1934). *The Philosophy of Spinoza*, 2 vols. Cambridge: Harvard University Press.

Chapter 6
Hume as a Western Mādhyamika: The Case from Ethics

Jay L. Garfield

6.1 The Irrelevance of LaFlèche

I am not the only person to have argued that Hume is a kind of Western Mādhyamika (Garfield 1990, 2011, 2015). And indeed, in teaching Hume at Tibetan universities in India, I have found that Tibetan scholars instantly recognize him as a *kind* of Mādhyamika, even if they are not sure that there is a ready-made *grub 'mtha* (doxographic) box within that camp into which to fit him. Most of the grounds for this classification are metaphysical, concerning Hume's accounts of causation, the nature of personal identity and his account of the construction of the idea of external objects, each of which is strongly redolent of the thought of Candrakīrti, although with hints of Bhāvaviveka as well.[1]

Alison Gopnik has recently argued that this is no accident of history (Gopnik 2010). She points out that Hume was resident at La Flèche Abbey at precisely the time that Ippolito Desideri was in residence following his remarkable sojourn in Tibet, and hypothesizes that Hume in fact borrowed all of his apparently Buddhist

---

Thanks to Gordon Davis for helpful comments on an earlier draft of this essay.

[1] My Tibetan colleagues note that in certain respects—e.g. Hume's taking convention as a kind of explanatory bedrock, and his refusal to take it for granted that we always have concepts corresponding to our words—he appears to be a good thal 'gyur pa/Prāsaṅgika; but in other respects, e.g. his apparent willingness to accept some convention-independent phenomena for granted—such as impressions or events—he appears more like a rang gyud pa/Svatantrika.

J. L. Garfield (✉)
Smith College, Northampton, MA, USA

Harvard Divinity School, Cambridge, MA, USA

University of Melbourne, Melbourne, VIC, Australia

Central Institute of Higher Tibetan Studies, UP, India
e-mail: jgarfield@smith.edu

ideas from Buddhism as related to him by Desideri.[2] Were this true, it would be one of the more remarkable instances of direct borrowing of Buddhist ideas by an early modern philosopher, alongside that of Leibniz's virtual plagiarism of the *Huayan (Avataṃsaka) Sūtra* from rough translations sent to him by his Jesuit correspondents in China.[3]

Unfortunately, however, Gopnik's historical argument is at best tendentious. For one thing, every one of the Humean ideas that Gopnik urges is borrowed from Tibet is also present in very much the form that Hume develops it in the Western skeptical tradition, developed at length by Sextus Empiricus and reported by Bayle. We know that Hume read Bayle and Sextus with care, and so there is no reason to think that he would not simply have borrowed the arguments he advances from them. So the Tibetan hypothesis is not necessary in order to explain the phenomenon.

For another thing, Hume, as we know, was a merciless critic of the Christian church, and particularly of Catholicism, and was more than willing to bite the hand that fed him. If he had discovered at LaFlèche that ideas he was advancing were endorsed by Buddhists—those condemned as pagan heretics by the church—he would surely have reveled in the opportunity to elevate pagan learning over Catholic doctrine. That he does not suggests strongly that he was not in fact aware of the affinities of his own ideas to those of Buddhism.

Nonetheless, as McEvilley (2002) and Beckwith (2015) have each persuasively argued, there is *something* to Gopnik's claim of influence. It is just that the links in this chain are older than she imagines. There is good (but again, not demonstrative) reason, including the testimony of Diogenes Laertius, to believe that there was interaction—perhaps mediated by Alexander's campaigns, perhaps by the Persian court, perhaps in Greek Bactria—between classical Greek and Indian Buddhist philosophers. Indeed, as Beckwith argues, classical skepticism may be an Indian import to Greece. Hume sits firmly in the Western skeptical tradition and borrows not only a general Pyrrhonian outlook, but many specific Pyrrhonian dialectical tropes. So there is good reason to believe that the confluence between Humean and Buddhist insights is not accidental, even if not mediated by Desideri's time in Tibet and Hume's sojourn in LaFlèche.

6.2   Metaphysics and Ethics in Hume and Madhyamaka

I am not interested here in exploring further the metaphysical affinities between Hume and Madhyamaka philosophers such as Nāgārjuna, Āryadeva or Candrakīrti. But it is worth thinking for a moment about the connection between metaphysics and ethics, both in Hume's philosophy and in the Indian Madhyamaka tradition.

---

[2] See Desideri (2010) for a detailed account of Desideri's time in Tibet and fascinating observations on Buddhism.

[3] See Liu (2002) for more on this affinity.

The homologies are striking and they set the stage for further reflection. In each case we find that the account of the status of the self and of the role of convention (or custom) in constituting both our social phenomenology andontology is fundamental to developing ethical theory. Let us take the Madhyamaka case first. Both Āryadeva and Śāntideva take the emptiness of the self and the failure to find any substantial referent for 'I' ethically significant.

Āryadeva argues that the emptiness of the self renders all self-grasping irrational, and hence egoism irrational. On the other hand, in chapter VI of *Catuḥṣataka (Four Hundred Stanzas)*, he takes the fact that persons exist conventionally to be a good reason to care about sentient beings. The fact that we do not exist ultimately hence defuses egoism; the fact that we do exist conventionally grounds the possibility of care (Cowherds 2016).

Śāntideva takes a similar route, but goes further along it. In chapter 8 of his *Bodhicaryāvatāra* (90–103), he argues that the absence of any self means that suffering, *per se,* is the object of care, and hence there can be no question of the ontology of selves grounding ethics. Instead, he argues, we construct sentient beings and perceive them as loci of suffering or happiness only through the force of mundane convention. Seen through the lens of convention there is compelling reason to relieve suffering and so to posit sentient beings as its bearer; seen from the ultimate point of view, there is no rational basis for preferring self, or one's own happiness or relief from suffering over others, or theirs. Śāntideva argues that it follows that universal concern is the only rational moral response. (*Ibid.*)

So, whether we think of conventional existence as the *absence* of any ultimate reality of self or others, or as the *positive reality* of the mundane world as a locus for moral action, Indian Mādhyamikas take convention to structure the way we experience the world morally and the way we respond to the world we experience. The union of emptiness and conventional reality, and the emptiness, but conventional reality of suffering and of sentient beings together ground the bodhisattva's ethics of *karuṇā* or care, and its universal scope.

Hume agrees that metaphysics grounds ethics. Despite the remarkable convergence between Humean and Mādhyamika accounts of the self, however, and despite remarkable convergences in their respective approaches to ethics, Hume's account of the role of metaphysical ideas in ethical thought is different. Hume urges that we begin with natural sympathy, a biological response of care for those close to us. But natural sympathy, like gravity, Hume believes, obeys an inverse square law. In order to extend that sympathy into a sense of justice—that is, to universalize concern— serious moral education and the cultivation of the moral imagination is necessary. (*Treatise 2.1.7, 3.2.1, 3.3.1*).[4]

---

[4]One must be careful not to oversell this disanalogy, however. Śāntideva devotes chapter 8 of *Bodhicaryāvatāra (How to Lead an Awakened Life)* to meditation precisely because he believes that it is important to repeatedly visualize the consequences of vice and virtue, and the interrelatedness of sentient beings, in order to counteract egoism by cultivating care. So Hume and Śāntideva agree about the need for cultivation, and indeed about the role of the imagination in that cultivation. They disagree about the nature of that cultivation, with Hume taking that process to be social, and Śāntideva taking it to be contemplative.

6.3   Moral Perception in Hume and Madhyamaka

Moreover, for both Hume and the Mādhyamikas, ethical training is directed at the reform of moral *perception* through the recruitment of the *moral imagination* (Cowherds 2016, Garfield 2012a, 2012b, 2015). Once again, let us begin in India. The bodhisattva comes to *see* herself as empty of intrinsic reality; comes to *see* other sentient beings as empty, interdependent loci of suffering, and responds ethically to those perceptions. This transformation is accomplished through meditation on emptiness, meditation devoted to the cultivation of awareness of others, and meditation directed specifically at the development of *muditā* (sympathetic joy), *metta* (beneficence) and *karuṇā* (care). The first leads one to see others' achievements and happiness as sources of one's own; the second leads one to take others' well-being as one's own ends; the third leads one to take others' suffering as one's own motivation for action. The consequence is the transformation of one's experience of the world from that conditioned by egocentricity and egoism to one permeated by a sense of interconnection with and concern for others.

It is important to note that in these Mahāyāna practices, the principal vehicle for reforming perception, for eliminating the superimposition of self-grasping, and of positing intrinsic identity, of seeing oneself as the unique subjective center of an objective universe, is the imagination. We *imagine* that all sentient beings are our mothers; we *imagine* ourselves and other as corpses, as collections of parts and even particles, as propelled by our *kleśas, etc.* (Garfield 2010/2011).[5]

Hume also recruits the moral imagination in the transformation of moral perception. He argues that when we develop a sense of justice, we extend natural sympathy to others by imagining them to be like us, by focusing on that we share with them. This imaginative reconception of others leads us in turn to see them as objects of sympathy, and so to respond morally to others. It is hard to overstate how unusual Hume's approach to ethics is in the Western tradition, grounding moral sensibility in the imagination and perception. The affinity to Madhyamaka ethical theory as set out by Śāntideva and his commentators Prajñākaramati and Kamalaśīla, who ties moral development even more explicitly to imaginative meditative practice, is striking.[6]

6.4   The Cultivation of Passions in Hume and Madhyamaka

A second analogy between Hume's approach to ethics and that of Mādhyamikas such as Candrakīrti and Śāntideva is their shared commitment to the view that the cultivation of the passions is central to ethical development. Note that this is a very

---

[5] Of course this is not unique to Mahāyāna ethical cultivation. We also see the imagination at work in tantra.

[6] See Prajñākaramati's *Pañjika* to the *Bodhicaryāvatāra* (Oldmeadow 1994) and Kamalaśīla's *Bhavanākrama (Stages of Meditation)* (Sharma 1997).

particular way of understanding the process of ethical maturation and the subject matter of ethics. While in the West the view that the cultivation of the passions is ethically important is not original with Hume—we find anticipations in Aristotle and especially in Stoic and Epicurean ethical theory—it is in Hume's work that we find the most comprehensive and sophisticated account of ethics as *principally* a discipline of affective cultivation.

For Kant, ethical development involves the subordination of the will to reason and the elimination of the passions as springs of action. For Mill and the consequentialists, as well, moral maturity involves a disposition to rational calculation of the consequences of actions. And while Aristotle, Epicurus, Epictetus and Marcus Aurelius would all agree that ethical cultivation involves the transformation and shaping of the emotions, each of them also sees the development of knowledge, and such capacities as moral strength as central to that enterprise.

Hume, on the other hand, urges that morality begins with our natural sentiments, our affections for those close to us, and develops by extending those sentiments to encompass others. Once again, it is the imagination, and not reason, that is the engine for this extension, as we learn to see those more distant from us as akin to those more proximal. Although reason plays an important role in this transformation, that role is instrumental, not constitutive. Reason is useful in transforming the tendencies of our passions, but it that affective transformation in which moral development consists. The imaginative exercises that Śāntideva urges on us (imagining other sentient beings as our mothers; imagining the suffering of others, imagining our own death, etc) are exactly the kinds of exercises we can imagine a Humean parent employing in raising and socializing her children.

In *Enquiry V,* Hume remarks that these moral sentiments must be originally natural, both in order for the raw material for moral development to be present and for the very practice of regarding such motives as benevolence as good, and motives such as malice as morally bad. For, he argues, to take an affective response as morally salutary is just for us to take it as a source of natural pleasure on contemplation; to take a response as morally vicious is to recoil from it. If these antecedent individual and collective tendencies were not generally present, morality could never get off the ground. Moreover, he points out (p. 47) someone who has the opposite view of moral sentiments is not so much deficient in understanding as *inhuman.* But of course to get from natural sympathy to a universal sense of justice takes work, and that is the work of reason. But even to value that work requires antecedently that we see it as worthwhile.

Moreover, the important role Hume assigns to reason in this process has an important parallel in Buddhist literature. Hume famously argues that "reason always is, and must be, a slave to the passions," and it might therefore be thought that on a Humean account reason can provide no guidance at all in moral development. But this would be wrong. As Hume makes clear, reason has an important, although *indirect* role here. It is reason that tells us that the cultivation of the passions in the service of the extension of natural sympathy into justice and benevolence is a good thing. That is why we bother to do it. As Hume remarks, it makes civilization, commerce and a truly human life possible. While reason may not be the spring of action, it is a guide to policy.[7]

Things aren't much different on the Madhyamaka side. Once again, Śāntideva aims to cultivate our passions and our ways of seeing. When I encounter someone I might plausibly take to be an enemy, I should see a friend; when someone harms me, I should receive that harm as a benefit, as a chance to practice patience. These reactions are cultivated ways of perceiving, cultivated emotional response. My own actions in return are driven by these perceptions and affective responses. The affective side, for Śāntideva, holds the reins in the chariot of action, just as it does for Hume.

Nonetheless, Śāntideva *argues* that we ought to adopt these attitudes, and convinces us using *reason* that we ought to cultivate our perception and affective responses in this way (Cowherds 2016). Moreover, in *Bodhicaryāvatāra* (particularly in chapter VI) he offers us a multitude of arguments to use in meditation and in action to restrain ourselves from overhasty responses to insult and to lead us to act with beneficence. So, while reason may not in the end hold the reins, the charioteer is certainly trained by, and makes use of reason.

6.5   Taking the Conventional Seriously in Hume and Madhyamaka

There is one final homology between the Humean and the Madhyamaka ethical traditions, and it may be the most important of all, lying at the foundation of all of those just scouted. Hume, like any good Mādhyamika, establishes ethical truth at the conventional level of discourse, and regards ethical practice as dependent entirely on human conventions. Justice and benevolence, he argues, are artificial virtues, instituted by conventions, cultivated by social conventions and have no basis outside of those conventions.[8] Hume argues that while we have natural motives to pursue our narrow self-interest, and even that of those immediately near to us, but no natural motive to justice in general. He concludes the astute discussion in *Treatise* 3.2.1 as follows:

> From all this it follows, that we have naturally no real or universal motive for observing the laws of equity, but the very equity and merit of that observance; and as no action can be equitable or meritorious, where it cannot arise from some separate motive, there is here an

---

[7] We might also note that there is a parallel in the Humean and Madhyamaka accounts of the role of reason in action selection itself. In each case, *what* we desire or reject is determined by the moral passions. Reason (*upāya,* or practical wisdom) enters the picture to determine the means by which we can achieve those ends. This is the point of the "slave of the passions" remark.

[8] This, as I argue in 2012a and 2014, is a major difference between a Humean or Buddhist and a Kantian approach to ethics. For Kant, ethics is grounded in a transcendental realm, and in the reality and freedom of a unified self—a transcendental ego and ethical agent. For Hume and his Mādhyamika forebears, ethics is grounded in an understanding of the emptiness of the person, of the absence of such a self, and in the conventional reality of persons and suffering.

evident sophistry and reasoning in a circle. Unless, therefore, we will allow, that nature has establish'd a sophistry, and render'd it necessary and unavoidable, we must allow, that the sense of justice and injustice is not deriv'd from nature, but arises artificially, tho' necessarily from education, and human conventions. (*Treatise* 483)

But of course Hume mitigates this conclusion almost immediately, in a justly famous passage:

To avoid giving offence, I must here observe, that when I deny justice to be a natural *natural* only as oppos'd to *artificial*. In another sense of the word; as no principle of the human mind is more natural than a sense of virtue; so no virtue is more natural than justice. Mankind is an inventive species; and where an invention is obvious and absolutely necessary, it may as properly be said to be natural as any thing that proceeds from first principles, without the intervention of thought or reflexion. Tho' the rules of justice be *artificial*, they are not *arbitrary*. (484)

And this is how it has to be for Mādhyamikas as well. After all, persons have only conventional existence, actions have only conventional existence, as do their effects. Ethical cultivation is about cultivating our ability to engage with each other, and to proceed on the path to awakening. It is a matter for those of us in a conventional world, and ethical truth can only be conventional truth. As Āryadeva puts it in *Catuḥśataka VI*:

8. Whatever concerns the everyday world
    Is said to involve engagement.
    Whatever concerns the ultimate
    Is said to involve relinquishment.

9. When you Say "since everything is nonexistent, what's the use?"
    You have become afraid.
    But if actions existed [ultimately],
    This dharma could not engender abandonment.[9]

And to engage in the world ethically requires, both Āryadeva and Śāntideva emphasize, the understanding of selflessness in very much the sense of Hume, but also the cultivation of sentiments such as benevolence and justice. Just as Hume argues that the rejection of justice would be unnatural and irrational, Śāntideva, in Chapter VIII of *Bodhicaryāvatāra* argues that egoism would be fundamentally irrational[10]:

90 First, one should earnestly meditate
    On the similarity of self and others:
    Everyone, subject to similar happiness and suffering,
    Should be protected by me like myself

---

[9] Translations my own from the sDe dge edition.
[10] Translation from Cowherds 2016, pp. 59–60. See pp. 68–74 for the detailed reading of this passage as an argument for the irrationality of egoism.

91   Just as the body, having many parts, divided into hands etc.
      Should be protected as one.
      The world, though divided, is undivided
      With respect to the nature of suffering and happiness.

92   Even if my own suffering
      Does not hurt others' bodies,
      That suffering is still mine and is hard to bear
      Because of self-love.

93   Just so, even though
      I do not experience
      The suffering of another myself, it is still his;
      His suffering is hard to bear because of self-love.

94   The suffering of others should be eliminated by me,
      Because it is suffering like my own suffering.
      I should help others
      Because they are sentient beings, as I am a sentient being.

95   When the happiness of myself and others
      Are pleasing in the same way,
      Then what is so special about me
      That I merely strive for my own happiness?

96   When the fear and suffering of myself and others
      Are not pleasing in the same way
      Then what is so special about me
      That I defend myself, but not others?

97   If they are not defended
      Because their suffering does not hurt me,
      So why defend against the suffering of a future body
      That does not hurt me?

98   It is vain fantasy
      To think "that is me then."
      Only another died
      From which only another is born.

99   If it is thought that only the suffering which is his
      Should be protected,
      When a pain in the foot does not belong to the hand,
      Why should it protect that?

100 Even though it is wrong,
This happens because of self-construction [ahaṃkāra]."
But that which is wrong, whether one's own or others',
Should be avoided as far as possible.

101 A continuum and collection,
Just like such things as a series or an army, are unreal.
The one for whom there is suffering does not exist.
Therefore to whom will that suffering belong?

102 Since all ownerless sufferings are
Without distinction,
They should be alleviated just because of being suffering,
What restriction can be made in that case?

103 "Why should suffering be alleviated?"
Because it is undisputed by everyone that
If it is to be alleviated, all of it is to be alleviated.
After all, I am just like everyone else.

So there is another deep affinity between Hume's approach to ethics and that of the Indian Mādhyamika ethicists: While neither Hume nor Śāntideva takes reason to provide original ethical motives, and while each takes ethical cultivation to be a cultivation of the passions, each takes that cultivation itself to be rational, and a refusal to do so to be fundamentally irrational. That is, while each analyzes *being morally good* affectively, each answers the question "why be good?" by arguing that it is the only rational option for human beings.

6.6 What It Is to Be a Mādhyamika Ethicist

What is distinctive about Madhyamaka ethics? We might say that it is the installation of *karuṇā*, or *care,* as the central ethical virtue, and of engaged *bodhicitta*[11] as the central mode of ethical being. Here is a way to make that explicit. The fundamental ethical stance for a Madhyamaka is one of *care* for others, and one in which we find ourselves connected directly to the wellbeing and the suffering of others in perception and immediate affective response. It is to *see* the world through the eyes

---

[11]As I argue in 2010/2011, Śāntideva distinguishes in the first chapter of *Bodhicaryāvatāra* between *aspirational* and *engaged* bodhicitta on the basis of whether or not the agent has cultivated a perception of phenomena as empty of intrinsic reality and so a spontaneous attitude of care towards others issuing from a decentering of the self.

of a bodhisattva; to *respond* to it with the heart of a bodhisattva; and to *act* in it with the commitment of a bodhisattva. And it is to cultivate that stance because on reflection it is the most reasonable one to adopt.

This account centers our interconnections, our joint membership in human and animal communities and the plasticity of our perceptual and affective responses to one another. It is also to take a world in which we engage for one another's benefit as a better world than one in which we engage egoistically, not simply because the world is happier that way, but because the nature of human reality demands that as a rational response to our shared humanity. This is Śāntideva's insight, and it is Hume's. Annette Baier (1987) once remarked that Hume is the ideal feminist philosopher precisely on the grounds that he fronts our social relations, the importance of childrearing in moral development and the centrality of affect in ethics. He is also the ideal Buddhist philosopher, not merely as a metaphysician, but also as an ethicist.

6.7   The Passions and the Self

I conclude with what might be the deepest connection of all between Hume and the Buddhist tradition, the remarkable insight that our sense of self is not the *cause* of our passions, but is rather their *effect*. This is a profound idea and is not immediately apparent. There is good reason on the Buddhist side even to doubt it. After all, the primal confusion that lies at the root of *samsāra* is often represented as the cause of attraction and aversion, and hence of the other *kleśas*, or dysfunctional cognitive states. But this is overhasty. For one thing, it is worth noting that even on the *Bhāvacakra*—the Buddhist representation of the wheel of life—the three are represented at the hub of the image as *mutually reinforcing*. The point of that remarkable graphic map of human moral psychology (which I discuss at greater length in 2010/2011) is that moral immaturity is due to the mutually reinforcing effects of these primary *kleśas*, and the resultant incessant cycling through maladaptive emotional states grounded in an egocentric view of our place in the moral universe.

And when we turn to Śāntideva's exposition of this view in *Bodhicaryāvatāra*, especially in the first three chapters of that text, we see passions such as fear and anger as giving rise to the sense of ego, not necessarily arising from it. Fear of death causes us to posit something permanent, a self, which taken to be continuous in life, and perhaps even surviving death, a self that then becomes the anchor of egoism at the center of each of our respective universes. An emotion of anger arises; we justify it by positing a self that has been offended. This is what Śāntideva has in mind when he says, in chapter VI, on patience and anger.

24.   Nobody becomes angry having formed
      The intention to become angry;
      Nor does anger simply occur having formed
      The intention for it to occur.

Here, rGyal tshab comments, "…Moreover, it is explained that it (anger) is the condition first of the arising of the self, and then of the arising of the dysfunctional states." (1999, p.188)

25. All vicious and evil deeds
Of whatever kind
Arise from circumstances and conditions.
Nothing exists independently.

26. Nor does the collection of conditions form
The intention, "I shall come into being."
Nor does that which produces it do so
Having formed the intention, "I will produce."

27. Neither the so-called fundamental substance one might posit,
Nor the self one might imagine to exist
Comes into existence having formed the intention,
"Now I will come into existence."

rGyal tshab explains (pp, 189–190) that this means that it makes no sense to think that the self comes into existence by itself or from antecedent conditions, since it itself is non-existent. Instead, the idea that there is a self is what requires explanation, and the explanation of that is not the intention to posit the self, but rather the egocentric affective states themselves. The illusion of self, after all, like any illusion, requires explanation, and when we press hard in Buddhist philosophy, that explanation lies, as rGyl tshab's teacher Tsongkhapa (2006) emphasizes, not in bad philosophy, but in an innate tendency to reify, and that tendency is called into action not by reason, but by affect.

Hume agrees, and pushes even deeper into the matter than do most Buddhist philosophers. In the *Treatise,* considering the relation of the passions to the self, he writes:

> 'Tis evident that pride and humility, tho' directly contrary, have the same OBJECT. This object is self, or that succession of related ideas and impressions of which we have in intimate memory and consciousness. (277)

…

> But tho' that connected succession of perceptions, which we call *self,* be always the object of these two passions, 'tis impossible that it be their CAUSE, or sufficient alone to excite them. (277–278)

That is, even though the contents of the passions are always *directed towards* the self, they are not brought about *by* the self. And one reason for that, on a Humean view, as on a Buddhist view, is simply that while intentional contents can be non-existent (and the self as an intentional content must be),[12] only that which exists can be causally efficacious, and the self, according to Hume, and according to his Buddhist forebears, does not exist. Hume emphasizes the creative power of the passions to bring about this illusion:

> We must therefore make a distinction betwixt the cause and the object of these passions; betwixt that idea that excites them, and that to which they direct their view, when excited. Pride and humility, being once rais'd, immediately turn our attention to ourself, and regard that as their ultimate and final object, but there is something farther that is requisite in order to raise them: Something, which is peculiar to one of the passions... (278)

It is when the passions arise that we are tempted to posit this object for them, an object that we then take to be the center of our world. This, Hume observes, in a reprise of the idea that to posit a self is an act of reflex primal confusion, is always a confusion of object with cause. The causes of the passions, he observes, in complete agreement with Śāntideva, lie without:

> To begin with the causes of pride and humility; we may observe, that their most obvious and remarkable property is the vast variety of *subjects* on which they may be plac'd. Every valuable quality of the mind, whether of the imagination, judgment, memory or disposition; wit, good sense, learning, courage, justice, integrity; all these are the causes of pride; and their opposites of humility. Nor are these passions confin'd to the mind, but extend their view to the body likewise. A man may be proud of his beauty, strength, agility, good mien, address in dancing, riding, fencing...But this is not all. The passions looking farther, comprehend whatever objects are in the least ally'd or related to us. Our country, family, children, relations, riches, gardens, houses, horses, dogs, cloaths; any of these may become a cause either of pride or of humility. (278–279)

And like Śāntideva and Tsongkhapa, Hume thinks that it is part of our biological (or what we might call in Sanskrit our *karmic)* inheritance that we respond to these causes by positing the self. Here is Hume on primal, innate *ahaṃkāra:*

> That we may comprehend this the better, we must suppose, that nature has given to the organs of the human mind, a certain disposition fitted to produce a peculiar impression or emotion, which we call *pride:* To this idea, she as assigned a certain idea, *viz.,* that of *self,* which it never fails to produce. (287)

It is one thing to see Hume as a Buddhist metaphysician. That view has become commonplace. It is still more interesting, I think, to see him as a Buddhist ethicist. But the deepest affinity of all, I conclude, is in the way that Hume and the most sophisticated Buddhist moral psychologists see the imagination and the passions working together to join these two domains of our lives. As Hume himself puts it:

> Tis remarkable, that the imagination and affections have a close union together, and that nothing, which affects the former, can be entirely indifferent to the latter. (424)

---

[12] Though this is not the place to go into this, there is a further nice affinity here: for, just as rGyal tshab claims (190) that the very idea of a self "makes no sense" and that the self "is incoherent, like the horns of a rabbit," Hume, of course, argues that we have no idea of a self in the first place. So, according to both Hume and rGyal tshab, this is an instance where the intentional content of our passions is not only non-existent, but *impossible*. And each explain this possibility through a nominalist understanding of conception and intentionality.

References

Baier, A. 1987. Hume, the Women's Moral Theorist. In *Women and Moral Theory*, ed. Eva Feder Kittay and Diana T. Meyers. Totowa: Roman and Littlefield.

Beckwith, Christopher. 2015. *Greek Buddha: Pyrrho's Encounter with Early Buddhism in Central Asia*. Princeton: Princeton University Press.

Cowherds. 2016. *Moonpaths: Ethics and Emptiness*. New York: Oxford University Press.

Desideri, I. 2010. *Mission to Tibet*, Trans. M Sweet and L Zwilling. Boston: Wisdom Publications.

Garfield, J. 1990. Epoché and Sunyatā: Scepticism East and West. *Philosophy East and West 40* (3): 285–307.

———. 2010/2011. What is it Like to be a Bodhisattva? *Journal of the International Association of Buddhist Studies* 33(1–2): 327–351.

———. 2011. *Western Idealism and its Critics*. Sarnath: Central University of Tibetan Studies Press.

———. 2012a. Mindfulness and Ethics: Attention, Virtue and Perfection. In *German as Achtsamkeit als Grundlage für ethisches Verhalten*, ed. M. Zimmermann, C. Spitz and S Schmidtt, Achtsamkeit, 227–250. Stuttgart: Hans Huber. 2012. and *Thai Journal of Buddhist Studies* vol. III, pp. 1–24.

———. 2012b. Buddhist Ethics. (in German as "Buddhistische Ethiks)" in *Polylog* 27: 98–110. (2012).

———. 2014. Just Another Word for Nothing Left to Lose: Freedom, Agency and Ethics for Mādhyamikas. In *Freedom of the Will in a Cross-Cultural Perspective*, ed. M. Dasti and E. Bryant, 164–185. New York: Oxford University Press.

———. 2015. *Engaging Buddhism: Why it Matters to Philosophy*. New York: Oxford University Press.

Gopnik, A. 2010. Could Hume have Known about Buddhism. *Huem Studies 35*: 5–28.

Hume, D. 1978. *A Treatise of Human Nature*, ed. P.H. Nidditch. Oxford: Oxford University Press.

———. 1983. *An Enquiry Concerning the Principles of Morals*, ed. J. Schneewind,. Indianapolis: Hackett.

Liu, Y. 2002. *Jesuits and Anti-Jesuits: Two Different Connections of Leibniz with China*, The Eigtheenth Century vpl. 34, n0, 2, 161–174.

Oldmeadow, P. 1994. *A Study of the Wisdom Chapter (Prajñāpāramitā Pariccheda) of Bodhicaryāvatārapañjikā of Prajñāpāramitā*. Unpublished doctoral dissertation, The Australian National University. https://openresearchrepository.anu.edu.au/handle/1885/110199.

rGyal tshab darma rinchen. 1999. *Byang chub sems pa'i spyod pa la 'jug pa'i rnam bshad rgyal sras 'jug ngogs (Entering the Great Bodhisattva Path: An Explanation of Bodhicaryāvatāra)*. Sarnath: Gelugpa Student Welfare Committee.

Sharma, P. 1997. *Bhavanakarkama of Kamalasila*. New Delhi: Aditya Parakashan.

Chapter 7
Anattā and Ethics: Kantian and Buddhist Themes

Emer O'Hagan

Are persons best understood as a series of happenings, or as having a kind of unity that merits the appellation "self"? Or to put the question another way: Is the self explainable entirely by reference to temporal units constitutive of it, or are these units better understood as temporal parts of a whole? In recent discussions of the nature of the self in Western philosophy, the distinction between constructionist and non-constructionist views marks these two options.[1] A constructionist like Derek Parfit argues that because the self is not united over time in any deep metaphysical way, it is not real, and a person is just the subject of experiences.[2] This view of persons is said to have moral implications because if persons aren't discrete wholes but merely a series of happenings, then it seems arbitrary to privilege the happenings in one series rather than another. It is morally problematic to concern myself with my own future states over others' future states; they are not really mine.

Christine Korsgaard, a non-constructionist, challenges Parfit's un-argued assumption, that it is only legitimate to treat future experiences as mine, and so serving as reasons for me, if metaphysically authorized.[3] Her Kantian position, acknowledging the significance of the practical standpoint denies that we are forced by the dictates of metaphysics to give up on the pragmatic unity of the self. Selves, she argues, are united by the unavoidable activity of practical reason; in deliberative choice we ask ourselves how to proceed and in doing so we adopt reasons for action

---

[1] As Marya Schechtman puts it: "Constructionist accounts view persons as constructs out of temporal parts, while non-constructionist accounts see these parts as abstractions from a unified person." In Schechtman, "Diversity in unity: practical unity and personal boundaries," *Synthese*, 162(3), 2008, 405–423; 406.

[2] Derek Parfit, *Reasons and Persons* (Oxford: Clarendon Press, 1984), 223.

[3] Christine Korsgaard, "Personal identity and the unity of agency: A Kantian response to Parfit," in her *Creating the Kingdom of Ends* (New York: Cambridge University Press, 1996), 363–397, 371.

E. O'Hagan (✉)
University of Saskatchewan, Saskatoon, SK, Canada
e-mail: emer.ohagan@usask.ca

© Springer International Publishing AG, part of Springer Nature 2018   145
G. F. Davis (ed.), *Ethics without Self, Dharma without Atman*, Sophia Studies
in Cross-cultural Philosophy of Traditions and Cultures 24,
https://doi.org/10.1007/978-3-319-67407-0_7

and simultaneously create a (more or less) united self. There are practical reasons for regarding myself as the same person who will occupy my body in the future: in order to act, it is practically necessary that I identify with some inclinations and not others, and in so doing I forge a connection between present and future selves. The unavoidable standpoint of choice thus provides grounds for commitment to a unified sense of self over time; the experience of deliberative choice is not the experience of something happening to oneself. One's reasons are themselves expressions of value that shape and connect present and future selves. Self-creation of this sort is simply a consequence of our nature as practically rational beings.

This distinction in Western philosophy's analysis of the self can also be seen in discussions of Buddhist views of the self which seem to be based on, or reject, an entirely metaphysical analysis of the nature of the self. In the next section, I will make a case that a distinction of this sort underlies two ways of understanding the doctrine of no-self: as a contemplative strategy, and as a metaphysical fact. I will not defend one view over the other, though I will offer some support for the contemplative strategy interpretation, aligning it with the practical standpoint. I will argue that within Kant's accounts of the self and ethics, we find something like the contemplative strategy in his duty of self-knowledge and his recognition of the existential significance of the individual's struggle to see and understand herself clearly. I will conclude by taking up some objections grounded in the claim that the Kantian emphasis on agency is inimical to the no-self doctrine. I hope to demonstrate that comparative studies of the nature of the self and ethics should go beyond metaphysics to address the standpoint of the agent who must choose how to think and act. Once we bring to the comparative project the relevance of the standpoint of action, Kantian affinities are illuminated, as are under-discussed aspects of Buddhist moral psychology.

7.1   No-Self and Norms Within Buddhist Thought

In all versions of Buddhist philosophy the nature of the self is a fundamental philosophical teaching, often drawn upon to understand practical matters, including how we should conceive of and respond to particular situations. The doctrine of no-self is the view that there is no self that is permanent, unchanging, or that identifies the essence of a person. The Pali Canon's "Anatta- lakkhana Sutta"[4] defends a form of anti-essentialism by pointing out that the five aggregates that constitute the basic parts of a person are impermanent, cannot be controlled, and so do not provide evidence of a stable self and thus cannot properly be considered "mine". What appears to us as a self is multiply conditioned by other factors, and so the belief in an essential self is a kind of delusion. According to Peter Harvey, in early Buddhism

---

[4] "The Characteristic of Nonself," in Bhikkhu Bodhi (trans.), *The Connected Discourses of the Buddha: A Translation of the Samyutta Nikaya*, (Boston: Wisdom Publications, 2000), 901–903. SN 22.59 (PTS: S iii 66).

the no-self doctrine is a rejection of the conception of self present in Brahmanical Upanishads and in Jain texts. He claims that it is a mistake to interpret the doctrine as explicitly asserting that there is no self, as this way of conceptualizing it short-circuits the process of coming to fully understand the doctrine: "the not-Self teaching is not a bald denial of Self, but a persistent undermining of any attempt to take anything as "Self," and thus be attached to it. It is a contemplative strategy to induce, in the end, a letting go of everything."[5]

This "contemplative strategy" view of the doctrine subordinates ontology to pragmatics. The point of the doctrine is to advance a method of coming to see more clearly the absence of an essential self in one's experience; the ethical implications are therefore primarily existential. On this interpretation, no-self is a technique of perception,[6] it endorses metaphysical quietism about the self, and is more like practical reasoning (reasoning aimed at what to do) than theoretical reasoning (reasoning governing belief). This quietist interpretation of the doctrine accords with the Buddha of the Pali Canon's refusal to answer the question whether or not there is a self[7] when asked outright, and with the *Majjhima Nikaya's* description of the person inappropriately caught in either the conviction that she has a self, or the conviction that she has no-self as in a "thicket of views, a wilderness of views, a contortion of views, a writhing of views, a fetter of views."[8] When Vacchagotta questions the Buddha as to whether or not the soul and body are the same the Buddha replies only that the speculation that soul and body are the same or different is a fetter of views beset by suffering – speculation is something that the Buddha has "put away".[9]

But while Early Buddhism advised against deeper inquiry into the nature of the self, not all Mahāyāna texts are steadfastly quietist. Some Scholars of Buddhism tell us that Aśvaghosa's *Buddhacarita* is among the first extant Buddhist texts to explicitly claim that there is no self.[10] Śāntideva's metaphysics of no-self in the *Bodhicaryāvatāra* offers a clear statement of no-self: "The notion 'it is the same me even then' is a false construction, since it is one person who dies, quite another who

[5] Peter Harvey, "Theravada Philosophy of Mind and the Person," in *Buddhist Philosophy: Essential Readings*, eds. William Edelglass and Jay Garfield (New York: Oxford University Press, 2009), 267.

[6] Ven. Thanissaro Bhikkhu argues for anattā as a "technique of perception" in "No- self or Not-self?", in *Noble Strategy* (Valley Center, Ca.: Metta Forest Monastery Publisher, 1999), 71–4.

[7] "Ananda (Is There a Self?)", in Bhikkhu Bodhi (trans.), *The Connected Discourses of the Buddha: A Translation of the Samyutta Nikaya* (Boston: Wisdom Publications, 2000), 1393–4. SN 44.10. By "quietism" I refer to the position in contemporary analytic philosophy that rejects the development of substantive philosophical theories, proposing instead that philosophical inquiry at best rids us of confusion, but does not provide knowledge.

[8] "All the taints," in Bhikkhu Nanamoli and Bhikkhu Bodhi (trans.), *The Middle Length Discourses of the Buddha: A Translation of the Majjhima Nikaya*, 3rd edition (Boston: Wisdom Publications, 2009), 91–96.

[9] "Aggivacchagotta Sutta," in Bhikkhu Nanamoli and Bhikkhu Bodhi (trans.), *The Middle Length Discourses of the Buddha: A Translation of the Majjhima Nikaya*, 3rd edition (Boston: Wisdom Publications, 2009), 590–602.

[10] Richard Robinson, Willard Johnson, and Thanissaro Bhikkhu, *Buddhist Religions: A Historical Introduction*, 5th edition (Toronto: Wadsworth Publishing, 2005), 91.

is born."[11] According to Śāntideva, the impersonal badness of suffering shows the irrationality of prioritizing ways to alleviate my own suffering over the suffering of others and helps us to see that we stand in the same relation to our future self that we stand in relation to others. For good reason this position has been compared to Derek Parfit's analysis of the self. As my philosophical focus is not whether the move beyond quietism is legitimated or required, but is rather how the analysis of the doctrine is shaped by the standpoint (theoretical or practical) brought to bear on the analysis, I will bypass these metaphysical and interpretive issues. Is the anattā doctrine completely explained by the (so called) metaphysical facts, or does it allow, or even require that the question of whether or not the self is real be addressed from the standpoint of practical reason?

To see the relevance of this distinction, consider Charles Goodman's view that a proper and complete understanding of the no-self doctrine leads to a theoretical, metaphysical stance which imposes constraints on ethical practice, and requires a consequentialist meta-ethic.[12] Goodman understands the doctrine to reject the reality of all composite entities, including persons, the relations between parts and whole being a function of how they are conceived by minds. Composite things can be said to exist as conventional truths, as they feature usefully in our lives, but selves and other composite entities "do not exist from the perspective of ultimate truth."[13] Goodman's interpretation of the doctrine rejects metaphysical quietism, claiming no-self as a metaphysical truth. Like Parfit, he holds that consequentialist ethical implications follow from this metaphysical fact. Because there are not ultimately any experiencers it cannot matter who experiences particular benefits and burdens, so we can ignore the distributive effects of our actions and simply maximize the good.[14]

However, we can agree with Goodman that we lack warrant for belief in an essentialist, non-composite view of the self without granting the necessity of the metaphysical claim or its normative consequences. The metaphysical interpretation of the no-self doctrine does entail that harms cannot *ultimately* be regarded as *mine* or *theirs*, but does not entail either that harms should be diminished, or that the good should be maximized. From a theoretical stance, we might just give up on the notion of ethical obligation; if there are no agents, there can be no sensible talk of moral responsibility, and no moral good that ought to be promoted.[15] Similarly there is no

---

[11] Śāntideva, "Excerpt from the *Bodhicaryavatara*" in William Edelglass and Jay Garfield eds., *Buddhist Philosophy: Essential Readings* (Oxford: Oxford University Press, 2009), 388–399.

[12] It should be noted that not all Mahāyāna approaches to the no-self doctrine are put in straightforwardly metaphysical terms. Some, relying on the doctrine of upāya, or skillful means, introduce a comprehensive strategy which acknowledges that teachings of the Buddha and Bodhisattvas will be adapted to the capacities of the hearers in order to be effective and of benefit.

[13] Charles Goodman, *The Consequences of Compassion* (New York: Oxford University Press, 2009), 11.

[14] He writes: "Once we bring to bear on ethics the teaching that there are no metaphysically important differences between different sentient beings, it cannot ultimately matter whether harms are compensated by benefits to the same beings or to others; nor can it ultimately matter who it is that carries out a harmful action." Goodman, 97.

[15] I am not here claiming that Goodman cannot account for moral responsibility, just claiming that nothing about the good is entailed by the metaphysical reading of the no-self doctrine.

logical entailment from the truth of no-self to an indiscriminate concern for all states of affairs. Those committed to diminishing suffering are likely to find it helpful to develop a diminished sense of the self, but the commitment is not forced upon us by metaphysics. Buddhist ethics supports the claim that the internalization of no-self will lead to the development of compassion, but we should not assume that the justification for compassion lies entirely in the logic or metaphysics of no-self.[16] The question of what ought to be believed, or attended to in thought, cannot be fully answered without acknowledging the practical standpoint. We may recall that in the "Kalamas Sutta", the Buddha responds to the Kalamas' expressed confusion over the differing doctrines advanced and criticized by visiting Brahmins and contemplatives by telling them to focus on what they find to be skillful and unskillful in their experience and to avoid supposing that doctrine is authoritative.[17]

It should be clear that the contemplative strategy interpretation of the doctrine, while not denying the significance of metaphysics, nonetheless denies that metaphysics alone settles the issue. The agent, faced with the question of what she is to do, how she is to think about what is likely to happen, or what has happened, faces a choice. No-self forms of thinking about how a situation is being perceived and how it should be responded to, are means for identifying and reducing stress and suffering. On the contemplative strategy view, what will be of interest is whether the sense of self is skillful or unskillful with respect to recognizing and responding to suffering, and the question of what is skillful or wholesome (kusala) is not the same as the question of whether or not the self is metaphysically real. There are clearly times when it would be unskillful for a person to see herself as simply a series of happenings and not as an agent. For example, in the wake of the uncomfortable feeling one might experience after having lied out of self-interest, it would not be skillful to take refuge in the sense of oneself as simply having been subject to a dishonest experience. We are notoriously prone to describing ourselves and our experiences as happenings when we are trying to avoid responsibility, so the question of when it is appropriate to relate to one's experiences as a series of happenings without self-identification is rather complicated.

If the arguments of this section are convincing it would follow that the practical standpoint is significant in a discussion of the no-self doctrine, that it supports the contemplative strategy interpretation, and that the doctrine of no-self *per se* does not support consequentialist ethics.

---

[16] Owen Flanagan makes this point in *The Bodhisattva's Brain: Buddhism Naturalized* (Cambridge, Mass.: The MIT Press, 2011), 131.

[17] "Now look you, Kalamas. Be ye not misled by report or tradition or hearsay. Be not misled by proficiency in the collections, nor by mere logic or inference, nor after consideration reasons, nor after reflection on and approval of some theory, nor because it fits becoming, nor out of respect for a recluse (who holds it). But, Kalamas, when you know for yourselves: These things are unprofitable, these things are blameworthy, these things are censured by the intelligent; these things when performed and undertaken, conduce to loss and sorrow – then indeed do ye reject them, Kalamas." See *Anguttara-Nikaya*, Woodward trans. (Oxford: The Pali Text Society, 2000), pp.171–172, PTS: A i 188.

7.2   The Self in Kantian Thought

In this section I will argue that the limits Kant places on theoretical knowledge of the self, along with his moral duty to understand the empirical self, can be seen as structurally similar to the contemplative strategy interpretation of the no-self doctrine. Kant's focus on the empirical sense of self that accompanies action coheres with the Buddhist recognition that the senses of self that we inhabit are deeply important aspects of our moral development.

Roughly put, Kant is famous in Western philosophy for seeing a way beyond theories of the mind and world which resulted in problematic gaps between the world and our ideas of it. If in perception we are acquainted with subjective representations of the world, then the world may be entirely other than we perceive it to be. Moreover, if what we are aware of is only our ideas, then we aren't actually aware of the world at all. Kant attempts to navigate toward a way of thinking that respects that we are both subjects (experiencers of the world) and objects (parts of the world governed by natural laws). He holds that a representation is an object of subjectivity that is represented as empirically real and transcendentally ideal. From one standpoint it makes sense to say that the world as perceived by us is real, and from another it makes sense to say that the world as perceived by us is ideal.[18] Kant argues that our minds shape our experiences, and his critiques are attempts to determine the limits of what we can know, beyond that interaction.

In particular, Kant holds that it cannot be known whether the self as a persistent, independent thing is ultimately real. To know this one would have to be able to have access to things in themselves (the noumenal) without the mind's intervention, and Kant takes this to be impossible.[19] Knowledge of events in the realm of experience (the phenomenal) is possible if it respects that it is a description of the realm of appearances. Our experience is the experience of a "thinking thing", the existence of the self being known in relation to its thoughts which are "its predicates", and this is the limit of our knowledge of a persistent self. In his discussion of whether the soul is substance in his "Paralogisms", Kant writes: "Through this I or he or it (the thing) which thinks, nothing further is represented than a transcendental subject of the thoughts = X. It is known only through the thoughts which are its predicates, and of it, apart from them, we cannot have any concept whatsoever, but can only revolve in a perpetual circle, since any judgement upon it has always already made use of its representation."[20]

---

[18] Jay Garfield discusses the similarities between Kant's transcendental idealism and Vasubandhu's Citta-matra Idealism in "Western Idealism through Indian Eyes," in his *Empty Words: Buddhist Philosophy and Cross-Cultural Interpretation* (Oxford: Oxford University Press, 2002), 152–169.

[19] By contrast, the Buddhist position is that it is both possible and desirable to attain access to a dimension unfabricated by the mind.

[20] Immanuel Kant, *Critique of Pure Reason*, trans. Norman Kemp Smith, (New York: St. Martin's Press, 1965), B404/A346.

Kant argues that it must be possible for the "I think" to accompany one's representations, for in the absence of the "I think" there would be representations "which could not be thought at all, and that is equivalent to saying that the representation would be impossible, or at least would be nothing to me."[21] For the representations to be representations, a unification within consciousness seems required; the "transcendental unity of apperception" operates as a unifier that makes coherent conscious experience possible, making that experience mine. In this sense we can think of a self which transcends our empirical experience – to this extent a unified self is part of our experience. It could be that there is a substantial self (though we cannot know this) and Kant claims, while the phenomenal realm indicates that we are governed by natural laws, unfree, and without a substantive self, it is not self-contradictory to suppose that there might be free causality in the noumenal realm. Kant's position thus respects a distinction between ultimate and conventional truths.

The relationship between noumenal and phenomenal selves is nonetheless a vexed part of Kant's philosophy. In places Kant himself makes claims about the noumenal which seem to overstep his own limits on the scope of knowledge. For example, he brings Christian assumptions to his analysis of the highest good (the ultimate end advanced by moral conduct), when in the *Critique of Pure Reason* he claims that the convergence of happiness "distributed in exact proportion to morality....is possible only in the intelligible world, under a wise Author and Ruler."[22] The attempt to secure a kind of eternal justice of happiness in proportion to virtue, seems to privilege one of a number of metaphysical possibilities. The question of whether Kant's considered judgement is that the highest good is brought about by God in another, non-natural world, or that the highest good it is brought about in the natural world through human efforts is debated within Kant scholarship.[23] While Kant clearly recognizes the importance of identifying our limited knowledge about the self, both in life and death, his own discussion, unsurprisingly, is conditioned by his cultural context. It is worth noting in the context of comparative philosophy, that one of Kant's few references to non-Western philosophy is a criticism of its failure to respect the limits of what can be known concerning the self through eternity, and the highest good.

In a rare instance of cross-cultural reflection, Kant remarks on a type of no-self view in Chinese philosophy, in his essay "The End of All Things." The remark is made in passing in a satirical essay whose indirect target is religious censorship, and in which Kant promotes a liberal Christian position, one that circumscribes what can be known about the afterlife and eternity. Brooding over unknowable final ends leads to mysticism, Kant writes, wherein "reason does not understand either itself or what it wants, but prefers to indulge in enthusiasm rather than – as seems fitting for an intellectual inhabitant of a sensible world – to limit itself within the bound of

---

[21] *Critique of Pure Reason*, B131–2.

[22] *Critique of Pure Reason*, A811/B839.

[23] Andrews Reath, for example, clearly distinguishes "secular" and "theological" interpretation of the highest good as presented across Kant's works. "Two Conceptions of the Highest Good in Kant," *Journal of the History of Philosophy*, 26(4), 1988, 593–619.

the latter."[24] Here Kant describes as "monstrous" what he takes to be Lao-Tzu's conception of the highest good as nothingness itself: "that it consists in *nothing*, i.e., in the consciousness of feeling oneself swallowed up in the abyss of the Godhead by flowing together with it, and hence by the annihilation of one's personality." He suggests that the 'pantheism' of the Tibetans and other 'oriental' peoples arises from this commitment to nothingness and to the conviction that the self is ultimately reabsorbed into the whole, and remarks that "in consequence from its philosophical sublimation *Spinozism* is begotten."[25] It is, perhaps, ironic that Kant charges this non-Western philosophy with disregarding the legitimate bounds of reason out of a desire for a blessed end of all things, an eternal tranquility, when his own conception of the highest good as happiness-in-proportion-to-virtue is fraught with Christian assumptions.

To return to the main line of discussion, for the purpose of demonstrating a parallel between Kantian and Buddhist metaphysics of the self, it will suffice here to note that Kant's argued for position is clear: we cannot know anything of the constitution of the soul "so far as the possibility of its separate existence is concerned" nor can we know whether we exist as substance or as accident.[26] I am not here advancing a defense of Kant's metaphysics, nor am I arguing that Kant's metaphysics is entirely analogous to Buddhist metaphysics. As all comparative projects are shaped by specific interests, it is worth clarifying some disanalogies as well.

Kant claims to have determined the limits of our knowledge of the self, but the Buddhist view of no-self does not make this claim. On the contemplative strategy interpretation it is claimed that an essential self does not exist, but it is not claimed that from the theoretical standpoint we see the limits of what is knowable. Rather, it claims that we are unwise to engage in deep metaphysical speculation about the nature of the self beyond a certain point, and instead wise to find repeatedly in our own experience the impermanence and instability of the self, the suggestion being that metaphysical speculation obstructs a better understanding of the nature of the self. So Kantian and Buddhist commitments to quietism concerning the ultimate truth about the self have different grounds, and different aims. This difference, while noteworthy, should not lead us to overlook the remarkable similarities, which arise from a shared commitment to the standpoint of agency. Neither for Kant, nor for contemplative strategy accounts of no-self, is the question of the nature of the self to be fully determined by its metaphysics. On both views, the nature of the self found in experience demands attention and critical scrutiny. To this topic I now turn.

---

[24] Immanuel Kant, "The End of All Things," in *Religion and Rational Theology*, trans. Allen Wood and George Di Giovanni, (Cambridge: Cambridge University Press, 1996), AK 8: 335.

[25] See the Spinoza chapter (ch. 5) in this volume for a discussion of related issues.

[26] Kant, *Critique of Pure Reason*, B420.

7.3 Kant's Contemplative Strategy

If we think of the contemplative strategy version of the no-self doctrine as a process in which one undertakes to free oneself from delusion, and to see things more objectively in order to promote right action, then we find a clear parallel in Kant's duty of self-knowledge. As outlined in the *Metaphysics of Morals*, an agent's two basic ends are self-perfection and the happiness of others. The duty of perfection involves the cultivation of one's natural predispositions so that one's will and understanding are developed in order to satisfy the requirements of duty.[27] Of Kant's specific duties to the self, the first duty is to develop self-knowledge. It is a wide duty to seek moral perfection: "'*know* (scrutinize, fathom) *yourself*,'... in terms of your moral perfection in relation to your duty. That is, know your heart – whether it is good or evil, whether the source of your actions is pure or impure."[28] This moral self-knowledge provides the start of all human wisdom and is aptly described by Kant as hellish but necessary.

As Kant understands us, we are by nature dissemblers who, even when we attempt to scrutinize our hearts, do not get easy or direct access to our own motives; we are prone to 'discovering' simply what we have ourselves put on view.[29] Our vulnerability to the opinion of others makes it impossible for a true self to be revealed and because our capacity for empirical self-knowledge is deeply limited, Kant is not entirely optimistic about our prospects for self-knowledge. Still, despite his pessimism, Kant does not renounce self-knowledge but understands it to be a necessary condition of moral development; it is a practical, not a theoretical pursuit.

Unlike most other thinkers in the Western tradition, Kant recognizes that it is dangerous to ignore or leave unchecked the empirical sense of self accompanying one's deeds. He promotes the development of an honest picture of oneself in action, one that counters the human tendency to exaggerated self-promotion. Accurate self-perceptions require that we observe our intentions and avoid self-identification with our "mere wishes" which provide a distorted sense of what we are like, our "pious ejaculations" being a better indication of how we like to think of ourselves, than what we are actually like.[30] Self-knowledge is a practical endeavor aimed at ridding oneself of false senses of self and constructing increasingly skillful senses of self as they apply to the aim of moral action. While in Buddhism the aim is a selflessness that liberates one from suffering, for Kant the aim is an agency free of the conceit that interferes with clear moral vision, sound judgement, and dutiful action.

---

[27] Immanuel Kant, *The Metaphysics of Morals*, Trans. Mary Gregor (Cambridge: Cambridge University Press, 1991), AK 6:386.

[28] *The Metaphysics of Morals*, AK 6:441.

[29] Immanuel Kant, *Anthropology from a Pragmatic Point of View*, trans. Robert Louden, (Cambridge: Cambridge University Press, 2006), AK 7:133.

[30] Immanuel Kant, *Lectures on Ethics*, trans. Peter Heath, eds. Peter Heath and J.B. Schneewind, (Cambridge: Cambridge University Press, 2001), AK 27:365.

Although his detractors like to present Kant as a fetishist about duty, there is point in his emphasis on clear recognition of the ground of one's action. It is morally dangerous, for example, to conflate the satisfaction of a basic duty with the feeling that one has done something noble. It is important to keep a close watch on our intentions and aspirations as they are strongly influenced by the "dear self"[31] and its improbably positive self-presentation. Moreover, Kant recognizes that awareness of one's actions as selfless is morally fraught, when he criticizes moral enthusiasts (such as religious fanatics) who lose sight of their obligations, focusing instead on the perceived merit of their actions, and in so doing "flattering themselves with a spontaneous goodness of heart."[32] These moral enthusiasts conflate the required satisfaction of the demands of duty with the pathological feeling of moral prowess and thereby construct a false sense of their own magnificence that diminishes virtue. Hence, Kant warns against the "exhortation to actions as noble, sublime, and magnanimous" when they are simply required.

For Kant, the self-knowledge which is our first duty is not theoretical knowledge regarding a metaphysical self, it is rather an internal self-accounting aimed at the production of a more authentic or autonomous self. Moral self-knowledge functions to remove the evil which is an obstacle to the natural development of a good will, and it helps both to destroy self-contempt and "egotistical self-esteem". Of course Buddhist philosophy does not suppose that humans are innately evil, merely that we have defilements, and the details of the Kantian and Buddhist accounts of delusion differ greatly, as do their accounts of objectivity and right action. But it is noteworthy that for Kant "evil" is a kind of corruption of the person marked by the subordination of morality to self-conceit, and that it is "radical" in the sense that all other evils stem from it. Both within Buddhist and Kantian ethics, ethical agency requires the cultivation and purification of the mind and heart, and this requires self-knowledge.

Kantian self-knowledge promotes the demise of mental habits that obstruct morality. As a kind of contemplative strategy it involves forms of recognition and de-identification with what might be thought of as deluded or unskillful self-conceptions (including self-aggrandizement, righteousness, self-conceit, magnanimity, and so on). A more refined self-conception is constructed over time by identifying with the thought of giving others their due, obedience to the moral law, and sympathy for the plight of others. This sort of moral development is social and includes attention to, and refinement of, character traits through emotional development. The conditional duty to develop sympathetic feelings (joy and sadness), for example, is described by Kant as a means of promoting benevolence by utilizing our natural tendencies to sympathy with others in order to achieve what "the representation of duty alone would not accomplish". He explains that it is "a duty not to avoid the places where the poor who lack the most basic necessities are to be found but

---

[31] Immanuel Kant, *Groundwork of the Metaphysics of Morals*, trans. Mary Gregor, (New York: Cambridge University Press, 1998), AK 4:408.

[32] Immanuel Kant, *Critique of Practical Reason*, trans. Mary Gregor (Cambridge: Cambridge University Press, 1997), AK 5:85.

rather to seek them out, and not to shun sick-rooms or debtor's prisons and so forth in order to avoid sharing painful feelings one may not be able to resist."[33] Clearly Kant recognizes that moral emotions shape an agent's experience for good or ill and that they need to be cultivated accordingly. In Buddhist thought vices are tied to misperceptions or wrong view, a failure of right thinking which promotes suffering. Interestingly, Kant identifies the vice of envy as a kind of misperception. It "is a propensity to view the well-being of others with distress, even though it does not detract from one's own," and so envy counts as a kind of malevolence, grounded in the mistake of comparing one's well-being with that of others, instead of acknowledging one's own intrinsic worth.

Kant's account of this phenomenal self is not naive; neither is it as sophisticated as its Buddhist counterpart. Kant fails to recognize that self-loathing is detrimental to morality, and over- estimates the constructive capacities of the thought of duty.[34] Nonetheless, his account of the duty of self-knowledge has noteworthy Buddhist affinities. It is not easy to acquire, given self-conceit. It is not awareness of a permanent self, and it is skillful when it serves to diminish a sense of self that is an obstacle to duty and recognition of what is, for example, owed to others. The view that agents need to become aware of the sense of the self that accompanies our moral actions, and that it needs to be refined in order to promote objectivity and moral action is part of what motivates the contemplative strategy interpretation of the no-self doctrine. Whether or not there is a self from the perspective of the ultimate dimension is relevant to this project *only* to the extent that it is useful to think of oneself in no-self terms.

7.4 Self-Legislation and Self-Identity

It might be objected that the Kantian focus on agency is difficult to square with Buddhist philosophy, that the contemplative strategy reading of the doctrine seems inconsistent with the Kantian focus on agency in two ways. First, even granting that Kant advances a distinction between the conventional and the ultimate, the Kantian appeal to synthetic *a priori* truths forces Kant and Kantians to commit to the noumenal as the real source of morality. If understood as a technique of perception, it seems that the no-self doctrine problematically divorces the phenomenal self from the noumenal in the activity of practical reason. If the ultimate self is the rational will, and free action is action governed by pure practical reason, then free, moral action is action governed by the intellect. This may be thought to be antithetical to a Buddhist conception of moral action, which does not hold reason in similarly high regard. Along these lines, Charles Goodman has argued that Kant's self must iden-

---

[33] *The Metaphysics of Morals*, AK 6:457.

[34] I have argued for this in "Kant and the Buddha on Self-Knowledge," in Stephen R. Palmquist (ed.), *Cultivating Personhood: Kant and Asian Philosophy* (Berlin: Walter de Gruyter, 2010), 695–708.

tify with the rational will, not with anything empirical, and that this seems to be at odds with Buddhist thinking which neither conceives of the ultimate self as reason, nor conceives of freedom as rule by reason.[35] However, it is not clear that Kant's conception of morality requires identification with the noumenal.

Julian Wuerth, for example, draws on an extensive range of Kant's writings to argue that Kant's own account of practical agency allows for free action from sensibility and does not equate action that is not governed by pure practical reason with unfree, immoral action.[36] The issue is significant because if Kant holds that free, moral action is the action of the noumenal self (because it is governed by pure practical reason), then it is unclear how people can legitimately be held responsible for immoral actions, as they are unfree. As my purpose here is neither a defense of Kant's metaphysics, nor engagement with disputed ideas in Kant scholarship, I will set aside the issue of whether or not Kant's own position founders on its *aprioristic* metaphysics. The point of this Buddhist-Kantian comparison is not to claim that the theories have identical, unproblematic, metaphysics of the self, nor is it to claim that Buddhist ethics is structurally Kantian. Kant's account of the noumenal self and agency doesn't forestall a fruitful comparison with Buddhist thought. Indeed, the relation between the phenomenal and the noumenal is not unlike the relation between present selves tied by karmic consequences to future selves. So the first objection does not derail the Buddhist-Kantian comparison.

The second objection to the comparison I have presented is that the Kantian focus on agency as self-legislation in the phenomenal realm opposes Buddhist ways of thinking about ethics; Kant and Kantians understand practical reasons as law-like modes of self-causality, while Buddhist ethics encourages us to be wary of forming rigid identities which must be, after all, grounded in delusion. To see why this objection doesn't pose a problem for the Buddhist-Kantian comparison, recall Korsgaard's Kantian position on personal identity. In response to the view that the self is best understood as a series of happenings, she argues that the lack of a deep metaphysical self does not force the conclusion that there is no self. Firstly, the practical necessity of eliminating motivational conflict in this body provides a practical reason for regarding myself as the same self in the future. Secondly, from a standpoint of deliberative choice we require reasons which express commitments which shape the responses of our future selves. In this manner we are by nature self-legislating, and it is in self-legislation that we create identities; this defense of the self is consistent with the claim that the self is not metaphysically deep.[37]

---

[35] Goodman, 201.

[36] Wuerth argues that thinkers like Henry Sidgwick and Christine Korsgaard have failed to properly mark Kant's distinction between *Wille* and *Willkur*, and that this has led to confusion about Kant's position. "Sense and Sensibility in Kant's Practical Agent: Against the Intellectualism of Korsgaard and Sidgwick," *European Journal of Philosophy*, 21(1), 2010, 1–36.

[37] As Mark Siderits notes, the reductionist version of the no-self doctrine denies that persons are completely distinct existences but does not deny the distinctness of the causal series that a person may experience as herself. So it makes sense to designate one series as me and the other as you by reference to the relations between earlier and later parts of the series. See Siderits, *Buddhism as Philosophy: An Introduction* (Indianapolis, Indiana: Hackett Publishing Company, Inc., 2007), 83.

On Korsgaard's Kantian view of agency, to determine your actions through self-legislation is to give expression to a way in which you value yourself, sometimes as a friend, or feminist, or parent, or perhaps as a citizen of the kingdom of ends.[38] These practical identities make our reasons apparent to us partly through self-awareness. To be a loyal, sympathetic friend, for example, is not to cold-heartedly apply the rule of sympathy in friendship to one's situation. Rather, it is to find oneself searching for a way of understanding of a friend's predicament and to have one's sense of self rebel against the inclination, say, to blame her for being foolish. A friend who lacked this sense of loyalty would not experience the tendency to blame as problematic; to invest in loyal friendship is to leave oneself open to finding oneself engaged in disloyal activities. Identities are created around the laws we give ourselves and may be morally skillful or unskillful ways of perceiving ourselves. To think of ourselves as law-governed in this way is not to suppose that we are rule-bound extremists who lack the capacity to recognize how and when these practical identities conflict. To be a thoughtful citizen and parent, for example, is to be open to feeling the competing demands of those identities when they conflict, as they surely will.

Charles Goodman has objected to Korsgaard, arguing that her conception of self-legislation promotes a self that Buddhism cannot endorse, as her agents will be bound by their own rules even when they should clearly abandon them: "if I view a particular decision rule as expressive of my self, I will be unwilling to abandon that rule, and make decisions in accordance with another rule, even when switching decision rules would produce much better consequences."[39] He sees the identities that naturally arise as we engage in self-legislation as obstructions to morality because he supposes them to be inflexible and dogmatically imposed. Goodman acknowledges that the phenomenology of deliberation suggests that there is someone involved in choice and that long-term planning involves an extended sense of self, and even acknowledges that a functional unity of the person seems required for action, but he goes on to assert that philosophers in the Buddhist tradition simply deny that the practical standpoint is the only or best way to live. By contrast, he writes, Buddhism demands "rejecting and abandoning the psychological processes that, for Korsgaard, help to constitute a persisting self."[40] In this respect Buddhist philosophy and Kantian philosophy are clearly at odds. The alternative to the practical standpoint, he writes, is the enlightened state, in which there are no decisions: "In this state, there is theoretical cognition, or perhaps nonconceptual intuitive insight, which clearly sees how things are."[41]

But Goodman's objection fails to recognize that the tendency to be caught by one's identity and act badly as a result isn't a problem merely for Kantian theory; it is a problem for all moral actors. This is what it is like to be a person, not what it is

---

[38] This form of identity is practical in that it marks "a description under which you find your life to be worth living and your actions to be worth undertaking." Christine Korsgaard, *The Sources of Normativity* (Cambridge: Cambridge University Press, 1996), 101.

[39] Goodman, 211.

[40] Goodman, 213.

[41] Goodman, 212.

like to be a Kantian. All agents are prone to acting from false perceptions of their situation and of themselves. With this Buddhist philosophy is entirely in agreement. Furthermore, the appeal to the possibility of enlightenment does not defeat the Kantian position that an agentially constituted self (or series of selves) can be pragmatically vindicated and is unavoidable for natural, rational creatures like us. Because life for all non-enlightened beings includes the construction of selves, morality for non-enlightened beings involves identity creation, and this can be usefully illuminated by the contemplative strategy interpretation of the no-self doctrine. Kantian agency and self-legislation are not undermined by the doctrine of no-self.

In conclusion, I have argued that the standpoint of agency has a place in our comparative studies of the nature of the self, and that it underlies some of the tension between the contemplative strategy and the metaphysical interpretations of the no-self doctrine. It is important that the contemplative strategy view be part of our comparative discussion, not only because it has a plausible textual defense, but also because it accords with the existential heart of Buddhism's soteriological project. The contemplative strategy interpretation of the no-self doctrine allows for clear parallels to be drawn between Kantian and Buddhist philosophy, specifically the importance of moral self-development by way of self-knowledge. Considered from the standpoint of agency, the doctrine of no-self illuminates aspects of moral psychology involved in the purification of the heart and mind that might have otherwise gone unnoticed.

References

Anguttara-Nikaya. 2000. Trans. F.L. Woodward. Oxford: The Pali Text Society.

Connected Discourses of the Buddha: A Translation of the Samyutta Nikaya. 2000. Trans. Bhikkhu Bodhi. Boston: Wisdom Publications.

Flanagan, Owen. 2011. *The Bodhisattva's Brain: Buddhism Naturalized*. Cambridge: MIT Press.

Garfield, Jay. 2002. Western Idealism Through Indian Eyes. In *Garfield, Empty Words: Buddhist Philosophy and Cross-Cultural Interpretation*. Oxford: Oxford University Press.

Goodman, Charles. 2009. *Consequences of Compassion*. New York: Oxford University Press.

Harvey, Peter. 2009. Theravada Philosophy of Mind and the Person. In *Buddhist Philosophy: Essential Readings*, ed. William Edelglass and Jay Garfield. New York: Oxford University Press.

Kant, Immanuel. 1965. *Critique of Pure Reason*. Trans. Norman Kemp Smith. New York: St. Martin's Press.

———. 1991. *The Metaphysics of Morals*. Trans. Mary Gregor. Cambridge: Cambridge University Press.

———. 1996. The End of All Things. In *Religion and Rational Theology*. Trans. Allen Wood and George Di Giovanni. Cambridge: Cambridge University Press.

———. 1997. *Critique of Practical Reason*. Trans. Mary Gregor. Cambridge: Cambridge University Press.

———. 1998. *Groundwork of the Metaphysics of Morals*. Trans. Mary Gregor. Cambridge: Cambridge University Press.

———. 2001. *Lectures on Ethics*. Trans. Peter Heath, ed. Peter Heath and J.B. Schneewind. Cambridge: Cambridge University Press.

————. 2006. *Anthropology from a Pragmatic Point of View*. Trans. Robert Louden. Cambridge: Cambridge University Press.

Korsgaard, Christine. 1996a. Personal Identity and Unity of Agency: A Kantian Response to Parfit. In *Creating the Kingdom of Ends*, ed. Korsgaard. Cambridge: Cambridge University Press.

Korsgaard, Christine. 1996b. *The Sources of Normativity*. Cambridge: Cambridge University Press.

Middle Length Discourses of the Buddha: A Translation of the Majjhima Nikaya. 2009. Trans. B. Bodhi and B. Thanissaro, 3rd ed. Boston: Wisdom Publications.

O'Hagan, Emer. 2010. Kant and the Buddha on Self-Knowledge. In *Cultivating Personhood: Kant and Asian Philosophy*, ed. S.R. Palmquist, 695–708. Berlin: Walter de Gruyter.

Parfit, Derek. 1984. *Reasons and Persons*. Oxford: Clarendon Press.

Reath, Andrews. 1988. Two Conceptions of the Highest Good in Kant. *Journal of the History of Philosophy* 26 (4): 593–619.

Robinson, R., W. Johnson, and Thanissaro Bhikkhu. 2005. *Buddhist Religions: A Historical Introduction*. 5th ed. Toronto: Wadsworth Publishing.

Sāntideva. 2009. Excerpt from the *Bodhicaryāvatāra*. In *Buddhist Philosophy: Essential Readings*, ed. William Edelglass and Jay Garfield. Oxford: Oxford University Press.

Schechtman, Marya. 2008. Diversity in unity: practical unity and personal boundaries. *Synthese* 162 (3): 405–423.

Siderits, Mark. 2007. *Buddhism as Philosophy: An Introduction*. Indianapolis: Hackett.

Thanissaro, Bhikkhu. 1999. *Noble Strategy*. Valley Center: Metta Forest Monastery Publisher.

Wuerth, Julian. 2010. Sense and Sensibility in Kant's Practical Agent: Against the Intellectualism of Korsgaard and Sidgwick. *European Journal of Philosophy* 21 (1).

Chapter 8
The Contingency of Willing: A Vijñānavāda Critique of Schopenhauer and Nietzsche

Douglas L. Berger

Much has been written in the past century, and particularly in the last few decades, on the degrees to which Schopenhauer and Nietzsche were influenced by their acquaintance with South Asian Buddhist thought.[1] In addition, comparative philosophy scholars have, apart from historical issues of influence, speculated about various ways in which Schopenhauerian or Nietzschean thought might have some significant resonance with various systems of classical Buddhism.[2] These strands of investigation and reflection have been fruitful and suggestive, both for their insights into the hermeneutics of nineteenth-century Continental receptions of Asian thought and how they were colored by Orientalist interpretations, as well as how they have expanded the West's philosophical horizons. However, considerably less has been written about how the works of Schopenhauer and Nietzsche might be assessed

---

[1] There is an extensive literature on Schopenhauer and Indian thought that stretches all the way back to the late nineteenth century, but some of the most thorough studies recently have been done by App (1998a and b) and myself (Berger 2004). In the case of Nietzsche, a number of insightful investigations can be found in Graham Parkes' edited volume *Nietzsche and Asian Thought*, including Hulin (1993) and Sprung (1993). Incisive hermeneutic analysis of their respective receptions of Indian thought can always be found in the work of the late Wilhelm Halbfass (1988).

[2] Once again, the literature comparing Schopenhauer's system to classical Hindu and Buddhist thought has a longer history, but the quality of these efforts is often low, as for instance in the work of Dauer (1969). Recently, Nietzsche's work has received more comparative attention on the part of predominantly East Asian thinkers, but there have been some interesting attempts to find affinities between his ideas and some South Asian Buddhist systems, such as in Martin (1993), Morrison (1999) and van der Braak (2011).

D. L. Berger (✉)
Leiden University, Leiden, The Netherlands
e-mail: d.l.berger@phil.leidenuniv.nl

© Springer International Publishing AG, part of Springer Nature 2018   161
G. F. Davis (ed.), *Ethics without Self, Dharma without Atman*, Sophia Studies
in Cross-cultural Philosophy of Traditions and Cultures 24,
https://doi.org/10.1007/978-3-319-67407-0_8

from Buddhist perspectives.[3] In this essay, I wish to critically examine these two seminal nineteenth century thinkers on the basis of what ended up becoming one of the most important schools of Buddhist thought, namely early South Asian Vijñānavāda. I will take this approach because I think that, in contrast to Schopenhauer's and Nietzsche's emphasis on the centrality of will in human life, and in light of the ways in which Vijñānavāda both retains and modifies various elements in early Buddhist Abhidharma analysis, we can appreciate the centrality of the Buddhist claim that human will(s), or the psychological impetuses of willing, are contingent. And, of course, for Buddhists, it is a most fortunate fact that willing is causally contingent, as this is the primary reason that awakening and perfection are live possibilities for human beings.

There can be no doubt that Schopenhauer and Nietzsche, for somewhat contrary reasons, believed that classical Buddhist thought and practice presented a fundamental challenge to various patterns of foregoing European philosophy and so would elicit a response from "modern" Europeans that would represent a fateful choice about its cultural trajectory. The great seriousness with which both thinkers take Buddhism, even given their limited degrees of familiarity with the latter's vast philosophical literature, is a sign of their basically open hermeneutical stance towards it. They treat Buddhism not as some dead, ossified body of texts or irrelevant religious practices, but as a provocative and formidable candidate, so to speak, to address the gloomy state of the human existential and civilization conditions. After all, Schopenhauer believed that the new avenues being opened up by the investigation of ancient Indian thought, particularly because of its resonance with how he read Plato and Kant, would prompt a new "Renaissance" on the Continent.[4] He speculated in his late works that Christianity, whose pessimism about the world proved it had "Indian blood in its veins," had long since been ruined in Europe through theological dogmatism and would not only fail in its missionary attempts in India but may be outshined by Hindu and Buddhist insights.[5] For his own part, Nietzsche lauded Buddhism for the "honesty" with which it faced down the nonexistence of a supreme deity and the "purposelessness" of the eternal cosmos, and even sometimes mused that the nihilism he propounded could make him both the "Buddha of Europe" as well as Buddhism itself an inevitable stage of nihilism through which Europe itself would have to travel.[6] Of course, ultimately, both of these partners and antipodes of pessimism believed that their own visions surpassed what had been achieved by Buddhist religious principles. Schopenhauer considered notions like *nirvāṇa* in the end to be nothing more than "symbol" and "metaphor," while his own "systematic" thought revealed the real nature of the world through

---

[3] A bit more critical assessment of Schopenhauer's characterizations of Brāhmiṇical thought has been undertaken, including comments by Radhakrishnan (1929) and a brilliant essay by Hacker (1995). Interestingly, Jay Garfield (2002) has offered a kind of stage theory about how Berkeley, Schopenhauer and Nietzsche came close to approximating positions taken in Vijñānavāda.

[4] Schopenhauer 1966a, xv–xvi.

[5] Schopenhauer 1974, 187; see also 1966a 356–7 and 1966b, 584.

[6] Nietzsche 1967b, 161, 1990, 42, 1967c, 180.

conceptual clarity.[7] In his turn, Nietzsche ultimately considered *nirvāṇa* to be the kind of decadent life-denial that all his philosophical energies, seeking affirmation of worldly life, were directed to overcome, and so he considered the Buddha to be "weak-willed."[8] Nonetheless, both surely were convinced that they understood Buddhism well enough to accurately assess it philosophically, existentially and civilizationally. But, as we shall see, in the final analysis, it must be said that Schopenhauer's and Nietzsche's most characteristic philosophical convictions about human willing were profoundly un-Buddhist.

8.1 Schopenhauer's Will as Ground of Being

Schopenhauer is certainly best known for his contention that will, as the ground of all individual beings, destines those beings to constant conflict, and this in turn makes the world a place that should never have existed; this is often thought the crux of his pessimistic perspective. In his early years as a philosopher, Schopenhauer, perhaps partly inspired by the very lectures of Fichte he attended at Göttingen which he claimed later to despise, and also due to his own ruminations, came to the conclusion that will was the most immediate and direct kind of self-knowledge that there is for us. Schopenhauer's modified Kantianism led him to believe that, merely following the logic and limits of representational knowledge, we could never know the true nature of appearances, including ourselves, but could only know the relations between one representation and another. However, in the movements of our bodies, the pains and joys we feel, in the powerful rush of various kinds of energies we observe in nature, we encounter not merely the spatial, temporal and causal relation of representations to one another, but an "unmediated" manifestation of our own and the world's reality.[9] This unmediated knowledge of will makes it, in Schopenhauer's early system, the "thing in itself" of the world. He expands this argument in the 1830s to various aspects of the then-developing fields of the natural sciences, where will explains everything from gravity and heliotropism in plants to psychic phenomena like telekinesis in his work *On the Will in Nature*. Will, for Schopenhauer, is at bottom the impetus to existence, the drive that impels everything to perpetuate its own being, even when this comes at the expense of others, and different kinds of inanimate and animate creatures alike are nothing but manifestations of the will at what he calls different "grades of objectification." In Schopenhauer's early thought, will is a metaphysical absolute; given that we know it as unlimited by the representational forms of space and time, it is the eternal, indestructible ground of being.

---

[7] 1966a, 411–12; 1966b, 629.

[8] 1967a, 59; 1964a, 74; 1974, 165–6.

[9] Schopenhauer 1966a, 100, 105, 110–11.

Nonetheless, there are indeed several important mitigating factors that qualify the characterization of will as a metaphysical absolute in Schopenhauer's philosophy. For one thing, beginning in his notes of 1824 and until the publication of the second edition of his major work *World as Will and Representation* in 1844, this arch-pessimist begins to relent on applying the label "thing in itself" to will.[10] This concession is prompted in view of the realization that we cannot help but know our individual wills, in the acts of our bodies and the unfolding of our individual characters, through time, and so, while the Kantian form of spatial intuition does not mediate our knowledge of the will, time must mediate it.[11] And so, in his late works, Schopenhauer is, at least sometimes, given to calling will "the nearest and clearest" appearance of the thing-in-itself, which, in its pristine essence, being one and undifferentiated, cannot quite be described.[12] However, at yet other moments in these same late works, he frequently reverts to calling the will the "thing-in-itself" anyway, which is "entire and undivided in every being."[13] This gradual shift in Schopenhauer's position on the ultimate metaphysical status of the will coupled with his persistent return to his early formulations of will as thing in itself has prompted recent commentators to argue over which construal represents "the sage of Frankfurt's" genuine position and arguments. At the very minimum, at any rate, we can say that our experience of willing brings us closest to the metaphysical basis of ourselves as beings and of the world as a whole, a basis which is unaltered by any happenings in space or time.

However, a more continuous qualification attaching to Schopenhauer's conception of the will was his abiding belief that, on the one hand, the compassionate person could surrender their egoism to help others, and on the other hand the mystic could transcend the compulsions of and domination by the will. The ways Schopenhauer referred to this admittedly rare occurrence are revealing. In terms of ethics, he appropriates the notion of the "intelligible character" in Kant to talk about the personality traits, desires, preferences, unique attachments and relative ethical comportments of each individual. Every person, in the typology he offers in the main argument to his 1840 essay *On the Basis of Morality*, is possessed of a specific kind of moral character.[14] There are evil and bad characters, who seek their own benefit over the benefit of others, in the case of the evil person by actively harming others and in the case of the bad person by being indifferent to the welfare of others. Then there are *just* (or justice-oriented) characters. They too see their own benefit, but only on the condition that their benefit does not come at the expense of others. All these types of characters are, however, primarily motivated by egoistic concerns. A compassionate character, by contrast, makes less of a distinction between themselves and others, and counts another's "weal and woe" as their own given the fact

---

[10] This slow but sure shift in Schopenhauer's position on will has been convincingly demonstrated in the works of Julian Young (1987) and John Atwell (1995).

[11] Schopenhuaer, 1966b, 35; 196–7.

[12] Schopenhauer 1966b 197.

[13] Schopenhauer 1966b, 325.

[14] See Schopenhauer, 1999, 69; 136–45 and 1964a, 363–73.

that both self and other are nothing more than different individuated manifestations of a unitary underlying will.[15] It may look here as if Schopenhauer is suggesting that a complete relinquishment of ego-identity is possible in moral conduct, a principle which a Buddhist could agree with. But the details of Schopenhauer's conception of compassion here curtail the possibility of much overlap between his beliefs and those of Buddhists. For one thing, the recognition of the oneness of self and other that Schopenhauer emphasizes as the necessary component of a compassionate character is a metaphysically specific realization, in that it is *only* this fact – that self and other are in essence the same will – that verifies the recognition.[16] Secondly, compassion predominates, in Schopenhauer's quasi-Kantian character analysis, only because compassionate people have certain kinds of fixed characters that others don't; one does not transform into a compassionate person, one simply is one because of the intelligible character that lies at the heart of what one is.[17] Finally, even a compassionate act is still an act that affirms the will. It distinguishes itself from a selfish act only in that it affirms the will of another instead of one's own. Therefore, even if there is a way in which the ego loses its axiological priority in Schopenhauer's depiction of the compassionate person, the essence of will is still taken to be affirmed and preserved by the compassionate act. In Schopenhauer's system, an ego-less act is every bit as grounded in the metaphysical unity of will as is a selfish act; the former merely sees into the unity of will instead of ignoring it, and benefits others instead of oneself.

Similarly, it may look, and has appeared to some readers, like Schopenhauer's ascetic notion of "denial of the will to live" strikes a chord with Buddhist ideas of renunciation. In the ascetic "renunciation of the will-to-live," in which all attachments and sense of ego-identity are surrendered, the intelligible character is not just temporarily set aside as it is in great experiences of beauty or compassion, but is permanently "destroyed."[18] However, while such descriptions are usually carefully enough phrased to make clear that the character being "destroyed" by the mystic is only their "individual" will and not the will of the world as a whole, Schopenhauer's portrayals of the renunciant do depict them as being centers of pure knowing of the world, "unspotted" in their mirror-like reflection of the reality of things.[19] He goes on to distinguish the views of the world held respectively by one still in the throes of the will's tumult and one who has left them behind, saying that they regard their respective "worlds" as "nothing." That is to say, the worldly person finds the mystic's unitary vision a "nothingness" just as the mystic sees "this very real world of ours with all its stars and galaxies" and all other manner of phenomenal differentiation as "nothing."[20] This language about the mystic makes it seem like there are states of life in which the will can be "abolished" and so not an absolute datum of

---

[15] 1969a, 365; 1999, 209.

[16] 1969a, 372–3.

[17] 1999, 193.

[18] 1966a, 378–9; 403.

[19] 1966a, 411.

[20] Schopenhauer 1966a, 412.

existence. This is also what makes Schopenhauer's conception of mystical knowledge somewhat of an oddity, insofar as it represents the sage uncovering the nature of being and then turning away from it rather than identifying with it.

But even here, and Schopenhauer occasionally admits as much, the formulations he gives of both the "denial of the will-to-live" and the "mystical view" of the world are never altogether consistent. In the former case, Schopenhauer describes the renunciation of willing as a "voluntary" and a "free act of will," and it is so presumably because the mystic does not will from within the limits of representation, but acts willfully nonetheless.[21] In the case of the latter, there is an overarching sense that, even though a mystic may be able to escape the compulsive clutches of the body's and the world's demands, there are yet many more creatures still living in the world who do not share the mystic's point of view; the will is still their driving force and the world of lifeforms, stars and galaxies persists in being. The renunciation of the will, in this case, while it does presumably effect a startling psychological, behavioral, epistemological and ethical transformation of a person, does not obliterate the world as a whole, for as long as there remain will and representation, the world goes on even if the mystic refuses to go on with it.

All this leads to several conclusions that reveal the manner and degree to which the will is made into a metaphysical absolute in Schopenhauer's thought. In the weakest sense, willing is the most immediate and direct experience we have that approximates the thing-in-itself, the inner nature, of the world, though most of the time Schopenhauer declares forthrightly that the will is the ground and basis of all that exists. Willing is the impulse of all our bodily movements and desires, the impetus that can be seen in the movements of all phenomena, be they animal or plant life or inanimate things. To varying extents, will underlies all of our motives, be they morally "good" or "evil." In the holiest of human beings, mystical sages, the will can be "turned away from," "denied," "resigned" or perhaps better suspended until bodily death in the individuals of those persons, but it continues to be the font of all continuing existence.

8.2   Nietzsche's Project of the Affirmation of Will

There are two overriding features of Nietzsche's treatment of willing that bring into focus how he prioritizes it above all else in life and nature. Nietzsche certainly does come to reject Schopenhauer's contention that there is but one undifferentiated will that grounds all existence and all individuals, in favor of a great plurality of wills both in the cosmos and in each person. But this shift in emphasis to a plurality of wills in no way dilutes the manners in which Nietzsche insists that willing is the decisive force in human events, both in their civilizational manifestations and in the psychological functioning of individuals. This insistence is at the forefront of both Nietzsche's lifelong attempts to find a formula for the "affirmation of the will

---

[21] Ibid., 391–2.

to life" and his analysis of how willing functions in the historical and natural life of human beings.

There is a sense in which Nietzsche, for the entirety of his philosophical career, was fighting a battle with Schopenhauer, whom he nonetheless considered a German thinker of outstanding merit. He engaged in repeated attempts to find a winning formula for the affirmation of the will to life, particularly in the face of Schopenhauer's trenchant conviction that everything from tragedy to history, from religion to human conduct, from historical to interpersonal conflict proved that only a pessimistic assessment and turning away from human willing was the key to whatever kind of human "salvation" could be found.[22] This project begins in *The Birth of Tragedy*, when Nietzsche argues that the combination of the Apollonian intellectual and Dionysian visceral elements in the musical chorus of Greek tragedy produced a cathartic release that headed off "the danger of a Buddhistic longing for a negation of the will" and enabled the spectator to affirm life, even with all its pain and loss.[23] A second major attempt at finding such a formula can be found in *The Joyful Science*, where the first version of Nietzsche's notion of "eternal recurrence" can be found. At this point, "eternal recurrence" is thematized as nothing more than a hypothetical "test" of a reader's ability to affirm life just as it is. In this test, as is well-known, a demon steals into one's "loneliest loneliness" in the dead of night, saying that a person will be doomed to live the very life they have lived countless times forever, and the reader who can take joy in the pronouncement is one who can affirm life unconditionally.[24] Indeed, there is some evidence that the source of the idea for this "test" of life-affirmation was Schopenhauer himself, as the latter at one point in his first edition of *The World as Will and Representation* had speculated that no one, who on their deathbed were given the chance to relive their life, would choose to do so, but would prefer complete non-existence to that chance.[25] In the section "On Redemption" in *Thus Spoke Zarathustra*, Nietzsche once again overtly assails Schopenhauer's recommendation that human beings deny the will to life, referring to it as a kind of self-imposed capital punishment, and himself urges that everything that has ever happened must be affirmed with an "I willed it so."[26] Indeed, given the close association Nietzsche makes between Schopenhaurian and Buddhist thought, especially since he assumed the former was a reliable interpreter and representative of the latter, Nietzsche, in the 1886 preface to the second edition of *The Birth of Tragedy* labels the "decadent" Schopenhauerian and Buddhist form of pessimism a "pessimism of weakness" in contrast to his own "pessimism of strength." The former's rejection of willful life is a sign of decay while his own

---

[22] The notion that the various attempts by Nietzsche to affirm the will to life were alternative "formulae," sidestepping the question of how much metaphysical currency should be put into any of them, was argued by Maudmarie Clark (1990, 282) some time ago, and I find this analysis of Nietzsche's works convincing.

[23] 1967a, 59.

[24] Nietzsche, 1964b,270–71.

[25] 1966a, 140–41.

[26] 1995, 137–42.

equally pessimistic outlook on life is nonetheless "prompted by well-being, by overflowing health, by the fullness of existence."[27] In order, then, for human beings to live a joyful life in spite of the modern collapse of Christian transcendent ideals, the loss of meaning and absolute morality and the unstoppable contests for power that constitute all human history, the will to live must be affirmed, preserved, celebrated and embraced as the root of all one's efforts.

Of course, as noted above, the will as conceived by Nietzsche is not the underlying unitary metaphysical essence or force that is shared by all beings. It is instead diversified both among individuals and within them as the entire array of physiological and psychological impulses that make up all their yearnings and ambitions. As early as the composition of *Daybreak*, Nietzsche describes the phenomenon of "self-mastery" as one set of drives trying to overpower another set of drives, which demonstrates that there is hardly one center of willing in any individual.[28] Other formulations in "late" works like *Beyond Good and Evil* associate will with the "plurality of feelings" in both the "muscles" and in the "affect" toward a thing which either repels us from or draws us to it.[29] Nietzsche extrapolates that it is through believing that we, our innermost egos, are the unitary causal agents of such willing that we gain a feeling of "power" over ourselves and our world, even though this belief about unitary agency is a psychological fiction. Indeed, in both his main works and his *Nachlass* from the mid 1880's onward, Nietzsche continuously attests to the multiplicity of wills within each person.[30] In the midst of these conclusions, Nietzsche finds Schopenuhauer to be doing little more than perpetuating a well-worn myth about unitary subjectivity, only replacing the "ego" or transcendental "self" with the undifferentiated will of each person and the cosmos in general. So, obviously, it is important to always keep in mind that Nietzsche frequently tries to speak of the will in overtly limited biological and psychological and not metaphysically absolutist terms.

Nietzsche's proclivity to see operating in each person not merely a multiplicity of wills but a multiplicity of subjectivities that serves those wills occasionally gives his pronouncements an air of the Buddhist conception of "no-self." For instance, in section 16 of *Beyond Good and Evil*, Nietzsche assails the Western philosophical tendency, especially aggravated since the days of Descartes, Kant and Fichte, to unify subjectivity and thought in the form I-consciousness and make of the latter an "unmediated certainty." Though, Nietzsche argues, senses of personal identity are taken for granted in "folk" thinking, the philosopher has no warrant to simply assume, let alone make axioms to the effect, that judgments like "I think" are not themselves based on feeling and willing. Whatever senses of self we have, be they commonplace or philosophical, Nietzsche continues, only serve when examined to raise more questions about ourselves than provide foundations to our lives. The generic Buddhist philosopher could easily concur with such passages in isolation.

---

[27] 1967a, 17.

[28] 1997, 110.

[29] Nietzsche, 1964a, 26–7.

[30] 1990, 11 (40)42 and 12 (1)58.

But we must consider them in the context of Nietzsche's overarching body of thought. He is generally given to seeing the roots of all thought, whether reflective thought is directed toward the world or the self, in feelings, drives, and will, as he does in this very section of *Beyond Good and Evil*. So, we are still left with the task of closely examining what Nietzsche is tying to get at with this focus on drives and will, and why the latter were, for him, so philosophically crucial. That is where the ways in which Nietzsche and Buddhist thought are importantly incompatible become more marked.

The fastidiousness with which Nietzsche insists that the will is heterogeneous in each of us does not prevent him from considering the will an incorrigible element of our experience (as we may put it), both descriptively and prescriptively. Obviously, this incorrigible nature of the will is insisted upon not only in Nietzsche's pursuit of a "formula" for life-affirmation, but also in his changing speculations about the "will to power." It is not necessary for our purposes to take sides on the long-debated issue of whether or not "will to power" represents, despite Nietzsche's overt abandonment of traditional metaphysics, yet another iteration of a metaphysical thesis.[31] Part of the fundamental reason that this debate between the "axiological" and "cosmological" readings of will to power has arisen in the first place is that Nietzsche almost always weaves elements of these two aspects of the phenomenon together. Certainly, Nietzsche often means by "the will to power" very specifically the will to "might" (*Macht*), as when he writes in *The Antichrist* that what we consider "good" is whatever increases our feeling of might, whereas what we deem "bad" is whatever weakens us.[32] Nietzsche occasionally speaks of this aspect of will to power as a "primary organic function" of bodies that seek to dominate one another, and in this respect, "life is precisely Will to Power."[33] Indeed, in the notes collected in *The Will to Power*, Nietzsche characterizes our internal lives as a kind of politics in which these different wills are seeking "might" over the other. Each bodily and psychological drive (*Trieb*), including the drive to think, is a "kind of lust to rule," each "has its perspective that it would like to compel all the other drives to accept as a norm."[34] And yet, in other notes of the very same work, will to power is also described as at once the "play of forces" in the natural order and the "joy" of the life-affirmer that "knows no satiety, no disgust, no weariness" that together make up "the world."[35] This is the famous passage that ends in the pronouncement: "This world is the will to power—and nothing besides! And you yourselves are this will to power—and nothing besides!"[36] Insofar as will to power is the play of energetic forces in the natural order, Nietzsche writes that it can be analyzed in terms of

---

[31] This debate was to a large extent initiated by the variant readings of Nietzsche in Heidegger (1979), Foucault (1984) and Derrida (1989) but continues to be waged in the secondary literature in the works of such scholars as Nehamas (1985) and Richardson (2002).

[32] 1974, 128.

[33] 1964a, 226.

[34] Nietzsche 1967c, 267.

[35] 1967c, 550.

[36] Ibid.

certain "dynamic quanta" that are "in a relation of tension" with one another and work "effects" on one another.[37] On the other hand, from an "inward" perspective, Nietzsche just as dramatically declares that, since "thinking is only a relation of… impulses to one another" and since will can only effect will and not matter, we must conclude that it is will and not any external factors that determine our generation and lives.[38]

On balance, Nietzsche tends to revert to the inner, psychological associations of will to power when he is in the mood to warn philosophers to be "cautious" about overextending their categories. It is, after all, the will to power itself as Nietzsche conceives it that drives us to interpret the world, and whether those interpretations are errant or careful, they serve the purpose of providing conditions within which our lives can be lived and through which, in the absence of any credible objective teleology, we can make our lives meaningful.[39] Ultimately, just as physicists do with the categories of "nature," Nietzsche admits he does with the "will to power," erecting an "interpretation" that endorses certain prescriptions for life-affirming behavior, and even if the latter are themselves "found to be "also only an interpretation," the philosopher shrugs, "so much the better."[40] Even though, that is, the very notion of the "will to power" can itself be circumscribed within an analysis that renders it merely another perspective on human existence that commands no more warrant than the foregoing social, religious and philosophical perspectives that Nietzsche dismisses, that is no reason that the will to power should be abandoned. It is the purpose that is served by the idea in our historical epoch, enabling human beings to embrace the world and their own finitude despite their loss, even their active murder, or "eternal" ideals, and not its descriptive truth, that lends it credibility.

I have described Nietzsche's position as one in which the will to life, or will to power, is *incorrigible*. It is not incorrigible in the recent epistemological sense that generally means indubitably certain, but is rather incorrigible in a more colloquial sense of being irresistible, persistent or indominible. I choose this term purposefully because, for one thing, I want to distinguish Nietzsche's approbation of will from Schopenhauer's metaphysical absolutization of will. Even the latter absolutization, as we saw in the preceding section, needed some qualification when it came to Schopenhauer's shifting position on defining will and to his belief that mystics could at least transcend being compelled by willing. Nietzsche's pluralistic, shifting and self-circumscribing thematizations of will must preclude us from claiming that he makes willing into some kind of metaphysical absolute akin to Schopenahauer's will as "thing in itself." And, perhaps surprisingly, not unlike Schopenhauer, Nietzsche admitted occasionally that those who, in a triumph of "decadence," achieved the 'ascetic" way of life could as a matter of fact and conduct live un-impelled by the will to live. But none of this ever entailed for Nietzsche that human

---

[37] Ibid., 339. These "quanta" in Nietzsche's ruminations take the place of classical mechanistic "atoms" when nature is considered most carefully.

[38] 1964a, 51–2.

[39] 1964b, 164.

[40] 1964a, 32–3.

beings *ought* to live without willing the persistence, enhancement and even the tragedy of their earthly lives. The will to live is, for Nietzsche, axiologically incorrigible; in most cases we cannot, but in all cases we should not, even must not, abandon it, deny it, or in any way say "no" to it. Indeed, the "no" to life that Nietzsche believed *nirvāṇa* represented is exactly what makes Buddhism so dangerous to modern Europeans. Nietzsche thought that Buddhism was a foreboding visitor to Europe for the very reason that Schopenhauer believed that Buddhism would be appealing to contemporary philosophers, namely because it held out the possibility that a will-dissolving ascetic spirituality that both spurned theism and traditional metaphysics and offered a "pessimism" that rightly attuned people to the hard realities of life.

8.3   Vijñānavāda and the Causally Conditioned Will

For all the limitations of their different levels of acquaintance with Buddhist thought, Schopenhauer and Nietzsche did basically understand that the most prized goal of South Asian Buddhist thought and practice was the quenching of desire and escape from rebirth. Schopenhauer believed that this main tenet of Buddhism represented a "wondrous" accord with his own system, while Nietzsche took it to be classical India's most triumphant form of "decadence." But even beyond this identification of desirous craving as the cause of life's most difficult problems and the goal to eliminate it found in the "Four Noble Truths", early Buddhism features detailed analyses of the structure of human desire in both its earliest *Discourses* and early philosophical Abhidharma commentaries. One of the aggregates (*kkhanda*) that make up the psychophysical constitution of the human being in early Buddhist thought is the collected habit formations (*sānkhārā*) that are shaped out of our likes, dislikes, attachments and indifferences that are built up through time, and indeed from the life of one individual to another in the next generation. The Buddha himself, in the *Samyutta Nikāya*s, is said to have identified these habit formations as the six kinds of volition (*cetanā*) that are associated with the eyes, ears, nose, tongue, skin and inner feelings and thoughts and are sparked by bodily contact with things.[41] They are also grouped into bodily, verbal and mental kinds of volition that ossify into psychological dispositions.[42] But, given the regularity offered by the process of causally conditioned co-arising (*paticca-samuppada*), though these complexes of volition will keep one "tumbling down the precipice" of rebirth as long as they are left to continue, they can be extinguished (*nibbana*) through the prolonged cultivation enjoined by the eightfold path of Buddhist praxis. In the intervening centuries that passed between the thematization of the early Buddhist position on volition and the writing of Vijñānavāda treatises, the notion that the motivational force or power (*śakti*) of these dispositions of will was transferred from past to future through the medium of psychic seeds (*bija*) had been promulgated by advocates of the

---

[41] Bodhi (2005) 337, Kochumuttom (1982), 64, 66.
[42] Bodhi (2005) 333, Kochumuttom (1982), 135.

Sautrāntika school.[43] But, given internal and external critiques of how well this model of the temporal transference of dispositions from past to future lives comported with the Buddhist doctrine of impermanence, the Vijñānavādins presented an elaborate explanation for the accretion and contingency of human volitions.[44]

In both their general theory of cognitions (*vijñāna*) and specific theory of their complex transformations, the most important early authors of Vijñānavāda, Vasubandhu and Sthiramati, locate volitional activities within consciousness. This seemingly straightforward point has a significant bearing on our present context, as it demonstrates firstly that, for Vijñānavāda, will is not a pervasive force in nor the ground of the natural order, but is instead only one of several causal conditions (*pratyaya*) for certain kinds of experiences to occur. A distinction is made between the six kinds of sensory cognition that merely present experiential content to awareness and the "enjoyment" (*upabogha*) and motivational (*preraka*) cognitions that are strictly mental conditions (*cittasāḥ*).[45] Furthermore, the character of motivation is not homogeneous between one individual and another, but is specific to every person. Each individual's will, though categorizable in terms of extremely general features, is particular or unique (*viśeṣa*) to that person because they associate different kinds of affective and dispositional ideations (*parikalpa*) with sensory cognitions, ideations of pleasantness, unpleasantness. Different people also respond with reactive behaviors that are not drawn from the mere physical existence (*abhuta*) of things. Willing, then, is but one function of our psychological complex that supplies us with our dispositional habits, both affective and actional, in interacting with things in our experience.

Furthermore, while our habits of willing accrete and are accumulated through time in the form of the aforementioned psychic seeds in the "storehouse consciousness" (*ālayavijñāna*), this repository of all cognitions is not itself, by nature, necessarily driven by any state of willing. On the contrary, Vasabandhu claims, the "storehouse consciousness," although it maintains a connection (*anvita*) with all manner of cognitions including volitions (*cetanā*) as long as these are operative, is on its own indifferent (*upekṣa*) to them and merely presses on, like onrushing water, in accord with whatever causal precedents determine how consciousness may unfold.[46] Now, the kinds of cognitions that facilitate the arising of desire and will are only those which feature an internally generated distinction between the grasped content (*grāhya*) of an experience and a putative grasper (*grāhaka*) or self (*ātman*) that "owns" that content in some way. On the grasped side of the equation, the sensory contents of a cognition, whether they be visual, tactile, gustatory or whatever are apprehended in this case not only in terms of sensation, but also in terms of their affective qualities, literally their "touch" (*sparśa*), which all differ from one

---

[43] Waldron 1994, 230, Kochumuttom (1982), 68.

[44] See Jiang (2006), 41–6 on how the Vijñānavādins better addressed "the problem of continuity" created by the Buddhist doctrine of impermanence than other scholastic movements of Buddhist thought (Kochumuttom 1982), 136.

[45] *Madhyānta Vibhāga* 1:9–10 (Kochumuttom 1982), 136.

[46] *Trimśātika* 2–4 (Kochumuttom 1982), 138.

individual to another.[47] That is to say, while visible things have a surface of some kind, they are not "really" orange or blue, while things have ingredients of various kinds, they don't "really" taste bitter or sweet, and while touchable things do have surfaces and contours, they are not "really" rough or smooth, as different persons and different creatures will experience distinct affective states when in contact with the same physical things. But these differences are not really the problem, as it were, with experience. The problem arises on the "grasper" side of the equation, which is produced by another unique and itself contingent type of cognition called the "deliberatively naming cognition" (*manonāmavijñāna*). This "deliberatively naming cognition" artificially produces a sense of selfhood by apprehending all the contents of the storehouse consciousness at any given time and saying the words "I" or "mine," identifying with or appropriating to itself those contents.[48] It is this act, primarily, that creates a fissure or a gap between a fictive self and experience, and it is that gap, wherein identity or possession is either present or not present, which lights the spark that sets aflame the appropriative or acquisitive desires we experience.

Now, according to Vijñānavādins, desires and volitions can cease in the case of those who are able, through certain kinds of Buddhist praxis and cultivation, to eliminate (*nirodha*) this connection (*sannipate*) between the manufactured "grasper" and the "grasped" content of experience, by effectively ridding themselves of ego-consciousness.[49] This is quite a crucial point in the "Cognition School's" portrayal of the person and experience, for the idea here is that it is not that we find experiences pleasant or unpleasant, joyful or sad, attractive or repulsive, that is by itself a karmic affliction (*kleśa*). It is only when such affective habits are permeated by the craving manufactured by the "grasper-grasped" distinction that they are considered "impure" (*akuśala*).[50]

The Vijñānavādins then identify volition or willing as a very specific kind of cognition that contingently arises within a certain causal nexus, as unique to each individual, and as subject to elimination given certain practices. Indeed, the mere "materiality" or "nature" (*prakritya*) of embodied cognition is not itself fundamentally desirous; the "storehouse consciousness" simply proceeds in accordance with whatever foregoing causal conditions happen to predominate in the entire psychophysical complex, and can be purposefully transformed in any possible direction.[51] Willing, therefore, is neither some absolute ground of life or existence for all things in nature nor an incorrigible aspect of human awareness and activity. Even when consciousness is affectively disposed toward the world (and even when it continues to use language to specify what things are and differentiate among them, and even when we interact with others in daily business), willing may or may not be operative in our experience.

---

[47] See Sthiramati's *Madhyānta Vibhāga Kārika Bhāṣya Tikā* 1:11 (Kochumuttom 1982), 138.

[48] *Trimśātika* 5–6.

[49] *Trimśātika* 7.

[50] *Trimśātika* 9–11.

[51] Ibid.

This latter conviction of Vijñānavāda can be taken to indicate a particularly crucial difference between their worldview and those of Schopenhauer and Nietzsche. For Schopenhauer, with the exception of fleeting experiences of beauty or compassion and permanently achieved states of mysticism, all representational experience, in which the correlativity of subject and object is always present, is dominated by willing.[52] There are several interrelated reasons for this in Schopenhauer's system. For one thing, we do not merely experience our objective surroundings as representations appearing before us, but rather, these representations have "significance" or "meaning" (*Bedeutung*) for us; they "do not pass us by like an empty dream or a ghostly vision not worth our consideration," and we do not live in the world of our representation as if we were merely disembodied knowing beings.[53] This indicates for Schopenhauer that, in its natural condition, representational knowledge is "grounded" in willing, for it is precisely the will that makes things interesting and meaningful to us, and which underlies the feelings and actions of our bodies. Furthermore, representational knowledge, in its "objective" aspects, is characterized by the Kantian forms of intuition, space, time and causality, and these "individuating principles," though they "ground" explanations of the relations of things to one another, are themselves "ungrounded" or unexplained unless will serves as their basis.[54] Predominantly, then, the natural, embodied state of human consciousness is one in which willing serves as its fundamental and universal impetus for Schopenhauer. Now, there may be certain achieved states of awareness, as just mentioned, in which willing can be suspended for the particular person who has realized them, though willing has not thereby been eliminated at the underlying level of their ultimate nature. But even when states of refined aesthetic enjoyment, self-sacrificing compassion or mystical triumph are realized, it is *these* exceptional states that are contingent and follow only in certain circumstances. Absent these circumstances, willing dominates consciousness, not only when the subject-object distinction permeates it, but also on the level of solely objective experience, since spatiality, temporality and causality must, according to Schopenhauer, be grounded in will, in order to be at all intelligible.

The explanation differs for Nietzsche but the direction of his arguments ultimately amounts to the same thing. Even when Nietzsche admits that people may occasionally be able to renounce their will-to-live in "ascetic" lifestyles, the very inclination to do so is not only an act of "emasculating the intellect," but it assumes an old philosophical ideal that supposes that consciousness can in such ascetic states be purely reflective of the world. This presumption, for Nietzsche, defies credulity, for it assumes that an "eye" can be turned "in no particular direction," in which the active, interpreting forces of willing, for which "alone seeing becomes seeing something" are somehow supposed to be inactive.[55] But this is simply, under all natural circumstances, not the case for Nietzsche, since seeing, interpreting and willing are

---

[52] 1966a, 141–2.

[53] Schopenhauer 1966a, 98–9.

[54] 1966a, 105.

[55] 1967b, 119.

all necessarily incorporated in every cognitive act. And this is, as we've already seen, as it should be, since for Nietzsche living is willing, and sometimes nature as a whole is "the will to power and nothing besides." Indeed, Nietzsche sometimes more forcefully claims that even when ascetics believe that they are engaging in will-denying behaviors, they are still getting something out of their conduct. In the case of Buddhist ascetics, they actually make religion into "health" and "hygiene" by embracing a "life in the open" of "travel, moderation" and a remarkable lack of "*ressentiment*," but what they are not doing is completely obliterating will even in their professed denial.[56]

The Vijñānavādins do not, by contrast, make the kinds of "essentialist" or "incor-rigible" associations between consciousness and willing that Schopenhauer and Nietzsche far more often than not offer up. For Vijñānavādins, consciousness is simply like "onrushing water" (*srotasauga*), and its transformations (*pariṇāma*) merely proceed from whatever causal conditions happen to prevail at any given moment, and this precludes us from saying that the "primordial nature" (*prakritya*) of conscious life in the world is one of willing. Indeed, one may, according to all Vijñānavāda texts, continue to have both experiences of phenomena and individuals in the world as well as experiences of pleasure and pain in the complete absence of both the subject-object distinction and volition itself. On this matter, what often may look to many like a point of accord between Schopenhauer, Nietzsche and Buddhism on "representational" experience and its permeation by will is actually a point of important divergence between them.

In a more general sense, this contingency of willing that we find enunciated in both early Buddhism and Vijñānavāda texts is not just what distinguishes their worldviews from the nineteenth century's two great "philosophers of will," but is also what makes Buddhism as a whole so provocative for Westerners in the first place. Buddhists claim that it is possible to live in the world as something other, something more, than merely creatures of desire. There is, in the Buddhist view, nothing inevitably natural about specifically human desire or human will. Of course, one must always be mindful in saying this of the Buddhist emphasis on another important distinction between physiological need and desire, where the former requires of life adequate food, shelter and protection and the latter demands acquisi-tive possessiveness in excess of such needs. We cannot continue to survive in the world without fulfilling our physiological needs, and so these needs can be consid-ered natural conditions of life. But we can live in the world without desirous attach-ments and the perturbations of will. For Buddhists, a life unburdened by will is far better; a life free of anxiety, enmity and unfulfilled regrets far healthier than a life dominated by these perturbations. Perhaps, for the Buddhists, it is no surprise that Schopenhauer and Nietzsche are such pessimists, for their pessimism does not lie in their inability to believe in an eternal God or eternal values, but rather is produced by their conviction that a natural human life must be one of principally insatiable willing. Were the Vijñānavādins to have written a philosophical historiography of nineteenth-century European thought, Schopenhauer and Nietzsche may well have been lamented by them as the century's two most ravenous of hungry ghosts.

---

[56] 1974, 148, 49.

References

App, Urs. 1998a. Notes and Excerpts by Schopenhauer Related to Volumes 1-9 of the *Asiatick Researches*. *Schopenhauer Jahrbuch* 79 (1998): 11–33.

———. 1998b. Schopenhauers Begegnung mit dem Buddhismus. *Schopenhauer Jahrbuch* 79 (1998): 35–56.

Atwell, John E. 1995. *Schopenhauer: On the Character of the World: The Metaphysics of Will*. Berkeley: University of California Press.

Berger, Douglas L. 2004. *"The Veil of Māyā:" Schopenhauer's System and Early Indian Thought*. Binghamton: Global Academic Publications.

Bodhi, Bhikkhu. (trans.). 2005. *In the Buddha's Words: An Anthology of Discourses from the Pāli Canon*. Boston: Wisdom Publications.

Clark, Maudmarie. 1990. *Nietzsche on Truth and Philosophy*. Cambridge: Cambridge University Press.

Dauer, Dorothea. 1969. *Schopenhauer as Transmitter of Buddhist Ideas*. Berne: Herbert Lang.

Derrida, Jacques. 1989. Interpreting Signatures (Nietzsche/Heidegger): Two Questions. In *Dialogue and Deconstruction: The Gadamer-Derrida Encounter*. Trans. Diane P. Michelfelder and Richard E. Palmer. Albany: SUNY Press.

Garfield, Jay L. 2002. *Empty Words: Buddhist Philosophy and Cross-Cultural Interpretation*. Oxford: Oxford University Press.

Hacker, Paul. 1995. Schopenhauer and Hindu Ethics. In *Philology and Confrontation: Paul Hacker on Traditional and Modern Vedānta*. Ed. and Trans. Wilhelm Halbfass, 273–318. Albany: SUNY Press.

Halbfass, Wilhelm. 1988. *India and Europe: An Essay in Understanding*. Albany: SUNY Press.

Heidegger, Martin. 1979. *Nietzsche*, vol. I–IV. Trans. David Farrell Krell. San Francisco: Harper.

Hulin, Michael. 1993. Nietzsche and the Suffering of the Indian Ascetic. In *Nietzsche and Asian Thought*, ed. Graham Parkes, 64–75. Chicago: University of Chicago Press.

Jiang, Tao. 2006. *Contexts and Dialogue: Yogācāra Buddhism and Modern Psychology on the Subliminal Mind*. Honolulu: University of Hawai'i Press.

Kochumuttom, Thomas A. 1982. *A Buddhist Doctrine of Experience: A New Translation and Interpretation of the Works of Vasabandhu the Yogācārin*. Motilal Banarassidas: Delhi.

Martin, Glen T. 1993. Deconstruction and Breakthrough in Nietzsche and Nāgārjuna. In *Nietzsche and Asian Thought*, ed. Graham Parkes, 91–113. Chicago: University of Chicago Press.

Morrison, Robert G. 1999. *Nietzsche and Buddhism: A Study in Nihilism and Ironic Affinities*. Clarendon: Oxford University Press.

Nehamas, Alexander. 1985. *Nietzsche: Life as Literature*. Cambridge, MA: Harvard University Press.

Nietzsche, Friedrich. 1964a. *Beyond Good and Evil*. Trans. Helen Zimmern. New York: Russell and Russell.

———. 1964b. *The Joyful Wisdom*. Trans. Thomas Common, New York: Russell and Russell.

———. 1967a. *The Birth of Tragedy and the Case of Wagner*. Trans. Walter Kaufmann. New York: Random House.

———. 1967b. *On the Genealogy of Morals/Ecce Homo*. Trans. Walter Kaufmann, New York: Random House.

———. 1967c. *The Will to Power*. Trans. Walter Kaufmann and R.J. Hollingdale. London: Weidenfeld and Nicholson.

———. 1974. *The Twilight of the Idols/The Antichrist*. Trans. Anthony M. Ludovici. New York: Gordon Press.

———. 1990. *Sämtliche Werke, Kritische Studienausgabe*, vol. 10 of 15, ed. Georgio Colli and Mozino Montinari. München: Deutscher Taschenbuch Verlag.

Radhakrishnan, Sarvapali. 1929. *Indian Philosophy*, vol. 1 of 2. Delhi: Oxford University Press.

Richardson, John. 2002. *Nietzsche's System*. Oxford: Oxford University Press.

Schopenhauer, Arthur. 1966a and b. *The World as Will and Representation*, vol. 1 and 2. Trans. E.F.J. Payne. New York: Dover Publications.

———. 1974. *On the Fourfold Root of the Principle of Sufficient Reason*. Trans. E.F.J. Payne. La Salle: Open Court.

———. 1999. *On the Basis of Morality*. Trans. E.F.J. Payne. Cambridge: Hackett Publishing.

Sprung, Mervyn. 1993. Nietzsche's Trans-European Eye. In *Nietzsche and Asian Thought*, ed. Graham Parkes. Chicago: University of Chicago Press.

van der Braak, Andre. 2011. *Nietzsche and Zen: Self-Overcoming Without a Self*. Plymouth: Lexington Books.

Waldron, William. 1994. How Innovative is the *Ālayavijñāna*? The *Ālayavijñāna* in the Context of Canonical and Abhidharma *Vijñāna* Theory. *Journal of Indian Philosophy* 11: 199–258.

Young, Julian. 1987. *Willing and Unwilling: A Study in the Philosophy of Arthur Schopenhauer*. Dordrecht: Martinus Nijhoff.

Chapter 9
Selfless Care? Heidegger and *anattā*

Sonia Sikka

Although parallels have been drawn between Heidegger and Buddhist thought, the portrait of the self given in Heidegger's most well-known work, *Being and Time*, seems to be diametrically opposed to the Buddhist doctrine of *anattā* (Sanskrit *an-ātman*) in virtually every significant respect. *Being and Time* describes "Dasein" – the entity that I myself am – as intrinsically possessing "mineness." The existence of Dasein, moreover, is defined as "care," *Sorge*, a term that in German suggests being troubled or worried. Dasein is said to be a being for which its own being is an issue. In other words, it matters to itself, fundamentally and essentially, and encounters what is within the world on the basis of this care for its own being. That care has an inescapably temporal structure. On Heidegger's analysis, Dasein is never just here now. It is projected towards the future in which it may accomplish possibilities of its own being, while recalling what it has been and understanding what it can and must do in its current situation. While Heidegger does, in *Being and Time*, characterize absorption in everyday concerns as "inauthentic," the contrasting mode of being, "authenticity," involves a greater, not lesser, degree of individualization, as well as a proper assumption of responsibility for my (and it is always *my*) own most potentiality for being. Thus, it would appear, given this analysis, that the self in *Being and Time* is as real as real can be and that the corresponding ideal of existence involves not a negation of individual selfhood, but a conscientious willingness to accept its burdens.

At the same time, though, *Being and Time* does challenge the idea of the self as a substance, an underlying thing that remains present over the course of time and is supposed to be the unchanging ground of transient properties. In addition, Heidegger's later writings exhibit a marked shift, at least in tone and arguably also in content, away from a self-assertive, anxious model of human existence in favor

S. Sikka (✉)
University of Ottawa, Ottawa, ON, Canada
e-mail: ssikka@uottawa.ca

© Springer International Publishing AG, part of Springer Nature 2018   179
G. F. Davis (ed.), *Ethics without Self, Dharma without Atman*, Sophia Studies
in Cross-cultural Philosophy of Traditions and Cultures 24,
https://doi.org/10.1007/978-3-319-67407-0_9

of one that, while it still involves effort and struggle, is articulated in terms suggesting serene reception as opposed to aggressive imposition. Throughout his writings, moreover, Heidegger rejects the conception of human beings as a self-enclosed subject, confined to the inner space of consciousness. He insists, against this conception, that Dasein, or in his later works just "man," is actually a "clearing," a space within which things come to light and is therefore more "outside" than "inside," insofar as this distinction remains appropriate.[1]

With an orientation to these features of Heidegger's analysis, I approach the issue of his relation to *anattā* from two directions in this chapter. First, I examine Heidegger's analysis, early and late, of the ontology of the self, asking not only how it compares with the thesis that the self does not truly or ultimately exist, but also what critical questions it raises for such a thesis. Second, I explore the existential implications of being, or not being, a self. By this I mean prescriptions for how one ought to be that are correlated with judgments about whether or not there "is" a self, or different ways of being that intrinsically follow from realizations about the self's (non-)existence. My focus in this second section is not on moral, in the sense of other-regarding, consequences of the self/no-self debate, important though these are. It is on the question of how "I" am to be, or on what is "my" good, given the true nature of the self. I have opted to call this topic "existential" rather than, for instance, soteriological or eudaemonic, as my approach is limited to this world, putting aside questions about a possible afterlife, and does not take it for granted that the good is identical with happiness, even broadly defined.

9.1   A Metaphysical Question: Is the Self "Real"?

Heidegger states at the beginning of *Being and Time* that his goal in this treatise is "to work out the question of the meaning of being and to do so concretely" (BT 1).[2] The fact that Heidegger takes this to be a novel question requires some explanation. It might seem that all metaphysics is concerned with the question of being, since it asks what really *is*, arriving at competing answers formulated in positions like materialism, dualism, idealism and so forth. Part of Heidegger's point, however, is that such answers reach conclusions about what is real and what is merely apparent without making explicit and examining critically the criteria being used to determine what counts as true being, and the warrant for the application of these criteria. Metaphysical speculations, that is, generally leave unclarified the idea of being that

---

[1] Reinhold May suggests that Heidegger's understanding of the "clearing" was indebted to Leon Wieger's interpretation of the Chinese character *wu* (May 1996, 31–34). I am less certain but in any case my objective in this essay is to draw conceptual comparisons rather than establish points of historical influence. Heidegger was certainly influenced by East Asian sources, however, and May provides a helpful survey of his contact with Chinese and Japanese thinkers and texts. See also Parkes 1987, 1993.

[2] "BT" refers to *Being and Time* (Heidegger 1962); page numbers refer to the German text, cross-referenced in the margins of Macquarrie and Robinson's translation.

they are employing to discriminate between different ranges of entities and to rank them with respect to their type and degree of being. As a result, an essential ground of metaphysical judgments is left unthematized.

Heidegger aims to make this ground his explicit theme in *Being and Time*, asking what is meant by "being" in various instances and from where these notions of being are derived. His approach is phenomenological, seeking to bracket assumptions and inherited theories while paying close attention to "the things themselves," i.e. to the phenomena as they present themselves to us. While ontological investigations are often oriented towards "objects," Heidegger's investigation takes Dasein, this entity that I myself aim, as its primary theme, attempting, first, to provide an adequate analysis of its being. Heidegger gives Dasein priority in this context because it is the entity that understands being, the one that makes judgments about the "what," "how" and "that" of things, and it therefore seems reasonable to focus on the character of its understanding of itself and the world in approaching the question of the meaning of being. It might be complained that such an approach is "subjective," being limited to how things appear to us rather than asking what *really* is. But such a complaint would be, from Heidegger's methodological perspective, philosophically naïve, making assumptions about how one determines what really is without having secured those assumptions through a critical investigation of their phenomenological basis. The thought here is that all decisions distinguishing reality from appearance still have to be based, ultimately, on conclusions drawn from the way entities present themselves to us. We need to be sure that our representations of those entities capture them accurately in the first place and are then deployed in an appropriate manner.

With respect to the being of Dasein, the critical point Heidegger makes, and stresses repeatedly, in *Being and Time*, is that we tend to misconceive the being of this entity – i.e. our own being – by interpreting it as a kind of thing. Put simply, we reify our own being, but this simple expression requires some unpacking. Heidegger writes that "the kind of being which belongs to Dasein is. .. such that, in understanding its own being, it has a tendency to do so in terms of that entity towards which it comports itself proximally and in a way which is essentially constant – in terms of the 'world'" (BT 15). In other words, we have a natural tendency to conceive of ourselves on the model of the things we encounter within the world, towards which we are oriented most of the time. Traditional philosophical ontologies of the subject suffer from this mistake in a special manner, for not only do they derive their conceptions of being from an orientation towards *things*, but they are in addition focused on things as given to detached observation, which is only one way, and not the primary way, we engage with entities within the world.

Heidegger offers Descartes as a primary example. Descartes' interpretation of the self as a "thinking thing," Heidegger argues, involves a way of picturing the being of the self which is rooted in a particular, and questionable, interpretation of the being of things within the world. In both cases, for Descartes, "the being of an entity that is in itself, is 'substantia'" (BT 89), and the concept of "substance," which literally means "standing underneath," involves "remaining constant" (BT 92). "Extension" is that which, on Descartes' account, remains constant in corporeal things, "underneath" their changing properties, and the being of these things is therefore taken to be "extended substance." "Thinking" is analogously taken to be the defining property of the "ego," the subject of *ego cogito*, "I am thinking." The difference between the properties of extension and thinking is supposed to define the radical difference between the "I" and its objects, but that "I," Heidegger notes, is still conceived, without adequate questioning or analysis, on the model of substantiality, and thus as a kind of constantly present underlying thing. Rather than looking clear-sightedly and without preconceptions at the being of the entity that I myself am, allowing its character to present itself as it is, Descartes "takes the being of 'Dasein' (to whose basic constitution being-in-the-world belongs) in the very same way as he takes the being of the *res extensa* – namely, as substance" (BT 98). Later in *Being and Time*, Heidegger contends that Kant understands the being of the subject in the same way: "… 'Consciousness of my Dasein' means for Kant a consciousness of my being-present-at-hand in the sense of Descartes," so that "when Kant uses the term 'Dasein' [existence] he has in mind the being-present-at-hand of consciousness just as much as the being-present-at-hand of things" (BT 203). Kant may reject the idea of reducing the "I" to a substance, but he still understands it as "the selfsameness and steadiness of something that is always present-at-hand" and accompanies representations, and so in essence as "something substantial" (BT 320–321).

On such ontologies, the "I" is understood as "what maintains itself as something identical throughout changes in its experiences and ways of behaviour, and which relates itself to this changing multiplicity in so doing." It is, in other words, conceived as "something which is in each case already constantly present-at-hand" and maintains itself in this being as the "selfsame in manifold otherness" (BT 150). Heidegger adds that "even if one rejects the 'soul substance' and the thinghood of consciousness, or denies that a person is an object" – as many philosophers do – "one is still positing something whose being retains the meaning of present-at-hand whether it does so explicitly or not" (BT 150). Heidegger rejects this manner of defining the self, claiming that "presence-at-hand is the kind of being which belongs to entities whose character is not that of Dasein" (BT 150). It follows that the self should not be conceived as a kind of substance, some "thing" that stays the same and is supposed to be the underlying ground of experience and action.

Does this mean that, for Heidegger, the self is not "real"? The answer is yes, and no, depending on the interpretation of this question. If to be real means to be a substance of some sort, where substantiality has been conceived as presence-at-hand, a kind of constant occurring, then no, the self of Dasein is not "real".[3] And indeed

---

[3] Anthony Traylor argues, on the other hand, that Heidegger acknowledges in *Being and Time* that Dasein is also, in a way, present-at-hand, and that in general "far from being relegated to the onto-logical periphery, *Vorhandenheit* as pure presence-at-hand stands at the epicenter of Heidegger's problematic" (Traylor 2014, 464). However, while I agree with Traylor that a basic sense of in fact being there, common to Dasein and the things it encounters, is presupposed in Heidegger's account but not adequately thematized, in my view this sense has to be differentiated from the concept of *Vorhandenheit* as intrinsically involving substantiality. It may be that this basic sense of "being" that is common to Dasein and things simply cannot be explicated, from which it would follow that the ultimate project of *Being and Time*, "to work out the meaning of being and to do so concretely" cannot in principle be completed.

Heidegger points out that this is precisely how traditional ontologies have understood "reality," which literally means being like a *res*, a thing (BT 201). But if one means to ask whether the self truly exists, then Heidegger's answer is certainly yes, as he emphatically rejects "the unexpressed but ontologically dogmatic guiding thesis that what *is* . . . must be *present-at-hand*, and that what does not let itself be objectively demonstrated as *present-at-hand*, just *is not* at all" (BT 275). That the being of Dasein cannot be understood in terms of concepts derived from the observation of objects, and that the "self" of the entity that I myself am does not exhibit itself as a substance or collection of substances, does not mean that the "I" lacks genuine being and is instead merely apparent. It means only that our schematizations of the being of "things" do not fit the character of our own being.

This is so far only a negative characterization of that being – Dasein is not a present-at-hand thing; the self is not a substance. It remains to be determined what it then "is," according to Heidegger's phenomenological findings. Now, Heidegger cannot just be saying that insofar as I am, my consciousness is there. He cannot be agreeing with the sort of positions presented by Descartes, Kant and Husserl, which suggest that the existence of my consciousness is transparently undeniable, or that self-consciousness accompanies all representations, or that the presence of a consciousness that is inherently first-personal is the condition for the possibility of apprehending anything else. Whether or not these views are legitimate, Heidegger's point must be a different one, since he problematizes and ultimately rejects the notion of the self as an underlying consciousness on which such arguments seem to depend.

Understanding why Heidegger rejects the concept of "consciousness" as an adequate characterization of the being of Dasein is helpful in understanding his own positive description. Two central reasons for this rejection need to be underlined. One is that "consciousness" suggests an "inner" space, whereas Dasein is defined as "being-in-the-world." It is always already "outside," in the world, concernfully occupied with things and engaging in solicitous relations with others, and this being in the world is an essential constituent of its existence. Second, the being of "consciousness" is associated with the idea of substance and connotes something still and permanent. But Dasein is no permanent unchanging substance; it is dynamic and constantly in process, though not, it should be stressed, in the same way that something observed might be apprehended as always in flux. Dasein is not, for instance, a "stream of consciousness," for it does not, when it is genuinely itself, just stream along. It *projects* possibilities of its own being into the future, seizes upon a range of these in decision, and chooses to realize them in action. It thereby *makes* something of itself, bringing into being what it had envisioned as possible. On Heidegger's phenomenological analysis in *Being and Time*, Dasein is fundamentally a "potentiality-for-being" (*Seinkönnen*). Accordingly, the truth of its being is most clearly disclosed to it not through a detached awareness of itself as aware, but through a sense of its own capability for effecting change. Heidegger privileges the mood of *Angst*, anxiety, in *Being and Time* because this mood especially brings Dasein before itself as responsible for the task of its own individual becoming and called upon freely to assume this task. Genuine "self-constancy," Heidegger therefore writes, consists not in the persistence of some "I"-substance (BT 322), but in the resolute decision to be true to oneself in heeding this call. It is the constancy of a self that properly grasps not the unity of consciousness, but the unfolding and unfinished story of its own individual existence. That requires an authentic anticipation of what it may do, given what it has been and in light of the demands of the situation into which it has been thrown.

In view of this analysis, how would Heidegger, at this stage of his thinking, judge Buddhist arguments regarding the existence of the self? There is of course no single Buddhist position on this issue, but from the vast array of options offered by the history of Buddhist philosophy, I want to focus on two arguments that represent central lines of thinking in at least a substantial number of Buddhist discourses affirming the unreality of the self. The first of these is the argument from parts and wholes. A well-known version of this argument is presented in *The Questions of King Milinda*, employing the analogy of a chariot. In this work, which takes the form of a dialogue, the Buddhist sage Nagasena is asked who he is by the Bactrian King Milinda (in Greek, 'Menander'). He responds that he is called "Nagasena," but that this is only a conventional designation for what is in fact a multiplicity of elements. "Nagasena," moreover, is neither identical with these elements – he is not nails, teeth or kidneys; feeling, perception, or ideas – nor is he something apart from these elements. Therefore, it is concluded, "Nagasena is only a sound" (*Questions of King Milinda* 1993, 29). The text draws an analogy between this case and that of an object like a chariot. The term "chariot" neither names the parts of this (alleged) thing – the yoke, wheels, reins and so forth – nor does it name something beyond these parts. Thus, drawing a parallel between the composition of the chariot and the composition of the self, Nagasena argues that in an ultimate sense there is in both cases no being there, although by convention we may give a single name to such organizations of elements:

> Just as when the parts are rightly set
> The word 'chariot' is spoken,
> So when there are the aggregates
> It is the convention to say 'a being'. (*Question* 1993, 31)

The so-called "self" is composed of aggregates like material form and mental formations, just as the "chariot" is composed of parts like axle and wheels, and neither of these conventionally designated wholes has any real being above and beyond "its" constituents.

From the perspective of Heidegger's analysis in *Being and Time*, this argument could only be judged as profoundly flawed, in its interpretation of *both* the being of the chariot and the being of the self. *Being and Time* actually contains an extended analysis of things like chariots; such entities are what Heidegger calls *Zeug*, tools or equipment. Their being is constituted by an "in-order-to"; that is, they are what they are, and are grasped as what they are, by being referred to an aim that Dasein has and which they serve. The chariot is for conveying persons from one place to another and this is what explains the design and organization of its parts. The purpose it serves, when put together properly, is also what makes it a single thing rather than a collection of parts. To the objection that it "is" nothing other than the parts, one might ask why its form, which is a product of its function, is not counted in establishing its reality as a single being. And to the objection that this function is "subjective," a "projection" of human interests, so that the whole to which it gives rise is merely convention, a Heideggerian response would be that this so-called "subject" is not something that stands outside of being so as to impose its fictional designs upon it. Dasein is in the world, and it acts in the world by projecting designs and making them actual. Some existing people did actually design the chariot to serve an end, after all, and hammered it together out of wood and metal and other natural materials. These are facts about the chariot, not conventions, and the existence of the chariot's makers and users, along with their goals and the place of such instruments in relation to those goals, is also a fact. To suppose that the truth about the being of the chariot must be determined independently of these facts, as if no human beings existed in the world and as if chariots were not actually constructed things within that world, is an odd and objectionable move.

The being of the self cannot be analyzed in such a manner, on Heidegger's account, as it is not a "ready to hand" thing like the chariot. But the nature of things like chariots indicates something fundamental about the being of Dasein, for they reveal its character as an entity that projects possible designs of being into the future and produces actual beings in accordance with these designs. Dasein is at the same time already in a world and occupied with what is presently before it. The unity of these dimensions, which describe the self-realizing of Dasein as being-in-the-world and as an entity for which its own being is an issue, constitutes Dasein in its "wholeness." Heidegger writes in *Being and Time*: "Dasein's totality of being as care means: ahead-of-itself-already-being-in (a world) as being-alongside (entities encountered within-the-world)" (BT 375). Dasein's unity does not consist in being a sum of present-at-hand parts,[4] nor is it the functional unity of a designed thing. It is, rather, the unity of a being that is always in the process of accomplishing itself, and so, in this sense, never *just* present, and also never finished, but nonetheless absolutely singular in its existence.

The inescapability of the "I" lies here not in the primordiality of the first-person perspective on the world (though Heidegger does not deny this aspect of "mineness") but in the fact that I, and only I, have my own being to be.[5] Only I can decide *how* to be; no one else can decide this for me. I can evade the call of my conscience, for instance, or be willing to listen to it. I can choose to face my mortality and to do what is concretely possible for me in the time and place where I find myself to be thrown, or I can lose my time in entertaining distractions and daydreaming and addiction to whatever is tempting at the moment. Others can make such decisions for *themselves*, but they cannot make them for me. In relation to questions about the

---

[4] Heidegger is explicit on this point: "In our existential interpretation, the entity which has been presented to us as our theme has *Dasein*'s kind of being, and cannot be pieced together into something present-at-hand out of pieces which are present-at-hand." (BT302)

[5] This emphasis differentiates Heidegger's account from that of Husserl, and also makes the point here a different one from that on which current debates about the self's existence usually focus. See, for instance, Zahavi 2005 and Fasching 2009.

reality of the self as a unified whole, the point here is that Dasein's being an individual does not consist in the unity of a bunch of parts, or in the perdurance of a substance over the course of a lifetime. It consists, rather, in the constancy of the thrown potentiality-for-being that binds Dasein into a narrative from birth to death, and is revealed in anxiety as a "naked 'that it is and has to be'" (BT 173). It may seem that talk of "individuality" changes the subject, from what is essentially a concern about numerical identity to a more "existential" sense of "being myself" rather than following the crowd. Heidegger's point does not, however, only concern possible forms of comportment. *Angst* genuinely reveals the singularity and "mine-ness" of the self as a free, responsible and individual entity. If what it reveals about the character of Dasein's being as such an entity does not readily fit concepts and categories derived from the observation of objects, that is to be expected. To assume beforehand and without warrant that those concepts and categories define "true" being, and then to reject, as not really real, any kinds of being that do not get captured by them, is just bad philosophy.

Thus, while *Being and Time* also rejects the concept of the self as a separate substance and in this respect agrees with the doctrine of *anattā*, it challenges the view that arguments demonstrating the incoherence of this concept of the self show that the term "I" is a mere convention. Explicating Nāgārjuna's arguments for the ultimate unreality of the self, Jay Garfield writes that "the hypothesis for *reductio* is that over and above (or below and underneath) any composite of phenomena col-lectively denoted by "I" or by a proper name, there is a single substantial entity that is the referent of such a term" (Nāgārjuna 1995, 246). There is, on Heidegger's analysis indeed no such "single substantial entity," but nor is the self a conventional designation for a composite. The self is decidedly a single entity that exists, but it *is* in its own way, and that way is different from the being present-at-hand of a sub-stance. What Heidegger's analysis invites us to see is that the equation of presence-at-hand with true being is not obvious. It involves the transference of a schematization of the being of entities that is derived from a specific region of our experience, into another region which it does not fit. That is like deriving one's idea of a living being from the model of plants and then "demonstrating" that, since an animal does not have leaves or flowers or roots, it cannot be a living thing.

The second, and related, Buddhist argument I want to consider is the argument from transience. In one early Buddhist discourse, it is said that none of the five aggregates thought to compose the self – body, feeling, perception, disposition and consciousness – are permanent, nor are any of them under my control (Holder 2006, 83–86). It follows, the argument goes, that none of these aggregates should be viewed as my permanent self, for if they were, they would not pass away, thereby causing affliction, and the "I" would be able to determine them.[6] If the question at issue here is about the existence of something like a soul, a permanent individual being that "has" a body, feelings, perceptions, dispositions and consciousness, and whose identity could conceivably survive into an afterlife with at least some of these elements intact, then Heidegger's account in *Being and Time* offers no conclusions

---

[6] See Peter Harvey's interpretation of the *Anatta-lakkhana Sutta* in Harvey 2009, 268–269.

one way or another. As a phenomenological analysis, it eschews speculation and has nothing to say about souls or the hereafter. But if the question is about the self that exists between birth and death, then Heidegger's analysis suggests that its being constantly in a state of becoming in no way demonstrates lesser being, let alone non-being.

Indeed, the equation of being with permanence, in the sense of constant sameness, is a central target of Heidegger's critique of traditional ontology in *Being and Time*. Even in his analysis of things within the world, Heidegger takes Descartes to task for his interpretation of the being of things as "extended substance," emphasizing the connection between substantiality and remaining constant, and he notes along the way that for Descartes "nothing like 'force' counts for anything in determining what the *being* of this entity is" (BT 91). For Descartes, what is real is what remains the same no matter what, with the consequence that properties like "hardness" and "color" are judged to be not really real, and processes of change, towards which concepts like "force" are oriented, can only be understood as the change in location of an entity that, insofar as it *is*, remains the same. Extension is judged to be the real being of the world because it is conceived as remaining constant "behind" the changes. Similarly, the being of Dasein is taken to be some other kind of permanent substance, rather than the dynamic process of self-determination that truly constitutes the existence of the "I-myself."

In relation to the argument for *anattā* from transience, therefore, Heidegger's response would be that a) the changing character of the so-called aggregates does not demonstrate their unreality, nor the unreality of the self they are said to compose, and b) the "I"-ness of the "I" is demonstrated not through reflective observation of the aggregates and not even through the observation that it is "I" who observe them, but through the fact that I *can* regard them in one way or another, which the argument itself presupposes. The very capacity to detach from these elements if they are found to be unsatisfactory and disillusioning and to turn away in the course of a search for liberation from the vicissitudes of life and death – a choice that numerous individuals over the course of human history have made – is, on this account, what truly reveals the being of Dasein. I *may* do this, and that is a decision only *I* can make, regarding how to be, which then determines the shape of my life. My power over myself is limited, certainly, for I am a finite being and do not make myself from the ground up. But I am nonetheless answerable for what I make of the life that is given to me, and it is my grasp of that answerability, of responsibility, that best lights up the character of my being.

9.2 An Existential Question: How Should "I" Be?

These last considerations, however, draw attention to the practical aspect of Buddhist arguments for *anattā*, which by and large differentiate these discourses from debates about whether the self is a real entity within modern Western metaphysics. The latter do also have some practical implications - for instance, in our attitudes towards the question of moral responsibility.[7] Occasionally, parties to the debate even report extraordinary experiences or changes to their lives as a result of the conclusions they have reached about whether or not the self is really real.[8] However, metaphysical debates about the self's existence in Western philosophical discourses tend to be conducted independently from discussions about how a person should live and act. They are certainly not themselves transformative exercises in the way that Buddhist reflections are.

In fact, the way in which I have presented the Buddhist "arguments" above is misleading, for this not the way they are told within the traditions to which they belong. The *Questions of King Milinda* actually relates a lengthy and detailed contemplation of how each "part" of Nagasena is not Nagasena. Likewise, the early Buddhist discourse on transience involves a concentrated meditation on the impermanence of every aspect of the self and the painfulness that inevitably ensues from regarding any impermanent property as mine. These reflections are not designed merely to convince someone of the correctness of a particular view of the self at a cognitive level. They map, and *enact*, a "view of the self," one that paradoxically both leads to and is the product of detachment *from* the self. The liberation that this detachment brings is intimately connected with the "rightness" of the view. As stated in another discourse:

> For the most part, the world is bound by approach, attachment, and inclination. But one who does not follow that approach and attachment, that determination of mind, that inclination and disposition, who does not cling to or adhere to the view 'this is my self,' who thinks 'the arising of suffering is what arises, the ceasing of suffering is what ceases' – such a person does not doubt and is not perplexed. Herein, one's knowledge is not dependent on others. To this extent, there is 'right view.' (Holder 2006, 83)

I want now to compare this "right view" with Heidegger's view of the self as care in *Being and Time*, which I began to sketch above. At first glance, there would seem to be a sharp contrast here as well. Surely, arriving at the Buddhist view of no-self involves, above all, a liberation from anxiety about the fate of the self? Heidegger's existential ideal of authenticity, by contrast, describes a willingness to assume that anxiety, and so to shoulder the burden of free self-realization in the face of death, against the temptations of the everyday world with its temporarily comforting pursuits and distractions.

But the contrast is not quite as stark as it first appears to be. Heidegger does define Dasein as "care," *Sorge*, a term whose usual meaning in German is "worry." Supporting his point through a non-philosophical illustration, he alludes to a Latin fable about the creation of human beings, in which it is decided that the spirit of this

---

[7] In *An Essay Concerning Human Understanding* (1690), John Locke discussed the question of the self's continuity and identity in terms of personhood, describing "person" as "a forensic term, appropriating actions and their merit," and therefore applying "only to intelligent agents, capable of a law, and happiness, and misery" (Book II, Ch. 27, "Of identity and diversity," Locke 2010–2015, 120). This dimension of the question about the "real" existence of the self remains important in current debates; see, for example, Korsgaard's critique of Derek Parfit in Korsgaard 1989.

[8] Examples are Parfit 1984, 281, and Harris 2014 (though the latter case is ambiguous, since Sam Harris had also been engaged in Buddhist meditative practices for many years).

creature will be given to Jupiter after death and its body to Earth, but that it shall be named after "care," *cura*, for "she shall possess it as long as it lives" (BT 198). This fable characterizing the essence of man, Heidegger writes, brings into view "the kind of being which dominates his *temporal sojourn in the world*, and does so through and through," for "man's *perfectio* – his transformation into that which he can be in being-free for his ownmost possibilities (projection) – is 'accomplished' by 'care'" (BT 199). "Care" has many modalities, however, and is by no means equivalent to concerned preoccupation with one's worldly affairs. Heidegger differentiates the anxiety that belongs to authentic being-in-the-world, which is one modality of care, from fear as another modality. *Angst* is not "anxiety" in the sense of being worried about this or that eventuality or outcome; it is not fear of something threatening *in* the world. *Angst* is, rather, anxious before "being-in-the-world as such," and Heidegger suggests that resolute willingness to be anxious in this sense actually liberates a person from fear, for it renders inconsequential the everyday "cares" in which we are usually absorbed (BT 266).

One should also notice the following sentences in *Being and Time*, on the relation between indifference, equanimity and resoluteness:

> Indifference (*Gleichgültigkeit*), which can go along with busying oneself head over heels, must be sharply distinguished from equanimity (*Gleichmut*). This latter mood springs from resoluteness (*Entschlossenheit*), which, in a moment of vision, looks at those situations which are possible in one's potentiality-for-being-a-whole as disclosed in our anticipation of death. (BT 345)

Heidegger must then think that authenticity, made possible by anxiety about one's being-in-the-world, is compatible with equanimity as a way of being emotionally attuned to the world. "Resoluteness" is the term Heidegger uses to describe the kind of decidedness he associates with authenticity. It may seem to denote an assertive act of willing, but the term is ambiguous as Heidegger uses it in *Being and Time*, since it means a *willingness* to follow the call of conscience.

In the shift Heidegger undergoes during the period marking the transition between his earlier and later thought, this ambiguity is resolved and the emphasis increasingly falls on a mode of being that is the opposite of worried, egoistic assertion. Accompanying this shift is a reinterpretation of ideas Heidegger had developed in *Being and Time*, as one can see from this notebook entry on "care," written in the late 1930's:

> "Care" – the awkward space for that in-standing of humanity in the there – almost the opposite then of what "one" knows as "cares" – hurrying and attachment in desire and acquisition. Care – but it means the gatheredness of human beings from the simplicity of that undriven simple–creative relation to being – almost releasement (*Gelassenheit*).. .
> (Heidegger 2014, 495)

By this point, Heidegger remarks on the difficulty of describing properly the mode of being that he has in mind and the consequent need to use traditional terms like "cura," though they might be misleading (Heidegger 2014, 495). In the *Letter on Humanism*, written a few years later still, Heidegger describes man as "the shepherd of being," whose existence is charged with guarding and preserving the truth of being, and says that this is what he meant by "care" in *Being and Time* (Heidegger 1993, 234). *Gelassenheit*, "releasement," "letting-go," or, in its common meaning, "serenity," is the term that eventually comes to replace "resoluteness" in Heidegger's understanding of the way of being that accords best with the mission of humanity as "the shepherd of being." And *Gelassenheit* is, he insists, *not* a form of willing; it involves a renunciation of willing and remains absolutely outside any kind of will (Heidegger 1966, 59).

So how does this conception of *Gelassenheit* relate to Buddhist ideals of *anattā* as detachment from self? *Gelassenheit* does not renounce action, nor does it abandon being-in-the-world. It is not *nirvana*, if that means an extinction of the "I" in every sense and a going beyond any form of care for existence. There is still "care" in *Gelassenheit* and a link with the ideal of authentic being one's self in *Being and Time*, and yet *Gelassenheit* does involve relinquishing the "I" in *some* sense. It is not anxious attachment to the "ego"; it is neither anxious, in fact, nor attached, nor concerned about oneself. Care has now given way to the ideal of a gracious and patient acceptance to think what needs to be thought and do what needs to be done at the moment in which one stands. This is not conceived as an assertion of the "I" imposing its will, including its designs and representations, onto the world and others. It is the opposite of such imposition, a gentle accordance that is nonetheless in its own way stilll active and effortful, since it involves a struggle to bring to fruition what is given to it as a requirement and a need. Whereas *Being and Time* describes authenticity as an anxious resolve for my ownmost potentiality-for-being, then, suggesting a kind of self-realization over time, *Gelassenheit* points to a calm tending of the possibilities of being that are given to me to be realized. The difference is subtle, and *Gelassenheit* could be described as a form of care, while care could be described as a form of willingness.

Perhaps the ideal of *Gelassenheit* is in some respects more like that of *karma yoga* presented in the *Bhagavad Gita* than it is like the detachment required to reach either *moksha* or *nirvana*, conceived as involving a complete renunciation of action (where thinking is also an action). For there is still action here, and struggle, and even the possibility of success and failure. Only, the motivation for such action is not the selfish desires of the "I", concerned about whether or not it will get what it wants and therefore constantly unsettled. It is rather, a willingess to serve, to be a kind of medium through which what needs to be accomplished, in view of the distresses and wrongs one perceives, may in fact be done. Without such willingness, after all, no lack in being would ever be filled through the actualization of a better possibility.

There is, however, a sense in which the possibility of *Gelassenheit*, as Heidegger describes it, does demonstrate that the existence of the self is "conditioned." The reality of the "I" that is motivated by desire and fearfully preoccupied with preserving and enhancing its being in the world is indeed a conditional one. Its being is dependent upon willing. If willing ceases, it does not arise. On Heidegger's analysis, what is always "there" in the world between birth and death, however, whether willing or not willing, is an individual site for the "clearing" of being. At this site, things come to light within a space that Heidegger prefers not to call "consciousness," for reasons discussed earlier, but that nonetheless "is" and could still be called a "self" if one can understand that term in a sense where it is emptied altogether of the representing, calculating assertion that constitutes its typical being. Heidegger describes it as a kind of openness, other to the ego, which is prior to thinking and being (Heidegger 1966, 83). It is especially this aspect of Heidegger's later thought that has been compared with the Buddhist idea of no-self (see Zimmerman 2006, 309).

The ordinary "self" would then be a strange sort of creature, dependent, peculiarly, on the act of asserting its existence, an act that may or may not be performed by an agent that cannot quite be called "myself". One might pause here and ask whether that makes the existence this "self" a matter not of fact but of value, as its being would appear to depend upon a kind of decision – to will, or not to will. At the same time, if, on one ideal, ultimate liberation is thought to consist in a cessation of *all* activity, effecting a complete closure of being-in-the-world, its accomplishment, too, would seem to rest at least in part on a value. B.K. Matilal suggests that the very idea of life as *dukkha* – an idea central to all Indian religions, in his view, and not only to Buddhism – centrally involves a judgement of value rather than only of fact. According to Matilal, life is judged to be *dukkha* if and only if, one seeks *nirvana*; otherwise, and ordinarily, it is reasonable to see life as a mix of pain and pleasure. "Or, to see the point in another way," he writes, "the noble truth [i.e. that life is *dukkha*] is a truth of ethics and religion rather than of metaphysics" (Matilal 2004, 23). If Matilal is right, the question about the existence of the self that cares about itself, whose being is actually produced by that caring, cannot be dissociated from this judgement about life, which in turn is grounded in the quest for a cessation of *dukkha*.

Matilal does not argue that *no* factual judgement is involved in the declaration that life is pain, for he acknowledges that "if, for example, every man desires *nirvana* then to the extent his worldly life is antagonistic to this goal, the pain-thesis, all is *duhkha*, would be both factual and evaluative" (Matilal 2004, 22). His point is that the desire for *nirvana* conditions the judgement that life is *dukkha*, though there may be a fact of the matter about this desire. My additional point is that the actual existence of the self is dependent upon a decision that is in turn dependent upon the goal of *nirvana*, so that it is also a "truth of ethics and religion rather than of metaphysics," involving a judgement of value.

A comparison with Nietzsche, whose ontology of the self has affinities with the doctrine of *anattā* but whose ideals of life are starkly different, helps to illustrate this point. Nietzsche also argues that there is no independent entity, no single unified substance, corresponding to what we call the "self" (*Beyond Good and Evil*, 12, 16, 19; Nietzsche 2003, 43, 45–46, 49). The self is, rather, on Nietzsche's analysis, an epiphenomenal product of a multiplicity of forces, which manifest themselves within living beings as will to power, the desire of every living being to exert its strength (BGE 13; Nietzsche 2003, 44). This is not a drive that a living being "has," as if the being were a subject possessing this property.[9] Will to power constitutes the

---

[9] Nietzsche challenges the idea that there is any such "subject" from a number of directions, arguing in one place that "'the doer' is merely a fiction added to the deed" (*Genealogy of Morals*, First Essay, 13; Nietzsche 1989, 45).

being of the entity, and if "it" is itself a multiplicity, as Nietzsche asserts, then the entity is itself only a multiplicity organized in a certain way; it is not ultimately real. Moreover, following Schopenhauer, who was himself influenced by the Buddhist as well as Vedantic ideas, Nietzsche affirms that will to power inevitably subjects living beings to conflict and suffering. And yet, Nietzsche is a champion of will to power and a critic of philosophies and worldviews that seek release from it.

There are some questions about matters of fact, psychological and metaphysical, at issue in Nietzsche's decision on this point. Nietzsche is sceptical about metaphysics generally, and would not assent to doctrines like karma and reincarnation. He is also a monist about will to power at the level of psychology, which means that non-willing is not a possible condition for a living being. Nietzsche therefore explicitly rejects the interpretation of religious asceticism as involving a renunciation of will, arguing instead that it is in fact a will to nothingness rather than a non-willing (*Genealogy of Morals*, Third Essay, 1; Nietzsche 1989, 97). In line with these metaphysical and psychological views, Nietzsche interprets Buddhist and Vedantic notions of liberation as achieving only a state of unconsicousness, by individuals who are weary of life. Alluding to passages from Shankara quoted by Paul Deussen, a contemporary Indologist who was at one time also his close friend, Nietzsche writes: "But it is not easy for us to take seriously the high valuation placed on *deep sleep* by these people, so weary of life that they are too weary even to dream – deep sleep, that is, as an entry into Brahma, as an *achieved unio mystica* with God" (GM III:17; Nietzsche 1989,133). Nietzsche's understanding of Buddhism is similar; it is a nihilistic worldview, born of a hypersentisitivy to pain and seeking release through a cessation of suffering (*The Anti-Christ*, 20; Nietzsche 1990, 142–143), radicalized in the will to nothingness. Nietzsche is known for interpreting many allegedly "wise" worldviews, Western no less than Asian, as products of this reaction to life, whose goal is, as he sees it: "the hypnotic sense of nothingness, the repose of deepest sleep, in short *absence of suffering* – sufferers and those profoundly depressed will count this as the supreme good, as the value of values" (GM III:17; Nietzsche 1989, 134).

One might dispute Nietzsche's claims about the inescapability of willing, which Heidegger, for one, does not share, as we saw above. One might also dispute his view of states like *nirvana* as involving a mere death-like absence of suffering, an interpretation Nietzsche inherits from Schopenhauer. But if I may be permitted to hazard a slightly bizarre counter-factual, I think that even if Nietzsche had accepted the possibility of non-willing, and had access to more complex and nuanced understandings of the soteriological goals of Buddhist philosophy, he would still have rejected a doctrine like *anatta* as an existential goal, in spite of holding similar, though not identical, ontological views about the self. That is because Nietzsche values positively the productions of will to power, including contestation and even suffering, and therefore sees only enervation and decline in worldviews seeking to escape these productions, in whatever fashion.

The fact of transience, moreover, constitutes for Nietzsche no objection to the desire to expand, enhance and enjoy one's worldly life, and not even where that requires some forgetfulness. Consider the following passage on death from *The Gay*

Science, so starkly different in its sensibilities from either Heidegger or Buddhist thinkers:

> Living in the midst of this jumble of little lanes, needs, and voices gives me a melancholy happiness: how much enjoyment, impatience, and desire, how much thirsty life and drunkenness of life comes to light every moment! And yet silence will soon descend on all these noisy, living, life-thirsty people. ... How strange it is that this sole certainty and common element makes almost no impression on people, and that nothing is further from their minds than the feeling that they form a brotherhood of death. It makes me happy that men do not want at all to think the thought of death! I should like very much to do something that would make the thought of life even a hundred times more appealing to them. (*The Gay Science*, 278; Nietzsche 1974, 225)

That the "self" is a temporary amalgamation of elements sustained by thirst provides no argument, in Nietzsche's judgment, for letting go of it. Thirst for life yields new life, new forms of becoming, and if one values becoming, as Nietzsche emphatically does, then the constancy of this thirst is a fact to be celebrated rather than adduced as a reason to judge that life is *dukkha*.

Heidegger's notion of *Gelassenheit*, I propose, actually provides a sort of middle way between these extremes of self-denial and self-affirmation. I leave it as an open question whether there are versions of *anattā* that do so in a similar sense.[10] Many Buddhist philosophers, including Nāgārjuna, also articulate a middle way between affirming and denying the "existence" of the self, of course, but Heidegger's notion of *Gelassenheit* has nothing to do with any metaphysical distinction between "ultimate" and "conventional" reality. It points, rather, to a distinction between possible *ways of being*. One of these ways of being is concerned with securing the world for itself, and constructs the "self" of such concern. The other has no such self-concern, no worry or *cura*, but still in a way "cares" for the fulfillment of those possibilities of being that are given to it in the time and place where it finds itself. This is why I suggested earlier that the path of *karma yoga* as depicted in the *Bhagavad Gita* might provide a better parallel for such a way of being than does the Buddhist ideal of realizing the emptiness of *anattā*. Or it is, at least, a better parallel than are the world-renouncing styles of life that originally accompanied the doctrine of *anattā* in the Indian context where Buddhism was born. *Karma yoga* also involves a kind of letting go of the self, which does not renounce action but does renounce attachment to the fruits of action, resulting in equanimity. It is, furthermore, *niskama*, "desireless" and therefore calm, yet still dutiful, motivated to act, although not from any self-concerned striving to achieve goals.[11] In short, it is a kind of selfless readiness for service, as is Heidegger's notion of humanity as "the shepherd of being."

---

[10] The following description of *nirvana* by Miri Albahari suggests there are: "There is a radical shift in motivational structure: no longer do such persons seek gratification from any state of affairs. Losing family or suffering illness fails to dent their equanimity. The arahant operates from a different basis: no more identifying with the 'I' of such situations than most of us would identify with burning leaves on a fire. Yet they still act fluently in the world – with great joy and spontaneity and compassion" (Albahari, 79). Heidegger was himself admittedly not much like an arahant, but then *Gelassenheit* describes a possible way of being rather than an achievement of this particular man.

[11] For an extended analysis and defense of the coherence of this idea, see Framarin 2009.

The latter conception turns human beings from subjects seeking to satisfy their wants, and calculating best how to do so, to (non)-selves cleared of such egoism but still able to perceive what is needed and to respond. This is a kind of realization of truth, for Heidegger, a realization of the true nature of being and of being human. Only, a decision is required to stand within this truth, and that decision determines the "existence" of the self.

9.3   Conclusion

Through the foregoing comparative discussion of Heidegger and *anattā*, I have meant to highlight multiple ways in which the self can be said to "be" or to "exist," while drawing attention at the same time to different possible meanings of "self." My objective has not been merely to draw parallels and contrasts, in itself not so interesting an endeavour, but to shed light on the philosophical question about the existence of the self, particularly on the relation between its metaphysical and existential dimensions. Implicitly, this has also been an exercise in comparative religion, for Heidegger's earlier understanding of being a self, in *Being and Time*, is clearly inspired by a Christian model of anguished responsibility before God (see Kisiel 1993, van Buren 1994), while his later thought is just as clearly marked by Asian influences (May 1996). Relating Heidegger's earlier and later positions on the self to the idea and ideal of *anattā* therefore also brings Christianity into complex dialogue with Buddhism. I conclude by suggesting that setting up dialogues of this sort is a valuable aspect of "inter-faith" conversation. In the interests of accuracy and genuine mutual understanding, it is important that such conversation not always proceed by downplaying or leveling differences though bland appeals to religions as different paths to the same goal. Nor should it assume a hostile opposition, though, as if it were obvious that there is only one best path to one best goal. Rather, inter-religious conversation needs to involve a charitable but also critical confrontation between different ideas about what is and how to be, among human beings struggling to find a way to deal with being in - perhaps by not being *of* - the world.

References

Albahari, Miri. 2011. Nirvana and Ownerless Consciousness. In *Self, No Self? Perspectives from Analytical, Phenomenological and Indian Traditions*, ed. Mark Siderits, Evan Thompson, and Dan Zahavi. Oxford: Oxford University Press.

Fasching, Wolfgang. 2009. The mineness of experience. *Continental Philosophy Review* 42: 131–148.

Framarin, Christopher. 2009. *Desire and Motivation in Indian Philosophy*. New York: Routledge.

Harris, S. 2014. *Waking up: A Guide to Spirituality without Religion*. New York: Simon & Schuster.

Harvey, Peter. 2009. Theravada philosophy of mind and the person: *Anatta-lakkhana Sutta, Mahanidana Sutta*, and *Milindapanha*. In *Buddhist philosophy: Essential readings*, ed. William Edelglass and Jay Garfield, 265–274. Oxford: Oxford University Press.

Heidegger, Martin. 1962. *Being and Time*. Trans. John Macquarrie and Edward Robinson. Oxford: Basil Blackwell.

———. 1966. *Discourse on Thinking*. Trans. John M. Anderson and E. Hans Freund. New York: Harper & Row.

———. 1993. *Basic Writings,* ed. David Farrell Krell. New York: Harper Collins.

———. 2014. *Überlegungen II–VI (Schwarze Hefte 1931–1938),* ed. Peter Trawny. Gesamtausgabe 94. Frankfurt: Vittorio Klostermann.

Holder, John J. 2006. *Early Buddhist Discourses. Indianapolis.* Hackett.

Kisiel, Theodore J. 1993. *The Genesis of Heidegger's Being and Time*. Berkeley: University of California Press.

Korsgaard, Christine. 1989. Personal Identity and the Unity of Agency: A Kantian Response to Parfit. *Philosophy and Public Affairs* 18 (2): 103–131.

Locke, John. 2010–2015. *An Essay Concerning Human Understanding. Book II: Ideas*, ed. Jonathon Bennett. http://www.earlymoderntexts.com/pdfs/locke1690book2.pdf.

Matilal, B.K. 2004. *Logical and Ethical issues: An Essay on Indian Philosophy of Religion*. New Delhi: Chronicle Books.

May, Reinhard. 1996. *Heidegger's Hidden Sources: East-Asian influences on his work*. New York: Routledge.

Nāgārjuna. 1995. *The Fundamental Wisdom of the Middle Way*. Trans. and Commentary Jay L. Garfield. New York: Oxford University Press.

Nietzsche, Friedrich. 1974. *The Gay Science*. Trans. Walter Kaufmann. New York: Vintage Books.

———. 1989. *On the Genealogy of Morals and Ecce homo*. Trans. Walter Kaufmann and R.J. Hollingdale. New York: Vintage Books.

———. 1990. *Twilight of the Idols and The Anti-Christ*. Trans. R.J. Hollingdale. London: Penguin.

———. 2003. *Beyond Good and Evil*. Trans. R.J. Hollingdale. New York: Penguin Books.

Parfit, Derek. 1984. *Reasons and Persons*. Oxford: Clarendon Press.

Parkes, Graham, ed. 1987. *Heidegger and Asian thought*. Honolulu: University of Hawaii Press.

———. 1993. Heidegger and Japanese Thought – How Much Did He Know, and When Did He Know It? In *Heidegger: Critical assessments*, ed. Christoper McCann, 377–406. London: Routledge.

Questions of King Milinda: An Abridgement of the Milindapanha. 1993. Ed. N.K.G. Mendis. Sri Lanka: Buddhist Publication Society.

Traylor, Anthony. 2014. *Vorhandenheit* and Heidegger's Predicament over Being-in-Itself. *American Catholic Philosophical Quarterly* 88 (3): 439–464.

Van Buren, John. 1994. *The Young Heidegger: Rumor of the Hidden King*. Bloomington: Indiana University Press.

Zahavi, Dan. 2005. *Subjectivity and Selfhood: Investigating the First-Person Perspective*. Cambridge, MA: MIT Press.

Zimmerman, Michael E. 2006. Heidegger, Buddhism, and Deep Ecology. In *The Cambridge Companion to Heidegger*, ed. Charles B. Guignon, 293–325. Cambridge: Cambridge University Press.

Chapter 10
Echoes of Anattā and Buddhist Ethics in William James and Bertrand Russell

Nalini Ramlakhan

10.1 Introduction

Many of the essays in this volume highlight the distinctive argument in Chap. 8 of Śāntideva's *Bodhicaryāvatāra*, which supports impartial altruism by appealing to a form of the Buddhist doctrine of no-self.[1] Such radical scepticism about selfhood was, by contrast, quite rare in Western philosophy, especially prior to the nineteenth century, but became fairly common – or at least familiar – following the impact of writers such as Schopenhauer, Nietzsche and some of the British idealists. Prior to the last century, one of the best known sceptics about traditional accounts of selfhood was William James; another, following fast on his heels (but also more ambivalent) was Bertrand Russell. Historians tend to emphasize their differences over the matter of pragmatism; but here I consider some of their common ground, as well as some key differences, in light of parallels with Śāntideva and other Buddhist writers.

In fact, it is natural to wonder whether James or Russell or both may have been influenced by the Buddhist writings that were published for the first time (in the West) in the mid-nineteenth century. In the case of James, for example, many of his writings seem to reflect Buddhist ideas, and not only regarding the ontology of selfhood; his theory of morality[2] resembles one sort of consequentialism that some commentators have identified as also playing a role in the development of Mahāyāna Buddhist ethics.

---

[1] For the full argument, with translation and discussion, see Jay Garfield's essay (Chap. 6) in this volume; see also the essay by Stephen Harris (in the next chapter).

[2] While some draw a distinction between ethics and morality (in various contested ways), I shall use these terms interchangeably in this paper. (The chapters in this volume by Mills and Sikka mention some ways of distinguishing them, and I do not wish to contest their usefulness; let us say my focus here is on *other-regarding* ethics.)

N. Ramlakhan (✉)
Cognitive Science Department, Carleton University, Ottawa, ON, USA
e-mail: nalini.ramlakhan@carleton.ca

© Springer International Publishing AG, part of Springer Nature 2018   197
G. F. Davis (ed.), *Ethics without Self, Dharma without Atman*, Sophia Studies
in Cross-cultural Philosophy of Traditions and Cultures 24,
https://doi.org/10.1007/978-3-319-67407-0_10

In *The Varieties of Religious Experience*, James makes reference to Buddhism and kindred religions, suggesting that, at the very least, he was aware of Buddhist ideas and principles. As we shall see, his friend and colleague Bertrand Russell was even more clearly influenced by certain Buddhist ideas, which suggests that there may have been some mutual reflection about these ideas, between these two influential figures.

The purpose of this chapter is to draw parallels between the ideas of James and Russell and certain elements of Buddhist doctrine. In particular, I aim to draw parallels on the one hand between James's conception of selfhood and the Buddhist doctrine of no-self and, on the other hand, between James's theory of morality and Buddhist ethics. I will also discuss the importance of the denial of selfhood in both theories of morality, as well as in certain phases of Russell's thinking on ethics. While there is little evidence to suggest that James was directly inspired by Buddhist ideas, the parallels between the two are striking and worth exploring for both their historical significance and philosophical value. There is more historical evidence available in Russell's case, but in some ways the most interesting comparisons are philosophical, including those that bring James and Russell together, and those that set them apart on these issues.

This chapter begins with a detailed account of James's analysis of selfhood as presented in *Principles of Psychology*, where I suggest that James holds a reductionist view of the self. I then discuss one formulation of the Buddhist doctrine of no-self, one that has famously been developed by Mark Siderits, and draw parallels between these two analyses. Following this, I provide an account of James's theory of morality, arguing that his theory is consequentialist in nature. I label his theory 'impartial moral consequentialism.' Then, I turn to Buddhist ethics, and suggest that Buddhist ethics endorses a similar form of consequentialism. In doing so, it will be apparent that James's view of selfhood and the Buddhist doctrine of no-self play significant roles in both theories of morality. Following this, I briefly turn to some of James's arguments in *The Varieties of Religious Experience* where he argues that religion (a kind of therapeutic religion in particular, including a spiritual practice along Buddhist lines) can benefit the individual in various ways. I do this simply to draw further parallels between James's philosophy and Buddhism. The final section of this paper then discusses the possible relations and influences between James, Russell, and Buddhism. I will discuss parallels between Russell's philosophy and Buddhism and draw further comparisons between James's philosophy and both – i.e. both his contemporary and his ancient precursor.

10.2   James's Analyses of 'Selfhood'

James claims that the only thing that we can positively assume in psychology is that some sort of thinking goes on.[3] Almost as certain, but perhaps deceptively so, is the idea that our thoughts belong to our own consciousness and cannot belong to

---

[3]According to Blackmore (2011), central to James's theory of personal identity is the idea that there is a phenomenology of psychical unity; but as James acknowledges, this does not settle the

another's consciousness. Be that as it may, thoughts are always in flux. James claims that there is an ongoing stream of thought for every individual thinker, as "experience is remoulding us every moment, and our mental reaction on every given thing is really a resultant of our experience of the whole world up to that date" (James 1890, p. 234). Whereas Hume considers consciousness to be a succession of ideas, James considers consciousness to be a stream of experiences.[4] Even transitive states, which James defines as relations between objects, are a part of the stream of consciousness because they give rise to feelings.

James splits the 'self' into two dimensions. There is the empirical self and the pure ego. The empirical self includes what James calls the material self, the social self, and the spiritual self. On James's model of the 'self', the empirical self is known objectively, while the pure ego is known subjectively. With regard to the empirical self, James claims that it is difficult to draw the line between what we call 'me' and 'mine'. This is because we tend to appropriate. This is similar to the Buddhist conception of the conventional 'I', and how we reach the conclusion that a 'self' exists in the conventional sense. For James, the things that we appropriate give rise to similar emotions to the things that we consider 'me', such as our bodies.

The first part of the empirical self, the material self, involves our body and bodily features, such as the way that we dress. The second part of the empirical self, the social self, involves the way that we present ourselves to others. The third part of the empirical self, the spiritual self, involves a person's inner or subjective being, their psychic faculties or dispositions taken concretely. Considering ourselves as spiritual selves requires that we think of ourselves as thinkers. On James's model, thoughts have a different existence than other things because thoughts can be of no one thing in particular, can be merely symbolic, or can even relate to non-existent things, like fictions. James claims that "whilst in the thoughts that do resemble the things they are 'of' (percepts, sensations), we can feel, alongside of the thing known, the thought of it going on as an altogether separate act and operation in the mind" (1890, p. 297). For James, all that the spiritual self really consists of is feelings, and these feelings include bodily feelings as well as abstractions.[5]

---

question of whether unity or continuity *exists*. James even seems to deny the existence claim when he says that "the thought itself is the thinker," suggesting, perhaps, that among our cognitive states and sense data there is no separate 'owner' of those states.

[4] James also disagreed with Hume in another regard, despite the fact that their theories of personal identity are quite similar. While Hume dismissed the concept of the 'self' as a mere fiction, James acknowledged that such a view runs against "the entire common sense of mankind" (Blackmore 2011, p. 122). In outlining a sort of compromise view, James invokes this metaphor: in order to have a herd, there must be a herdsman that owns and holds the cattle together. There is no permanent herdsman, however, but rather a series of passing owners who inherit the cattle. Thus, "each Thought is born an owner and dies owned, transmitting whatever it realized as its self to the next owner. In this way is the apparent unity created" (Blackmore 2011, p. 123).

[5] According to Blackmore (2011), the spiritual self is the name given to "mental dispositions and abilities, and intellectual, moral and religious aspirations, together with moral principles, conscience and guilt" (p. 121). The spiritual self also includes subjective experience.

James defines the pure ego, the second dimension of 'self' that is known subjectively, as everything that an individual is conscious of at any given time (which may not, after all, include a real ego, so this is more about purity, perhaps, than about ego). At times, he acknowledges other conceptions of selfhood. For example, when discussing the stream of conscious thought, he says that "in the other sense of continuity, the sense of the parts being inwardly connected and belonging together because they are parts of a common whole, the consciousness remains sensibly continuous and one. What now is the common whole? The natural name for it is *myself, I,* or *me"* (James 1890, p. 238). He also seems to accept some conception of a 'soul' in *The Varieties of Religious Experience.* However, it is clear that he does not accept the conventional conception of 'self'. In his chapter "The Consciousness of Self" in the *Principles of Psychology,* he claims that there is nothing more to a spiritual self than a series of bodily movements, such as head movements, which give rise to feelings. And referring to both Humean and Buddhist views, in *The Varieties of Religious Experience,* James ([1902] 2012, p. 195) adds that:

> When I say 'Soul', you need not take me in the ontological sense unless you prefer to; for although ontological language is instinctive in such matters, yet Buddhists or Humians[*sic*] can perfectly well describe the facts in the phenomenal terms which are their favourites. For them the soul is only a succession of fields of consciousness; yet there is found in each field a part, or sub-field, which figures as a focal and contains the excitement, and from which, as from a centre, the aim seems to be taken. Talking of this part, we involuntarily apply words of perspective to distinguish it from the rest, words like 'here', 'this', 'now', 'mine', or 'me'; and we ascribe to the other parts the positions 'there', 'then,' 'that,' 'his' or 'thine,' 'it,' 'not me.'

Whether or not there is more to a self than this is a key question with respect to the diachronic dimension of personal identity. That there may not be is suggested, perhaps, by James's emphasis on the role of *feeling.* In attempting to determine what the 'self' may feel, James claims that we must "settle for ourselves as definitely as we can, just how this central nucleus of the Self may *feel,* no matter whether it be a spiritual substance or only a delusive word" (1890, p. 298). James acknowledges that we seem to have direct acquaintance with the 'self', and apparently cannot have direct acquaintance with any other 'self' but our own; but this too is (perhaps no more than) a feeling, i.e. a pervasive but fallible phenomenology.

Surveying these reflections on 'selfhood', we can conclude that James's conception of personal identity reduces it to the collection of an individual's mental states and thoughts, which are constantly in flux, but nonetheless thought of as a continuous stream of consciousness. For James, there is no more to selfhood than this. Similar to the conception of selfhood in Buddhism, the 'self' exists purely in the conventional sense and there are conventional truths about our various selves, but the 'self' does not exist at the ultimate level of truth.[6] This suggests that James held a *reductionist* view of personhood. A reductionist view of the self holds that "there

---

[6]As Ashwani Peetush points out in Chap. 12 in this volume, there are also Hindu systems of thought (e.g. Advaita Vedanta) that offer a split-level treatment of individuality and selfhood, ultimately debunking any ontology of the latter. Given that James was also aware of Hindu thought, more needs to be said to motivate special attention to the *Buddhist* parallels.

are no facts about persons and personal identity beyond facts about brains, bodies, and mental or physical events" (Shoemaker 2009, p. 248). One way of probing or testing this categorization is to compare James's analysis to others; and we may learn more if we notice parallels with analyses from outside the Western tradition.

10.3   The Buddhist Doctrine of No-Self (Anattā)

In seeking to formulate the Buddhist conception of personhood in modern terms – and somewhat controversially invoking the notion of reductionism[7] – Mark Siderits points out that "to be a reductionist about a certain kind of thing is to hold that things of that kind do not exist in the strict sense, that their existence just consists in the existence of other kinds of things" (2007, p. 69). In the words of another writer, someone who is a reductionist about selves or persons holds that "*persons are like societies* [in that] individual lives are really like sets of lives" (Shoemaker 2009, p. 248) – 'lives' that may themselves consist in other kinds of things (where 'lives' would, in a fuller description, be replaced by e.g. *experiences*). And as Derek Parfit famously infers, there is therefore no deep distinction *between* individuals (Parfit 1984). Glossing Parfit's view of personhood, David Shoemaker adds that "what makes you and me different is just that you've got a different body, brain, and stream of consciousness from me, but that's just not a significant difference between us, and it certainly doesn't call for there to be any deep *moral* difference between us" (ibid, 248). With regard to the 'self', Buddhists seem to hold a similar view. As Siderits and Katsura (2013) put it, "all Buddhists agree that there is nothing in reality that is the basis of our sense of 'I' and 'mine'. They agree that it is our mistaken belief in the existence of something behind this sense of 'I' and 'mine' that brings about suffering" (2013, p. 193).

The Buddhist view of personhood is often called the 'no-self' view. It is called 'no-self' because Buddhists do not believe that a 'self' exists at the ultimate level of truth. By the same token, 'persons' do not exist at the ultimate level of truth, though they do exist at the conventional level of truth. Conventional truths are really just fictions that many people (e.g., those who are not on the path to nirvana) believe to be true. The no-self thesis says that "we are empty persons, persons who are empty of selves" (Siderits 2007, p. 32). According to Siderits,

> … by 'the self' what Buddhists mean is the essence of a person—the one part whose continued existence is required for that person to continue to exist…to say that there is a self is to say that there is some one part of the person that accounts for the identity of that person over time. If there were a self, then the person whose self it was would continue to exist as long as that self continued to exist. The self would then be the basis of a person's identity over time… [But instead] the Buddhist view [is]… that the existence of a person just consists in the occurrence of a complex causal series of impermanent, impersonal *skandhas*. (2007, pp. 32–33 & 69)

---

[7] See n. 10 below, on the role of reductionism in his approach; see also the chapter by Stephen Harris in this volume (Chap. 11).

The five *skandhas* include *rupa* (anything physical or bodily), feeling (sensations), thirdly perception, fourthly *sankhara/samskara* (sometimes called 'mental forma-tions'), and finally consciousness (awareness). The early Buddhist defence of the of no-self doctrine is supported by the exhaustiveness claim, which is the claim that "every constituent of persons is included in one or more of the five *skandhas*" (Siderits 2007, p. 37), and no other mental component can be found in an ultimate analysis. While this claim calls for elaboration and defence, my aim here is not to defend reductionism, but instead to draw parallels between Buddhist views and James's philosophy. (A comprehensive defence of not one, but two, versions of the no-self claim, can be found in Siderits (2015).)

Just as James argued that 'self' boils down to a collection of thoughts and other mental states, early Buddhists argued that 'persons' reduce to complex causal series within the five *skandhas*. (As noted below, this is an Abhidharma-based formula-tion; but the no-self conclusion has wider application, as we shall see.) Naturally, such a reconceptualization of personhood will have implications for the scope and content of ethical thought, which suggests another place to look for parallels between James's philosophy and Buddhist philosophy. We will now turn our discus-sion to James's theory of morality and then consider similarities with Buddhist ethics.

10.4   James's Moral Theory

The key elements of James's moral theory can be found in his essay "The Moral Philosopher and the Moral Life", published at the end of the nineteenth century. The normative part of James's theory is, I shall argue, a form of consequentialism. Although James does not offer a label for his theory, we can call it 'impersonal moral consequentialism', in light of the following features of his approach.[8] At first, it appears that James endorses utilitarianism (a specific form of consequentialism) when, in describing what 'the best' is, he says that "the best, on the whole, of [vari-ous] marks and measures of goodness seems to be the capacity to bring happiness" ([1897] 2010a, b, p. 201). However, we notice that his conception of consequential-ism is more axiologically open-ended (than utilitarianism) when he says that "in seeking for a universal principle we inevitably are carried onward to the *most*

---

[8] In its most basic form, consequentialism is a normative theory that holds that 'the good' should be maximized. A consequentialist is someone "who holds that what makes an action wrong is its failure to maximize the good, that is, its failure to bring about the best consequences" (Shoemaker 2009, p. 242). Unlike utilitarianism, which is a strict form of consequentialism that focuses on the maximization of pleasure or happiness, consequentialism more generally is open regarding whether the maximized good should consist of pleasure, pain-avoidance, virtue, wisdom, equity, or whatever. It leaves open what exactly 'the good' is and therefore what should be maximized. As David Shoemaker remarks, "consequentialism is a kind of placeholder theory, neutral with respect to a variety of possible valuable things one might maximize" (2009, p. 242).

universal principle, – that *the essence of good is to simply satisfy demand...* [where] demand may be for anything under the sun" (201).

I use the term 'impersonal' to describe James's consequentialism because he believes we should not prioritize – or give any sort of greater normative weight to – any particular person's 'demands', not even (to) ourselves, from our own point of view as agent. That is, his view is 'agent-neutral', in the sense that we should "bring about the very largest total universe of good which we can see" ([1897] 2010a, b, p.209) – not only giving peasants' interests (in his example) a priority that is at least equal to those of aristocrats, but more generally, giving those of others a priority equal to ones' own. Meanwhile, on James' theory of morality, moral considerations apply only to sentient beings. As James puts it, "surely there is no *status* for good and evil to [have] in a purely insentient world" ([1897] 2010a, b, p. 185). Insofar as the relation between 'good' and 'obligation' is vague and contested, things are murkier in the curious hypothetical scenario James considers, where there exists just one sentient being. James calls this scenario a 'moral solitude', and claims that "in such a moral solitude it is clear that there can be no outward obligation, and that the only trouble the god-like thinker is liable to have will be over the consistency of his own several ideas with one another" ([1897] 2010a, b, p. 191). However,

> if we now introduce a second thinker with his likes and dislikes into the universe, the ethical situation becomes much more complex, and several possibilities are immediately seen to obtain. One of these is that the thinkers may ignore each other's attitude about good and evil altogether, and each continue to indulge in his own preferences, indifferent to what the other may feel or do. In such a case we have a world with twice as much of the ethical quality in it as our moral solitude [had], only it is without ethical unity. (ibid, 191, 192)

James continues by stating that such a world would be a moral dualism rather than a moral universe because there is no single point of view from which the morality of both beings can be judged. However, "multiply the thinkers into a pluralism, and we find realized for us in the ethical sphere something like that world which the antique sceptics conceived of, – in which individual minds are the measures of all things, and in which no one 'objective' truth, but only a multitude of 'subjective' opinions, can be found" (ibid.). Later, I consider how this reflects James's pragmatism; but for now, we should bear in mind that the subjectivity here may relate to what is 'good' rather than what is 'right'. Since 'impersonal moral consequentialism' is a theory of the latter, it remains an open question whether a Jamesian should consider this view as having an objective or a subjective status.

In "The Moral Philosopher and the Moral Life", James claims that the words 'good', 'bad', and 'obligation' "have no absolute natures... [t]hey are objects of feeling and desire, which have no foothold or anchorage in Being, apart from the existence of actually living minds" ([1897] 2010a, b, p. 197). Furthermore, he states that "wherever such a mind exists, with judgments of good and ill, and [making] demands upon... other[s], there is an ethical world with its essential features" (ibid, p. 187). Many Buddhists would agree with these meta-ethical claims; but they are perhaps not as fundamental as his normative claims, which show an even deeper affinity, with at least one moral view in the Buddhist tradition (as we shall see in the next section).

In attempting to determine what morality consists of and what the 'good' is, James notes that

the Benthams [and] the Mills… have done a lasting service in taking so many of our human ideals and showing how they must have arisen from the association with acts of simple bodily pleasures and reliefs from pain. Association with many remote pleasures will unquestionably make a thing… significant of goodness [sic] in our minds; and the more vaguely the goodness is conceived of, the more mysterious will its source appear to be. ([1897] 2010a, b) p. 186)

For James, the moral ideal requires: 1) satisfying as many 'demands' as possible, and 2) minimizing dissatisfactions. This sounds once again like utilitarianism, but James points out that the things that make us feel good can be things like "the passion for poetry, for mathematics, or for metaphysics" (187) or even "the love of drunkenness" (186). He also claims that "a vast number of our moral perceptions… are certainly of this secondary and brain-born kind… [t]hey deal with directly felt fitness between things, and often fly in the teeth of all the prepossessions of habit and presumption of utility" (187). As we shall see, in contrast to early utilitarians, James included spiritual experiences in this extended category of goods (and thus counted them among legitimate 'demands' within the aspiration for a good life).

Nonetheless, James's kinship with classical utilitarianism is evident when he writes that "nothing can be good or right except so far as some consciousness feels it to be good or thinks it to be right" (James 1890, pp. 192, 193). Despite this epistemic limitation – or perhaps because of it – his main argument for impersonal moral consequentialism involves reasoning by elimination, and a shifting of the burden of proof in moral theory. He contends that the burden of proof is on the opposition to prove his claim wrong. In a move reminiscent of Bentham's approach, he challenges his opponent to consider "any claim, however slight, which any creature, however weak, may make. Ought it not, for its own sole sake, to be satisfied? If not prove why not…" ([1897] 2010a, b, 195). He then asks: "since everything that is demanded is [*pro tanto*] a good, must not the guiding principle for ethical philosophy (since all demands conjointly cannot be satisfied in this poor world) be simply to satisfy at all times *as many demands as we can*" (p. 205)? When it comes to discriminating between various demands, he claims that "that act must be the best act, accordingly, which makes the *best whole,* in the sense of awakening the least sum of dissatisfactions…those ideals must be written highest which *prevail at the least cost,* or by whose realization the least possible number of other ideals are destroyed" (ibid.).

Perhaps reflecting the post-classical shift from direct to indirect forms of consequentialism, James adds:

The best, on the whole of these marks and measures of goodness seems to be the capacity to bring happiness. But in order not to break down fatally, this test must be taken to cover innumerable acts and impulses that never *aim* at happiness; so that, after all, in seeking for a universal principle we inevitably are carried onward to the *most* universal principle, – that the *essence of good is simply to satisfy demand.* The demand may be for anything under the sun.[9]

---

[9] One reader has remarked that this seems to veer towards Spinoza (who claimed that *what is good is whatever one desires*), albeit on a matter about which Spinoza seems to diverge from most

What is significant in this passage is James's claim that the acts and impulses that lead to happiness (or more generically, satisfaction) need not *aim* at happiness (or indeed, presumably even at satisfaction). The general underlying principle may be the same—moral rightness is determined by the good, even though this is now thought of as overall maximum satisfaction in a broad sense. Thus James adopts a *consequentialist* approach, and though he was influenced by utilitarians such as Bentham and Mill, he does not believe that our acts must always aim directly at the good, a good which is meanwhile not quite happiness in any narrow sense. Rather, we should develop systems of belief and value such that their application leads (experimentally, and perhaps indirectly) to the maximization of life-satisfaction. Here, we can see how James's moral theory accommodates the role of habits and other (indirectly justifiable) personal patterns in ethical life, as it is lived in practice. A utilitarian might agree: if you act and live your life in such a way that your actions produce the greatest amount of happiness, your actions will be justified, whatever the proximate intention may have been. Insofar as James's consequentialism is open to a greater range of 'goods', however, the role of happiness can be replaced here with a broader notion of 'satisfaction'; and this may bring it closer to Buddhist axiology, which adds a range of spiritual goods to the ones that utilitarians have more typically associated with happiness.

10.5 Buddhist Ethics (from Abhidharma to Mahāyāna Altruism)

As we have seen, one of the central doctrines in Buddhism is the doctrine of no-self. Stated in Abhidharma terminology, this means that the *self* does not exist, except in a conventional sense when used to refer to 'my' person or another's 'individuality', whose parts exhaust what there is in the way of both appearance and reality (only the parts exist, in any ultimate sense). The worst of human suffering is ultimately explained by widespread belief in a *real self*, and the most significant step towards attaining nirvana consists in realizing that this ultimate truth explains (and explains away) the conventional truths.

This Abhidharma system of thought serves to reinforce the ethics of the *brahmaviharas*, of which the most famous has been *compassion*. Mahāyāna Buddhism, meanwhile, is well-known for an even more demanding (or at least more expansive) conception of compassion. Practicing Mahāyāna Buddhists, such as the Dalai Lama,

Buddhists, for whom the most justifiable demand is not for 'anything under the sun', but rather, for spiritual liberation. See the chapter on Spinoza (Chap. 5 in this volume) for discussion of this point; the authors there question whether Spinoza could really have meant for his claim to be applied to the sense(s) of 'good' that seem to open up common ground between Western and Buddhist ethicists (and in attenuating the claim, they suggest a reconciliation with Buddhist ethics). Similar concerns may apply to James, although the neutrality of James's assessment of 'demands' may, at least, helpfully reinforce the *impersonal* nature of his consequentialism.

are often used as examples of the ambitious humanitarianism that is bound up with such Buddhist ideals. However, the question arises, if the 'self' does not exist, why should we be moral toward others at all?

Most Buddhists claim that "becoming enlightened [and in particular realizing that the 'self' does not really exist[10]], relieves existential suffering… [and] makes us more concerned about the welfare of others" (Siderits 2007, p. 69, parentheses mine). Although the 'self' does not actually exist, there are ethical obligations that we have towards sentient beings, and the doctrine of no-self reinforces our obligations towards all these beings. Because Buddhism is traditionally atheistic in nature, the moral values that stem from Buddhism are not thought of as corresponding to some divine law. According to Siderits (2007), Buddhist morality has three layers. The first (putative) rationale for morality is based on karmic causal law; you reap what you sow, and sowing the seeds of immorality will grow into sources of suffering for the agent. However, as Siderits (2007) points out, this layer only seems to apply to individuals whose primary aim is to attain pleasure and happiness, rather than those actively seeking nirvana. This leads to the second layer of morality. According to early Buddhism, there are three poisons that fuel *samsara*, the cycle of death and rebirth (which stands between us and nirvana, so to speak); in classical Abhidharma, these three poisons are greed, hatred, and delusion. We should be moral beings and avoid the three poisons because doing so is part of the training needed to attain nirvana. "[T]he claim is that by following this regime of retraining our emotional habits, we will ultimately become able to fully grasp the truth about ourselves—that there is no self—and thus attain nirvana" (Siderits 2007, p. 80).

There is also the question of why those who have already attained nirvana should be moral. If those on the path to nirvana are moral because the immoral 'poisons' interfere with the liberating insight of non-self, then why should those individuals who have already been liberated be moral? As Siderits (2007) puts the question, "is there anything about enlightenment that could constitute a source of moral motivation" (p. 80)? This is where the third, and final, layer of morality comes in. Here, we find "an argument for an obligation to be benevolent: whenever we are able to prevent others from experiencing pain or suffering we must do so" (Siderits 2007, p. 80). Here we may detect the rudiments of yet another form of impersonal moral consequentialism:

> [T]o the extent that morality consists in giving equal consideration to the welfare of others, this can be seen as an argument for an obligation to be moral. The immorality of stealing, for instance, can be explained by the fact that the thief intends to benefit while causing others pain. To be moral is to give others' welfare no less weight than one gives one's own welfare. (p. 80)

When we become enlightened, then, we see that the good of promoting the welfare of others needs no ulterior motive or explanation. Explicable or not, there is nonetheless a kind of moral truth acting as both standard and guide – the truth that everyone's happiness deserves equal consideration. And if that is the moral standard

---

[10] Siderits's phrase, omitted here, which is a gloss on *becoming enlightened*, is "coming to know the truth of reductionism", but in citing this way of formulating my own understanding, and that of 'most Buddhists', it is perhaps worth exercising some caution about the label 'reductionist'.

regardless of the pattern of intuitions that may motivate an enlightened being,[11] then it would seem that such a standard would also indirectly justify the other layers of morality, to the extent that they do effectively channel our social impulses in the right direction; but on this point, Buddhist ethicists have differed about how best to interpret Buddhist values.

In a recent book advocating wider application of the lessons of Buddhist ethics, Charles Goodman comments that "there has been some controversy, and much confusion, about which Western ethical theories resemble Buddhist views, and in what respects" (2009, p. 3). Undaunted by this formidable interpretive challenge, he tries to show in his *Consequences of Compassion* that Buddhist ethics is most akin to consequentialism. According to Goodman,

> Buddhist ethics is based on compassion… [but if we] define compassion simply as a motivation to promote the welfare of others… the fundamental basis of the various forms of Buddhist ethics is the same as that of the welfarist members of the family of ethical theories that analytic philosophers call 'consequentialism'. (ibid., p. 5)

The phrase used earlier to label James's view, 'impersonal moral consequentialism', is perhaps even more apt here, given that Buddhist ethics is literally impersonal – that is, committed to a *no-self* or *non-self* understanding of the totality of sentient beings (a totality, or *dharmadhatu*, that is *anātman*: without self or selves). Inspired by Sāntideva, Goodman invokes the no-self insight to reinforce his 'agent-neutral' understanding of consequentialism.

Goodman also emphasizes three forms of compassion found in Buddhist ethics that directly relate to the doctrine of no-self. First, there is compassion toward living beings, which is the lowest form of compassion. Goodman claims that this "compassion toward living beings…is a feeling or emotion that generates a motivation to promote the welfare of others, but constrains that motivation with considerations depending for their validity on the distinction between different persons" (Goodman 2009, p. 6).

The second form of compassion is directed toward impersonal events and is based on the realization that the 'self' does not exist. That is, it is based on the realization that "the boundaries between the lives of sentient beings are conventional, and do not reflect any really existing unity of an individual life, or separateness of distinct lives" (Goodman 2009, p. 6). As we have seen, this realization also informs James's moral theory. James argues that the 'self' does not exist, and that 'individuals' can be reduced to collections of mental states. Insofar as we can see James's theory of selfhood as a form of reductionism, we can then attribute this same premise to both Buddhist ethicists and James: "not only is there is no deep metaphysical difference between individuals, there's also no deep metaphysical unity within individual lives" (Shoemaker 2009, p. 249; here Shoemaker is echoing Derek Parfit's

---

[11] Leaving aside some complications as to how Mahayanists describe bodhisattvas and buddhas as enlightened without being liberated in an *absentee* sense, we could gloss how such an enlightened being proceeds, using more classical terminology: such a being would enjoy *nirvana-with-remainder*, not the sort of 'nirvana-without-remainder' that would efface all agency (not to mention all being) from the path that the person had occupied.

famous version of this view). This line of thinking implies that there is nothing more to a person than various experiences that are related to one another in different ways—which implies that there is no deep distinction between persons. And there is a further implication, which is that "what makes you and me different is just that you've got a different body, brain, and stream of consciousness from me, but that's just not a significant difference between us, and it certainly doesn't call for there to be any deep *moral* difference between us (as there might be if we had souls)" (Shoemaker 2009, p. 248). It would seem that Buddhists and Jamesians should agree on this, given their views on both selfhood and morality.

Meanwhile, according to Goodman, the third form of compassion "depends on the realization of emptiness" (2009, p. 6). Going beyond the prior stages, the bodhisattva who has reached this level intuits the emptiness of not only persons but of all objects, concepts and thoughts. Interestingly, he adds, "those who [operate at this level] do not believe any ethical theory at all; indeed, they are not committed to any theory about anything… [W]ithout any need for deliberation, they behave as if they were act-consequentialists" (Goodman 2009, p. 6). On the one hand, this raises important questions about the extent to which 'moral theory' is a desideratum of advanced Buddhist practice (though, for that matter, we could ask the same question about pragmatists like James, quite reasonably second-guessing the application to James of a notion of 'moral theory'). On the other hand, Goodman stresses that even after abandoning a 'theoretical' approach to moral decision-making, something like act-consequentialism is still in the picture, even for bodhisattvas – perhaps as a moral *standard*.[12]

In any case, while bodhisattvas who are guided by the third form of compassion may not be 'committed' to any ethical theory, they nonetheless automatically behave in a consequentialist manner (on the interpretation that is shared by Siderits and Goodman). That is, in a way that echoes what James says about moral action, they do not *aim* to maximize the good — they simply do (perhaps within the constraints of *samsara*). Goodman adds that "Buddhists texts claim that this form of compassion is expressed in the minds of enlightened beings: Buddhas, Tantric *siddhas,* and other advanced bodhisattvas" (2009, pp. 6–7). When such beings act *selflessly,* this now has a double meaning: they act on behalf of a greater whole, and whatever they channel in doing so is not channelled through any 'self'.

To my knowledge, James did not link – with anything like that degree of explicitness – his analysis of personhood and his ethics; and yet, his ethics offers many parallels to this consequentialist interpretation of Mahāyāna Buddhism. There is one further parallel worth noting. Some may object to my approach by arguing that James merely glimpsed the same sort of structural outline of an ethical theory that some Buddhists (and *only* some, such as Sāntideva) seem to have developed, and

---

[12] This latter possibility is suggested by a more recent proposal offered by Goodman (2016), though it is not the only way of reading the above claim; it could be that act-consequentialist *success* is just an unpremeditated outcome of bodhisattvas' actions. The question of why this might *matter* is addressed in Goodman (2016).

that a key element that is missing from James is the spiritual dimension of Buddhist axiology. But I shall argue that this element was not overlooked by James after all.

10.6   Other Parallels Between James's Philosophy and Buddhism: The Varieties of Religious Experience

Buddhists claim that existential suffering is caused by ignorance about the truth (most crucially, the truth that there is no such thing as a 'self'). Yet existential suffering can also be compared to the pathology of clinical depression.[13] Early reflections on the depressive aspects of existential suffering (early in the Western tradition, that is) can be found in thinkers such as Schopenhauer.[14] Seeking nirvana, even if never reached, can release individuals from existential suffering (or alleviate it), and this is meant to be the ultimate goal of meditation and other forms of Buddhist practice. Given this, we can understand Buddhism as a 'way out' of existential suffering where Buddhism gives life a 'deeper meaning'. As Siderits states, "the point, for Buddhism, is to attain nirvana, to bring suffering to an end" (2007, p. 8). Although the quintessentially religious theme of soteriology is present here, it is important to keep in mind that Buddhism lacks many features of religions that are known as 'faiths', and is often seen as a form of atheism (especially early Buddhism). According to Siderits, "if we think of religion as a kind of faith, a commitment for which no reasons can be given, then Buddhism would not count… [Buddhists do not] accept a bundle of doctrines solely on the basis of faith [and]… salvation is not to be had just by the devout belief in the Buddha's teachings" (2007, p. 7). As Hanson and Jones put it: "Buddhism encourages people to take nothing on faith alone and does not require a belief in God" (2009, p. 8). The point here is that even though Buddhism differs in this way from other religions, Buddhist practice can be seen as a way to release oneself from existential suffering, and allows practitioners to find 'deeper meaning' and to purge various pathologies, including perhaps many that are diagnosable by modern methods, leaving it an open question whether existential suffering itself can be or not. Many people who have suffered from depression or existential suffering, such as Tolstoy, turn to religion for this sort of release. In *The Varieties of Religious Experience,* James discusses how religion can benefit these sorts of individuals.

James labels individuals like Tolstoy, those who suffer from existential angst but then find meaning in life, as 'twice-born' ([1902] 2012). In this category of 'twice-born', he includes 'Brahmins' – apparently simply meaning Hindus – as well as Buddhists and some Christians, and 'Mohammedans'. James calls individuals that are twice-born 'sick souls'. They are sick souls because they suffer from existential angst. That is, they look for a meaning in life and cannot find one, and thus become

---

[13] See Hanson and Jones (2009).

[14] See the essay by Douglas Berger (Chap. 8) in this volume, on Schopenhauer.

alienated and discontented with life. When they eventually find meaning in their life, usually through religion, they are 'born again', and this is why they are 'twice-born.' These individuals are contrasted with the 'healthy-minded', who have always been optimistic about life and find meaning and purpose in it. James cites the philosopher Baruch Spinoza and the poet Ralph Waldo Emerson as examples of the healthy-minded. Speaking of an early kind of psychotherapy (known simply as 'mind-curing'), in which a restored healthy-mindedness takes on a spiritual dimension, James notes that:

> The results... [of] combined optimism and expectancy [and associated] regenerative phenomena... remain firm facts of human nature, no matter whether we adopt a theistic, a pantheistic-idealistic, or a medical-materialistic view of their ultimate causal explanation... The theistic explanation is by divine grace, which creates a new nature within one the moment the old nature is sincerely given up. The pantheistic explanation (which is that of most mind-curers) is by the merging of the narrower private self into the wider or greater self, the spirit of the universe (which is your own 'subconscious' self), the moment the isolating barriers of mistrust and anxiety are removed.[15] ... Whether the third [materialistic] explanation might, in a psycho-physical account of the universe, be combined with either of the others may be left an open question here. ([1902] 2012, pp. 91–92.)

James adds that "the completest religions would... seem to be those [with]... pessimistic elements... Buddhism, of course, and Christianity are the best known to us of these... religions of deliverance: the man must die to an unreal life before he can be born into the real life" (ibid., p. 131). In this sense, Buddhists can be seen as twice-born since they initially experience existential suffering, and then after realizing that the self does not exist, are born again into a real life where happiness becomes possible. Again, we see that James was quite aware of Buddhist teachings, and elements of those teachings surface at various key junctures in his writings.

James argues in *The Varieties of Religious Experience* that religion can be useful because it can help sick souls. This is one function of religion according to James. Suspending the question of whether the experiences correspond to objectively real phenomena, James concludes that the effects of religion on the mind are real. As he put it,

> [T]he experiences are only psychological phenomena. They possess, it is true, enormous biological worth. Spiritual strength really increases in the subject when he has them, a new life opens for him, and they seem to him a place of conflux where the forces of two universes meet; and yet this may be nothing but his subjective way of feeling things, a mood of his own fancy, in spite of what is produced. (2012, p. 385)

In the same way that Buddhism relieves existential suffering and depression, James believes that religion, whether it holds any truth or not, has a healing effect on the mind. James even suggests that "God is real since he produces real effects [mental

---

[15] The merging of the 'narrower' private self into the greater self can be seen as a realization of what might already be a *fait accompli*: the unity of many selves in one stream of consciousness, akin to what some pantheists describe as the unity of everything in the universe, such that persons and other things are not ultimately differentiated at all. This may call to mind Advaita Vedanta, but when we consider James's phrase – "the isolating barriers of mistrust and anxiety are removed" (p. 91n.) – there is a strong resonance with Buddhist themes here as well.

ones]" (ibid., p. 391), where the effects evidently involve the release of existential suffering. It would appear that a Jamesian would have to accept a similar line of reasoning about the notion of *nirvana* (and its reality).

In this section, I have tried to show that there are similarities between Buddhist practice and meditation and James's view of the benefits of religion with regard to sick souls. In some passages, it is evident that James was exposed to some Buddhist teachings. Although it would be going too far to say that James was inspired by Buddhism, it appears that he was familiar with many of its key ideas; and in any case, the parallels between Buddhism and James's philosophy are striking.

10.7   Russell and Buddhism

In light of our discussions of James's moral philosophy and of moral ideals in early Buddhism, it is clear that there are striking parallels between the two. What is more, it is likely that James's view of selfhood influenced his moral philosophy, just as the doctrine of no-self shaped Buddhist morality—another parallel between the two. And there is reason to believe that James was influenced by Buddhism to an extent, although the evidence is scattered and indirect. It is quite likely that James was exposed to Buddhist writings given that such writings had been read and discussed by his friends and colleagues, one of whom was Bertrand Russell.

Russell's *Autobiography* reveals some intriguing connections with both Buddhism, on the one hand, and with William James, on the other. Russell reports that his older brother thought of himself as a Buddhist of some sort,[16] and it is possible that Russell, who as we shall see was sometimes inspired by Buddhism himself, discussed Buddhist philosophy with James.[17] In this final section, I turn to the influence of Buddhism on Russell's philosophy, and after comparing the similar impact of such influence on James and Russell, I acknowledge a difference between James and Russell that reveals the latter to be perhaps even closer to the Buddhist sensibility. In particular, I will contrast James's fundamentally pragmatic attitude towards belief-systems with what appears to be Russell's emphasis on a strong form of objectivity (echoing the epistemic ideal of 'seeing things as they really are'), as the goal of philosophy and science.

In the Pali Canon, *'yatha-bhuta-dassana'* means 'seeing things as they really are'. When a Buddhist approaches nirvana, or when a bodhisattva is far along the path of wisdom, they aspire to see things as they really are (e.g., that the 'self' is only real at the conventional, and not the ultimate, level of truth). The ultimate aim of Buddhist meditation and practice, as discussed above, is to attain the ability to see things as they really are. When *yatha-bhuta-dassana* is attained, existential suffering is extinguished.

---

[16] As Russell mentions in his *Autobiography* (1967), vol. 1, p. 46.

[17] There are references to James (and correspondence between the two) in *ibid.*, vol. 1, pp. 80, 167, 197 and 211.

These two goals, however, are not necessarily equivalent. When James endorses religious belief, this is because it can cure 'sick souls' of existential suffering, not because it will necessarily capture reality as it really is. While James seems to accept both a no-self view and some form of impartial consequentialism, and while he emphasizes the ethical importance of religion, he reduces the soundness of such views to their pragmatic value. Russell, on the other hand, entertains a no-self view, and a similar impartial consequentialism, not solely with a view to their practical or pragmatic significance, but also in the hope of reflecting the reality of things ('seeing things as they really are'). Part of this orientation stems from Russell's views on metaphysics and science. Before showing that Russell endorses the aim of *yatha-bhuta-dassana* (albeit in a more scientific idiom), I will first offer a survey of some of Russell's works, which will show that he was influenced by Buddhism and favoured some key Buddhist ideas.

In "Greek Exercises", one of Russell's journals when he was sixteen years old (in 1888), he writes,

> I think there is much in Buddha's *nirvana*, where the good sleep in peace. For is not a good night a most pleasant thing, [being a] temporary cessation of the action of the mind? We are delivered from all troubles and anxieties, and are entirely forgetful of our existence…[I]t makes goodness a much finer thing, as it takes from it all possibility of reward beyond internal satisfaction. (Russell 1999, p. 13)

At this young age, Russell was already familiar with the notion of *nirvana* as a kind of inner tranquility, in which the mind is at peace. In his later writings, he deepens his affinity for Buddhist philosophy of psychology by putting in perspective what 'the mind' amounts to in the context of (so-called) individuals.

For instance, in his 1927 book, *An Outline of Philosophy,* Russell states that.

> The notion of substance, at any rate in any sense involving permanence, must be shut out from our thoughts if we are to achieve a philosophy in any way adequate either to modern physics or modern psychology…[T]he 'ego' has disappeared as an ultimate conception, and the unity of a personality has become a peculiar causal nexus. In this respect, grammar and ordinary language have been shown to be bad guides to metaphysics… And it must be understood that the same reasons which lead to the rejection of substance lead also to the rejection of 'things' and 'persons' as ultimately valid concepts. (1927, pp. 254–55)

'Substance' is a term used in philosophy to refer to something that is permanent and unchanging. When Descartes and others speak of substance, they are speaking about something that is permanent and persists throughout time. With regard to personal identity, Descartes claims that the 'self' is equivalent to a soul, which he believes to be unchanging and permanent throughout time. David Hume, on the other hand, argues that insofar as a self is supposed to be permanent and unchanging, such a self does not actually exist because our perceptions are always changing and are impermanent. Hume states that "I may venture to affirm of the rest of mankind, that they are nothing but a bundle or collection of different perceptions, which succeed each other with an inconceivable rapidity, and are in a perceptual flux and movement" (2008, p. 162). Similarly, Russell claims that.

[conscious perception, e.g., of colour] does not of itself involve that more or less permanent person whom we call 'I'. So far as immediate certainty goes, it might be that the something which sees the brown colour is quite momentary, and not the same as the something which has some different experience the next moment (1912, p. 19)

Again echoing Hume, he continues:

When we try to look into ourselves we always seem to come upon some particular thought or feeling, and not upon the 'I'…It does not seem necessary to suppose that we are acquainted with a more or less permanent person, the same today as yesterday, but it does seem as though we must be acquainted with that thing, whatever its nature, which…has acquaintance with sense-data. (pp. 50–51)

Russell appears to be endorsing a no-self view, or even a bundle-theory along the lines proposed by Hume, with regard to so-called personal identity. At least at this point in his development, he settles for the view that if there is such a thing as the 'self', it is merely a collection of sensory experiences.

In a 1927 essay on physics and metaphysics, Russell states that "our grammar is [mistakenly] based upon the belief in permanent things" (1996, p. 273). This belief leads people to believe that 'things', like tables, chairs, and persons, exist. Russell claims, however, that 'things' should be thought of as series of phenomena that are connected by causal connections and not unified by substantial identity. Russell admits that this scepticism about substance is not new, but was developed "by the early Buddhists in the time of King Asoka" (p. 274). He goes on to acknowledge that Buddhist metaphysics and ethics are deeply connected to an analysis of causation. Yet, in some ways, Russell also echoes later forms of Buddhist scepticism about time and causation (seen in Yogācāra, for example[18]), and then applies this revisionary metaphysics to a reconceptualization of personhood:

The normal beliefs of the normal man, as well as all his standards of value, depend on a radically different outlook. A man wants, we will say, to be a 'dynamic personality', but would perhaps feel this desire less strongly if he realized tht nothing is 'dynamic' and there are no 'personalities'…When we call a person 'dynamic', what we mean, as nearly as I can gather, is that he causes a great deal of motion in matter. Seeing that there is no such thing as matter, and that motion has become a completely vague idea, it is evident that the word 'dynamic' cannot retain the force that it used to have. (p. 275)

Even at a fairly late stage in his thinking, then, Russell was inclined to subvert the metaphysical status of 'selfhood', in the spirit of Hume and James. And like James, Russell applies the no-self insight to ethics. He had already done this in 1894, in his early essay "Cleopatra or Maggie Tulliver?", where he says:

[D]esires are of the Self, and…it seems, the satisfaction should be of the Self too… [but] personal satisfaction cannot be perfect until it is shared by all… [I]t is difficult to see how Ethics can…transcend the Self. But… I am vastly tempted to regard the Subject [i.e. Self] …as a mere fluid nucleus of Feeling, of uncertain and constantly changing boundaries, and so adopt an almost Spinozistic monism, in which our terms become merely [impersonal] Desire on the one hand and Satisfaction on the other—this would obviate all these ethical difficulties. (1999, pp. 97–98)[19]

---

[18] Cf. Jonathan Gold's survey of Vasubandhu's Yogācāra philosophy, *Paving the Great Way* (2015).

[19] For a survey of similar interpretations of Spinoza, see the essay by G. Davis and M. Renaud (Chap. 5) in this volume.

For Russell, once the 'self' is eliminated, or seen for what it is, which is "a mere fluid nucleus… of uncertain and constantly changing boundaries," we should consider the right moral focus to be the satisfaction of desires, with desires construed in an impersonal and impartial manner. Once the boundary of 'self and other' is abandoned, we will be able to pursue the good of everyone, rather than pursuing only (or even primarily) our own desires and satisfaction. Here, we see the same sort of impersonal consequentialism that makes its mark in the Buddhist writers discussed by Goodman (2009). Russell further emphasizes this when he states that

> … [some] hold that, although there is such a thing as the general good, and although this is not always best served by pursuing my own good, yet it is always right to pursue my own good exclusively…It is difficult to see what grounds there can be for such a view. If good is to be pursued at all, it can hardly be relevant who is going to enjoy the good. It would be as reasonable for a man on Sundays to think only of his welfare on future Sundays, and on Mondays to think only of Mondays. ([1910] 1994, pp. 50–51)

It is evident that Russell's reconceptualization of 'selfhood' (if not elimination of the concept) plays a role in his ethical theorizing. Echoing the sort of consequentialism we saw at work in (a version of Mahāyāna) Buddhist ethics, Russell believes that once the self is no longer seen as a fundamental factor in moral reasoning, the greater good must be pursued collectively, and for the collective. That is, the good cannot justifiably be pursued only for a particular person (since after all, in a sense, that person does not exist). Instead, the good is pursued 'impersonally', and it should be considered irrelevant as to who will end up participating in the optimal outcome. Drawing on both science and metaphysics, then, Russell tries to expose personhood *for what it really is* (and what it is not), thus echoing the ideal noted earlier, that of '*yatha-bhuta-dassana*'; and this appears to play a key role in the reasoning that leads him to entertain an impartial and impersonal form of consequentialism.

While it is clear that Russell's critique of the traditional selfhood-conception plays a role in his ethical theory, and while he does echo the '*yatha-bhuta-dassana*' ideal, it is less clear what Russell's own understanding of Buddhism was. Though he does appear familiar with many key Buddhist ideas (as seen above), it is unclear whether his understanding of Buddhism was duly informed by a knowledge of the unique cultural context of its origins and development. It is unclear, in particular, whether he appreciates that Buddhism is not (or at least not necessarily) religious in the way that Christianity or Islam are generally considered to be. In a talk addressed to a research group in Beijing (in 1921), Russell had the following to say about Buddhism:

> Among present-day religions Buddhism is the best. The doctrines of Buddhism are profound; they are almost reasonable, and historically they have been the least harmful and the least cruel. But I cannot say that Buddhism is positively good, nor would I wish to have it spread all over the world and believed by everyone. This is because Buddhism only focuses on the question of what Man is, not on what the universe is like. Buddhism does not really pursue the truth; it appeals to sentiment and, ultimately, tries to persuade people to believe in doctrines which are based on subjective assumptions[,] not on objective evidence. Generally, subjective opinions produce false beliefs. I think no matter what the religion, nor how ambiguously its faith is expressed, the same problem arises because of the substitution

of subjective sentiment for objective evidence. Sentiment might be taken as the dominant force in our daily lives. But, as for belief in facts, the further we distance ourselves from sentiment, the better. Never substitute sentiment for facts. It is absolutely harmful to do so. (Russell 1996, p. 432)

Here one might say that Russell uses the Buddhist notion of *yatha-bhuta-dassana* against itself, or at any rate against the 'religion' that domesticated it. But we may question Russell's classifying of Buddhism as a religion, unless we view religion as a 'way of life' or 'way of living.' Since Russell seems to have in mind the same sort of category that people commonly use to classify Christianity and Islam, we may wonder whether his familiarity with the Buddhist tradition(s) had advanced much beyond that of Schopenhauer and Nietzsche. On the other hand, that passage from his 1921 speech, which posits a kind of mindfulness (so to speak) that can prevail decisively over sentiment, seems to imply that he would not quarrel with the Buddhist notion of transcending conative forces in the way that Schopenhauer and Nietzsche both did.[20]

It is possible that Russell's views on Buddhism may have wavered throughout his life and career, which would explain the varied descriptions of Buddhism he offers. Even if Russell did have a somewhat distorted view of Buddhism at times, however, the point still remains that with regard to philosophy, psychology and science, Russell's intellectual aspiration was akin to that of the '*yatha-bhuta-dassana*' ideal. That is, his critiques of self and substance, his defence of the notion of objective truth, and his views on metaphysics are advanced in the spirit of 'seeing things as they really are'; and this same clinical and analytical spirit leads him to entertain a form of impersonal consequentialism. Nonetheless, despite convergences between the views of Russell and James, and despite common ground that both shared with Buddhist doctrine, there may ultimately be different strains of Buddhist philosophy that might most fruitfully be used for comparative purposes – namely, more realist strains in the case of Russell (such as Abhidharma philosophy) and more pragmatist strains in the case of James (such as Madhyamaka).[21]

---

[20] As Douglas Berger argues in his chapter in this volume (Chap. 8), on Schopenhauer and Nietzsche.

[21] Although there were some doctrines proposed by James that Russell was in partial agreement with, such as James's radical empiricism, it was not so with James's pragmatism. Acknowledging that James's theories on will and religious belief were not isolated from his pragmatism, Russell ([1945] 1972) notes that James "is prepared to advocate any doctrine which tends to make people virtuous and happy; if it does so, it is 'true' in the sense in which he uses the word" (p. 727). According to James's pragmatism, an idea is true so long as it is profitable in our lives. According to Russell, endorsing pragmatism means accepting that theories are instruments and not self-contained answers to pure enigmas. Russell admits that he finds fault with James's pragmatism because it assumes that a belief can be 'true' just because the effects of it (e.g. of a religious belief), are worthwhile or repeatedly fruitful in practice. It is evident that while James considers a theory to be true if it is useful, Russell is concerned with actual truth and not the effects of particular beliefs, which lends further support to the idea that Russell, unlike James, gives epistemic priority to the notion of 'seeing things as they really are'.

10.8   Conclusion

In this chapter, I have explored parallels between James's philosophy on the one hand, and Russell's on the other, to key ideas in Buddhist philosophy. After examining James's philosophy, we saw that there are striking parallels between James's conception of selfhood and the Buddhist doctrine of no-self. We have also seen that James's theory of morality is quite similar to one major form of Buddhist ethics, with both endorsing a form of impersonal moral consequentialism. In light of these convergences, we are able to appreciate the importance of revisionary conceptions of selfhood in kindred moral frameworks.

I have also shown that Russell's philosophical priorities are quite similar to the Buddhist ideal of *yatha-bhuta-dassana*, whereas James's pragmatism, while leading to some of the same moral conclusions that Russell reaches, offers a very different philosophical foundation (though one with its own Buddhist resonances, echoing other Buddhist ideals, e.g. the Mahāyāna ideal of *upāya*). Both philosophers were aware of, and more than likely influenced by, Buddhism to some extent. But influences aside, the *parallels* between the ideas of James and Russell and at least some strains of Buddhist philosophy are undeniable and deserve further examination and exploration.

References

Blackmore, S. 2011. *Zen and the Art of Consciousness*. London: Oneworld.

Blackwell, K. 1985/2013. *The Spinozistic Ethics of Bertrand Russell*. New York: Routledge.

Blackwell, K., A. Brink, N. Griffin, R.A. Rempel, and J.G. Slater. 2000. *The Collected Papers of Bertrand Russell*. London: Routledge.

Gold, J. 2015. *Paving the Great Way: Vasubandhu's Unifying Buddhist Philosophy*. New York: Columbia University Press.

Goodman, C. 2009. *Consequences of Compassion: An Interpretation and Defence of Buddhist Ethics*. New York: Oxford University Press.

Goodman, C. 2016. From Madhyamaka to Consequentialism: A Roadmap. In *Moonpaths: Ethics and Emptiness*, ed. Cowherds. New York: Oxford University Press.

Hanson, R., and A.B. Jones. 2009. *Buddha's Brain: Practical Neuroscience of Happiness, Love & Wisdom*. Oakland: Harbinger Publications.

Hume, D. [1739] 2008. *A Treatise of Human Nature*. Oxford: Clarendon Press.

James, W. 1890. *Principles of Psychology*. New York: Cosmio Classics.

———. [1897] 2010a. *The Will to Believe and Other Essays*. Seaside: Watchmaker Publishing.

———. [1897] 2010b. The Moral Philosopher and Moral Life. In *The Will to Believe and Other Essays*, ed. James. Seaside: Watchmaker Publishing.

———. [1902] 2012. *Varieties of Religious Experience*. New York: Oxford University Press.

Parfit, D. 1984. *Reasons and Persons*. Oxford: Clarendon Press.

Pigden, C., ed. 1999. *Russell on Ethics: Selections from the Writings of Bertrand Russell*. New York: Routledge.

Russell, B. 1927. *An Outline of Philosophy*. London: George Allen & Unwin.

———. 1967. *The Autobiography of Bertrand Russell*. New York: Little Brown & Co.

———. [1945] 1972. *The History of Western Philosophy*. New York: Simon & Schuster.

———. [1910] 1994. *Philosophical Essays*. London: Routledge.

———. 1996. *Collected Papers: A Fresh Look at Empiricism, vol. 10*. London: Routledge.

———. (1999). *Russell on Ethics: Selections from the Writings of Bertrand Russell* By C. Pigden. New York: Routledge.

Shoemaker, D. 2009. *Personal identity and ethics: A brief introduction*. Peterborough: Broadview Press.

Siderits, M. 2007. *Buddhism as Philosophy: An Introduction*. Cambridge: Hackett Publishing Company.

———. 2015. *Personal Identity and Buddhist Philosophy: Empty Persons*. 2nd ed. Surrey: Ashgate.

Siderits, M., and S. Katsura. 2013. *Nagarjuna's Middle Way: Mulamadhyamakakarika*. Boston: Wisdom Publications.

Chapter 11
Altruism in the Charnel Ground: Śāntideva and Parfit on Anātman, Reductionism and Benevolence

Stephen Harris

In the eighth chapter of his *Bodhicaryāvatāra*, or *Introduction to the Practices of Awakening* (hereafter, BCA), the eighth-century Indian Buddhist monk Śāntideva appeals to the nonexistence of any enduring self as a premise in his argument that we ought to commit to impartial benevolence. A striking feature of this argument is that it appears in a chapter that is otherwise comprised of meditations designed to develop disenchantment with samsara and increase compassion for others. Almost all of the verses preceding the argument, which begins at verse ninety and continues for about fifteen verses, focus on some unsatisfactory aspect of samsaric experience, like the unreliability of impermanent things like friendship and wealth. Particularly striking are a set of forty verses in which Śāntideva imagines himself in a charnel ground contemplating rotting corpses. It is rather jarring to find him transition from these graveside contemplations to an extended argument for benevolence.

In a past article, I argued that we can resolve this tension by treating the argument as a meditation designed to lessen selfishness (Harris 2011). Although this is one function of these verses, Garfield, Jenkins and Priest are right to point out that this is no reason to think the argument is not also meant to rationally convince (2016). In this essay, I reverse my former approach; rather than interpreting what appears to be an argument as an extended meditation, I show how the meditations of the first half of the chapter establish an important premise in the argument. Reading the text in this way shows how Śāntideva can respond to a potentially powerful objection which I develop by re-examining Śāntideva's premises through the lens of comparative philosophy. Like Śāntideva, Derek Parfit argues in his masterwork *Reasons and Persons* that if one accepts reductionism about personal identity, one ought to be less specially concerned about one's own future well-being, relative to that of others. In the first section below, I explain why the Buddhist rejection of

S. Harris (✉)
Leiden University, Leiden, Netherlands
e-mail: s.e.harris@hum.leidenuniv.nl

an enduring self is close enough to Parfit's reductionism to allow us to look at their arguments together. After discussing these arguments, I summarize a powerful response to Parfit by Susan Wolf that claims normative implications do not follow from Parfit's reductionism. This objection, I argue, also applies to Śāntideva. Although her argument is probably effective against Parfit, in the final section I explain how Buddhist claims about impermanence and suffering provide a response to Wolf. In other words, the verses of BCA's eighth chapter that develop these Buddhist themes also do philosophical work that strengthens the force of Śāntideva's argument.

11.1   Reductionism and Not-Self in Parfit and Buddhism

Parfit describes reductionism about personal identity as the view that "the fact of a person's identity over time just consists in the holding of certain more particular facts" and that "[t]hese facts can be described in an impersonal way" (Parfit 1984, 210). Likewise, for a reductionist, "each person's existence just involves the existence of a brain and a body, the doing of certain deeds, the thinking of certain thoughts, the occurrence of certain experiences, and so on" (Parfit 1984, 211). Parfit's own version of reductionism claims that the important facts in personal identity are primarily psychological connectedness and continuity.[1] Psychological connectedness "is the holding of particular direct psychological connections" such as memories, beliefs and desires (Parfit 1984, 206). When a sufficient number of psychological connections hold between persons at different times, they are said to be strongly psychologically connected. Psychological continuity "is the holding of overlapping chains of strong connectedness" (Parfit 1984, 206). Together, psychological connectedness and continuity make up what Parfit calls "Relation R" (Parfit 1984, 215). In ordinary situations, when persons at different times are psychologically continuous with one another, they are the same person.[2]

Buddhists claim that persons are comprised of five groups of momentary events, the aggregates (skandhas) of matter (rūpa), hedonic feeling (vedanā), recognition (samjñā), conscious awareness (vijñāna), and a category called samskāra that includes volition and karmic tendencies. One of the definitive Buddhist claims is that there is no enduring unitary self (ātman) aside from these groups of momentary constituents. They would, therefore, accept Parfit's central reductionist claim that persons are entirely reducible to their components and the causal relations between them. For Buddhists, the term "person" is a conventional designation (prajñapti) allowing us, for convenience, to refer together to discrete assemblages of causally related constituents. Likewise, they would claim that continuity of

---

[1] Parfit's argument for this position occupies much of part three of *Reasons and Persons*.
[2] Parfit also stipulates that identity must take a nonbranching form, but we can overlook this detail here. See Parfit 1984, 207.

identity over time involves nothing more than the occurrence of these causally related constituents.[3]

An important difference between Parfit's reductionism and the Buddhist rejection of the self (*ātman*) is that unlike Parfit, Buddhists are reductionists not just about persons, but about all partite objects. The classic example Buddhists give is of the chariot. The word "chariot" is simply a conventional designation (*prajñapti*) grouping together a causally related assemblage of chariot parts for convenience, since this configuration of parts allows us to access the function of speed. This difference will not affect my argument to come, however.

There are also several important differences in the doctrine of the nonexistence of an enduring self developed in early Buddhism and the doctrine accepted by Śāntideva's own school of Madhyamaka Buddhism. Most significantly, early Buddhists claim that everything that exists is reducible, finally, to *dharmas*, momentary physical and mental events such as color, shape, sensations of pain, ideas, memories and so on. The wheels of the chariot, for instance, can themselves be analyzed into the color and shape of the wheel, but these *dharmas* cannot themselves be further analyzed. They are therefore real entities that exist independently of our concepts. The distinctive claim of Śāntideva's Madhyamaka school is that even *dharmas* are analyzable into their causal conditions, and therefore are only conceptual entities. Some interpretations of Śāntideva's argument for impartial benevolence interpret him as provisionally accepting the early Buddhist view that pain is a *dharma* and is therefore real (Siderits 2003, Harris 2011). In this essay, I will construe Śāntideva's argument in a way that does not depend on this claim. Therefore, we can ignore this difference in what follows.

For both Parfit and Buddhists, being a reductionist about persons means rejecting the existence of what Parfit calls a "further fact", a "separately existing entit[y]" that is the person (Parfit 1984, 210). Like an immortal soul or Cartesian thinking substance, the self (*ātman*) rejected by the Buddhists is an example of a further fact. Since according to Parfit, facts about psychological connectedness and continuity account for continuity of identity, and since connectedness and continuity are a matter of degree, Parfit claims that there are times when personal identity can be unproblematically indeterminate. Parfit refers to the question of continuity of identity in such cases as "empty." To explain what an empty question is, he offers the example of a club that ceases to meet, then several years later reorganizes with many of the same original members. Is the second club numerically identical, that is the very same club, as the first? Parfit calls this an empty question, meaning that although we know all the facts, these do not give us an answer (Parfit 1984, 213–214).

---

[3] It is worth noting that Parfit was aware of Buddhist ideas about selflessness when he wrote *Reasons and Persons*, and interpreted these ideas as expressing a reductionism about persons (p. 273). I think his interpretation is correct, although below I will also suggest a couple of ways in which Buddhist reductionism differs from that of Parfit. See also *Reasons and Persons*, Appendix J (pp. 502–503), in which Parfit cites several Buddhist passages about the nonexistence of an enduring self. My concern, however, is about the conceptual relationship between Buddhist views about the nonexistence of an enduring self and Parfit's reductionism about persons, as well as the moral consequences each deduces from their respective positions.

Likewise, there are times when the identity of persons is indeterminate. Parfit's most famous example of this is his branch line teletransportation case. Imagine that humans invent transportation devices that copy our body's patterns, including the brain. The machines then destroy the original body, but beam the physical patterns to other planets, where they are used to recreate qualitatively identical bodies that preserve psychological continuity. One day, when I am teletransported to Mars in this way, my old body is not destroyed. There are now two physically and psychologically qualitatively identical versions of myself.[4] In cases like these, Parfit claims that there is no determinate answer as to which, if either, of the persons is numerically identical to the one who entered the teletransportation machine. Once we reject the existence of a further fact, it is unproblematic in cases like this to claim that questions about continuity of identity are empty.

The example of the teletransporter is somewhat reminiscent of the way Buddhists treat rebirth. When a person dies, all physical continuity ceases, but the stream of causally connected mental moments are united to a new body in the mother's womb. Some psychological continuity, such as habitual patterns of behavior, continues, but memories from the previous life are forgotten. A traditional Buddhist answer to the question of whether the person who is reborn is the same as the one who has died is that they are neither the same nor different (Rhys Davids 63). Buddhists would claim that cases like these provide examples of empty questions. Since psychological continuity comes in degrees, and since much of that continuity has been lost, there is no longer a determinate answer as to whether the reborn person is identical to the one who died.[5]

11.2   Śāntideva's Argument for Impartial Benevolence[6]

Śāntideva's argument for impartial benevolence spans about sixteen verses in the eighth chapter of his BCA. Below, I quote the parts that let us understand his appeal to selflessness. The early verses establish a *prima facie* reason to remove suffering, no matter to whom it belongs:

> One should first earnestly meditate on the equality of oneself
> and others in this way: "All equally experience suffering and
> happiness, and I must protect them as I do myself." (BCA 8:90)[7]

> I should eliminate the suffering of others
> because it is suffering, just like my own

---

[4] See Parfit 1984 pps. 199–202 for his account of the teletransporter thought experiment.

[5] See Harris (forthcoming) for a development of these ideas about continuity of identity and rebirth in Buddhist texts.

[6] See Garfield, Jenkins and Priest 2016 for a helpful summary of the range of interpretive possibilities of this argument.

[7] Translations are by Wallace and Wallace in Śāntideva 1997. I indicate any places where I have modified the translation.

suffering. I should take care of others
because they are sentient beings, just as I
am a sentient being. (BCA 8: 94)[8]

When happiness is equally dear to others and
myself, then what is so special [viśeṣa] about me that I strive after
happiness for myself alone? (BCA 8:95, my insertion of brackets)

When fear and suffering are equally abhorrent
to others and myself, then what is so special [viśeṣa] about
me that I protect myself but not others? (BCA 8:96, my insertion of brackets)

Śāntideva begins the argument by asking us to contemplate the way suffering and happiness feel. Our immediate reaction, when we experience pain, is to want to remove it. These four verses then remind us that the suffering of others feels just as bad to them as ours does to us. Since the badness of the suffering we and others feel is alike, Śāntideva concludes that we have a prima facie reason to remove any suffering, no matter to whom it belongs. The same holds true for the promotion of happiness.

In verses 90 and 94, then, Śāntideva establishes both that others abhor suffering and desire happiness as much as we do, and claims that this provides at least some reason to remove their suffering and promote their well-being. The argument continues in verses 95 and 96 by asking what distinction (viśeṣa) justifies my prioritizing my own welfare? If two persons were in agony and we could rescue only one of them, we should be able to provide some justification for our choice as to which one to help, such as the fact that one caused his own suffering through unethical behavior. Śāntideva, likewise, is asking whether we can provide some kind of rational justification for prioritizing our own well-being over the well-being of others.

These verses, then, provide Śāntideva's initial argument that we ought to commit to impartially removing everyone's suffering. First, we have a reason to remove suffering, no matter to whom it belongs, because of the badness of that suffering. Second, if we are going to prioritize removing our own suffering, we should be able to provide some kind of relevant distinction about ourselves that justifies this prioritization. For the remainder of the argument, Śāntideva considers and dismisses as irrelevant several potential distinctions that might justify prioritizing my well-being. Verses 95 and 96 also rule out one possible justification. Since suffering and happiness are equally dear to myself and others, it isn't the case that there is anything particularly repugnant about my own suffering that warrants its prioritization.

Śāntideva's appeal to the truth of not-self comes in verses 101–103, when he considers what is probably the most powerful distinction the opponent can appeal to as rationally justifying special concern for his own well-being. The opponent can claim that he is more concerned about his future suffering because it belongs to him. In reply, Śāntideva invokes the Buddhist doctrine of the nonexistence of an enduring self:

The continuum of consciousness, like a series, and the
aggregation of constituents, like an army and such, are
unreal. Since one who experiences suffering does not exist,

---

[8] "Sentient being" here translates "sattva," which in Buddhist thought refers to anything possessing consciousness.

to whom will that suffering belong? (BCA 8:101)

All sufferings are without an owner without exception.
They should be warded off simply because they are suffering.
Why is any restriction made in this case? (BCA 8: 102, translation modified)[9]

Why should suffering be prevented? Because everyone
agrees. If it must be warded off, then all of it must be warded
off; and if not, then this goes for oneself as it does for
everyone else. (BCA 8: 103)

In the first verse, Śāntideva reminds his opponent that the Buddhist commitment
to the unreality of partite objects entails that the self, which is composed of causally
connected mental and physical moments, is unreal. As a result, suffering is not
owned by anyone. The second verse goes on to claim that since all moments of suffering are ownerless, it is their intrinsically negative feel alone that should motivate
us to remove them. The last verse considers the possible objection that if there are
no selves, we have no reason to remove anyone's pain. Śāntideva replies that since
no one claims that pain should not be removed, we need not consider this objection.
Arguments must end somewhere, and the premise that we ought to remove suffering
because it is bad is as deep as we can or need to go. He concludes that since there is
no good reason to prioritize our own welfare, if we are to be rationally consistent we
must commit to removing everyone's pain, or care about none of it, our own
included. This last option has already been dismissed by his claim that everyone
agrees pain should be removed. Thereby a commitment to impartial benevolence,
which for Śāntideva would mean committing to the bodhisattva path as the way of
most quickly liberating sentient beings, seems to follow.

It is important to be clear about how much work the Buddhist rejection of an
enduring self is doing in this argument. Śāntideva is not arguing that because no self
exists, we are somehow metaphysically entangled in a way that prevents special
concern for our own future. Rather, he accepts that physically and psychologically
causally related streams can be conceptually distinguished and identified as particular persons. Instead, his basic argument has two steps. First, we have independent
reasons to remove suffering, no matter to whom it belongs. Śāntideva argues for this
in verses 90, 94 and 95 by appealing to the similar nature of pain and happiness for
all beings, and in 103 by appealing to the universal acceptance of the need to remove
pain. Second, the best potential justification for giving one's own well-being priority is blocked. Since we are not enduring selves, we cannot appeal to this fact as
rationally justifying self-interested action. A commitment to impartial benevolence
seems to follows. We are committed to removing everyone's pain, since it is bad, but
are blocked from prioritizing our own, since we have no good reason to justify this
prioritization.

---

[9] ... asvāmikāni duḥkhāni sarvāṇyevāviśeṣataḥl duḥkhatvādeva vāryāṇi niyamastatra kiṁkṛtaḥ
(Śāntideva 2001, 190). Wallace and Wallace translate "aviśeṣatah" as an ablative of reason,
"because they are not different." It is unclear, however, why Śāntideva would be claiming that suffering is ownerless because it is not different. Instead, I translate "aviśeṣatah" adverbially, as
"without exception."

11.3 Parfit, Reductionism and Morality

Although Parfit does not incorporate the nonexistence of a further fact into an argument for impartial benevolence, he argues that several important normative conclusions follow from reductionist premises.[10] Reductionism about persons entails that persons have no metaphysical depth; what really exists are a plurality of causally related physical and mental events, which are conceptually unified under the concept of "person."[11] Therefore, any normative positions that depend upon a thickness to the separation between persons become less plausible. In particular, the objection that it is unfair to redistribute wealth and resources loses much of its force.[12] Since what really exists are psychological events, it matters less to whom these events belong. As Parfit says, for reductionists "[i]t becomes more plausible, when thinking morally, to focus less upon the person, the subject of experiences, and instead to focus more upon the experiences themselves(341).[13]

We saw above that Śāntideva claims that accepting selflessness entails that we have no good reason to give any special concern to our own future well-being. Parfit calls this position the extreme claim, and suggests that it is one of two plausible attitudes that a reductionist can rationally hold towards his future. The other, which gives some importance to psychological connectedness and continuity, he calls the moderate claim.

> Extreme Claim: If reductionism is true, we have no reason to be specially concerned about our own futures. (307)

> Moderate Claim: Relation R [psychological connection and continuity] alone gives us a reason for special concern. (311)

Although Śāntideva would accept the extreme claim, it alone does not commit one to impartial benevolence. One might, instead, claim that if persons do not exist, we have no reason to care about anyone's future, our own included.[14] As Śāntideva himself claims, I must strive to remove all suffering, or none of it. (BCA 8:103) If we combine the extreme claim with a baseline commitment to removing everyone's suffering, however, impartial benevolence seems to follow.[15]

Parfit himself is neutral as to whether we should accept the extreme or the moderate claims (312). But even accepting the moderate claim would bring the

---

[10] Goodman 2009 argues that Śāntideva anticipates Parfit in this respect. See especially Goodman's fifth chapter (2009).

[11] This way of phrasing Parfit's reductionism about persons as unification of more basic elements under a concept is influenced by Korsgaard 1989, 103–104.

[12] See *Reasons and Persons* sections 111–117 for Parfit's full development of this view.

[13] See Goodman 2016 for an application of this point to Śāntideva.

[14] See Harris 2011 for a development of this possibility.

[15] One would, of course, have to rule out the possibility that we might have good reasons to prioritize the well-being of certain others, such as our friends, before impartial benevolence would be established. But the non-existence of any deep metaphysical fact of identity could be appealed to again in respect to these persons.

reductionist closer to impartial benevolence. The psychological continuity and connectedness to which relation R refers comes in degrees. I am less psychologically connected to myself ten years from now than I am ten weeks from now. If I accept the moderate claim, then I should vary the degree of my special concern depending on the strength of these psychological connections. This means that the reductionist will have far less special concern for his life overall; he will treat his distant future self more like another person. Special concern for his own future will decrease the further out that future is.[16]

One way to respond to Parfit's and Śāntideva's arguments is to reject reductionism about persons and personal identity. Many of the Buddhists' traditional opponents, including the philosophical school of Nyāya, took this approach. An alternative response, that I am interested in here, is to accept (at least provisionally) Parfit's reductionism, but reject his claims about its moral implications. Below, I examine one such argument, given by Susan Wolf in her defense of the importance of persons. Wolf's argument applies to Śāntideva as well, and before turning to it, I illustrate what I take to be her central point by reference to the Buddhist example of the chariot.

Remember that according to Buddhists, the conventional designation (*prajñapti*) "chariot" is a name used to group together a discrete collection of elements. Moreover, this unification under a concept has both a spatial and a temporal element. I could have used the name "chariot" to refer to an alternate spatial arrangement of the parts, for instance with the chariot wheels on top of the carriage. Instead, I restrict its use to the usual arrangement since it provides a useful function—quick speed. Likewise, the name "chariot" could have been used to refer to any temporal duration of the assembled chariot parts. We could have marked out ten second temporal slices of the chariot arrangement with the term, for instance. But instead we adopt the usual practice since it fits better into our conventions of ownership and possession.

What this means is that, although not dictated by any metaphysically unified object, our practices of spatially and temporally grouping chariot parts together are far from arbitrary. Although not constrained by metaphysical facts, our naming practices are constrained by practical facts. Thinking of this spatio-temporal plurality of chariot parts together lets us access the function of speed and fit these useful collections smoothly into our lives. Even though it is a conceptual construction, the chariot configuration has a kind of thickness, grounded in its being embedded within our practices and needs. So even if we are reductionists about chariots, we should still believe that chariots—as spatially and temporally extended causally configured collections of discrete parts-- are important.

The heart of Susan Wolf's critique of Parfit comes when she makes a similar claim about the importance of persons. Here is how she makes this point:

> [P]ersons live, or have the potential to live, richer lives than other
> beings. Persons are capable of aspiring to and achieving a diversity of
> Ideals, of developing physical and intellectual skills, of creating artistic

---

[16] See Parfit 1984, 312–314.

masterpieces and scientific theories. Perhaps more important, persons.
are capable of developing deep and rewarding interpersonal relationships
of exhibiting and appreciating moral virtue, and of understanding and
committing themselves to moral laws. (Wolf 1986, 708–9)

As Wolf points out, being a reductionist about persons does not settle the question of which arrangement of basic person parts should be important to us. We could care about temporal slices of person configurations, or, as in Parfit's Moderate claim, we could care about relation R, psychological connectedness and continuity. With Wolf, we can refer to a strongly psychologically connected being as an R-related being (Wolf, 710). A third possibility, defended by Wolf, is that even after becoming reductionists, persons as traditionally understood should continue to be our objects of concern. Wolf in the argument above provides good reasons for caring about temporally extended configurations of person constituents. Ten second persons slices cannot develop nurturing relationships, commit to long term projects and so on. Moreover, the desirability of ordinary person-formations over ten second persons has nothing to do with the truth of reductionism. Switching concern from persons to ten second person slices would not be a metaphysical mistake, but a practical one.

Unlike ten second person slices, R-related beings are capable of developing relationships, nurturing projects etc. But Wolf points out that there is a depth of value to our ordinary person conventions that would be lacking if we switched to caring about R-related beings. If we did this, then our concern for our own and other people's future would be contingent on their maintaining a strong level of psychological connectedness. One unwanted consequences of this is that parents of young children would have no great concern for the adult persons those children would become. Likewise, my commitment to my spouse and friends would be contingent on their retaining psychological connectedness with their present selves. But part of the richness of lifelong commitments, like marriage and parenthood, depends on the way its members care about each other throughout massive periods of psychological growth (Wolf 710–12).

A central point of Wolf's response to Parfit is that there is an integrity and coherence that human lives can achieve that goes beyond mere psychological continuity, and that this does not depend on metaphysical unity.[17] My commitments may outlast the reasons for which I take them on; I may marry for passion, but remain faithful out of deep and lasting love. I might start a support group to deal with my own trauma, but remain involved to nurture others. Such continuity of commitment is aided by thinking of long stretches of my life as one unified narrative in which growth, and even disintegration are seen as the transformation of a single person.

What Wolf's argument establishes, contra Parfit, is that our convention of treating persons as enduring (more or less) from the birth until the death of the body has a pragmatic value that cannot be matched by temporally shortened objects of concern. The unification of a human life has more value for us than that of R-related beings, 10 second person formations and so on. Persons matter, not for metaphysical

---

[17] My comments here are also influenced by Korsgaard 1989.

but for practical reasons.[18] Wolf's argument also suggests that we should reject the moral implications of reductionism suggested by Parfit.[19] For instance, our strong practical reasons for thinking of human lives as discrete unities entail concerns about the fairness of redistribution arising from the separateness of persons will have similar force for a reductionist as for one who accepts the existence of a further fact.

Wolf's remarks may also be adapted into an argument against what Parfit calls the 'Extreme Claim'. The Extreme Claim says that without the existence of a metaphysically real further fact, we have no good reason for special concern about our future well-being. Wolf can reply that the pragmatic importance of personal identity can rationally ground such concern. If continuity of identity based upon a metaphysical fact can justify special concern, then why not continuity of identity based upon practical considerations? A reductionist has good reason to view her future self's goals, aspirations, commitments and well-being as belonging to herself. These relationships I currently participate in will stretch out into my future. The valuable projects I have begun are ones that my future self can complete. Others have valuable relationships and projects of their own, but these projects are not mine. I have good reasons to identify with the entirety of my life that do not depend upon its metaphysical unity.

Of course, one can deny that the pragmatic unity of a life rationally justifies special concern for our future self. One might claim with Śāntideva that since all persons equally experience happiness and suffering, we have no reason to prioritize the well-being of our pragmatically unified self. But a parallel argument can be made against the non-reductionist. For since all persons equally experience happiness and suffering, what difference does it make that I am metaphysically identical to my future self?[20] What this suggests is that the truth of reductionism has little to do with whether we ought to commit to impartial benevolence. If metaphysical unity justi-

---

[18] In a reply to Wolf's article, Parfit agrees that we have practical reasons to care about persons, but claims such concern remains irrational since it is arises from the metaphysically mistaken belief in a further fact (Parfit 1986, 832–833). Most Buddhists, however, accept that persons do exist in the conventional sense, as conceptually unified synchronic and diachronic aggregations of mental and physical events, and so this critique would not apply to them. I do not think it applies to Wolf either, since I take her point to be that we have good practical reasons for extending our concern beyond the boundaries of strong psychological continuity stressed by Parfit. To put this in Buddhist terms, I have practical reasons to conceptually unify the aggregates (*skandhas*) from birth to death, regardless of partial psychological discontinuity within this time period. Wolf's claim is that I choose this stretch of mental and physical activity to care about because of the pragmatic value of doing so. This is not, however, irrational, in the sense of being a metaphysical mistake, since these mental and physical events do exist. Still, metaphysics may have nothing to do with my concern for persons, in the sense that the existence or nonexistence of a unified enduring further fact is irrelevant to why I care about them. Thanks to Oren Hanner for suggesting I engage with Parfit's reply.

[19] Wolf does not explicitly draw this conclusion, although Korsgaard 1989, whose argument partially overlaps with Wolf, does. See Goodman 2009, chapter eleven for a treatment of Korsgaard's argument in relation to Buddhism.

[20] See Martin 2009 for a development of this challenge.

fies special concern for my future, then so should pragmatic unity. The existence or absence of a further fact does little to settle the issue.

11.4 Siderits' Interpretation of Śāntideva's Argument

In my interpretation, Śāntideva's argument has two parts. First, the badness of pain provides good impersonal reasons to remove it, regardless to whom it belongs. Second, we have no good justification for prioritizing our own well-being. Since everyone's pain feels equally bad, the badness of my pain alone does not provide the needed justification. If the identity between my future and present self was a metaphysically deep fact, this might justify special concern. Because no such self exists, however, the fact of identity has no metaphysical depth.

Wolf shows what is wrong with Śāntideva's argument, when it is understood in this way. Persons do not have metaphysical depth, but they have pragmatic depth. I have good reasons to be concerned about persons, because there is a richness to living that would be lost if we took shorter identity configurations as our objects of concern. Special concern for my own future can be justified by the fact that my temporally extended identity is part of an unfolding set of developing relationships and projects. The fact that my current and future self are part of the same life is no less significant if I accept it on practical rather than metaphysical grounds.

Mark Siderits provides a stronger interpretation of Śāntideva's argument which, if successful, would answer Wolf's objection. As in my interpretation above, Siderits claims that Śāntideva argues that the impersonal badness of pain provides an impersonal reason to remove it. Like Wolf, Siderits next goes on to stress that we adopt the convention of treating causally related mental and physical moments as temporally extended persons for practical purposes. Unlike Wolf, however, Siderits does not claim this is because it allows us to enjoy particularly rich human forms of experience. Rather, we adopt the person convention because it helps us effectively lessen pain. Here is how Siderits puts the core of his argument:

> We commonly think that our reason to floss has to do with the fact that that future person will be me, that I am preventing my own future pain. The enlightened person knows that is false. It so happens that each of us is quite commonly in a position to prevent future pain in one particular causal series. That is why it was useful that we learn to think of that causal series as a person, me. That is why it was useful that we learn to identify with and appropriate future states in that causal series. Because that turns out to be a very efficient way of preventing a great deal of future pain. But that means that my reason to prevent what I think of as my future pain does not derive from the fact that it is mine; it stems from the fact that it is pain, which is bad, and the fact that I am usually better situated than others to prevent it. Adopting the personhood theory is a maximizing strategy. (Siderits 2007, 288–89)

Once we accept that the person convention is adopted merely to eliminate pain, Siderits claims, this entails a commitment to impartial benevolence. Since we adopt the personhood convention only to minimize impersonal pain, we should depart from this convention whenever doing so would result in a net loss of pain. If removing impersonal moments of pain was the only justification for adopting the person convention, then Siderits' argument would be effective. Moments of pain, taken in isolation, are qualitatively identical feelings of badness. Taken in isolation, why would the location of momentary pain have any importance?

As Wolf argues, however, our reasons to care about persons seem to go beyond the removal of pain. Considering my current and future self as being the same person helps me floss effectively, but it also helps me develop my musical talent and nurture lifelong relationships. There is a richness to human experience that cannot be achieved without treating persons as temporally extended beings. Moreover, my current and future self are involved in this same set of projects and relationships. This seems to provide justification for giving special concern to the well-being of the temporally extended person of whom my present self is a part. Contra Siderits, therefore, we have reasons for caring about persons other than the impersonal maximization of pain, based upon which it would seem to be rational to prioritize our own well-being.

11.5   Suffering and Impermanence in Chapter 8 of Śāntideva's *Bodhicaryāvatāra*

Together with impermanence (*anitya*) and unsatisfactoriness (*duḥkha*), the Buddhist doctrine of not-self (*anātman*), appealed to by Śāntideva in his argument, is one of the three marks (*trilakṣaṇa*) characterizing almost everything that exists.[21] An interesting feature of BCA chapter 8 is that many of the ninety verses preceding Śāntideva's argument focus on one or both of the other two marks. Buddhists texts claim that there is a close relationship between these three universal characteristics. In the early Pali canon, for instance, it is often claimed that the fact that objects and experiences are impermanent and unsatisfactory entails that we should not take them to belong to, or be part of an enduring entity (Ñāṇamoli and Bodhi 1995, p. 232: M i 139.) Likewise, one of the deeper forms of unsatisfactoriness, the suffering of change (*viparinama duḥkha*) refers to the fact that pleasant sensations are impermanent, and will cause pain when they end.[22]

One of the themes repeatedly emphasized early in BCA chapter 8 is the inability of impermanent relationships to provide lasting satisfaction:

> For what impermanent person, who will not see his loved
> ones again in thousands of births, is it appropriate to be
> attached to impermanent beings? (BCA 8:5)

> Failing to see them, one does not find joy nor does one
> abide in meditative concentration. Even upon
> seeing them, one does not become satisfied but is tormented
> by strong desire, just as before. (BCA 8:6)

---

[21] Nirvana is held to be selfless, but is not impermanent or unsatisfactory.

[22] See for instance Vasubandhu 905.

Both verses illustrate a facet of the connection between impermanence and dissatisfaction. In the first verse, Śāntideva draws our attention to the inevitable pain of impermanent relationships. The second verse emphasizes that even when I am with those I love, as long as my mind is still afflicted with craving, my longing will simply increase.

Other parts of the text emphasize how ordinary pursuits, such as wealth and honor, also bring no lasting satisfaction. Once more, the unsatisfying nature of samsaric pursuits is linked to impermanence in the form of death:

> A mortal who thinks, "I am rich and respected, and many
> like me," experiences fear of approaching death. (BCA 8:17)

> Many have become wealthy and many have become famous,
> but no one knows where they have gone with their wealth
> and fame. (BCA 8:20)

Perhaps the most striking set of verses in chapter eight provide an extended meditation in which Śāntideva imagines visiting a charnel ground and contemplating the rotting corpses strewn about. He begins this section by reminding himself that this will also be his fate:

> When shall I go to the local charnel grounds and compare
> my own body, which has the nature of decay, with other
> corpses? (BCA 8:30)

> For this body of mine will also become so putrid that even
> the jackals will not come near it because of its stench. (BCA 8:31)

> A person is born alone and also dies alone. No one else has a
> share in one's agony. What is the use of loved ones who
> create hindrances? (BCA 8;33)

His attention soon turns from his own radical impermanence to the inevitable destruction of those whom he loves.

> If the co-emergent pieces of bones of this single body will
> fall apart, how much more so another person whom one
> holds dear? (BCA 8:32)

In some of these verses, Śāntideva mocks his reader with an unnerving grim humor about how we hide the fact of death from ourselves.

> Either you have seen that bashfully lowered face before as
> being lifted up with effort, or you have not seen it as it was
> covered by a veil. (BCA 8:44)

> Now, that face is revealed by vultures as if they are unable to
> bear your anxiousness. Look at it! Why are you fleeing away
> now? (BCA 8:45)

Since we longed to see our lover's face when she hid it with a veil, Śāntideva urges, we should be ecstatic now that even the bones are revealed by the vultures. Śāntideva goes on to generalize these remarks to everyone we know:

> You fear a skeleton that has been seen like this, even though
> it does not move. Why do you not fear it when it moves as if

set in motion by some ghost? (BCA 8:48)

Seeing a few corpses in a charnel ground, you are repelled,
yet you delight in a village which is a charnel ground
crowded with moving corpses. (BCA 8:70)

All human goals, relationships and achievements are radically vulnerable to
gradual decay or immediate destruction. The threat and actuality of death brings
with it multilayered physical and emotional suffering. Moreover, even while we
possess or enjoy these objects and experiences of supposed value, Śāntideva claims
that the insatiable nature of desire, as well as our repressed fear of death makes any
deep enjoyment impossible. Consider again the central point made by Susan Wolf
in her defense of the importance of persons:

[P]ersons live, or have the potential to live, richer lives than other
beings. Persons are capable of aspiring to and achieving a diversity of
Ideals, of developing physical and intellectual skills, of creating artistic
masterpieces and scientific theories. Perhaps more important, persons
are capable of developing deep and rewarding interpersonal relationships,
of exhibiting and appreciating moral virtue, and of understanding and
committing themselves to moral laws.

But these early sections of BCA chapter eight suggest the Buddhist response to
Wolf's critique. Persons in samsara are not capable of living rich lives, because our
deluded cognitive systems that superimpose permanence and satisfactoriness on a
radically unstable and unsatisfying universe cannot achieve any lasting satisfaction.
The development of ordinary physical and intellectual skills, as well as aesthetic
achievement, is only a brief distraction from the coming of death.[23] Relationships,
except those supporting a commitment to liberation, are snares that set the stage for
deep emotional anguish. Regarding moral commitments, Śāntideva can respond
that the commitment to ending impersonal pain is the only one we need commit
ourselves to, and this can be motivated by the intrinsic badness of pain itself.

11.6 Conclusion

One reason to read Parfit and Śāntideva alongside each other is that drawing upon
the sophisticated contemporary responses to Parfit's claims can also help us assess
the reasonableness of Śāntideva's argument. As Susan Wolf forcefully argues, the
lack of metaphysical unity alone does not settle the question of the value of persons.
If we accept, with Wolf, that persons matter because of the way they let us access
the richness of human experience, then it is a small step to say that I have reasonable

---

[23] Śāntideva does place great value on developing a subset of intellectual knowledge that is relevant
to one's development on the Buddhist path. This is shown most clearly by his explanation and
defense of Buddhist philosophical positions about selflessness and emptiness in the ninth chapter
of the BCA. See Keown 2001 for an exploration of the moral significance of certain kinds of intellectual development in the Buddhist tradition. See Harris 2014 for a study of Buddhist positions on
the pervasion of ordinary experience by suffering (duḥkha).

grounds to prioritize the well-being of my future self with whose projects and relationships I am already deeply entwined.

Incorporating the meditations on impermanence and suffering from the first half of BCA chapter eight into Śāntideva's argument blocks Wolf's critique. If we accept, with the Buddhist, that human lives cycle through various levels of emotional and physical distress, then it will no longer seem plausible that the person convention is justified by the richness of human experience. Nevertheless, as Siderits points out, the human convention does have value in removing impersonal pain. Therefore, if we accept the Buddhist understanding of impermanence and suffering, then Śāntideva's argument becomes more plausible. The nonexistence of any deep metaphysical unity between my current and future self blocks the egoist's most obvious justification for special concern for her future. The pragmatic response developed out of Wolf's critique is blocked by the unsatisfactory nature of human lives. The remaining justification for adopting the person convention is to remove impersonally bad pain. But if this is our reason for adopting this convention, then as Siderits argues, we should depart from it whenever doing so will remove pain more effectively. It no longer matters to whom pain belongs, but only how successfully we remove it.

What this suggests, on the one hand, is that the Buddhist conception of ordinary experience being saturated by various forms of suffering does a good deal of philosophical work, even when it is not explicitly invoked in the form of an argument. Just as importantly, I hope to have helped demonstrate the value of looking at the context and background in which analytically framed arguments appear. Above, I have argued that it matters that Śāntideva's argument takes place in a chapter largely devoted to exploring the dissatisfactions of samsaric life. By resisting the philosophical urge to abstract, and by placing Śāntideva's argument back into the charnel ground, I hope to have helped show how it functions, not merely as an isolated fragment of reasoning, but as a deeply embedded part of an interconnected web of beliefs, assumptions and arguments designed to lead the practitioner from concern for himself alone to concern for everyone.

References

Garfield, Jay, Stephen Jenkins, and Graham Priest. 2016. The Śāntideva Passage. In *Moonpaths: Ethics and Emptiness*, ed. The Cowherds. New York: Oxford University Press.

Goodman, Charles. 2009. *Consequences of Compassion: An Interpretation and Defense of Buddhist Ethics*. Oxford University Press.

Goodman, Charles. 2016. From Madhyamaka to Consequentialism: A Roadmap. In *Moonpaths: Ethics and Emptiness*, ed. The Cowherds. New York: Oxford University Press.

Harris, Stephen. forthcoming. Promising Across Lives to Save Non-existent Beings: Identity, Rebirth and the Bodhisattva's Vow. *Philosophy East and West* 68: 2.

———. 2014. Suffering and the Shape of Well-Being in Buddhist Ethics. *Asian Philosophy* 24 (3): 242–259.

———. 2011. Does Anātman Rationally Entail Altruism? On *Bodhicaryāvatāra* 8: 101–103. *Journal of Buddhist Ethics* 18: 92–123.

Keown, Damien. 2001. *The Nature of Buddhist Ethics*, rev. ed. New York: Palgrave Macmillan.

Korsgaard, Christine. 1989. Personal Identity and the Unity of Agency: A Kantian Response to Parfit. *Philosophy & Public Affairs* 18 (2): 101–132.

Martin, Raymond. 2009. Would It Matter All That Much If There Were No Selves? In *Pointing at the Moon: Buddhism, Logic, Analytic Philosophy*, ed. Mario D'Amato, Jay L. Garfield, and Tom J. F. Tillemans, 115–134. Oxford: Oxford University Press

Ñāṇamoli and Bodhi. (trans.). 1995. *The Middle Length Discourses of the Buddha*. Boston: Wisdom Publications.

Parfit, Derek. 1986. Comments. *Ethics* 96 (4): 832–872.

———. 1984. *Reasons and Persons*. Oxford: Oxford University Press.

Rhys Davids, T.W.. (trans.). 1890. *The Questions of King Milinda*, 2 vols. The Sacred Books of the East; vols 35–36. Oxford: Clarendon Press.

Śāntideva. 1997. *A Guide to the Bodhisattva Way of Life (Bodhicaryāvatāra)*. Trans. Vesna and Alan Wallace. Ithaca: Snow Lion Publications.

———. 2001. *The Bodhicharyāvatāra of Ārya Śāntideva with Commentary Pañjikā of Śri Prajñākaramatiī & Hindi Translation*. Ed. and Trans. Swāmī Dwārikādās Śāstrī. Varanasi: Bauddha Bharati.

Siderits, Mark. 2003. *Personal Identity and Buddhist Philosophy*. Burlington: Ashgate.

———. 2007. Buddhist Reductionism and the Structure of Buddhist Ethics. In *Indian Ethics: Classical and Contemporary Challenges*, 283–296. Ashgate.

Vasubandhu. 1988. *Abhidharmakośa*. Trans. La Vallee Poussin. English translation by Leo M. Pruden. Berkeley: Asian Humanities Press.

Williams, Paul. 1998. *Studies in the Philosophy of the Bodhicaryāvatāra: Altruism and Reality*. Delhi: Motilal Banarsidass.

Wolf, Susan. 1986. Self-Interest and Interest in Selves. *Ethics* 96 (4): 704–720.

Chapter 12
The Ethics of Interconnectedness: Charles Taylor, No-Self, and Buddhism

Ashwani Peetush

12.1 Introduction

My aim in this paper is to chart what I see as parallels between the ontology of self in Charles Taylor's work and that of various Buddhist 'no-self' views, along with parallels between Taylor's commitment to reviving republican ideas (in a 'communitarian' form) and some aspects of Buddhist ethics. I see key resemblances and overlaps at the level of metaphysics as well as ethics. For Taylor, the sorts of atomistic accounts of self that have come to be accepted as natural and unquestionable in the West are deeply misguided. The dominant Hobbesian-Lockean procedural picture of selfhood blinds us to the intrinsic relatedness of self to others and has profoundly negative consequences for the kinds of shared conceptions of the good necessary for viable and functioning democracies to survive and flourish. For Taylor, we thus need to retrieve and rearticulate a more accurate understanding of the self (Taylor 1985a, c, d, 1989, 1995a, b, 2003). This conception acknowledges that the self is located in a web of locution, conversation, and social interconnectedness, a sense that gives rise to an expanded notion of our moral and political duties. I argue that such an understanding of the self and ethics has strong resemblances to the kinds of views of the self and ethics as articulated by various schools of Buddhism. Conceptions of anātman or no-self and pratītya-samutpāda (interconnectedness) similarly broaden the scope and domain of our moral concern to be more inclusive by interrogating perspectives that conceive of the self as a separate and isolated individual. This is illustrated by, for example, the Dalai Lama (1999),

I would like to thank Gordon Davis, Steven Thompson, Kathy Behrendt, Nigel DeSouza, Rebekah Johnston, Gary Foster, Renato Cristi, Emily Jull, John Abraham, Christopher F. J. Ross, and Angela Brown for sharing their insight and their helpful suggestions; of course, all shortcomings are my own.

A. Peetush (✉)
Wilfrid Laurier University, Waterloo, ON, Canada
e-mail: apeetush@wlu.ca

© Springer International Publishing AG, part of Springer Nature 2018
G. F. Davis (ed.), *Ethics without Self, Dharma without Atman*, Sophia Studies
in Cross-cultural Philosophy of Traditions and Cultures 24,
https://doi.org/10.1007/978-3-319-67407-0_12

who argues that a more accurate understanding of the self as empty of inherent and separate existence leads to adopting a more compassionate ethical stance towards others. I would suggest that, along the same lines, this understanding is required for a sustainable future for not only our communities, but that of an increasingly inter-related and inter-dependent world.

Indeed, this is not simply a matter of abstract theoretical concern, but of daily practice: how we see the other affects how we treat them. If there is anything to be learned from the 2008 global financial crisis, it is that an ethic rooted in a metaphysics of the self as an individual rational agent, seeking to contract with adversarial others for the sake of maximization of individual self-interest, has potentially devastating consequences for democracy and global equality. A constellation of current movements in the West, including Taylor's communitarian republicanism, deep ecology, feminism, and race theory, boldly challenge the distortion of narrow and truncated moralities to which individualistic ontologies of the self lead. These contemporary challenges in Western philosophies have deep resonances with a variety of Buddhist views. The chorus of these perspectives seek to show that a more perspicuous understanding of the self as part and parcel of a multi-faceted web of inter-relation of self to other guides us to see that the interests of others are indeed our own interests, and to see their suffering as our own suffering. Ontologies of inter-connectedness of self to other thus widen the range and depth of our ethical and moral concerns.

To be sure, I understand that there are profound differences between Taylor's view of the self and those of various Buddhist schools (and among Buddhist schools themselves); nevertheless, despite such divergences, I see common ground in their emphasis on an ontology of interconnectedness of self and other, and, in particular, the ethical, social, and political implications of this interconnectedness of self to other. This is, in broad strokes, the purpose and focus of this chapter: to map out some of these overlaps of insight and understanding.

12.2   The Punctual Self of Procedural Liberalism[1]

Taylor argues that the individualistic atomist ontological account of the self presupposed by modern Western liberal societies distorts our understanding of the nature of our interrelated being and is far from accurate, yet, it has become almost axiomatic, and its grip on the modern imagination nearly impossible to loosen. To begin to broaden one's understanding is to see its contingency and its history:

> To come to live by this definition of the [self] – as we cannot fail to do, since it penetrates and rationalizes so many of the ways and practices of modern life – is to be transformed: to the point where we see this way of being as normal, as anchored in perennial human nature in the way our physical organs are. So we come to think that we 'have' selves as we have heads. But the very idea that we have or are 'a self', that human agency is essentially

---

[1] Regarding one possible confusion about the term 'punctual', see note 2 below.

defined as 'the self', is a linguistic reflection of our modern understanding and the radical reflexivity it involves. Being deeply embedded in this understanding, we cannot but reach for this language; but it was not always so. (1989, 177; see also, 106)

The brand of liberalism from which this picture emerges, supported from leftist liberals, such as John Rawls (1999), to right-wing libertarians, such as Robert Nozick (1974), has its roots in Hobbes and Locke. This view sees society instrumentally: as a contract that individuals enter into with other individuals for the sake of their enlightened self-interest. Prior to society, such individuals exist in a "state of nature," in which there is no rule of law except that of power and violence – where individuals are isolated selves in conditions of competition for scarce resources. Such a situation is inherently unstable: each uses his right of nature and is free to do whatever he wants whenever he wants to get whatever he wants, by whichever means necessary. Violence and coercion reign supreme. To get out of this situation, for Hobbes, individuals purportedly contract with adversarial others and agree to lay down their natural freedom to use force to achieve their ends, as long as other individuals are willing to do the same, and, as long as there is an authoritative party to secure the agreement. We strive together to achieve convergent ends that we could not alone, as our individual self-interests in stability and security intersect.

The legacy of this picture is difficult to underestimate, especially in economics and politics. The putative purpose of the modern liberal state has come to be seen as procedural, with equal and maximal facilitation of individuals' desire-fulfilment as the convergent goal of the state. Such a state is "neutral" with regard to the individual values of citizens, for any conception of an individual's good is seen as being as valid or as admissible (qua good) as any other. It makes no value judgements regarding either the individual good or the common good of the community. For these are both private matters on this conception of society (or in the case of communal goods, perhaps a family-based or association-level matter). A life of courage and compassion is treated as though it is as worthy as a life of consumerist egoism. For to distinguish between higher or lower, more worthy and less worthy, might be discriminatory and might jeopardize the freedom of individuals to choose for themselves whatever it is that they desire. Such distinctions would be an assault on the foundational value of a liberal society, which is the equal individual autonomy of each to decide for oneself where one stands on such questions of value.

In Rawls's terms: the right takes priority over the good; the job of society is to figure out how to arbitrate between conflicting views of comprehensive notions of the good life and what equality requires in such terms, not to evaluate such notions or to promote any particular good. To endorse any particular view would be favouritism and discriminatory, and the worry – perhaps taken to an obsessive extreme – is that views not endorsed with official status would not be treated with equal respect. Fairness in such a view consists in coming up with the right decision-making procedures, not the right decisions – for there are no real right decisions, apart from what individuals choose for their own purposes (Taylor 1985b, 1989, 1995a).

Taylor contends that there are many profound problems with this model of liberalism. Such a model is not viable or realistic for a functioning democratic republic, which requires an extended and robust sense of ethical and political participation from its citizens, and some conception of the need for occasional self-sacrifice – at least with respect to any democracy that can flourish. The above liberal model presupposes a number of questionable assumptions about the self and its relationship to others that unduly narrow the range of potentially valuable ethical and political options for modern societies (1995a).

Let me begin with what I see as a deep problem with the contractual model, and something I see Taylor's communitarian republicanism, and forms of deep ecology, feminism, and Buddhism, as attempting to overcome. A critical issue here is one of moral and political motivation, and regard for the well-being of others. One of the key attractions of the contractualist model is that it purports to show how our duties towards others can be derived from individual self-interest and desire for individual security alone: it is in my enlightened self-interest, on this view, to take into consideration the interests of others because ultimately it will be of benefit to me. But this source of strength is its very weakness.

To see this, consider the following. On this model, why should I refrain from harming you and taking your possessions? If I do this, I will eventually be caught and imprisoned. In the long run, if we both agree to keep our contracts, then our individual convergent interests in individual security and property will be achieved; so it makes sense to obey the laws, they are always, in the end, a benefit for me – at least in the long run. A classic problem remains, however. What if I can be sure that no one is looking? Hobbes in such circumstances thought that it was imprudent to break the law because you could only get away with it once or twice, but that eventually you would be caught; this is not worth the risk. This response is weak: if moral, ethical, legal, and political obligation is grounded in my self-interest, there are times when the risk of getting caught will be sufficiently low that abstaining would be foolish (on a Hobbesian criterion of rationality). As long as I am clever enough, then it is in my interest to do whatever it takes to gain advantage. This is not simply an abstract concern, but one with which we are only too familiar: the world financial crisis of 2008 showed something along these lines. If the 'common good' is conceived of as (or reduced to) a deal struck between merely convergent self-interests, it would turn out to depend on everyone's simply calculating the risk of getting caught versus what they might gain from defecting from shared norms, undetected. What is in fact in my true interest is to deceive you, to convince you that it is in our mutual self-interest to obey the law, but stab you in the back when you are not looking, which is one way of describing attitudes that were pervasive on Wall Street in the period leading up to that crisis.

There are other dire problems, as Martha Nussbaum (2006) has pointed out, for such models: direct moral, ethical, and political obligation is only ever owed to those who are regarded as potentially threatening, given the adversarial nature of this view. The reason I am motivated to contract with you in the first place is because you present a threat to me, to my life, to my property, as I do to your life, liberty, and property. But what if you do not present a threat to me? What if you are too weak, too young, too old, mentally challenged, or disabled (let alone of non-human species)? I have no theoretical or practical reason to contract with you, and, hence no direct moral or political obligation to you. Any perspective that makes our ethical and political obligations to the weakest and most vulnerable in our society only derivative or optional (e.g., children are the children of an adversarial other – they are like property, to harm them is to harm their owner) is to distort the very nature of ethics.

Taylor argues that the kinds of deep ethical and political sacrifices that republican democratic regimes require of their citizens, including such sacrifices as paying taxes, following the rule of law, and being called on to protect and defend society, require a sense of belonging and attachment to our compatriots, to a common and shared good, that is not reducible to individual self-interest. Nor is the good of others dependent simply on my desiring or choosing it and nor – accordingly – should my respect for their dignity be so dependent. We need to distinguish between two senses of collective goods, what Taylor calls convergent goods (e.g., fire stations, a public policing system, paved roads) versus common or shared goods, such as friendship and republican citizenry. In the case of a commonly shared good, the value of the good sought can only be defined in relation to an *us*, in our connectedness and relationship as an us, whereas in the case of a convergent good no such relationship is necessary. All that is required for the latter is a 'me', and a narrow sense of self-interest. In a despotic society the kinds of sacrifices required for a political regime can be extracted from the ruled (via the threat of imprisonment for non-compliance) whereas this cannot be so for any free democratic republican regime. Coercion has to be replaced with an internal sense of motivation for acting out of genuine regard for the other, community, and the polis:

> This can only be a willing identification with the polis on the part of the citizens, a sense that the political institutions in which they live are an expression of themselves. The "laws" have to be seen as reflecting and entrenching their dignity as citizens, and hence to be in a sense extensions of themselves.. .. It transcends egoism in the sense that people are really attached to the common good, to general liberty. But it is quite unlike the apolitical attachment to universal principle that the stoics advocated or what is central to modern ethics or rule of law (1995a, 187).

Any flourishing democratic regime requires bonds of trust between citizenry, an attachment to the good of others as citizens of the same historical and cultural community, as interconnected patriots. Such bonds of trust and loyalty seem to lose their justification on the contractual model where the whole structure is based on the individual self-interest and separateness of isolated selves. However, the "very definition" of a free republican political regime requires an exploration of relationships of identity and community, an expansion of our moral concerns that move us beyond the false image of the self as some kind of discrete and unchanging individual entity (1995a, 192).

12.3   The Self in Webs of Interlocution

The critical problem for the contractual model of society, argues Taylor, is that it is grounded in an inherently problematic ontological account of the self. The self is understood as a sort of atom, analogous to a kind of extension-less point in space – what Taylor calls the "punctual" self, that is, from *punctum* or sharp point (1989, 159–176).[2] This ontological picture of the self originates from thinkers such as Descartes, Hobbes, and Locke. They take the self to be a separate, discrete, and essentialist entity with impermeable borders, that stands outside of the web of communal relationships, minimally defined by being self-conscious. A few Hobbesian reservations aside, this set of thinkers largely agreed on something along the lines of the *res cogitans* of Descartes, the thinking substance that can be defined in isolation from the physical body or the world (1989, 156). It is a self "unencumbered" by any constitutive purposes or meanings, an individual entity that exists prior to and apart from any bonds of community, to borrow Michael Sandel's phrase (1995). All life plans and goals are optional, matters of autonomous choice and desire, and thus such a self contracts for the sake of his individual interest, against those who potentially stand in his way. In fact, all judgments of value or worth, for the modern self, are a part of the purely subjective, projected onto an inherently valueless and disenchanted objective cosmos (Taylor 1989, 143–176). They are fabrications of the mind, colouring our understanding of an inherently objective, meaningless, and unordered universe. The primacy of rights and the value of individual autonomy and freedom take pride of place in this picture. It is alleged to be a distinct human trait to be able to fashion new identities and thereby create meaning within what is a meaningless world. In its ultimate and hyper-individualistic form, the self may aspire to become a Nietzschean *übermensch* by conquering others, by standing above and apart from the community and world. Taylor points out that this sense of the self has such a firm hold on the modern imagination that it seems self-evident, natural, and unquestionable.

Yet, there are deep problems with this view of the self. It is true that as a self, we are physically individuated in a body (1989, 112–113), but this individuation does not exhaust our sense of self or personhood. Physical individuation may differ, but selves are permeable and necessarily interconnected in frameworks of social meaning and significance. The atomist or punctual view of the self buries these in a silence of inarticulacy. The idea of an atomist self as a *punctum* that exists prior to society in some state of nature is not only a benign historical myth or some purely heuristic device; it distorts the very nature of our lives, being, and interconnectedness. The self, Taylor argues, cannot be properly understood without reference to the "web of interlocution" in which we exist: "One is a self only among other selves. A self can never be described without reference to those who surround it" (1989, 35).

---

[2] This is a different usage of 'punctual' than the one employed by Mark Siderits to spell out construal(s) of the no-self claim in Buddhism (a usage that is discussed above, in Chap. 5, by Gordon Davis and Mary Renaud).

We are intrinsically related to the self of others in multifaceted and dialogical relationships of conversation. We cannot be selves apart from such a web of relationships.

> This is the sense in which one cannot be a self on one's own. I am a self only in relation to certain interlocutors: in one way in relation to those conversational partners who were essential to my achieving self-definition; in another in relation to those who are now crucial to my continuing grasp of languages of self-understanding – and of course, these may overlap. A self exists only within what I call 'webs of interlocution' (1989, 36; see also 1985a, 267; 1995c, 25–26).

Taylor's account of the self as not merely exhausted by the idea of mere self-consciousness draws, in part, on Aristotle's insight that the human being is a social and political animal (1985d, 189); that indeed, contra the atomistic thesis, a self cannot be properly understood in isolation from the community. That is, person-hood requires being a part of rich frameworks of meaning and significance, which are only made possible in interrelation and conversation with a community of others. Indeed, a self could not develop its basic capacity for communication or acquire a language without being a part of a community of users. Using Wittgenstein's insight, Taylor argues that the transcendental conditions of learning and understanding a language require relating to others; this is necessary in coming to know that one's usage of a term, for example, is indeed correct (1989, 38). Without language and the rich vocabularies of expression for which it allows, self-understanding, frameworks of meaning, significance, and purpose cease for beings like us. Judgements of value about the right thing to do or what it is good to be, of what is higher or lower, better or worse, cannot be made. Indeed, the very ideals of freedom and equality require shared frameworks of meaning and significance in which these are shared goods for us, for which we must be willing to make sacrifices.

Such judgements of value provide the horizon of meaning and significance in which a person makes sense of her life; they provide independent standards by which one conceives of one's life as worthwhile. Taylor argues that such frame-works of "strong evaluation" are not contingent or subjective projections on our part, but that they are an intrinsic part of the inter-subjective/objective ontological furniture of the cosmos for beings like us (1989, 53–62; 2003). Indeed, selves and their actions can only be understood as located within a conceptual structure that links judgements of value to self-interpretation, within a teleological framework (contra behaviourism). That is, the self can only exist in relation to such a structure of questions about the nature of the good. The most urgent constellation of such values concerns "respect for life, integrity, and well-being, even flourishing, of others" (1989, 4); these are infringed upon in various authoritarian regimes where a person can be tortured, raped or murdered for merely criticising authority. The importance of human rights illustrates the necessity of coming to grips with rich frameworks of meaning and significance in providing justification for such basic rights. The egoist contractual model fails at the task of justification, both due to its conception of 'ego' and its conception of 'contract'.

This ontology of the self not only enlarges the circle of moral and ethical concern to our communities, but it goes beyond such parochial borders. Respect and recognition of cultural membership, against a background of normative pluralism, hold particular importance on Taylor's view, since such membership provides the rich language and the horizon of meaning and significance in which I locate myself and define who I am. The conditions of being a full agent or self require membership in a community, and these are some of the conditions that make possible the exercise of my autonomy and freedom (Taylor 1993, 53–54); such a horizon provides meaningful choices among which I can choose. This is why recognition and respect of diverse identities and pluralism in a liberal state is critical. As we have seen with the colonial and post-colonial treatment of indigenous peoples and other minorities, denial of such recognition and respect can often lead to real damage. Even when legal and formal obstacles to opportunities are removed, members of marginalized communities may simply be unable to take advantage of this due to internal hindrances caused by images of self-inferiority that they have come to adopt as a consequence of the structural domination that the majority has mirrored to them for centuries (Taylor 1995c, 225–227). But the modern self as *punctum* has a challenge in articulating such concerns, as it narrows the range of the ethical to the realm of formal equality and individual self-interest, thereby illegitimately limiting the scope and domain of ethical concern as a consequence of its distorted, inaccurate, and impoverished ontology. Such an ontology of the self leads to a closing of both the heart and the mind.

12.4   No-Self, Interconnectedness, and Compassion

It might appear as though there are few parallels between Taylor's ontology of the self and its implications for ethics and politics, and those of Buddhist views. In fact, the latter might seem quite the opposite: many Buddhist views of the self as no-self, or *anātman*, appear to be in stark contrast to Taylor's social ontology. This is certainly true when one thinks of various Abhidharma traditions, such as that of Sarvāstivāda and Theravāda schools. According to such schools, the self or the *ātman* understood as a substantial, separate, and permanent individual is a delusion.[3] Such a self does not exist. On the contrary, the self of everyday is but an

---

[3] There is a widespread and prevalent misconstrual of the Upaniṣadic notion of *ātman* as being identical with a substance-like eternal individual ego-self, purportedly held by "Hindus" versus the no-self views of Buddhists. No doubt some at the time of the Buddha employed the concept of *ātman* in this way; nevertheless, the concept of *ātman* is frequently used in many of the Upaniṣads to refer to exactly the *opposite* of the self as a substance-like individual ego-self with a unique essence. Rather, *ātman* is used to denote an unconditioned reality, or a pre-reflective form of pure consciousness, which gives rise to the *false sense* of individual ego-self; indeed, it gives rise to the very ideas of time and space themselves. Time- and space-dependent concepts, such as "eternal" and "substance," strictly speaking, fail to apply to *ātman*; see e.g., Bṛhadāraṇyaka Upaniṣad 3.4; see also Śaṅkara's (8th c. CE) later interpretation of *ātman* (no doubt influenced by Buddhists and sometimes derisively referred to as a crypto-Buddhist). For a contemporary discussion of this issue, see Albahari (2002), Werner (1996), and Lindtner (1999). I should also like to point out that Daisetz Suzuki, the eminent Zen philosopher, does not fall prey to any such misconception and is

aggregate of processes: the five *skandhas*, consisting of physical/bodily processes and the mental processes of consciousness, perception, emotion, and volition. What we think of as an individual self is simply a way to count things, which can be reduced to their various constituents. This becomes apparent in the *Questions of Milinda* (approx. 100 BCE) where the philosopher-monk Nāgasena argues in his conversation with Indo-Greek king Milinda, as there is no chariot over and above its constituent parts, there is no self over and above various physical and mental processes. Indeed, the chariot cannot be found in the wheels, the yoke, the axle, the goading-stick, or the banner-staff. It is merely but a "way of counting, term, appellation, convenient designation" (Koller and Koller 1991, 224). Analogously, there is nothing over and above individual parts that we could call a "self." This reasoning extends to all macroscopic entities for most Abhidharmists. Such entities can be reduced to their elemental parts, or momentary *dharmas* in time and space. We should note that at the microscopic level, such *dharmas* do have substantial self-existence (*svabhāva*) and unique characteristics (*svalakṣaṇa*).

This kind of reductionist view of the self has more in common with current cognitive science (and philosophers such as Derek Parfit or Daniel Dennett) than with Taylor's social ontology and anti-foundationalism. Taylor, in fact, explicitly rejects an almost identical analogy of the self when he denies that the self can be neutralized as a *punctum*[4] that can be compared to a car, for there are no comparatively meaningful questions to pose about the identity of a car, which is an assemblage of mechanical parts, in contrast to a self-interpreting being who inhabits the 'space of reasons' – a space of practical and moral considerations – i.e. someone who is an agent, for whom things have purpose and meaning, and for whom things matter (1989, 50).

However, these are not the only interpretations of the idea of no-self. In a similar anti-reductionist spirit to Taylor's metaphysics, some Mahāyāna traditions, such as that of the Chinese Hua-Yen school, the Chan/Zen school, and various Tibetan traditions, also interrogate reductive and essentialist interpretations of no-self. Such perspectives resonate with Taylor's views in a number of ways; in particular, the overlapping emphasis on the inter-relationship between self and other lead similarly to a broadening of the scope and domain of ethical and moral concern.

At the heart of various Mahāyāna perspectives and ontologies of the self is the notion of *pratītya-samutpāda* or interconnectedness (often termed 'dependent origination'), which is associated with the idea of anitya or impermanence, and *śūnyatā* or emptiness. As for Taylor, for Buddhists, the self exists in relation to the good; in the Mahāyāna context, the good is understood as nirvana and awakening for *all* sentient beings, free from all forms of suffering or *duḥkha* (or *dukkha* in Pali).

---

clear on the distinction between ātman construed as unconditioned being versus phenomenal ego-self (1900, 106). In addition, see Thompson (2015, 1–20) for a contemporary and insightful reading of some of the principal Upaniṣads with regard to *ātman* and consciousness.

[4] N.B. the footnote near the beginning of this chapter, in which this objection is dissociated from those that might be addressed to what Mark Siderits calls 'punctualism', a very different position in philosophy of mind.

Suffering is a result of not understanding and not coming to terms with the dynamic and connected nature of reality. It is perpetuated by *tṛṣṇā* (P. tanha) and *upādāna*: craving and clinging to a false sense of separate and permanent selfhood. An early formulation of the idea of *pratītya-samutpāda* was expressed this way:

> That being, this comes to be;
> From that arising, this arises;
> That being absent, this is not;
> From the cessation of that, this ceases. (Nidāna Saṃyutta)

Interconnectedness points to the dynamic and causally connected nature of reality as a process of becoming (rather than being); the claim is that nothing, including the self, can exist by itself. Nothing has permanent and unchanging self-existence/own-being or *svabhāva* or unique essence (*svalakṣaṇa*). Everything is dynamic and causally related. All things and events are dependent on the conditions and causes from which they arise, and when these conditions and causes cease, such things and events too will cease.[5] Abhidharmists have no issue with this, but they consider the ultimate constituents of causality, the *dharmas*, to be self-existentially real, which most Mahāyānists deny. The philosopher-monk Nāgārjuna (second century CE), who founded the Madhyamaka or middle way school, contends that all things and events, even *dharmas*, are *śūnya* or empty of any kind of inherent unchanging self-existence or unique essence. I read Nāgārjuna's arguments transcendentally: if change and becoming is possible, then there can be no ultimate constituents of conditions and causes that are assumed to have inherent self-existence or unique essence. If conditions and causes were indeed separate individuals with unique essence, then one could not explain their inter-relationship, and hence the possibility of transformation and change (see Nāgārjuna (1986), 105–117). Contemporary Zen master Thich Nhat Hanh explains Nāgārjuna's ideas in terms of the notion of "inter-being":

> So what permanent thing is there that we can call a self? ... Nothing can exist by itself alone. It has to depend on every other thing. That is called inter-being. To be means to inter-be. The paper inter-is with the sunshine and with the forest. The flower cannot exist by itself alone; it has to inter-be with soil, rain, weeds and insects. There is no being; there is only inter-being. Looking deeply into a flower, we see that the flower is made of non-flower elements. We can describe the flower as being full of everything. There is nothing that is not present in the flower. We see sunshine, we see the rain, we see clouds, we see the earth, and we also see time and space in the flower. A flower, like everything else, is made entirely of non-flower elements. The whole cosmos has come together in order to help the flower manifest herself. The flower is full of everything except one thing: a separate self, a separate identity. The flower cannot be by herself alone. The flower has to inter-be with the sunshine, the clouds and everything in the cosmos. If we understand being in terms of inter-being, then we are much closer to the truth. Inter-being is not being and it is not non-being. Inter-being means being empty of a separate identity, empty of a separate self (2002, 47–48).[6]

---

[5] For an insightful analysis of the differing and extended sense in which many Buddhist schools use the idea of causation, see Cook 1977, 67–74.

[6] I thank Emily Jull for bringing this passage to my attention.

The Chinese Hua-Yen school of Buddhism describes the inter-related nature of selves in the beautiful metaphor of the jewelled *Net of Indra*. In the Avataṃsaka Sūtra, the existence of selves and the cosmos or *suchness* (*tathātā*) is described in terms of an infinite and multi-dimensional net extending in all possible directions, with sparkling and multi-faceted diamonds of "blazing" "boundless" self-illuminating "Golden Light from a Spotless Sun" tied at each juncture or knot of the net (Avataṃsaka Sūtra 1984, 226, Cleary translation; see also 212–241). No individual self exists in and by itself; every slight ripple at any one juncture has an effect and reverberation for every other part of the net. Each facet of every diamond in the net reflects every other diamond like a mirror. As Francis Cook explains: the net represents the "infinitely repeated interrelationship among all members of the cosmos" and their "mutual identity and mutual inter-causality" (1977, 2; see also pp. 75–89). Analogous to what we find in Taylor's ontology of the self, there is the notion that the being of 'selves' is interpenetrated and interpenetrating; the self is reflected and mirrored in the lives of significant others and of the community, and of the globe. It is part and parcel of an entirety, of dialogical relationships with which, and to which, one is intrinsically tied. As Taylor would say, one can only be a self among others, intrinsically related to others; an individual always and only takes real shape as a 'self' when in sufficiently close relations with other selves.

What are the implications for ethics of such an ontology of the self? For Taylor, the rejection of an atomistic account of the self as a *punctum* (conceived of a separate and permanent individual *ātman*), in favour of a more web-like dialogical view of the self as interconnected to others, has ethical implications that are analogous to those recognized by some Mahāyāna schools. Insight into *pratītya-samutpāda* leads the philosopher-monk Śāntideva (8th CE), in his *Bodhicāryāvatāra*,[7] to posit the self as a part and parcel of an organic whole, intimately connected to all others. Just as the hand protects the foot (VIII. 99) and the integrity of the body, we should protect other sentient beings.

VII. 90
First, one should earnestly meditate
On the similarity of self and others:
Everyone, subject to similar happiness and suffering
Should be protected by me like myself.

VIII. 91
Just as the body, having many parts, divided into hands etc.,
Should be protected as one.
The world, though divided, is undivided
With respect to the nature of suffering and happiness. (Garfield et al. 2016, 59)

---

[7] See the Cowherds (i.e., Garfield et al. 2016, 54–76) for an illuminating history of this text; like most Indian philosophical texts, some passages may have been added later. Various different translations and readings of these passages depend on the exact nature of one's interpretation of anātman, the self that is the subject of suffering, and its relation to the other. My favoured reading is from a Chan/Zen perspective. See also Edelglass (2017) for an insightful contextualization of Śāntideva's ethics as embedded within a bodhisattva ideal.

Śāntideva implores us to move beyond the individualistic self-interest that is characteristic of a Hobbesian liberal contractual mentality: dividing the world into an isolated me and a you, forgetting that there is no me without you, nor you without me. The sharp lines drawn by such a picture are misguided, for the suffering of another is like my own suffering. Indeed, I should thus strive to eliminate the suffering of all sentient beings:

> VIII. 94
> The suffering of others should be eliminated by me,
> Because it is suffering like my own suffering.
> I should help others
> Because they are sentient beings, as I am a sentient being. (59)

It is only when I am in the grip of a false ontology, a false understanding of the reality of the self as a unique and permanent entity that I develop a deep and false sense of I-ness or *ahaṃkāra*, which is the cause (and at the same time, the result) of more separation, suffering, and misery in the world (see verse VIII.101, trans. Garfield et al.). This ontology perpetuates a vicious circle of alienation of self from other(s). Such misguided views are grounded in, and at the same time lead to, thinking and feeling that your suffering has no bearing on my own, and that our interests are completely separate. As Śāntideva brilliantly argues: "what is so special about me that I merely strive for my own happiness?" (VIII. 95). Is my hunger, pain, and isolation different from yours? Does it not hurt in the same ways? One might try to insist that another's pain is in her body, while my pain is in my own; but would I not feed my child because the hunger is in her body and not in my own? Of course I would feed her, regardless of our differing physical bodies. Our individuation may be separate but our selves are in common, our interests are in common.

Daisetz Suzuki interprets the *Awakening of Faith*, attributed to Aśvaghoṣa (second century CE)[8] from a Zen perspective in a similar manner. The realization of emptiness of the self as a separate and permanent being, and the attempt to understand the *dharmadhātu* or the totality of things, or *suchness* (*bhūtatathātā* or *tathātā*) at the level of ontology, leads one to broaden one's ethical perspective, broaden and develop a sense of *karuṇā* or compassion, and leads one to treat others as their own selves by a principle of equality:

> What is meant by the activity of suchness is this: all Buddhas, while at the stage of discipline, feel a deep compassion (*mahākarunā*) [for all beings], practice all *pāramitās*, the four methods of entertainment (*catvāri-sangrahavstūni*), and many other meritorious deeds; treat others as their self, wish to work out a universal of mankind in ages to come, through limitless number of kalpas; recognize truthfully and adequately the principle of equality (*samatā*); and do not cling to individual existence of a sentient being. (Suzuki 1900, 98–99)

The Dalai Lama uses almost an identical train of thought to argue that it is a misguided atomistic picture of the self that leads one to ignore others' interests apart from one's own:

---

[8] This attribution to Aśvaghoṣa is questionable because – among other reasons – no Sanskrit text has been found; however, the text is an influential work, and I take Suzuki's reading and interpretation as offering legitimate insight into Mahāyāna views of Suchness, *śūnyatā*, and ethics.

When we come to see that everything we perceive and experience arises as a result of an infinity of dependently originated and interrelated causes and conditions, our whole perspective changes. We begin to see that the universe we inhabit can be understood in terms of a living organism in which each cell works in balance cooperation with every other cell to sustain the whole. If just one of these cells is harmed, as it is when disease strikes, that balance is harmed and there is danger to the whole. This in turn suggests that our individual well-being is intimately connected both with that of all others and with the environment within which we live. It also becomes apparent that our every action, our every deed, word and thought, no matter how slight or in consequential it may seem, has an implication not only for ourselves but for all others too. Furthermore, when we view reality in terms of dependent origination, it draws us away from our usual tendency to see things and events in terms of solid, independent, discrete entities.. ... we come to see that the habitual sharp distinction we make between 'self' and 'others' is itself and exaggeration.. ... it is possible to imagine becoming habituated to an extended conception of self wherein the individual situates his or interests within the interests of others.. ... If the self had intrinsic identity, it would be possible to speak in terms of self-interest in isolation from that of others. But given that this is not so, given that self and others can only be understood in terms of relationship, we see that the self-interest and the interest of others are similarly interrelated. Indeed, within this picture of dependently originated reality, we see that there is no self-interest completely unrelated to others' interests. Due to the fundamental interconnectedness which lies at the heart of reality, your interest is also my interest.. ... And because, as we have seen, our interest are inextricably linked, we are compelled to accept ethics as the indispensable interface between my desire to be happy and yours (1999, 46–49).

I should again like to note the overlap of the way in which a rejection of the self as a kind of geometric *punctum* for Taylor, and the rejection of the self as a discrete entity with unique self-existence and essence for various Buddhist schools, leads to a broadening of ethical concern and obligation to and for others. Indeed, there is a growing global convergence here, which ranges across feminist views of the self to deep ecology (see e.g., Naess[9] 1985) in that the self cannot be severed from the other in a neat surgical fashion, or from the cosmos of which it is a part; or to put this differently, such a feat cannot be accomplished without distortion, and without profound cost and debilitating consequences for ourselves, our communities, and our natural environments.[10] The overlapping consensus of the chorus of such a challenge to individualist ontologies of the self, as they continue to manifest in economic greed, destruction of natural environments and cruelty to non-human animals, shows the urgency of re-thinking such views, and opening a necessary global, intercultural, and inter-philosophical dialogue and exploration of what is required for a sustainable future for humanity.

I take the purpose of all of these challenges to be that of conceptually widening the circle of our moral concern by chipping away at the false ontology of the self that divides us from the other. The purpose of Buddhist philosophical arguments how-

---

[9] See also the discussion of Naess and deep ecology in the chapter following, by Gordon Davis and Pragati Sahni.

[10] I argue elsewhere that toleration, as a *political* phenomenon, apart from being simply an individual virtue, was first constructed by Emperor Aśoka (268–232 BCE) based on Buddhist interpretations of *ahiṃsā* or non-violence long before it was constructed as such in Europe (see Peetush 2015).

ever is not simply intellectual. The philosophical enterprise is conceived not merely as conceptual, but as a contemplative practice (at least, for many schools in India, China, Japan, and Tibet); its aim is to deepen and widen understanding so as to improve lived experience and to lessen suffering in the world. This is one reason that a practice such as mindfulness, *dhyāna* or zazen, may be intrinsic to such an enterprise. Philosophy cannot be neatly isolated from practice, as most modern Western philosophers would have it. Indeed, to paraphrase Marx, the purpose of philosophy is not simply to interpret the world, but (also) to change and transform it.

While one might grant that, in broad strokes, the logic of interrogating ontologies of atomistic accounts of selves as separate, unchanging, and disconnected entities lead both Taylor and Buddhists, and indeed many others, to broaden the scope and domain of the ethical, there are admittedly some deep dissimilarities that I have set aside here. Buddhist notions of self and interconnectedness, the Net of Indra, and emptiness, are ontologies and concerns about the ultimate basis of the real, the *dharmadātu*, the totality of being and our place in it. Their aim is to get behind conventional truth, to get behind our phenomenal existence, to the underlying reality that exists behind the world of appearance or *saṃsāra*. One might object that there is a contrast here with Taylor, who is a realist of a different kind. For him, there is no reality that is somehow more real than the one we experience now. For many Buddhists however, the everyday self and world reflect *māyā*, or illusion. Of course, we might deceive ourselves about our real motivations (or have false sense impressions, etc.), as Taylor would admit, but this is not the same sense of deception, in degree or kind, that these Buddhists would posit. Even Taylor's belief in God would, presumably, be of a divine source standing in a benevolent relationship to our world, a world of His own creation. In fact, Taylor says little about the nature of the soul as providing a defining feature of the ontology of selfhood. Taylor's ontology of the self is but a *social* ontology with the potential to correct complex and sophisticated fabrications and distortions that have arisen in the West, which need to be exposed as misguided and false – distortions that have the potential to lead to the fragmentation and demise of flourishing democratic regimes, but nothing more. My analysis, some will thus say, glosses over this critical difference.

In response, I want to reemphasize that for Taylor, the dialogical nature of the self is an ontological feature of selfhood. This characteristic is not merely a historical, social, and political contingency, as some might take Taylor to be saying. Furthermore, and as importantly, that such a self can only be understood teleologically in relation to the good – a self-interpreting being for whom things have significance, meaning, and purpose – is also an ontological feature of selfhood. For Taylor, the best possible explanation of such meaning and significance is that these are part and parcel of the intersubjective ontological furniture of the real world. It may be that, if beings like us ceased to exist, the good would also cease to exist; nonetheless, the good is not merely a projection on to the world, according to Taylor; it is not a "subjective" property mapped onto a neutral cosmos (2003). This general conception of a middle way bears some resemblance to the ontological orientation of various Buddhist schools.

Secondly, while I certainly agree that some Buddhist schools adopt an anti-realist and reductionist stance towards the phenomenal self and world, it is far from accurate to claim that these are representative of all Buddhist views. Indeed, many of the Tibetan and Zen schools reject the idea that we can somehow ignore the phenomenal world as simply illusory. What is required is not a repudiation of our shared common-sense world, but a transformation of how we come to see this world, and the place of our selves in it; the aim is to break through the distortion of separateness; and this is much like Taylor's view. As the Dalai Lama remarks:

> … while acknowledging that there is often a discrepancy between perception and reality, it is important not to go to the extreme of assuming that behind the phenomenal is a realm which is somehow more 'real'. The problem with this is that we may then dismiss everyday experience as nothing but an illusion. This would be quite wrong. Similarly, accepting a more complex understanding of reality, in which all things and events are seen to be interdependent, does not mean we cannot infer that the ethical principles we identified earlier cannot be understood as binding. (1999, 48)

Dependent origination and the emptiness of self-existence, on this interpretation, is not meant to undermine the reality of our everyday lives, but to provide a more perspicuous framework in which to locate ourselves and others:

> Far from undermining the notion of phenomenal reality, the concept of dependent origination provides a robust framework within which to situate cause and effect, truth and falsity, identity and difference, harm and benefit. It is therefore quite wrong to infer from the idea any sort of nihilistic approach to reality. (1999, 45)

Indeed, nirvana is not separate from *saṃsāra*, as the practice of emptiness and Zen (among other schools) teach; it is attained by fully living and being present in the moment: in washing your dishes, sweeping the floor, eating breakfast, listening to your daughter or son, and talking with a friend.[11] Nirvana is not an otherworldly heaven, it exists in the here and the now; it is the lived experience of the interrelatedness of the web of life or the Net of Indra. Compassion awakens one to such interconnection and, at the same time, is rooted in such interconnection; it is nothing if only in the mind and the intellect. It has to be in the heart, in the act, and in the daily practice of relating oneself to others. None of this is to deny the various differences between the ontologies of the self found in Taylor and Buddhism (nor, to be sure, those among Buddhist schools themselves). My point is that some of these differences may not be as deep or as wide as they may at first appear. Indeed, such ontologies of the self, and their ethical implications, are complementary in significant respects.

---

[11] Daisetz Suzuki utilizes R.H. Blyth's reading of Bashō's haiku in a similar regard:

> *Fleas, lice,*
> *The horse pissing*
> *Near my pillow*
> – Bashō

We are urged to understand that "these things too," the fleas, the lice, the horse urinating, as well as "butterflies," are an intimate part of the real, a part of what it is to live in the real world, a part that cannot simply be dismissed in favor of some heavenly realm (Suzuki 1973, 237–238; see also Cook 1977, 11).

References

Albahari, Miri. 2002. Against No-Ātman Theories of Anattā. *Asian Philosophy* 12 (1): 5–20.

Cleary, Thomas. 1984. *The Flower Ornament Scripture: A Translation of the Avatamsaka Sutra*. Boulder: Shambhala Publications.

Cook, Francis. 1977. *Hua-Yen Buddhism: The Jewel Net of Indra*. New York: Pennsylvania State University.

Edelglass, William. 2017. Mindfulness and moral transformation: Awakening to others in Śāntideva's ethics. In *The Bloomsbury Research Handbook of Indian Ethics*, ed. S. Ranganathan, 225–248. New York: Bloomsbury Press.

Garfield, Jay, Stephen Jenkins, and Graham Priest. 2016. The Śantideva Passage: *Bodhicāryāvatāra* VII.90–103, 55. In *Moonpaths: Ethics and Emptiness*, ed. Cowherds. New York: Oxford University Press.

Gyatso, Tenzin. (His Holiness the Dalai Lama). 1999. *Ancient Wisdom, Modern World: Ethics for a New Millennium*. London: Little, Brown and Company.

Koller, John, and Patricia Koller. 1991. *A Sourcebook in Asian Philosophy*. Upper Saddle River: Prentice Hall.

Lindtner, Christian. 1999. From Brahmanism to Buddhism. *Asian Philosophy* 9 (1): 5–37.

Naess, Arne. 1985. The World of Concrete Contents. *The Trumpeter* 22 (1): 43–55.

Nāgārjuna. 1986. *Nāgārjuna: The Philosophy of the Middle Way*. Trans. D. Kalupahana. New York: State University of New York Press.

Nhat Hanh, Thich. 2002. *No Death, No Fear: Comforting Wisdom for Life*. New York: Riverhead Books.

Nozick, Robert. 1974. *Anarchy, State, and Utopia*. New York: Basic Books.

Nussbaum, Martha. 2006. *Frontiers of Justice: Disability, Nationality, Species Membership*. Cambridge, MA: Harvard University Press.

Peetush, Ashwani. 2015. Human rights and political toleration in India: Multiplicity, self, and interconnectedness. In *Human rights: India and the West*, ed. A. Peetush and Jay Drydyk, 205–228. New Delhi: Oxford University Press.

Rawls, John. 1999. *A Theory of Justice*. Cambridge, MA: Belknap Press.

Sandel, Michael. 1995. *Liberalism and the Limits of Justice*. New York: Cambridge University Press.

Suzuki, Daisetz [Teitaro]. 1900. *Açvaghosha's Discourse on the Awakening of Faith in the Mahâyâna*. Chicago: The Open Court Publishing Company.

——— [Teitaro]. 1973. *Zen and Japanese Culture*. New York: Princeton University Press.

Taylor, Charles. 1985a. The Concept of a Person. In *Philosophy and the Human Sciences: Philosophical Papers 2*, 58–90. New York: Cambridge University Press.

———. 1985b. Neutrality in Political Science. In *Philosophy and the Human Sciences: Philosophical Papers 2*, 58–90. New York: Cambridge University Press.

———. 1985c. What's Wrong with Negative Liberty. In *Philosophy and the Human Sciences: Philosophical Papers 2*, 211–229. New York: Cambridge University Press.

———. 1985d. Atomism. In *Philosophy and the Human Sciences: Philosophical Papers 2*, 187–210. New York: Cambridge University Press.

———. 1989. *Sources of the Self: The Making of the Modern Identity*. Cambridge, MA: Harvard University Press.

———. 1993. *Reconciling the Solitudes: Essays on Canadian Federalism and Nationalism*, ed. Guy Laforest. Montreal: McGill-Queen's University Press.

———. 1995a. Cross-Purposes: The Liberal-Communitarian Debate. In *Philosophical Arguments*, 181–203. Cambridge, MA: Harvard University Press.

———. 1995b. Irreducibly Social Goods. In *Philosophical Arguments*, 127–145. Cambridge, MA: Harvard University Press.

———. 1995c. The Politics of Recognition. In *Philosophical Arguments*, 225–256. Cambridge, MA: Harvard University Press.

————. 1999. Conditions of an Unforced Consensus on Human Rights. In *The East Asian Challenge for Human Rights*, ed. Joanne R. Bauer and Daniel A. Bell, 124–144. New York: Cambridge University Press.

————. 2003. Ethics and Ontology. *The Journal of Philosophy* 100 (6): 305–320.

Thompson, Evan. 2015. *Waking, Dreaming, and Being*. New York: Columbia University Press.

Werner, Karel. 1996. Indian Conceptions of Human Personality in Relation to the Doctrine of the Soul. *Journal of the Royal Asiatic Society of Great Britain and Ireland* 1: 73–97.

Chapter 13
Variations on Anātman: Buddhist Themes in Deep Ecology and in Future-Directed Environmental Ethics

Gordon F. Davis and Pragati Sahni

Ashwani Peetush's discussion of Buddhist resonances in Charles Taylor's work, in the previous chapter of this volume, raises an important problem about the ideal scope of selfless engagement with others. The framing of the question there has to do with collective action within a sovereign democratic society. Yet, despite agreeing that selfless compassion should constitute a key value in just societies, many Buddhists would take some critical distance from the concepts that Taylor and other communitarians treat as fundamental – namely, those of sovereignty, self-government, and related notions of legitimacy in public deliberation. Some Buddhists would be uneasy with any elevation of the political over the ethical, and some would also be concerned to warn us about the risk of reifying such abstractions. Their reservations would be all the more acute to the extent that any such concept depends on the putative moral salience of *borders*. A notable point of consensus across the many different Buddhist traditions is the idea that selfless compassion is owed to *all* sentient beings, be they fellow citizens or not. To some outsiders this is a sign of moral robustness in Buddhism; to some it is a weakness. Indeed, some have seen it as a weakness of Buddhist philosophical traditions that they seem to have lacked (at least until modern times) a well-developed discipline of political philosophy. But in light of the global vision of well-being that seems historically to have favoured other normative foci, one might well wonder whether the paucity

The authors wish to thank Chris Framarin, Ashwani Peetush, Noah Quastel, Noel Salmond, Sonia Sikka and Mark Siderits for many helpful exchanges and conversations on the topics and themes of this chapter.

G. F. Davis (✉)
Department of Philosophy, Carleton University, Ottawa, ON, Canada
e-mail: Gordon.Davis@carleton.ca

P. Sahni
University of Delhi, Delhi, India

© Springer International Publishing AG, part of Springer Nature 2018   253
G. F. Davis (ed.), *Ethics without Self, Dharma without Atman*, Sophia Studies in Cross-cultural Philosophy of Traditions and Cultures 24,
https://doi.org/10.1007/978-3-319-67407-0_13

of 'political theory' in Buddhist sources could simply be a collateral effect of something ultimately salutary: a borderless ethical perspective.

In this chapter, we turn to a normative discourse that is not only transpersonal, but also deeply transnational: that of environmental ethics, and specifically the ethics of global ecology. We do not aim here to settle the relative importance of ethics and politics in Buddhist philosophy; rather, we undertake to highlight the ways in which some ethically motivated ecologists have taken inspiration from Buddhist perspectives, as well as to outline what some neglected strands in Buddhist ethics might contribute to environmental ethics. Our aim is not to defend a view in environmental ethics, but rather to expose, once more – along the lines of other chapters in this volume – the role of Buddhist writing in the development of Western philosophy. In highlighting deep ecology, for example, our aim is not to endorse it, let alone glorify it; on the contrary, like other philosophers we acknowledge its problems and paradoxes. The point is rather that deep ecology has served as a bold and novel philosophical framework for environmental ethics, something with a unique place in twentieth-century history of ideas, and perhaps even a unique place in the story of modern Western philosophy. And yet, the Asian sources in its wells of inspiration have only partially been examined and discussed.

We do not restrict ourselves to deep ecology, however. After discussing Arne Naess's bridging of Asian philosophy and 'deep ecology', or 'ecosophy' (terms he was the first to use), we consider the views of a somewhat more moderate – and more explicitly Buddhist – theorist, Joanna Macy. Finally, we turn to consider the implications that may be in store for environmental ethics when the perspectives of some more specialized Buddhist ethicists are applied in that area. These contemporary philosophers – Mark Siderits and Charles Goodman in particular – mark an apt closing point for this volume, being Western philosophers in the same sense that the other modern figures in this volume are or were, and being influenced by Buddhism just as every figure since Schopenhauer (in this volume) has been, but notably, drawing on a more extensive knowledge of Buddhist texts, languages and traditions than any previous generation of philosophers has had the fortune of possessing.

A fundamental feature of the deep ecological tradition is a resistance to separating questions of animal welfare from questions of global biospheric integrity. On the one hand, Buddhist sources – especially the Mahāyāna ones that informed Naess's views – stress *advaya* (non-duality, known in Hindu sources as *advaita*), and thereby reinforce the bridging of those concerns, and possibly even the bridging of the sentient and the non-sentient sphere(s). On the other hand, Buddhist ethics can mitigate some of the vagueness of deep ecology, in part by highlighting the concreteness of animal suffering and – some would argue – the particular salience of animal welfare relative to more abstract concerns. When a Buddhist pledges to 'benefit all sentient beings', she is likely to welcome an open mind about what qualifies as 'salience'; and yet, the concern for sentient beings, both within and beyond our anthropogenic borders, remains a salutary starting point for ethics.[1]

---

[1] This transnational concern for welfare could of course be combined with an approach like Peetush's in the previous chapter (our remarks at the outset were not intended to imply that a 'sovereigntist' bias must be inherent in a Taylorian approach).

As most of our colleagues have done here, we approach this discussion wearing philosophers' hats, so to speak, rather than those of ecologists or doctrinaire Buddhists. Having said that, there is at least one strand in Buddhist ethics that we join Naess and Macy in finding particularly instructive. Many of the other chapters here have mentioned the ideal of the bodhisattva figure: the sage who accepts even the greatest self-sacrifice (even sacrificing liberation) for the sake of others. But fewer mentions have been made of a moral skill attributed to bodhisattvas, known in Pali and Sanskrit as *upāya* (skilful means).[2] An *upāya* is a strategy for alleviating suffering in the world. Such strategies can involve practical compromises, doctrinal adaptations or even heterodoxies; can bend rules, principles and precepts; and/or can flirt with ideas and values that may serve a purpose for a time but would eventually need to be corrected or jettisoned, i.e. when the risks of speaking the plain truth – perhaps ultimate truth – are finally lifted. As philosophers, our aim is not to judge the successes of 'ecosophies' *qua strategies*, let alone to indulge their rhetorical agenda, e.g. by sparing them critical scrutiny. But we acknowledge, in advance, that the strictly *philosophical* merits and demerits of deep ecology do not necessarily tell the whole story, particularly with respect to those for whom the demands of activism may sometimes justify glossing over philosophical intricacies. If Arne Naess, for example, shared some of the spirit of the bodhisattva – in a social 'activist' guise – his ideas should also be judged by their fruits; and we hardly wish to deny that the tradition of ecological writing he spawned has been fruitful in many ways. Indeed, this is one important reason for his inclusion in this volume.

13.1 Arne Naess and the Origins of Deep Ecology: Buddhism, Spinoza and Anātman

In his first exposition of 'deep ecology', Arne Naess emphasized what he called "biospherical egalitarianism" ([1973] 1995a, 4). We shall work up to an explanation of what this might imply in practice; but in theory, it is the belief that every organism across space and time has equal value. (We shall return to a Spinozist understanding of 'across space and time', and also return to the concept of 'value' in connection with the notion of *intrinsic* value.) As we shall see, more than simply 'organic' beings are involved in what Naess had in mind. But two genealogical questions arise, the first causal: (1) What inspired Naess to embrace ecological egalitarianism?; and the second justificatory: (2) what line of reasoning could ground or justify the egalitarian conclusion? A third question is about methodology

---

[2] Damien Keown was among the first to highlight the potential importance of this concept for a modernized Buddhist moral theory, though he also flags it as a potentially divisive concept; he suggests that in one sense, *upāya* is related to traditional moral cultivation (and thus implies, indirectly, that it may be akin to *phronesis*); but he also admits that some see *upāya* as licensing exceptions to moral rules (2001, 157–60).

or epistemology: (3) what is the role of metaphysical reasoning – in principle and/ or in his philosophical practice – in a Naessian defence of ethical principles?

Many of the essays in this volume have wrestled with what might be called the question of what it is to be *'self-sceptical'*.[3] Two of Naess's middle-period essays, composed not long after his 1973 exposition of deep ecology, illustrate several ways of being 'self-sceptical'. In "Through Spinoza to Mahāyāna Buddhism", Naess wrote that the "status of self is precarious… both for Spinoza and for Mahāyāna Buddhism… [In light of] human and nonhuman [solidarity]… the term *self* can, and ought, to be avoided" ([1977] 2008a, 272–73). There is no facile anti-realism about selfhood here, though, and we may note the word 'problem' when Naess later broaches "the difficult problem of how to interpret the Buddhist *anātmavāda*, the negation of the existence of selves" ([1985] 2008b, 197). The context of this is Naess's attempt to explain "how wide a range of beings may be meaningfully said to realize themselves. Animals, yes; plants, yes; but including a wider range… dilutes the very concept of… Self. There is a limit here, but it is not definite" (196). Naess here expresses a salutary scepticism about his own claims (even if one hears his 'dilution' as accompanied by a Buddhist *'tant mieux'*) – which nonetheless, for argument's sake, we will try to organize along the sort of Spinozist lines that Naess himself would recognize.

Signalling some limits to his readiness to tackle question (3) above, Naess acknowledges the role of *feeling* in both the Buddhist (in particular, Zen) approach and his own approach to nature; but on the other hand, this feeling is incorporated into the reasoning he offers. An "antihierarchical way of feeling things" ([1985], 202), he argues, is warranted in light of a duly sceptical treatment of human self-hood (inspired by both Spinozist and Buddhist analyses of our organic nature). In other words, Naess felt that subverting Cartesian and kindred conceptions of self-hood would support some version of his egalitarian principle. Yet it seems that he may have directed more of his mature philosophical scepticism at his own earlier egalitarian position than at the no-self premise that had come to serve as almost an axiom in his ethical reflections. In that same essay, "Gestalt Thinking and Buddhism", he ends with some awkward sceptical reflections about the implica-tions of putting all life forms on the same moral level. As he puts it, "[i]f we think of some of the cruelest parasites, inflicting slow, painful death… it is difficult to invest them with any sort of positive intrinsic value… [a point which] applies even more… to chemical and other weapons… [W]hat about [this] "problem of evil"…? Clearly, this concept [of equal intrinsic value] is as vulnerable as any other that tries to attach uniform positive value of some kind to all that is felt to be real" (203). There is some tension in Naess's philosophy, then, between his almost limitless

---

[3] See Chap. 1 for qualifications and reservations about the use of this and related terms. Most of our co-contributors here have sensibly favoured Pali and Sanskrit terms over English ones, i.e. *anattā* and *anātman* (though, in citing the secondary literature, it is impossible to avoid references to 'no-self', 'not-self', etc.).

embracing of ascriptions of intrinsic value throughout nature,[4] and his awareness of the philosophical vulnerability that emerges in the wake of critical reflection.

Our critical remarks will thus echo Naess's own, when we turn to consider the risk of deep ecologists' denying the difference between the evil of suffering and the ways or modes of being that limit suffering. But meanwhile, regarding the first question above, it is perhaps noteworthy that Naess edited the *Invitation to Chinese Philosophy* in 1972, the year before his original essay on deep ecology appeared. This was not his first foray into Asian philosophy (his early forays focused on the theory and practice behind Gandhi's non-violence); but to our knowledge it was his first – albeit as editor – that addressed Mahāyāna Buddhism. While Naess's own experiences in the wilderness of Norway clearly played a key role in the inspiration that led to his 'deeper' perspective on ecology, there was also surely an element of textual or intertextual inspiration. This may well have included exposure to a distinctively East Asian Mahāyāna idea: that all of nature is bound together, not just by organic microcosms, but *as* a microcosm, reflecting an inherently value-laden – sometimes called 'originally enlightened' – macrocosm. (This is our attempt at rendering an idea associated with the *Avatamsaka-Sutra* tradition, symbolized most famously by the metaphor of '*Indra's Net*', though we readily grant that this construal might be contested by certain Buddhists; for present purposes, in any case, we have simply invoked Naess's own terms for expressing this: "Self-realization in our world is increased by [symbiosis]... Each flower, each natural entity with the character of a whole (a gestalt) somehow mirrors or expresses the supreme whole... Microcosm is essential for the existence of macrocosm"[5] (1995b, 36–37).)

This identification of microcosm and macrocosm is important to understanding why Naess's retention of the term 'self' is ultimately akin to an *anattā*-based (i.e. no-self) ontology, which he calls a 'gestalt' ontology. The concept of 'self', for Naess, is to be superseded by a wider notion of 'Self', so much wider that it is no

---

[4] Describing his openness to such ascriptions – his and others' – as '*almost* limitless', rather than simply limitless, reflects his earlier hesitation about a 'wider range' than (e.g.) plants, but it may be rather charitable to Naess, seeing as a (less credible) *limitless* openness seems to follow from what he calls his 'gestalt ontology'. This is a relativist ontology that seeks to vindicate even the most emotive 'observations' of intrinsic value simply by situating those emotive claims within the observer's context, which is just the context of nature itself (see Naess 2008b and other essays in Devall and Drengson (2008)). With this 'gestalt' approach, Naess sought to defend himself and others against the charge that investing (e.g.) waterfalls with ethical significance was a merely subjective reaction to the environment. Just as he did not – ultimately – go through with investing *all* of nature with intrinsic value, however, he would surely not wish to extend ontological status to *all* reactions to features of the natural environment; and if that is right, then there would have to be limits to his gestalt ontology.

[5] Commenting further on this idea – the interdependence of microcosm and macrocosm – Naess adds: "Spinoza was influenced by the idea when demanding an immanent God, not a God apart" (ibid, 37). Cf. the discussion of the *Weltgeist* element in Spinoza's ethics (and the later concept of pantheism), in Chap. 5 of this volume.

less than the biosphere conceived as an 'ecological self'.[6] It is this 'ecological self' that is referred to in his ethical injunction to pursue 'Self-realization'. It is well-known that Naess was guided by the Spinozist view that (so-called) individuals are merely 'modes' of the one substance that is nature, not substances in themselves. Yet he also assimilated this view to a Mahāyānist framework that takes the idea of an enlightened macrocosm to supersede the notion of *ātman*, in the sense of an individually unified self, as evidenced in his essay "Through Spinoza to Mahāyāna Buddhism" ([1977] (2008a)). In other words, Naess assimilates much of the Buddhist critique of the selfhood concept, even though his terminology reflects a coalescence of Hindu and Buddhist ideas, which may explain his use of phrases like 'great Self' to refer to the ecological macrocosm.[7] In any case, the ethical upshot – or the appearance of such – seems natural enough, where the equation of microcosm and macrocosm may inspire an ecological form of egalitarianism, and where the notion of 'original enlightenment' may be felt to explain the 'intrinsic value' that each equal being is alleged to have.

We have already seen how Naess himself acknowledged problems with the notion of equal intrinsic value in nature. Some of these problems are analogous to the morally levelling effect that some see as following from radical versions of pantheism.[8] Here, though, we shall consider a less familiar example of the levelling effect, an example that can serve as a pivot towards a very different way of applying Buddhist philosophy to environmental ethics (which we develop in Sect. 13.3 below).

When Naess construes ecological egalitarianism in terms of the "uniform value of all that is felt to be real" (quoted above from his [1985], p. 203), he presumably means this to cover all that is, was, or will be. After all, in emphasizing the holistic and intuitive elements in Spinoza, Naess seems to share his aspiration to see things *sub specie aeternitatis* – that is, from the point of view of eternity. This is one reason for construing Naess as seeking to vindicate the value of 'every organism across space and time', as we put it earlier. But this seems to imply that our respect for things of the past should equal (in accord with this 'deep' egalitarianism) our respect for the rights or welfare of future organisms. Or, if one wishes to avoid the discourse of 'rights', one might simply say that, on this view, our assessment of the value in things should be blind to the distinction of past and future. (Some evolutionary

---

[6] Naess sometimes hints at intermediate stages of widened identification, possibly warding off charges of reductionism or eliminativism. A moderate widening of what might count as self or mind has also been proposed by externalists and enactivists in the philosophy of mind, going back to Hilary Putnam decades ago, and taken further recently by Alva Noë (2009) and Evan Thompson (2007), whose work also engages with themes in Buddhist philosophy and psychology (see also Varela et al. 1991).

[7] As Naess explains, though, "As I use the expression 'realizing the great Self', it does not correspond to a Hindu idea of realizing the absolute *Atman*. If I should choose a Sanskrit phrase for '*self-realization*', I might select 'realizing *svamarga*'... The *great Self* corresponds to the maximum deepening and extending of the *sva* through deepening and extending the process of identification" ([1985] 2008b, 198).

[8] Cf. Pierre Bayle's critique of Spinoza (discussed above, in Chap. 5).

biologists would applaud, particularly those who take the findings of paleontology as warranting a special kind of respect, or even reverence.) This generates, however, another iteration of the 'problem of evil', which worried Naess, as we have seen. The problem is not how to combat evils, but how to *explain* them, and in such a way as to avoid assuming that their repetition might be a good thing. The people of the past – not to mention other animals – generally faced short, fraught lives, whereas enlightened future policies may, just possibly, secure better lives for all terrestrial beings who will live in the future, or at least aim for this, for as many beings as possible. Naess's approach risks being unable to explain why the moral status of future beings would have an undeniable significance that long-gone cycles of species interaction do not.[9] In the final section, we consider a different Buddhist perspective that rectifies this by taking a 'future-directed' form.

It might be objected that, in practice, like almost every form of ecology, deep ecology would focus on improving our relationship to the environment and thus would be as 'future-directed' as any alternative framework. And if deep ecology would be future-directed in practice, then any practical defects in its normative platform must lie elsewhere. After all, critics of deep ecology have often preferred to question its egalitarian levelling of human and non-human interests, precisely because this seems apt to generate policies and practices that would limit concrete gains in human welfare for less concrete results among less sentient beings. (They may or may not be right, but – so the objection goes – at least this pinpoints a key *practical* divergence.) However, with a very general question in mind, that of the ethical upshot of a no-self ontology, our interest here is in the *theoretical* coherence or incoherence of Naessian deep ecology. Debating the relative importance of human and non-human flourishing may reveal no theoretical advantage on one side or the other, given that almost every ethicist is equally uncertain about how or where to draw such a line. But precluding the possibility of *progress* in overall well-being – due to an intertemporal neutrality that would ascribe equal intrinsic value to every segment of the geological timescale – seems by contrast to reveal a defect at the level of moral theory. It is not that Naess should be accused of dismissing future welfare considerations altogether; the question is rather how past and future could be properly weighed against each other if one were to accept the 'deepest' egalitarianism that his deep ecology has to offer.

Before turning to the work of another deep ecologist, Joanna Macy, it may be worth reflecting once more on the apparent synthesis of Hindu and Buddhist conceptions that Naess seems to have proposed. Reacting to this, J. Baird Callicott has recently argued that "the Deep Ecology tradition in environmental philosophy, spawned by Arne Naess, has exhibited a greater affinity for Buddhist ['relationalism' about selfhood] than to Hindu Universal Essentialism and its Western analogue in

---

[9] We take no issue here with the belief that past suffering can justify as much compassion as any other suffering (nor, in particular, with a bodhisattva's compassionate surveying of past lives); the question at hand is whether an acceptance of the reality of past suffering should mitigate the moral urgency of not repeating it.

the philosophy of Spinoza, despite Naess's claims to the contrary" (Callicott 2014, p. 388). If Callicott is right about the later trajectory of the deep ecology movement, this may have something to do with reservations that some have had about Naess's notion of intrinsic value. It is true that Naess's talk of intrinsic value sometimes seems more akin to the classical Hindu equation of self, Self and joy (i.e. ātman = brahman = ānanda"), and it is also true that some Buddhists, such as Madhyamikas, reject the idea that *any* property can be intrinsic (with *svabhāva*), let alone value, i.e. evaluative qualities.[10] Is Callicott right – and is he more thoroughly Buddhist – if he is indeed implying that Naess *should have* backed away from his conception of intrinsic value? The first is a key question; but we do not have space here to explore ways of defending the notion of intrinsic value in ethics. Our main concern has been to show that not only did Naess *believe* he was developing genuinely Buddhist ideas, but indeed, *some* strands in the Buddhist tradition correspond to premises he invoked. This is true of certain Mahāyāna conceptions of the relationship between dependent origination and anātman[11]; and it might also be true of a certain conception of intrinsic value in nature (as we suggest in Sect. 13.3 below).

13.2   Joanna Macy and the Ecosystem As Self: Ecology and Buddhist Syncretism

Joanna Macy is one of the writers in the deep ecology tradition whose Buddhist inspiration is most explicitly acknowledged and theorized. Along with philosophers such as Warwick Fox, George Sessions and Michael Zimmerman, she represents a stream of environmental philosophy that has drawn on Buddhist traditions of thought and practice for both moral orientation and activist inspiration.[12] Arne Naess's reflections on Buddhist philosophy, by contrast, were not well-known until his collection of essays *The Ecology of Wisdom* appeared at the end of

---

[10] See the discussions of Madhyamaka meta-ethics in the Cowherds' *Moonpaths: Ethics and Emptiness* (2016). One recurring thread in those essays – often assumed rather than argued – is that emptiness in relation to selfhood entails emptiness in relation to (all) postulations of intrinsic value. Contraposing that point, and putting it in the form of a critique, some might attempt a *reductio* of Naess's ethics on the assumption that notions of intrinsic value must be discarded along with the discarded bathwater of *ātmavāda*. This assumption is disputable, and can be dispensed with even within certain forms of Buddhist ethics that embrace the notion of intrinsic value (see Davis 2013b, 39–47).

[11] Cf. Ashwani Peetush's discussion of *pratītya-samutpāda* in the preceding chapter (Chap. 12 above).

[12] She has also drawn on Naess's work, going so far as to say that Naess's 'deep ecology' is an 'appropriate, secular referent for *dependent co-arising*' (1991a, p. xvi) – i.e. *paṭicca samuppāda* (*pratītya-samutpāda*) which we discuss below. One notable difference between Macy and the writers listed here is that, for better or worse, they have drawn inspiration from Martin Heidegger as well (for some related themes, see Chap. 9 by Sonia Sikka, in this volume).

his life[13] – and as we have seen, his Spinozist monism has often been seen through a Vedanta, rather than a Buddhist, lens. Macy's work signals a more intensive effort to build on specifically Buddhist concepts and values.

In this section we draw mainly on three of Macy's books: *Mutual Causality in Buddhism and General Systems Theory: the Dharma of Natural Systems* (1991a), *World as Lover, World as Self* (1991b) and *Active Hope* (2012).[14] These books are not concerned exclusively with environmental ideas, and even when they are, their scope reaches further. For example, her development of the Naessian notion of the 'ecological self' is an exploration in ontology as much as it is one in ecology.[15] Both rely, in any case, on her analysis of causality, which expands on the idea of *paṭicca samuppāda* (*dependent origination* or *dependent co-arising*) in Buddhism.

Macy argues that understandings of causality as linear (an assumption she sees extending from Aristotle to Marx and beyond) are not only philosophically problematic but also possibly at the root of environmental and other problems that plague the world today. Her work is devoted to defending a conception of causality along the lines of mutual interdependence. She finds that both General Systems Theory (GST) and Buddhism partake of this understanding; and her explication of the mutual causality view, as with much of her ecological framework, invokes both of these. She acknowledges nonetheless that it would be too facile to equate the two (granting that for one the focus is an understanding of natural events while for the other it is – in many cases – their transcendence). What she aims for is the elaboration of a 'reciprocal' hermeneutic. She describes many common patterns and principles underlying GST and Buddhism, referring to their confluence as the 'Dharma of Natural Systems' (in *Mutual Causality* (hereafter, MC)).[16] It is this *dharma* that she believes can serve as a philosophical and moral grounding for an ecological worldview according to which moral values "inhere in the fundamental causal interconnectedness of all phenomena" (MC 1991a, p. xiii).

This first book of Macy's was mostly rooted in early Buddhism (the *Suttas* and *Nikāyas*) and in it she cites the Pali Canon a great deal; but *World as Lover* and subsequently *Active Hope* also make reference to Mahāyāna themes. She emphasizes the impact that the Buddha's analysis in terms of *paṭicca samuppāda*

---

[13] Ed. Devall and Drengson (2008) – referred to several times in our Sect. 13.1 above.

[14] These books will be referred to as MC, WL and AH respectively from now on.

[15] WL and AH address environmental issues most explicitly. MC incorporates both Theravadin and Mahāyāna ideas; by contrast, AH is the most practically oriented, but also takes inspiration from the Mahāyānist bodhisattva ideal.

[16] GST describes causal networks as 'open' i.e. they are able to exchange energy, matter and information; due to this exchange, systems grow in complexity, opening up new possibilities and responses, yet they also display orderliness and equilibrium. To systems theorists, not only wholes, but social institutions and psychological processes can be viewed as systems as well. According to GST, cause and effect can modify each other; in such cases, feedback loops can be negative (which stabilize the system, maintaining equilibrium) and/or positive (which support deviations leading to 'novelty or instability' (MC 1991a, Chap. 4)). These processes manifest themselves equally in ecological systems and in any adequate process for gathering information about, and finding patterns in, our natural environment (ibid.).

(Skt. *pratītya samutpāda*) has had on her, writing that this "doctrine has provided me ways to understand the intricate web of co-arising that links my being with all other beings, and to apprehend reciprocities between thought and action, self and world." (WL 1991b, p. 63). At the end of *World as Lover*, she also refers to the eco-logical movements' embracing of the notion of far-reaching interconnection in nature and she calls this the 'third turning' of the wheel (echoing the Buddhist con-cept of turning the wheel of dharma). This idea figures in *Active Hope* as the "great turning", which refers to what she believes the modern ecological crisis calls for: "a collaborative model of power based on appreciating how much more we can achieve working together than as separate individuals" (AH 2012, p. 7).[17]

Macy's Naessian conception of a transpersonal consciousness, and the ethical conception she elaborates, come together in her conception of deep ecology as an expression of insight into *paticca samuppāda* (cf. again, 1991a, p. xvi). Macy claims that ecological destruction is rooted in a dysfunctional notion of self as causally isolated, autonomous and resistant to meaningful interconnection. If such a notion were the only option for us, any motivation to act for the sake of others would be severely limited, she claims. Once freed from this misconception, on the other hand, we are empowered to act for the sake of others; altruistic ethical engagement can then flow very naturally. Macy compares this aspiration to act for the sake of others with the motivation of the *bodhisattva*, whose legendary self-sacrifice was theorized by Mahāyānists, as we noted in our introduction, so as to formulate an ideal of self-less moral engagement.[18]

Macy seems to suggest that the kind of moral improvisation that is called for when such a person becomes an agent of social reform – albeit someone who is not an 'agent' as this term was typically used in early modern metaphysics (as we note below, Macy also invokes *anattā*) – can be facilitated by a consciousness of either 'general systems' causality or *dependent co-arising*, the complex causal framework already referred to by its Buddhist (Pali) name, *paticca samuppāda*.[19] As she says, "[i]n *paticca samuppāda* the [Buddha] presented causality… [as an] interaction of multiple factors where cause and effect cannot be categorically isolated or traced unidirectionally… [n]o effect arises without cause, yet no effect is predetermined, for its causes are multiple and mutually affecting" (1991a, p. 19).

---

[17] This 'great turning' can be seen as having three dimensions – direct action (actions that protect the earth), life-sustaining practices (building new institutions in the economy and in society) and an underlying shift in consciousness (a change in values and perceptions and the recognition that changing the self and the world is at root a single endeavour) – all implying the involvement of community rather than just the individual (AH, passim).

[18] See AH, passim; and cf. Goodman (2009). The aspiration to be 'liberated' from this world may seem contrary to an engagement with ecology; but some Mahāyāna traditions also offer an ideal of 'non-abiding' nirvana, which replaces the goal of liberation *from* the world with a goal of libera-tion *within* the world (cf. Davis 2013a).

[19] Of course, many Buddhists would strengthen 'can be facilitated by…' to 'must be guided by…' – but Macy is not so prescriptive, tending to favour an approach along the lines of Naess's 'platform' for collective ecological action (where the basic principles of ecology can be the object of a kind of overlapping consensus, instead of a doctrinal foundation).

Echoing classical Buddhist views, Macy notes that the notion of *paṭicca samuppāda* must be considered alongside an emphasis on *impermanence* in the midst of natural processes.[20] Meanwhile, echoing both the latter and a range of modern views, including General Systems Theory, she contends that experiences can have significance even in the absence of an experiencing subject (a 'self' in the Cartesian sense). The 'I' is not a substance, she argues, but rather part of a system "whose boundaries do not coincide with the boundaries either of the body or of what is popularly called the 'self' or 'consciousness'" (MC 1991a, p. 112). Borrowing a Buddhist metaphor, Macy considers the individual agent to be a *stream* of being – or a dynamic pattern of activity – that can interact with the environment to the point of *identifying* with the environment (thereby highlighting the latter half of her title: World as Lover, *World as Self*).[21]

A twofold problem arises here, however – a problem with an exegetical aspect and a philosophical aspect. Exegetically, we may note that in the early Buddhism that Macy often cites, the links (*nidānas*) in dependent co-arising (*paṭicca samuppāda*) are not salutary, but on the contrary, harmful – or, for lack of a better word, evil. She could sidestep this doctrinal inconvenience by, once again, switching to the Mahayanists' conception of (what they would generally sanskritize as) *pratītya-samutpāda*, which for them is often conceived in a more positive spirit. But before addressing that, let us consider the philosophical problem. This is similar to Naess's revived 'problem of evil', discussed above as an important objection that he himself posed to his own deep ecology. As well as there being a concern about how a deep ecologist can – as it seems she *should* – acknowledge that there are *some* evil (or simply bad) elements in the environment, the problem is replicated here, because a Theravādin might inadvertently be led to the conclusion that *everything* in the environment would have to be seen as evil rather than good. Now, some Mahāyāna approaches do indeed invert this valuation (or *valence*), making 'interdependence' a positive feature of existence.[22] But this does not seem to resolve the deeper problem. Naess's concession was that an important distinction seems to exist, between things that are intrinsically good and things that are either bad or neutral (even if we

---

[20] The Abhidharma tradition in Buddhism, Macy argues, diluted this understanding of mutual causality by focusing on *dharmas* (psycho-physical units of *svabhāva*), rather than the dynamic processes at work between them. Rejecting this in favour of a theory of dynamic causation and a praxis of compassion, indicates one source of attraction she acknowledges in Mahāyāna tradition; we discuss another below.

[21] *World as Lover, World as Self* contains one of her most relevant discussions in a chapter called 'The Greening of the Self'; here she blames the current planetary crisis on confusion about identity and self-identification. Echoing Naess's revisionist notion of 'self', she says the proper role of 'self'-identification is not to posit a substantial entity but to deploy metaphor(s) under whose guise we construct our identity and our place in the world; this understanding must open onto a wider 'ecoself' construct whereby the outlines of the 'old' self are extended to a being that is co-extensive with other beings and life on our planet. She credits Buddhist writings with praecursors of this extension of identification.

[22] Sometimes a different term is here substituted for *pratītya-samutpāda*, e.g. *yuganaddha*, a Sanskrit term used in Tibetan philosophy; cf. Odin (1982), who explores this Tibetan conception of interdependence.

are often unable in practice to discern which is which). Portraying all of nature as in some sense bad may be orthodox in some Buddhist circles; but doing so would counterintuitively undermine this distinction. By the same token, portraying all of nature as inherently *good* would make the same counterintuitive misstep, especially if what *makes* everything 'good' is – *ex hypothesi* – bound up with interdependence (in which case all things could not just turn out well contingently; rather, all would in a sense be *necessarily* good, making it difficult even to *describe* the evils Naess acknowledges, let alone to observe them). Calling anything 'good' would become tautological, and in effect, normative distinctions would be nullified despite the superficial retention of certain normative terms.[23]

A special case of the intuition that poses this problem for deep ecology is the one discussed earlier: it seems possible, at least, to describe patterns of behaviour in past societies as wrong, bad or evil, while envisaging future forms of life as progressively freed of such evils, even though the former were no less part of a functioning, integrated biosphere than the latter would be. The problem is that deep ecology risks levelling the past and the future in the same way that it – in this case, perhaps more justifiably – levels our species and other species (or to be more precise, risks making moral attitudes towards the past as important as a moral urgency about the future). The concern, in other words, is that deep ecology may not be sufficiently *future-directed*. We are not suggesting that Macy's 'active hope' is not, in some sense, future-directed in its compassionate quest for reform and improvement; but as with other deep ecologists, it is not clear that her premises are compatible with any form of ecological thinking that is future-directed in its foundational principles.[24] We turn now to consider how both Buddhist ethics in general and a no-self view, in particular, can support a more deeply future-directed moral framework for environmental ethics.

---

[23] Siderits (2016) offers a similar critique of what he calls the '*Indra's Net* strategy' in Buddhist environmental ethics, echoing kindred criticisms in Ives (2009, 2013) – the problem being due to this strategy's inadvertent 'erasing (of) all distinctions' (Siderits 2016, 135). Some Buddhists might reply that by shifting to an ultimate level of truth, terms like 'good' and 'bad' do not apply; and of these, those who shun transcendence (e.g. in the name of ecological engagement) might argue that interdependence is a reality rather than a norm. At that point, however, a different problem arises about why people, and especially those who need persuading, should care about the environment on this view – even if they accept its view of interdependence (cf. Gowans 2015, 178 – who connects this to the classical is/ought problem in ethical theory).

[24] At a theoretical level, Macy may end up precluding a robustly future-directed perspective for another reason, which is that she proposes a deconstruction of the means/ends distinction that underlies it: she believes it is a mistake to consider any 'end' to have an independent existence, whereas on the mutual causality view the goal cannot be seen as independent but only as interdependent with 'means' (MC 1991a). This may represent an interesting point of departure from Naess, whose focus on 'intrinsic value' (construed independently of biospheric egalitarianism) marks a degree of continuity with the 'future-directed' approach we will discuss.

13.3 Neither Deep Nor Shallow: Anātman and Future-Directed Ecology

Though he coined the term (and its more celebrated opposite), Arne Naess never clearly defined what constitutes 'shallow ecology'; but if nothing else, it is anthropocentric. That is reason enough, perhaps, to want to avoid it, but many would agree that what environmental ethics needs are more options that occupy the space *between* deep and shallow ecology. At the very least, we should consider what it would involve, as Christopher Ives has put it, to "steer a middle way between a staunch anthropocentrism that would take only human interests into account and a radical biocentrism that would see all animals, including humans, as equal" (Ives 2013, p. 558). Ives refers to Naess, Macy and other deep ecologists, and a host of others who have contributed ideas in Buddhist environmental ethics, but in outlining the approaches he himself favours, he does not attempt to set out from a theoretical basis, be it ontological (whether holism or reductionism about identity or some other alternative) or ethical. Some might say that doing so would fall too far outside the spirit of Buddhist praxis; but there are Buddhist philosophers who delve deeply into foundational moral theory, and we shall consider two, who have indeed already appeared in many of the chapters here: Mark Siderits and Charles Goodman. The main reason, of course, for highlighting the contributions of Siderits and Goodman is that they bolster their moral theorizing with metaphysical reflections on personal identity, mind, agency and anātman.

The notion of a 'middle way' in ethics often sounds tempting in itself, not to mention that it resonates with a major theme that goes back to the Buddha's first sermon on the four noble truths, a sermon that introduced the theme of a middle way between egoistic desire and a radical rejection of all things human. But one should not take it for granted that the poles at each end of a spectrum must always be wrong or evil; such judgments should depend on how each spectrum is characterized. Accordingly, we do not *assume* that biospheric egalitarianism is wrong or false.[25] To the extent that such an egalitarianism is based on a radical monism in ontology, we share doubts (including Naess's own) about that egalitarianism, based on considerations that vitiate the monist element – in particular, the theoretically undesirable prospect of losing all normative distinctions for those who plunge into such a monism. A parallel problem arose in an earlier chapter, in light of what Siderits has called the '*Weltgeist*' alternative to theories of unified selfhood.[26] On the *Weltgeist*

---

[25] Nor, for that matter, should any philosopher assume that egoism is false (if for no other reason than that philosophers should be wary of assumptions in general). Likewise, most major traditions of Buddhism offer *arguments* to demonstrate the dogmatism and/or the incoherence of egoism (cf. Siderits 2003 and Goodman 2009).

[26] Siderits (2003, 42). In Chap. 5, Davis & Renaud consider a '*Weltgeist*' construal of Spinoza's substance (akin to a common German Idealist reading of Spinoza). Here we should recapitulate the 'special case' of monism discussed above, which we might call the 'moral homogeneity of past and future'. The problematic consequence of deep ecology, in that context, was a disproportionate

model, the entire world constitutes a single, homogeneous spirit, and unlike the reality of its non-duality, *distinctions* are mere appearances, including (allegedly false) distinctions between good and bad, right and wrong, progress and regress. This model may provide one way of dissolving selfhood, but the problem is that it also seems to dissolve the values that even deep ecology – or perhaps especially deep ecology – seeks to embody and promote. Indeed, it may dissolve value distinctions of all kinds, quite possibly making environmental *ethics* futile.

We have not referred to the conceptions of interdependence advanced by Naess and Macy as versions of a *Weltgeist* model, partly because they leave indeterminate what ontological predicates might be fundamental in their ontology (e.g. physical versus mental)[27]; but their approaches fall broadly into this sort of category. As a result, they generally overlook other Buddhist models that Siderits explores, for example the 'punctualist' model, which instead of unifying multiple selves, analyzes – and in effect divides – persons into fine-grained temporal parts that are ultimately *impersonal* segments of experience.[28] It may be said that Naess and Macy do not *overlook*, but rather *reject*, what they would see as a form of reductionism. For several reasons, this would be too quick on their part; and in fact, they do not engage closely with such analyses of personal identity.[29] By '*punctualism*', Siderits usually means a simple reductionist analysis, but sometimes uses this term to refer to a normative application, which would prioritize the present moment, or the near-future (e.g. for broadly hedonic purposes).[30] We avoid the latter usage here; the

---

'respect for the past', but it is important to keep in mind that this is not just an abstract oddity of a general theory; it may also be connected to a traditional ecological ideal, the ideal of 'conservation'. Like many others, we develop ideas here that aim at disentangling worthwhile notions of conservation from some insidious forms of *conservatism* (insidious enough to creep even into deep ecology).

[27] Many ecologists taking a monistic perspective ('deep' or not) probably assume that the single being must be physical; but one reason for seeing Naess and Macy differently is their kinship with Buddhist views, most of which are not naturalistic, let alone physicalist.

[28] Views that are closely akin to punctualism are sometimes called 'time-slice theories', e.g. time-slice theories of rationality or of morality, which may in turn be based on a time-slice theory of the metaphysics of personhood. Brian Hedden (2015) has recently defended the former, borrowing ideas from Derek Parfit, but based more on a scepticism about settling the metaphysics of personhood rather than a full-blown theory of the latter. Parfit's approach remains influential in the contemporary literature (despite his having apparently marginalized it in his final work in ethics, i.e. Parfit (2011)); but see the reservations about time-slice-centric approaches in Stephen Harris's chapter (Chap. 11) above, in the section entitled 'Parfit, Reductionism and Morality'.

[29] It might be thought that their holist ontology would rule out such a model, but it is worth bearing in mind that (a) holism does not necessarily exclude every form of reductionism; (b) normative punctualism need not presuppose ontological reductionism; and (c) those who *are* reductionists about personal identity need not be physicalist reductionists about mental states (let alone other natural phenomena): Vasubandhu, for example, seems to have been a temporal-parts reductionist even though he rejected physicalism (cf. Oren Hanner's (2016) reductionist reading).

[30] The latter use appears later, not in Siderits (2003), but in Siderits (2007), thus avoiding some potential confusion.

variant we think worth exploring is the analysis in terms of moments or phases, which need not and does not discount the distant future in favour of the near future.[31]

Apart from invoking a neutrality with respect to future phases of life on our planet (without a moral neutrality with respect to *past* and future), this kind of punctualist perspective would put a decisive nail in the coffin of speciesism. From the punctualist viewpoint, it would appear that in some cases, a mature individual of another species should have equal or possibly greater moral status than certain humans – or at least, one could not reject this comparison merely by defining the status of a fetus or an infant in light of its anticipated adult phase, because the connecting threads in a lifespan would be seen as less important than experiential states in themselves. To be more precise, it is not the 'individual' of whatever species that weighs in here; it is the capacity within a *santāna* of awareness for rich, joyful experiences, however temporally finite they may be. Gauging this capacity – whether possible in practice or not – should not be constrained by assumptions about species or individuals. In many cases, the contingent capacities of humans may tip the moral balance in 'their' favour when it comes to ecological trade-offs[32]; but in many cases it will not, seeing as so many other sentient organisms carry equal – or sometimes greater – capacity for intrinsically valuable experience. An impersonal form of altruism would seem to follow from this, if not psychologically, then perhaps logically. If the balance of reasons (e.g. for assistance or protection) regularly weighs against favouring ourselves or our own kind, people would have altruist *reasons* for weighing their own welfare impartially relative to the welfare of other beings, whatever their *motivations* may be in their unenlightened state.

In light of the discussions of Śāntideva's argument for altruism throughout this volume, we can see an affinity here between that argument and this elaboration of punctualism; but the above elaboration, for better or worse, does not depend on any crude reductionism, either about mental states or about the nature of organic beings. When Siderits (2000) and Goodman (2009) appeal to Śāntideva's argument, on the other hand, they are cognizant both that the no-self premise there is invoked in a reductionist spirit and that this does not necessarily harmonize with their preferred Mahāyāna frameworks (or even with Śāntideva's own Madhyamaka framework). One motivation they share, for reconciling the reductionism and the Mahāyāna elements in Śāntideva and others, is based on the confidence that all these elements – and especially the bodhisattva vow to aid all sentient beings – resonate well with

---

[31] We ask the reader to bear with any apparent incongruity in the use of the term 'punctualism', which could be resolved with a more elaborate terminological apparatus (for another occasion). We are interested in something quite opposed to any ethic that would prioritize the nearest 'point' in time; such points may be fundamental to the framework, but the future-directed framework gives equal weight to all points where sentient beings exist.

[32] The reservation about saying 'their…' is parallel to a reservation that would be needed if one were to say *'certain* humans…', as the punctualist could not coherently say that some particular humans reach a pre-eminent standing (due to exceptional capacities) and then retain that standing through a lifetime. Again, the view does not fundamentally distinguish *between* different people, but rather *within* lives (and capacities will strengthen and weaken, not necessarily according to fixed patterns, through the course of any life, human or non-human).

universal moral consequentialism.[33] This consequentialist interpretation of Buddhist ethics has been controversial, and we are not endorsing it here; but it is worth recognizing not only the natural fit between consequentialism and the no-self premise, but also the possibility that Buddhist consequentialism could bolster a neglected alternative to deep and shallow ecologies. Indeed, the 'aggregative' focus of universal moral consequentialism dovetails with the punctualist analysis, which would renounce speciesism as firmly as it would renounce the moral elevation of non-sentient beings attempted by deep ecology.

To reiterate the central point here, the moralized punctualist perspective would weigh the relative moral significance of each episode (or even each *moment*) in every sentient being's life, rather than the moral significance of each individual.[34] From that perspective, moral trade-offs would have to transcend inter-species boundaries, and in many situations, non-human interests would outweigh human interests. For better or worse, this represents a clean break from any anthropocentric perspective. But it is an approach that does not ignore distinctions between phases of maturity in a life-cycle (and their possible moral significance, based on changes in capacity for pain or joy). Nor would it ignore distinctions such as that between the fundamental badness of pain and the fundamental goodness of joy. Most importantly, it is an approach that is future-directed – insofar, that is, as its moral counterpart takes a consequentialist form. It is a well-known problem that people will often pass up opportunities for improvement because they insist on following through with a pre-conceived plan, whatever its prospects for improvement may be. To put this another way, we risk making ourselves hostages of the past, because we feel a need to honour our past commitments (promises to *others* being a different matter, even if equally '*prima facie*' in their degree of bindingness). But it can be not only rational, but perhaps quintessentially Buddhist, to sever or loosen this kind of clinging to the past. Breaking down the (putative) unity and boundedness of (putative) selfhood can make this easier; meanwhile, the pressing need to make environmental progress makes this – or at least some form of breaking with the past – more important than ever.

Of course, consequentialism is not the only moral view that is fundamentally future-directed. Hans Jonas is widely respected as an environmental philosopher who frames our moral duties in terms of obligations to future generations (Jonas 1984, 1998). However, Jonas formulates these obligations in terms of Kantian categorical imperatives. So, indeed, there have been future-directed ecologies that do not rely on consequentialism – but alternatives like this one arguably tend in a direction that is quite remote from any Buddhist orientation.[35] Consequentialism has

[33] On this point, see Siderits 2003 (as well as Siderits 2000).

[34] This may – though not necessarily in all variations – amount to the diametric opposite of a narrative conception of personhood (which Peetush discusses in Chap. 12, above). It would be yet another indication of the rich diversity of Buddhist philosophical options, if indeed this punctualism could be formulated in Buddhist terms, just as some narrative accounts could be.

[35] See Goodman (2009, ch. 11) on some deep differences between Buddhist and Kantian moral philosophy. Keown and others take a different view of this; but many differences would remain even if such conciliatory efforts succeed.

always seemed closer to the spirit of Buddhist ethics, even if several prominent writers have argued that Buddhist ethics does not or should not ultimately content itself with a consequentialist form.[36]

In his book *Consequences of Compassion*, Charles Goodman mounts a robust defence of the aggregative framework of consequentialism, based on a synthesis of Theravāda and Mahāyāna elements in ethics, but also, and perhaps most crucially, on the no-self reasoning of Śāntideva (Goodman 2009, chapters 3–6). Unlike most previous defences, however, he broadens the appeal of his approach by favouring a form of consequentialism that is not narrowly utilitarian.[37] Utilitarianism focuses on either desire-satisfaction (naturally not the best fit for most forms of Buddhism) or pleasure, whereas a 'consequentialist', by virtue of preferring this term, will favour a pluralist axiology – a plurality of the kinds of things that can have value in experience.[38] Goodman considers the goodness of character traits, which opens up a possible reconciliation with virtue ethics, not to mention a special ethic of compassion *qua* virtue. But we might also consider positive spiritual states (not necessarily pleasurable) and other non-conceptual states of consciousness (again not necessarily pleasurable), where the latter, if not the former, could be attributed to non-human beings in morally relevant ways.[39] Hence, whereas utilitarianism risks being anthropocentric in its value theory, consequentialism does not, or at least not by default. And whereas the hedonic focus of utilitarianism exposes it to temporal discounting (i.e. discounting the future, as is standard in economic 'rational-choice theory' for example), universal consequentialism recognizes no reason to discount the future. In his book, Goodman says relatively little about the implications for an impersonal ecology,[40] but one implication is clear: rational altruism, on this view, would be fundamentally future-directed in its normative principles.

This rational altruism would be concerned with 'consequences', but would also be guided by the second element in Goodman's titular phrase 'consequences of

---

[36] As Damien Keown (2001) argues – who, nonetheless, discusses utilitarian interpretations quite extensively, precisely because many early writers on Buddhist ethics favoured this comparison. Keown (2007) applies his virtue-based approach to environmental ethics, as several other Buddhist philosophers have done in recent years. For a variety of other virtue-based approaches, see Sahni (2011).

[37] Knowingly or not, he thus echoes an idea shared by William James and Bertrand Russell; but it is worth bearing in mind, as Nalini Ramlakhan shows in Chap. 10 above, that James and Russell were themselves influenced by ideas in Buddhist ethics and/or Buddhist spiritual axiology (as these were (imperfectly) understood a century ago).

[38] Some will even go beyond experience, which is one reason why deep ecologists should not rule out consequentialist frameworks for their ethics (insofar as intrinsic value might be thought to reside in a non-sentient thing); but we set aside this possibility here.

[39] Only *some* of these states could have value, of course; otherwise, this approach would be vulnerable to the same sort of objection that Naess faced as a result of his axiological levelling of all things in nature (i.e. vulnerable to a 'problem of evil' that implies we must make room for conditions of the *possibility* of distinguishing good and bad).

[40] Though, like many Buddhist ethicists, he stresses the importance of animal welfare as being among the core practical concerns of Buddhist ethics (e.g. 2009, p. 3).

compassion', i.e. *karunā* (compassion). One might well wonder: does any Buddhist ideal of *karunā* correspond to this particular conception of altruism, focused as it is on *reasons* for assisting others?[41] One thing seems clear: these would not be *personal* reasons, so this kind of altruism fits, at least, with Buddhist *anātmavāda*. Beyond that, the larger question about *karunā* is one we cannot answer here. But if we were to ask whether Buddhists (or which Buddhists) treat *karunā* as having intrinsic or instrumental value, the answer would either be indeterminate, or perhaps both – possibly having intrinsic value as one of the *kusalamulani*, but certainly, in any case, as having instrumental value. Acts of compassion are or ought to be acts of *upāya*, and should be 'skillful' in relation to *results*; in other words, on this view, they should be future-directed.

The future-directed emphasis in this train of thought may give the impression that this style of ecology would merely instrumentalize measures to protect the environment, rendering it 'shallow'.[42] But on the contrary, it should not be regarded as shallow – in Naess's sense – for at least two reasons. One is that the 'selfless' orientation of this approach puts it in a different category from those that treat environmental justice as mainly concerned with certain kinds of human rights. The other is that Naess had implied, early on, that shallow ecology saw the natural environment as a kind of infrastructure whose maintenance was required for sustaining an economy in which consumer preferences were paramount. But future-directed ecology, if consequentialist, recognizes the finality of certain kinds of intrinsic value (which cannot be relativized to individual preferences, no matter how much free rein these preferences might be permitted at one time or another as part of the evolution of open economies). These items of intrinsic value would include experiences and joys of a kind that we may share with other animals. Nonetheless, the view would not be a form of 'deep ecology' either, because it would not advocate egalitarianism throughout the biosphere.

In setting aside biospheric egalitarianism, the future-directed approach is not necessarily anti-Naessian. After all, as we have seen, Naess eventually worried about a version of the 'problem of evil', which plausibly advanced the thought that disease-causing agents in nature could hardly be deemed as valuable as other beings (no matter how *sub specie aeternitatis* one's viewpoint may be).[43] It seems fair to

---

[41] One might contrast the somewhat less rationalist phenomenology of *karunā*, defended by Jay Garfield in ch. 6.

[42] A more disconcerting objection, meanwhile, would be that this approach is not fundamentally about *protecting* the environment, but about *optimizing* it, in a sense – e.g. at times, it could justify measures that would *enhance* the environment. Up to a point, this is true, as this is not a *conservative* philosophy. But to speak disparagingly of 'optimizing' would not be fair either: on this view, sentient beings should not be 'optimized' for ulterior purposes, unless those purposes return benefits to sentient beings.

[43] Of course, what is meant here is that microbial disease-causing agents have little or no *intrinsic* value; in other words, little or no additional value can be discerned after one has accounted for whatever instrumental value they may (sometimes) have. As for their potential instrumental value, this would need to be treated more delicately than we have space for here. Obviously we do not

say that this was not a mere afterthought; it was consonant with his philosophical commitments that he would highlight such a problem. It also seems fair to say, though, that he himself did not solve this problem, whereas the alternative derived from the ideas aired here may at least avoid it, by acknowledging that some sub-sentient beings will tend to do less good in nature than others and should not be assumed to compensate for this 'in their own being', precisely because they lack sentience. In any case, in outlining this alternative, we wish to be clear that we have not set out to defend it so much as to show how it can be extrapolated from the kinds of approaches in Buddhist ethics that are available in recent work by such writers as Mark Siderits and Charles Goodman.

Although we have not set out to describe a 'future-directed' alternative with the aim of endorsing it, we hope at least to have given a sense of the breadth and depth of philosophical vision that would be required to make this more than just a stab at a 'middle way' in environmental ethics. Its roots in Buddhist ethics would contribute as much breadth as they have already done in deep ecology; and its roots in *anatmavāda* would offer at least as much depth. We close this chapter, and the volume, on a more modest note, merely observing how these debates in environmental philosophy – and ethical theory more generally – may play a role in a historiography of the most recent phases of contemporary philosophy. Philosophy has not yet broken through to a global forum, for better or worse, nor have any local or national philosophical fora truly 'globalized' in the methods or contents of their own debates; but in some settings, cross-cultural philosophy has evolved significantly in recent decades. Any future history of philosophy, unless prefixed with the qualification 'Western', will have to trace this evolution and gauge its impact. We hope to have shown that cross-cultural philosophical inquiries have evolved and have been particularly fruitful in contexts where Buddhist and Western philosophies are brought together. This volume's survey of philosophers since Schopenhauer has highlighted two phases of this evolution in the modern context. Firstly, there has been a growing awareness, not only of contemporary Western philosophy in Asian countries, but of (especially but not exclusively) Buddhist ideas in Western settings. Meanwhile, with the philosophers discussed in this chapter, a second and perhaps more refined phase comes into view, insofar as these philosophers now proceed on the basis of a close familiarity with the canonical languages of Buddhist traditions, and a much closer familiarity with texts, both ancient and modern, written by Buddhist philosophers from within those traditions. This trajectory just happens to be eminently traceable in contemporary debates in environmental ethics – debates that are not just *within* Buddhist ethics, but also *between* pioneering figures in this area of ethics. It may well be that other areas of mainstream ethical theory will see similar injections of cross-cultural dynamism in the future.

---

have things like biological weapons in mind; but there are open questions about the ethical use of chemical or biological agents that allow a controlled eradication of disease-causing insects, as well as 'natural' examples (more openly contemplated by some ecologists) of diseases that have historically regulated wild populations of various species.

References

Callicott, J. Baird. 2014. Recontextualizing the Self in Comparative Environmental Philosophy. In *Environmental Philosophy in Asian Traditions of Thought*, ed. Callicott and J. McRae. Albany: SUNY Press.

Cook, Francis H. 1977. *Hua-Yen Buddhism: The Jewel Net of Indra*. University Park, Pennsylvania State University Press.

Davis, Gordon. 2013a. Traces of Consequentialism and Non-Consequentialism in Bodhisattva Ethics. *Philosophy East and West* 63: 275–305.

———. 2013b. Moral Realism and Anti-Realism outside the West: A Meta-Ethical Turn in Buddhist Ethics. *Comparative Philosophy* 4 (2): 24–53.

de Spinoza, Benedictus. [1677] 1985. *The Collected Works of Spinoza*, vol. 1. Trans. Edwin M. Curley. Princeton: Princeton University Press.

Devall, Bill, and Alan Drengson. 2008. *The Ecology of Wisdom: Writings by Arne Naess*. Berkeley: Counterpoint.

Fox, Warwick. 1995a. *Toward a Transpersonal Ecology*. Albany: SUNY Press.

———. 1995b. Transpersonal Ecology and the Varieties of Identification. In *The Deep Ecology Movement*, ed. A. Drengson and Y. Inoue. Berkeley: North Atlantic Books.

Goodman, Charles. 2009. *Consequences of Compassion: An Interpretation and Defence of Buddhist Ethics*. Oxford: Oxford University Press.

Gowans, Christopher W. 2015. *Buddhist Moral Philosophy: An Introduction*. London: Routledge.

Hanner, Oren. 2016. *Moral Agency under the No-Self Premise: A Comparative Study of Vasubandhu and Derek Parfit*. Doctoral dissertation, University of Hamburg.

Hedden, Brian. 2015. *Reasons without Persons: Rationality, Identity and Time*. Oxford: Oxford University Press.

Ives, Christopher. 2009. In Search of Green Dharma: Philosophical Issues in Buddhist Environmental Ethics. In *Destroying Mara Forever*, ed. J. Powers and C. Prebish. Ithaca: Snow Lion Publications.

———. 2013. Resources for Buddhist Environmental Ethics. *Journal of Buddhist Ethics* 20: 2013.

Jonas, Hans. 1984. *The Imperative of Responsibility*. Trans. D. Herr. Chicago: University of Chicago Press.

———. 1998. *Pour une éthique du futur*. Trans. S. Cornille and P. Ivernel. Paris: Payot-Rivages.

Keown, Damien. 2001. *The Nature of Buddhist Ethics*, rev ed. New York: Palgrave.

———. 2007. Buddhism and Ecology: A Virtue Ethics Approach. *Contemporary Buddhism* 8 (2): 97–112.

Macy, Joanna. 1991a. *Mutual Causality in Buddhism and General Systems Theory*. Albany: SUNY Press.

———. 1991b. *World as Lover, World as Self*. Berkeley: Parallax Press.

———. 2012. *Active Hope*. Novato: New World Library.

Naess, Arne. 1989. *Ecology, Community and Lifestyle: Outline of an Ecosophy*. Cambridge: Cambridge University Press.

———. [1973] 1995a. The Shallow and the Deep, Long-Range Ecology Movement: A Summary. Reprinted in *The Deep Ecology Movement: An Introductory Anthology*, ed. A. Drengson and Y. Inoue. Berkeley: North Atlantic Books.

———. 1995b. Self-Realization: An Ecological Approach to Being in the World. In *The Deep Ecology Movement*, ed. A. Drengson and Y. Inoue. Berkeley: North Atlantic Books.

———. 1995c. The Systematization of the Logically Ultimate Norms and Hypotheses of Ecosophy T. In *The Deep Ecology Movement*, ed. A. Drengson and Y. Inoue. Berkeley: North Atlantic Books.

———. [1977] 2008a. Through Spinoza to Mahāyāna Buddhism, or Through Mahāyāna Buddhism to Spinoza?. In *The Ecology of Wisdom: Writings by Arne Naess*, ed. B. Devall and A. Drengson. Berkeley: Counterpoint.

———. [1985] 2008b. Gestalt Thinking and Buddhism. In *The Ecology of Wisdom: Writings by Arne Naess*, ed. B. Devall and A. Drengson. Berkeley: Counterpoint.

Naess, Arne, and Alastair Hannay, eds. 1972. *An Invitation to Chinese Philosophy*. Oslo: Universitetsforlaget.

Naess, A., and G. Sessions. 1985. Platform Principles of the Deep Ecology Movement. In *Deep Ecology: Living as if Nature Mattered*, ed. B. Devall and G. Sessions. Gibbs Smith: Salt Lake City.

Noë, Alva. 2009. *Out of our Heads*. New York: Hill and Wang.

Odin, Steve. 1982. *Process Metaphysics and Hua-Yen Buddhism: A Critical Study of Cumulative Penetration versus Interpenetration*. Albany: SUNY Press.

Parfit, Derek. 1984. *Reasons and Persons*. Oxford: Clarendon Press.

———. 2011. *On What Matters,* 2 vols. Oxford: Clarendon Press.

Sahni, Pragati. 2011. *Environmental Ethics in Buddhism: A Virtues Approach*. Abingdon: Routledge.

Śāntideva. 1995. *The Bodhicaryāvatāra*. Trans. K. Crosby and A. Skilton. Oxford: Oxford University Press.

Sessions, George. 1994. *Deep Ecology for the Twenty-First Century*. Boston: Shambhala.

Siderits, Mark. 2000. The Reality of Altruism: Reconstructing Santideva. *Philosophy East and West* 50 (3): 412–424.

———. 2003. *Personal Identity and Buddhist Philosophy: Empty Persons*. Burlington: Ashgate.

———. 2007. *Buddhism as Philosophy: An Introduction*. Indianapolis: Hackett.

———. 2016. Does Buddhist Ethics Exist? In *In the Cowherds, Moonpaths: Ethics and Emptiness*. Oxford: Oxford University Press.

Taylor, Charles. 1989. *Sources of the Self*. Cambridge, MA: Harvard University Press.

Thompson, Evan. 2007. *Mind in Life*. Cambridge, MA: Harvard University Press.

Varela, Francisco, Evan Thompson, and Eleanor Rosch. 1991. *The Embodied Mind*. Cambridge, MA: MIT Press.

Zimmerman, Michael. 1994. *Contesting Earth's Future: Radical Ecology and Postmodernity*. Berkeley: University of California Press.

Index